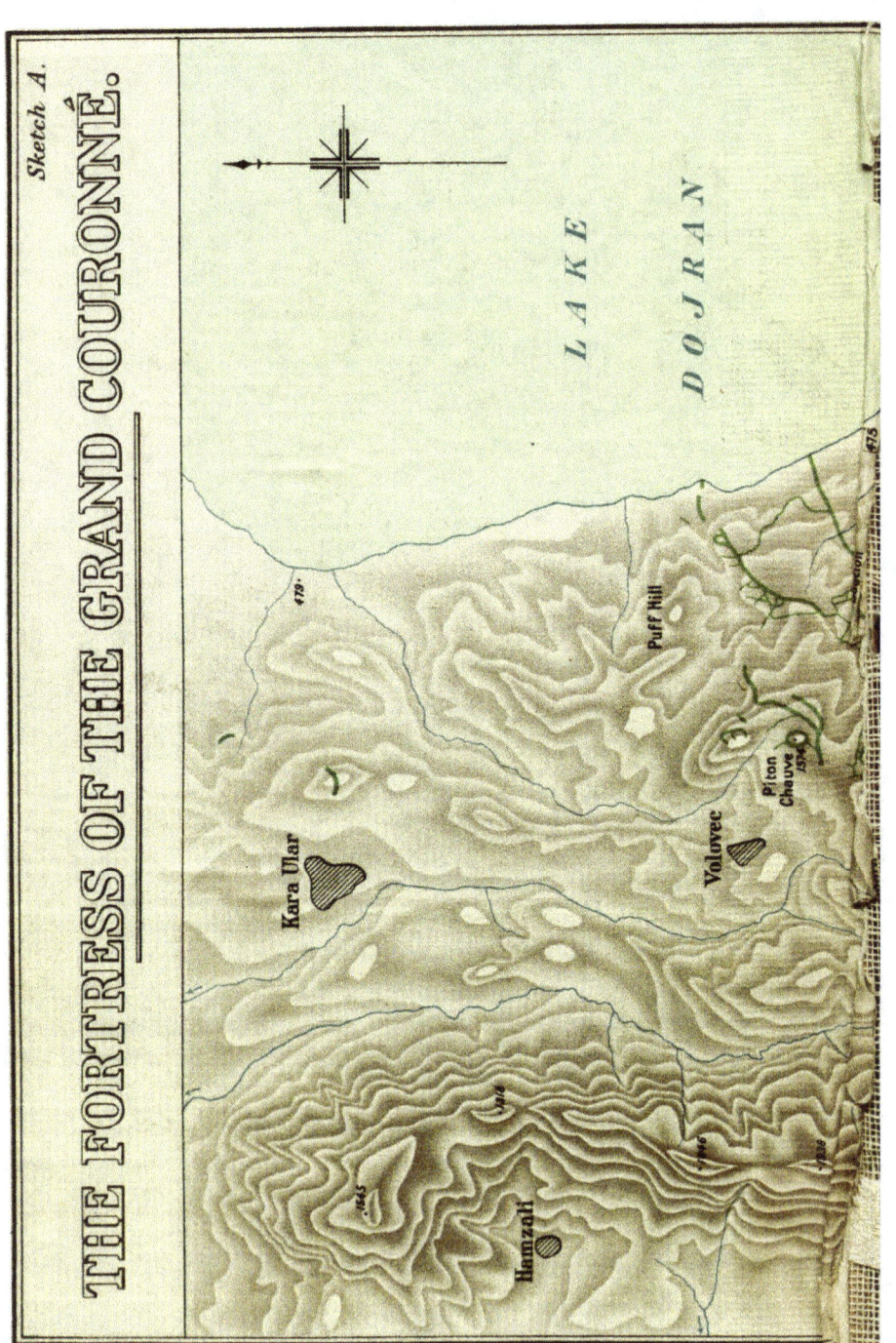

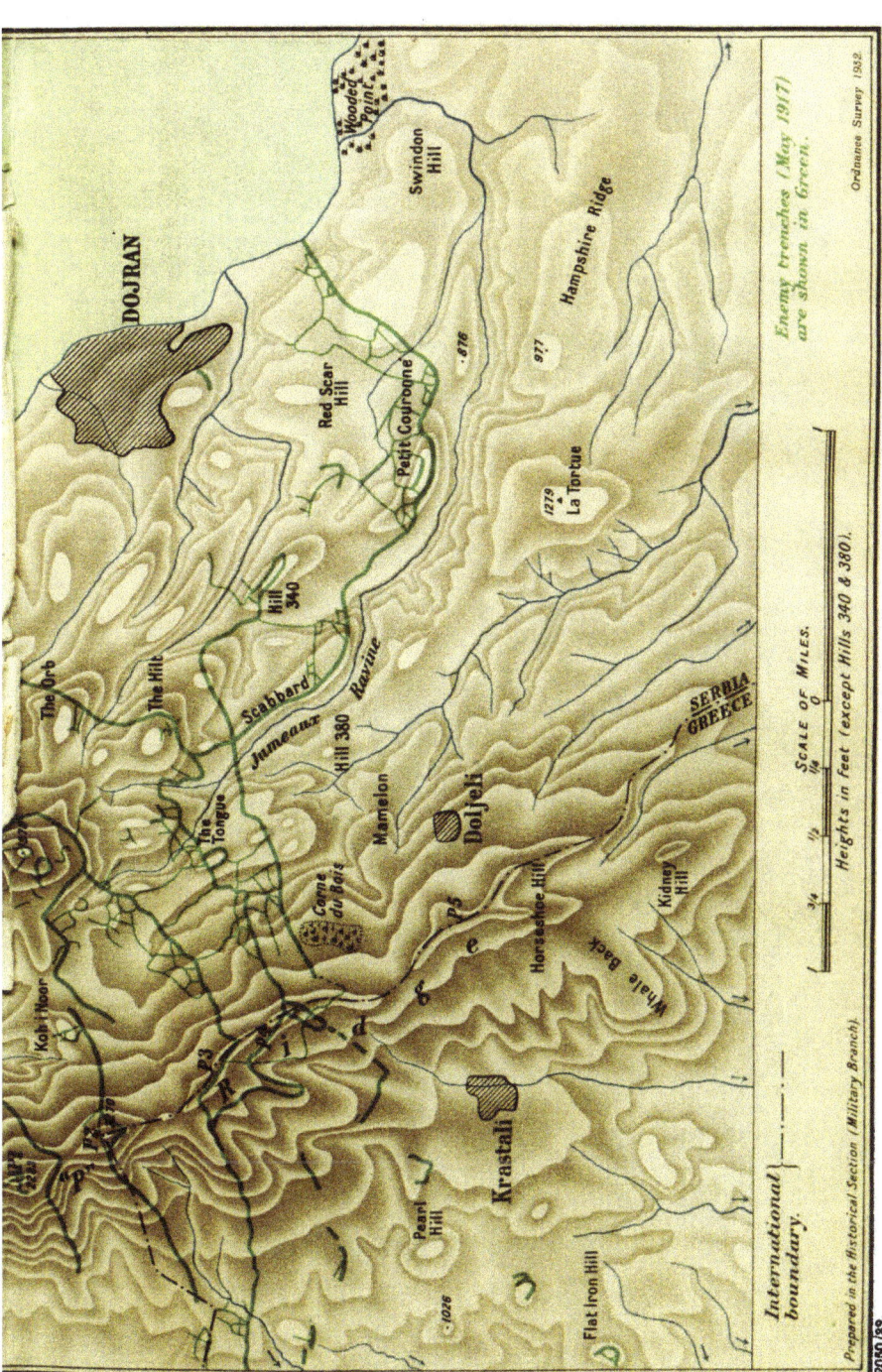

History of the Great War.

MILITARY OPERATIONS.

HISTORY OF THE GREAT WAR
BASED ON OFFICIAL DOCUMENTS
BY DIRECTION OF THE HISTORICAL SECTION OF THE
COMMITTEE OF IMPERIAL DEFENCE

MILITARY OPERATIONS MACEDONIA
FROM THE OUTBREAK OF WAR TO
THE SPRING OF 1917

COMPILED BY
Captain CYRIL FALLS
LATE R. INNIS. FUS. AND GENERAL STAFF

MAPS COMPILED BY
Major A. F. BECKE
R.A. (RETIRED), HON. M.A. (OXON.)

The Naval & Military Press Ltd

Published by

The Naval & Military Press Ltd
Unit 5 Riverside, Brambleside
Bellbrook Industrial Estate
Uckfield, East Sussex
TN22 1QQ England

Tel: +44 (0)1825 749494

www.naval-military-press.com
www.nmarchive.com

Cover image: The Salonika 1916 displaying soldiers of all Allied nations taking part in the campaign. From left to right standing: Montenegrin, British, Serbian, Italian, French Colonial Zouave, Indian, Greek. Kneeling: French Colonial Cochin Chinese, Russian, French, French Colonial.

In reprinting in facsimile from the original, any imperfections are inevitably reproduced and the quality may fall short of modern type and cartographic standards.

PREFACE.

THE history of British military operations in Macedonia will be completed in two volumes. The present volume covers events from the outbreak of the Great War to the spring of 1917, those prior to the landing of British and French troops at Salonika being only outlined. The last military operations described in it are those of the offensive of April and May, known officially as the Battle of Doiran, 1917. In the political field, however, the record is carried up to the dethronement of King Constantine of Greece in June, which ended the division of Greece into two hostile camps and brought her into the war on the side of the Allies. The second volume will not only conclude the military operations but, according to present intentions, contain a short sketch of post-war events—the record of the Army of the Black Sea, into which the British Salonika Army developed—probably in the form of an appendix.

On first examining the material, it appeared to the compiler that his method here would have to be the converse of that employed in the history of the Palestine campaign, on which he had previously been engaged.[1] There it was considered necessary to make only incidental allusion to politics; here it has seemed desirable to set the military history in a political framework and to trace all events from their political sources.

The Palestine campaign was fought almost exclusively by the troops of Great Britain and the Empire. To enable the operations to be understood it sufficed to give brief sketches of Britain's situation in Egypt, of the genesis of the Arab revolt, and of the conflict between French and Arab interests in Syria. In the Macedonian theatre, on the other hand, British, French, Serbian, Italian, Russian, and Greek troops served together, and the general control of operations was in French hands. The divergence of French and British policies affected the whole course of the campaign. The comparative inaction of the British contingent, which led to its being allotted a very large proportion

---

[1] "Military Operations, Egypt and Palestine." Vol. I (from the Outbreak of War with Germany to June 1917), by Lieut.-General Sir George MacMunn and Captain Cyril Falls; Vol. II (from June 1917 to the End of the War), by Captain Cyril Falls. (H.M. Stationery Office.)

of the front in order to release other troops, and entailed other embarrassments for its command, besides being contrary to British traditions, was due to instructions from Whitehall. These instructions cannot be comprehended unless the attitude of the Government and the General Staff, as revealed in summaries of discussions in the War Cabinet, correspondence with the French political and military authorities, and minutes of a long series of international conferences, is made clear. This attitude also helps to explain the treatment of the British Salonika Army, especially in the period with which the second volume begins, after May 1917. Perhaps it explains also the public's lack of recognition after the war of the Army's trials and endurances. An Army which, it may fairly be said, was expected not to give trouble or cause its distant theatre of war to be talked about could scarcely be crowned with laurel in an instant, however great its final achievement. The British Army was not alone in this fate. The French Army of the East, after having had a share of the limelight in the early stages of the campaign, was thereafter shrouded in a similar fog of misconception and ignorance, which not even victory completely swept away.

A second reason why it is necessary to study the political side of the campaign is that the relations between the Allies and Greece had a very important effect upon it. And while the military operations have already been shortly described in the Commander-in-Chief's despatches, there is no authoritative account, even so brief as this, of political events during the war. The negotiations with Greece, and with France on the subject of Greece, have therefore been recorded here in some detail.

The British military records are generally adequate; where they are wanting, gaps have been filled with the assistance of officers who took part in the campaign. Chapters in draft have been circulated to about two hundred of these officers, many of whose criticisms and suggestions have been invaluable. The official histories of the British operations in France, Egypt and Palestine, and Gallipoli, as well as the Naval, Royal Air Force, Medical, and Veterinary official histories, have been drawn on where necessary.[1]

---

[1] They are referred to as "France and Belgium," "Egypt and Palestine," "Naval Operations," "Medical Services," etc. There is no reference to the Royal Air Force history in the text, because the volume consulted was in course of preparation at the same time as this.

The works consulted for information about the Allies of Great Britain and about the enemy are given in the list of books which follows.

A word must be added about the last published volume of the Austrian official history, "Österreich-Ungarns Letzter Krieg," Dritter Band, Das Kriegsjahr 1915, Zweiter Teil. This admirable volume, which, except that it is without orders and appreciations, may well be described as a model of what official military history should be, appeared while the present volume was in the press, and could therefore not be made full use of. It may be said, however, that both text and maps point to the conclusion that the intervention of the Allies in Macedonia, tardy as it was, contributed even more to saving the remnant of the Serbian Armies than has been suggested in the account given here. The last and most promising of Mackensen's attempts to encircle and completely destroy the Serbians was made in the third week of November. But at that time the greater part of the Bulgarian *Second Army* was heavily engaged with the French in the Vardar–Crna loop. Had it been free to take part in the encirclement of the Serbians in the Kosovo Polje, it is probable that their forces would indeed have been destroyed, and that instead of 150,000 men escaping to the Adriatic shore there would not have been 20,000 survivors.

As in previous volumes issued by the Branch, two sets of maps are included : " sketches " which are bound in the volume, and larger " maps " issued in a separate case. A general map covering the whole British front and extending as far west as Vodena has been placed in a pocket of the text volume. Maps 8 and 10, showing respectively the operations in the Struma valley from September 1916 to May 1917 and the Dojran front in April 1917 will, it is hoped, be particularly useful. Though reference to them is not made in the margin of the text prior to the events which they are especially intended to record, they can be consulted for all operations from the time of the British advance to their respective areas.

The maps and sketches, with the exceptions of Maps A and 2, which are parts of existing publications, have been prepared by Major A. F. Becke. Probably only the compiler knows how many difficulties Major Becke has had to contend with owing to the indifferent quality of the survey work in areas beyond the British lines, or how skilfully he has overcome them. Sketches A, 4, 13, and 14 have been drawn by Mr. H. Burge ; all the other sketches and all the maps (with the two exceptions mentioned above) by Mr. J. S. Fenton.

Of the illustrations, the panorama of the western shore of Lake Dojran is reproduced from a photograph taken by the Italian troops when they were in the line east of the lake. This was lent for the purpose of reproduction by Field-Marshal Sir George Milne. The panorama of the Struma valley is from a pencil and water-colour sketch by Lieut.-Colonel S. G. R. Willis, late R.A., and lent by him. The photograph of the Belašıca Planina is the copyright of the Imperial War Museum, and those of the Demir Kapija defile and the Kajmakčalan are reproduced by arrangement with the Geneva publishing firm, Les Editions d'Art Boissonnas.

The writer has worked without an assistant in the compilation of this volume, so has no acknowledgements to make on that score. He is, however, indebted, as he was in the case of the Palestine volumes, to Mr. W. B. Wood and Mr. C. T. Atkinson for their valuable commentary upon the final text.

October 1932.   C. B. F.

NOTES.

THE convention commonly observed in the British Army regarding the distinguishing number of Armies, Corps, Divisions, etc., is followed here as in previous volumes. That is to say, they are written in full for Armies, in Roman figures for Corps, and in Arabic figures for smaller formations and units, with the exception that in the case of Field Artillery Brigades and Heavy Artillery Groups the customary Roman figures are employed. We have thus, XII Corps, 22nd Division, 65th Brigade, XCVIII Brigade R.F.A., 99th Field Company R.E.

Bulgarian, German, Austrian, and Turkish formations and units are printed in italic characters to distinguish them from those of the British or their Allies, thus: Austrian *Fifth Army*, Turkish *XX Corps*, Bulgarian *9th Division*, German *146th Regiment*.

The conventional abbreviations of regimental names are employed, *e.g.* " 4/K.R.R.C." for 4th Battalion the King's Royal Rifle Corps.

The problem of the spelling of place-names appeared difficult enough in the Palestine volumes, but was child's play to that encountered here. The area with which the greater part of this volume is concerned is partly Greek, partly Serbian, while fairly frequent reference is made to place-names in Bulgarian territory. But all this area had only recently emerged from Turkish hands. One meets, therefore, not only intermingled Turkish, Greek, and Slav names, but frequently alternative forms. To add to the difficulties, the various maps of the area contain Austrian, Turkish, Greek, and French versions of place-names.

The principle adopted has been to use in general Serbian, or rather Croatian forms for names within the (pre-war) Serbian frontier, and Greek forms for those within the Greek frontier, except in cases where either only Turkish forms existed or where only Turkish or some other alien forms would be recognizable by British readers who took part in the campaign. Thus, Gevgeli (Turk.) is preferred to Gjevgjelija (Croat.), Gnoina (Turk.) to Palaiokhora (Gk.), Kaziköi (Turk.) to Vathylakkos (Gk.), Ortach (Turk.) to Khortiates (Gk.), etc. But Khirsova (Gk.) is retained in place of the better known Hirsova (Croat.) because there seems to be no possibility of mistake. Dojran is similarly preferred to Doiran, even though the latter form is on the Colours of so many British infantry regiments.

The pronunciation of the Croatian forms presents no great difficulty if the following points are kept in mind :—

c=ts ;
ć=t in tune ; when final almost ch ;
č=ch ;
j=the consonant y ; when preceded by a vowel the semi-vowel y ;
š=sh ;
ž=approximately z in azure, or the French j ;
A vowel sound frequently does not appear, as in Crna (pr. Tserna), Prsten (pr. Persten).

The compiler is indebted to the Secretary of the Permanent Committee on Geographical Names for British Official Use for assistance in this matter. He is also indebted to Madame Draga Ilić for many helpful suggestions of a similar kind, and perhaps especially for pointing out how strongly Yugoslavs object to their towns and districts being labelled with alien forms, as if they were still alien property.

CONTENTS.

Chapter I.
The Outbreak of the Great War.

Macedonia and its Neighbours	1
The Struggle between Serbia and Austria in 1914	8

Chapter II.
The Crushing of Serbia.

After the Victory	22
The Campaign against Serbia	29
The Landing of the Allies at Salonika	37

Chapter III.
The Expedition into Serbia.

The Campaign under Discussion	42
The Advance into Serbia	50
Notes: I. Reply handed to General Joffre on the 30th October 1915	62
II. Mr. Asquith's Statement at the Calais Conference, 4th December 1915	63

Chapter IV.
The Retreat from Serbia.

The Actions of Kosturino	64
The Retreat into Greece	71
The Retreat in Greek Territory	79

Chapter V.
The Entrenched Camp of Salonika.

The Formation of the Entrenched Camp	85
Command and Administration	95
Note: Instructions with Regard to the Command at Salonika	103

Chapter VI.
The Advance from the Entrenched Camp.

General Sarrail's Projects	104
The Advance to the Frontier	111
The Change in Command	114

CONTENTS

Chapter VII.
Events Leading to the Intervention of Rumania.

The General Situation: Fort Rupel	119
Greece and the Allies..	129
The Prospect of Rumanian Intervention	133
Preparations for an Offensive	140
Note: Telegrams between General Milne and the C.I.G.S.	150

Chapter VIII.
The Dojran and Struma Operations, 9th August to 23rd September 1916.

The Dojran Operations and the Bulgarian Advance on the Flanks	152
British Holding Operations—The Action of Machukovo	162
Note: Telegrams between General Milne and the C.I.G.S.	169

Chapter IX.
The Monastir Offensive and the Rumanian Campaign.

The Action of the Karajaköis and Capture of Yeniköi	172
The Progress of the Monastir Offensive	184
The Affair of Bairakli Jum'a	192
The Rumanian Campaign and its Influence on British Policy	196

Chapter X.
The Greek Imbroglio, August 1916 to January 1917.

Affairs in Old Greece..	208
Affairs in Macedonia and Thessaly..	225
The Rome Conference	230

Chapter XI.
The Winter of 1916–1917.

The End of the Monastir Offensive..	234
The British Front: November and December 1916	241
Policy and Organization	252
The Front during January and February 1917	259
Note: Dispositions of the Enemy during the Battle of Monastir..	267

Chapter XII.
The Working of the Machine.

Exterior Communications and Supply	269
Transport	274
Water Supply..	285
Medical Services	287
Veterinary Services	291

CONTENTS

Chapter XIII.
The Battle of Dojran, 1917.

	PAGE
Preliminaries of the Offensive	294
The Night Attack of the 24th April—the 26th Division	302
The Night Attack of the 24th April—the 22nd Division	312

Chapter XIV.
The Battle of Dojran, 1917 (*continued*).

The Night Attack of the 8th May—the 26th Division	317
The Operations of the 22nd and 60th Divisions	328
The Operations of the XVI Corps	334
The Offensive West of the Vardar	339
Note: I. Letter to Lieut.-General C. J. Briggs	346
II. The Enemy's dispositions in May 1917	346

Chapter XV.
The End of the Greek Imbroglio.

Reaching a Decision	348
The Abdication of King Constantine	354
Note: Note demanding the Abdication of King Constantine and the Reply	361

TABLE OF APPENDICES.

1. Order of Battle of the Allied Armies in Macedonia, December 1916 .. 363
2. Order of Battle of the British Salonika Army, December 1916 .. 365
3. Order of Battle of the Bulgarian, German, and Turkish Forces in Macedonia, December 1916 .. 371
4. Salonika Transport Establishments .. 372
5. Army Operation Order No. 22, 8th June 1916 .. 384
6. 27th Division Operation Order No. 40, 28th September 1916 .. 385
7. XII Corps Operation Order No. 24, 9th April 1917 .. 387
8. XII Corps Letter G/4/919, 2nd May 1917 .. 391

SKETCHES, MAPS AND ILLUSTRATIONS.

SKETCHES.
(*Bound in Volume.*)

Sketch A.	The Fortress of the Grand Couronné	*At beginning*	
,, 1.	Theatre of Austro-Serbian Campaign of 1914	*Facing p.*	9
,, 2.	Action of Kosturino, 7th December 1915	,,	63
,, 3.	Sea to Vardar, 20th April 1916	,,	111
,, 4.	Dojran—"P" Ridge Position, August 1916	,,	151
,, 5.	Sea to Vardar, 4th August 1916	,,	155
,, 6.	Action of Machukovo, 13th–14th September 1916	,,	165
,, 7.	Battle of Monastir, 20th August–19th November 1916	,,	171
,, 8.	Action of the Karajaköis, 30th September 1916	,,	175
,, 9.	Affair of Bairakli Jum'a, 31st October 1916	,,	191
,, 10.	Sea to Vardar, 1st January 1917	,,	251
,, 11.	General Sarrail's Projected Offensive	,,	293
,, 12.	Sea to Vardar, April 1917	,,	297
,, 13.	Battle of Dojran, 24th April 1917	,,	301
,, 14.	Battle of Dojran, 8th May 1917	,,	319
,, 15.	Capture of Ferdie and Essex Trenches, 15th May 1917	,,	337

ILLUSTRATIONS.

The Demir Kapija Defile	*Facing p.*	68
The Belašica Planina	,,	122
The Kajmakčalan	,,	184
The Struma Valley	,,	194
Looking west over Lake Dojran	,,	306

LIST OF BOOKS CONSULTED

(In addition to the British Official Histories mentioned in the Preface).

"Armées Françaises dans la Grande Guerre, Les." (Paris: Imprimerie Nationale.)
    This admirable and well-documented official history has unfortunately only reached August 1916 for the operations in Macedonia.

Barby: "Avec l'Armée Serbe." (Paris: Albin Michel.)
    Journalistic in character but full of useful information obtained from Serbian G.H.Q. during 1914.

Conrad: "Aus meiner Dienstzeit." (Vienna-Berlin: Rikola.)
    The papers of Field-Marshal Conrad v. Hoetzendorff.

Cordonnier: "Ai-je trahi Sarrail?" (Paris: Les Étincelles.)
    Polemical, but gives information about the Battle of Monastir.

David: "Le Drame ignoré de l'Armée d'Orient." (Paris: Plon.)
    Consulted for the movements and intentions of M. Jonnart during the Greek crisis in 1917.

Desmazes and Naoumovitch: "Les Victoires Serbes en 1914." (Paris: Berger-Levrault.)
    A good military account, based on official documents, of the operations of 1914 from the Serbian side.

Falkenhayn: "General Headquarters and its critical Decisions." (English Edition, Hutchinson.)
    Extremely valuable for the period during which the writer was Chief of the General Staff.

Feyler: (i) "Les Campagnes de Serbie, 1914 et 1915"; (ii) "La Campagne de Macédoine, 1916–1917"; (iii) "La Campagne de Macédoine, 1917–1918." (Geneva: Editions d'Art Boissonnas.)
    A valuable study of the whole series of campaigns by a Swiss officer. Wonderfully good photographs.

Gallwitz: "Meine Führertätigkeit im Weltkriege, 1914–1916." (Berlin: Mittler.)
    The commander of the German *Eleventh Army* gives a clear account of the offensive of 1915.

"Herbstschlacht in Macedonien, Cernabogen 1916." (Berlin: Stalling.)
    A German official monograph. Consulted for the Battle of Monastir.

"Historique des Troupes Coloniales pendant la Grande Guerre, 1914–1918 (Fronts Extérieurs)." (Paris: Lavauzelle.)
    An official work which has been found especially useful for the period after August 1916, where the official military history of the French Armies leaves off.

Kuhl: "Der Weltkrieg 1914–1918." (Berlin: Kolk.)
    A useful two-volume history of the Great War by a well-known German soldier.

Larcher: "La Grande Guerre dans les Balkans." (Paris: Payot.)
    A strategical and political study.

LON: "Bulgaria en la Guerra Europea, 1915–1918." (Madrid: Talleres del Depósito de la Guerra.)
    A curious work by a lieutenant-colonel on the Spanish General Staff, written on the spot. The account of the opening phases of the campaign is excellent and detailed. After the Allied advance from the Entrenched Camp the account, so far as Macedonia is concerned, tails off into a colourless and almost valueless summary, which looks as if it were derived from official wireless communiqués. The notes on the Bulgarian military organization are full.

NÉDEFF: "Les Opérations en Macédoine, l'Épopée de Doïran." (Sofia: Imprimerie Armeyski Voeno-Isdatelski Fond.)
    A translation by a French officer of the work of a Bulgarian lieutenant-colonel on the General Staff. The sub-title, "The Epic of Dojran," defines its scope. For the fighting on the Dojran front throughout the campaign it is invaluable.

"ÖSTERREICH-UNGARNS LETZTER KRIEG." (Vienna: Verlag der Militarwissenschaftlingen Mitteilungen.)
    The excellent official Austrian military history of the Great War has been found valuable for the operations of 1914 against Serbia. The volume covering the year 1915 on the Serbian front appeared while this work was in the press.

ROBERTSON: "Soldiers and Statesmen." (Cassell.)
    Field-Marshal Sir William Robertson's memoirs of the Great War show clearly the attitude of the General Staff with regard to the Macedonian Campaign.

SARRAIL: "Mon Commandement en Orient (1916–1918)." (Paris: Flammarion.)
    General Sarrail's defence is written in an angry tone and is often misleading, but contains information not so far available elsewhere.

SCHWARTE: "Der Grosse Krieg." (Leipzig: Johann Ambrosius Barth.)
    A ten-volume history of the Great War, edited by General Schwarte, the various sections being written by German or Austrian officers who took part in the campaigns which they describe.

VILLARI: "The Macedonian Campaign." (English Edition, Fisher Unwin.)
    A study of the Macedonian Campaign as a whole with special reference to the part played by Italian troops.

NOTE.—Reference to certain other works occasionally consulted is made in footnotes in the text. All German regimental and battalion histories available have been consulted.

CHAPTER 1.

THE OUTBREAK OF THE GREAT WAR.

(Maps 1, 2; Sketch 1.)

MACEDONIA AND ITS NEIGHBOURS.

JOURNEYING by railway northward from Athens, the traveller is borne by Helicon, by Parnassos, through the vale of Tempe below the peak of Ossa, and along the shoreward flank of Olympos. He passes through the birthplace of the fairest and most splendid mythology ever conceived, the finest source of inspiration to the poetry of all ages. As he continues on his way, Olympos behind him, Greek names, lovely as music, still accompany him, and still lofty peaks and bold ridges, with pine-woods and flowering shrubs on their flanks and green valleys between, look down upon the bright waters of the Ægean. Names and scenery alike still seem to belong to Hellas and to accord with its legacy of history and myth. Yet thenceforward, even upon the shore west of the isle of Thasos, names like Olympos, Aponomi, Kassandra, and Athos are mingled with those of the harsher Turkish tongue; east of Thasos the names are all Turkish. If he goes north from Salonika Slav names appear, holding divided sway with the Turkish, having driven out the Greek. He is reminded that Macedonia, not Greek in origin, has been mainly Slav under Turkish rule for hundreds of years.

Ancient Macedonia was first a kingdom, then a Roman province; but the district to which we now commonly apply the name has never been a national entity, though its natural boundaries are well enough defined. It may be said to consist of the valleys of four great rivers, the Mesta, the Struma, the Vardar, and the Vistritsa. Its eastern boundary is, first, the lower Mesta, then the Dospad range; its northern follows the lofty Rila Dagh, the heights, lesser but still almost impassable from north to south, between the Struma at Kyustendil and the Morava, and between the Morava and the Vardar; its western is the great chain of mountains beginning with the Šar Planina, which separate it from Albania and cut it off from the Adriatic. To the south there is no barrier comparable to these, and the boundary here may be described as running along Latitude 40 to the sea at Olympos. The mountains on three sides are of savage grandeur and as inaccessible as any in Europe, impassable for the purposes of trade or war except along the corridors cut by certain rivers. Those to the west form the strongest barrier of all, the peaks being 7,000 feet high and the steep-faced ridges all along from 4,000 to 5,000 feet. Hardly anywhere has Nature shut off one land from another more completely than here. It is true that the Romans, who were daunted by no gradients, made a military road from Dyrrhachium (Durazzo) through Salonika and Xanthi to Constantinople; but west of Monastir their *Via Egnatia* can no longer be traced. Modern engineering science, however, can find a way even through barriers such as this. As we shall see, Serbia, after the Second Balkan War in 1913, sought an outlet to the Adriatic, despite this barrier, when she found that Salonika was unattainable.

There is one immemorial highway from north to south which makes this district of strategic and commercial importance and gives a symbolic meaning to the trident-form of Khalkidike, poised above the Ægean. This route branches off at Niš from the still greater highway (along the Maritsa valley from Sofia to Adrianople) to Constantinople and the east. It follows the Southern Morava, crosses the watershed, and runs down the valley of the Vardar to Salonika. Along it is laid the Niš–Salonika railway. There is another north-and-south route down the Struma from Sofia to the Ægean at Salonika and Kavalla, but it is much more difficult and was not followed by a railway at the outbreak of the Great War. It is the Vardar corridor which gives Salonika its strategic significance, and would have made it perhaps the first port of the Near East but for national rivalries and their artificial barriers. When it is added that the city's immediate hinterland, the Macedonian plains, is rich agricultural land and that there is great, though as yet scarcely tapped, mineral wealth in the mountains, that it has the only good harbour between the Gulf of Volos and the Dardanelles, that it is only 250 miles from Piræus and from Smyrna, and about 800 from the entrance to the Suez Canal at Port Said, the possibilities of Salonika in peace and its importance in war can easily be grasped.

The city, which is surrounded by Byzantine walls,

had, at the outbreak of the Great War, a population of about 170,000. It had a safe harbour with good anchorage, a long quay and several piers, and ample warehouses, but no dock. It is built upon a natural amphitheatre, with a citadel at the top of the hill. On the higher slopes is the upper town, largely Turkish. The lower town, stretching to the water-front, is almost entirely Jewish and contains the business quarter. To the south-east is a residential suburb, in which are the foreign consulates. Its worst feature is its unhealthiness, due to the malaria-carrying mosquitoes of the neighbouring marshes; but this it shares in summer with most of the valleys of Macedonia.

Macedonia is populated by a medley of races. The three most important are the Serbians, who are Slavs; the Bulgarians, of Turanian origin but now largely of Slav blood and using a Slav language; and the Greeks. Even here there are sub-divisions; for example, a barrier as stiff as that of race divides the Bulgar Pomak mountaineers, who are Mohammedans, from their Christian brethren. The Greeks are concentrated mainly in the large towns and in the peninsula of Khalkidike. There are Turks—the former landed aristocracy, which was already disappearing in 1914, and the peasantry planted on its estates—Albanians from the western mountains, Vlachs, Jews, and Gypsies. To add to the Babel, the Salonika Jews speak fair Castilian Spanish, being mostly descendants of refugees from Spain, though there was a Jewish colony as far back as the day of St. Paul.

The mixture of the three chief races is largely the result of the long struggle in the dark ages for possession of the Vardar corridor and the access to the sea afforded by it. The history of the country is as tangled as its mountains, but a very brief sketch, avoiding all complexities, will help to make clear the situation at the outbreak of the Great War. It is the more necessary because aspirations and claims in this land of long memories are based upon very distant events, Basil the Bulgar-Slayer being as near to Macedonian Greeks as Gladstone is to Britons.

The victory of Philip of Macedon at Chæronea in 338 B.C. imposed the conqueror's will upon Greece and allowed his son to claim to be the representative of Greek culture. The untimely death of Alexander in 323 B.C. cut short the dominance of a civilization which might have changed the whole course of history; and by 168 B.C. Macedonia was in the hands of the Romans. It remained a Roman province for a thousand years, but passed to the Eastern Empire at the end of the fourth century A.D. In the sixth century the Slavs appeared, soon followed by the Bulgars; and from that time forward there was conflict between them and Byzantium. Twice Bulgar rule was established; the second empire, in the early thirteenth century, being followed by a Latin (Crusaders') Kingdom of Salonika. On each occasion the Byzantines regained control, on the first by the victories of Basil II, on the second by the absorption of the Greek Empire of Nicæa, the successor to the Angeloi dynasty, which had driven out the Latins. In the fourteenth century came the dominion of the Serbs, who, adding their conquests to the dowry of the Greek Emperor's daughter, finally, under the great Stephen Dushan, ruled nearly all Macedonia. But a still greater and a more stable power was approaching. In the latter part of the century the Ottoman Turks appeared on the scene, and overthrew both Serbs and Bulgars. Salonika, which had never, and has never been either Serbian or Bulgarian, was maintained by the Greeks for a short time and was for seven years held by the Venetians. From them the Turks captured it in 1430, to remain in possession of it and of all Macedonia for nearly five centuries.

Now night fell upon Macedonia, long veiling the woes of its peoples from the world at large. Only when the stirring of national consciousness began, first in Greece, then in the Balkan countries to the north, could its inhabitants make known their miseries and their aspirations to the Powers of nineteenth-century Europe. After the long War of Independence, Greece won her freedom in 1829. Serbia, after gaining a qualified measure of autonomy in the same year, saw the last Turkish garrisons depart in 1867. Bulgaria still remained beneath the yoke, to be set free after one of the biggest of the periodic Balkan conflagrations, lit by a rising in Bosnia and Hercegovina in 1875. That revolt was quickly put down by the Turks; nor was the Bulgarian rebellion in the spring of the following year any more successful. Immediately afterwards Serbia declared war on Turkey, and was in her turn swiftly defeated. The rapid expansion of the public Press made known to the conscience of Europe the terrible atrocities committed by the Turkish irregulars ; and in Britain especially the plight of the Bulgarians was regarded with popular indignation owing to the passionate eloquence with which Gladstone pleaded their cause. But Britain, jealous of the spread of Russian influence among the Slav peoples and of Russian designs upon Constantinople, retaining also some sympathy for Turkey, her ally against Napoleon and Mehemet Ali in Syria, and against Tsar Nicholas in the Crimea, was not yet prepared to see the Porte deprived of its sovereignty. It was Russia who took up arms in 1877 and, with the aid of Rumania and later of Serbia, defeated Turkey. By the Treaty of San Stefano on the 3rd March 1878 Bulgaria was constituted " an autonomous tributary principality," with boundaries extending to the Ægean to include most of Macedonia, and also taking in the valley of the Maritsa to just above Adrianople, before running eastward to the Black Sea.

The other Powers had previously announced that they would have to be consulted regarding the settlement ; and Russia agreed to the Congress of Berlin, at which the Treaty of San Stefano should be reviewed. Britain raised objection to certain of its clauses and notably to the extent of the new Bulgaria, which would contain great numbers of non-Bulgarian subjects and excite the jealousy of all the other Balkan peoples. Her strongest objection was doubtless that, on the one hand, the Vardar corridor and the access to the Mediterranean which it afforded, on the other, the Maritsa valley, within a hundred miles of Constantinople, would fall into the hands of a Slav State under the influence of Russia and owing to that Empire its very existence. Britain's view prevailed with the Congress, and as a result of the Treaty of Berlin Bulgaria found herself sadly shorn of her promised dominions, of which, indeed, she lost upwards of two-thirds. She was confined within the comparatively narrow limits of the Danube and the Balkan range. What has here been defined as Macedonia remained under direct Turkish rule, while a large area to the east, and south of the new Bulgarian frontier, was formed into a semi-autonomous province for which was invented the title of " Eastern Rumelia." It was " peace with honour," but peace infected from the first by the virus that was to breed future wars.[1]

---

[1] Other articles of the treaty provided for the transfer of Bosnia and Hercegovina to the administration of Austria ; formal recognition of

Unfortunate Macedonia was returned to the mercies of the Turks, having to be content with the promise of " special Commissions, in which the native element should " be strongly represented " to elaborate the details of its system of government. The Porte never appointed these commissions, and that article of the treaty was therefore useless. Rather more valuable was the appointment of foreign officers to the police force. Neither the Serbo-Bulgar War of 1885 nor the Græco-Turkish War of 1897 need concern us here ; for the first caused no transfer of territory and the second only a slight modification of the frontier between Turkish Macedonia and Greece near Larissa. In 1886 Eastern Rumelia was united with Bulgaria. The accession of the Karageorgević dynasty to the throne of Serbia after the murder of King Alexander in 1903 strengthened that country. The next great event was the Turkish Revolution. It was born in Macedonia, the Young Turk Committee of Union and Progress transferring itself from Geneva to Salonika in 1906, and it aroused the wildest enthusiasm there. Turks, Greeks, Bulgarians, and Serbs embraced publicly. The Jews of Salonika, good citizens under any authority and demanding only liberty to attend to their affairs, were equally overjoyed. A golden age seemed to be dawning. The sanguine Powers of Europe smiled benignantly—and withdrew the foreign police officers.

The reaction alas! was swift and bitter. The old Turkish administration had been marked by outbursts of savagery in times of threatened danger, alternating with long somnolence—a deadening somnolence, no doubt, but not quite unbearable. The new *régime* forthwith set about levelling races and abolishing national distinctions in pursuit of the policy of " Turkification " which it attempted to introduce all over the Turkish Empire. The Christian Balkan States watched with growing anger, and finally decided that they would settle the Macedonian problem once and for all for themselves. The Powers tried to preserve peace, promising that they would enforce the neglected clause of the Treaty of Berlin ; but Serbia, Bulgaria, and Greece considered with some justice that the promises of the Powers were apt to fade away when they brought them up

---

the independence of Rumania, Serbia, and Montenegro ; the cession of Bessarabia by Rumania to Russia in return for the cession of the Dobruja to Rumania, etc.

for discussion and found their own ambitions and rivalries in conflict. The First Balkan War broke out on the 17th October 1912.

The campaign brought overwhelming victory to the Allies, and resulted in Turkey being swept out of Macedonia. But the conquerors could not agree over the division of the spoils. Bulgaria, who had borne the brunt of the fighting, claimed Salonika and Kavalla, with all the coast between them, which Greece was determined to hold. Serbia, seeing that Bulgaria was obtaining unexpected gains to the east, including Adrianople, while she herself was denied by Austria access to the Adriatic, demanded that the secret pact between the two States, by which certain Macedonian territories were guaranteed to Bulgaria, should be revised. Once again the Powers failed to settle the quarrel, and in July 1913 Bulgaria declared war on Serbia and Greece. Despite her exhaustion and losses, she was quite confident of beating both single-handed. Any chance she may have had of doing so was, however, at once ruined by the sudden intervention of Rumania, who invaded her territories from the north. Turkey, in defiance of the Treaty of London, promptly recaptured Adrianople and invaded her from the east. Bulgaria was overwhelmed in a few days. The Treaty of Bucharest of the 9th August 1913 brought the Second Balkan War to an end. Serbia extended her territories to include northern Macedonia, to just south of Monastir. Greece got all southern Macedonia to Kavalla, including that port. Bulgaria, supported by Austria, was comparatively fortunate in being allowed to annex the valleys of the upper Struma and Mesta and also in obtaining egress to the Ægean between Kavalla and Dede Agach, though the latter was only an open roadstead; but she had to hand over to Rumania a large strip of the Southern Dobruja on the shore of the Black Sea.

Such was the situation resulting from the two Balkan Wars when the far greater struggle, of which they were in part the cause, burst out a year later. Greece was fairly satisfied. Serbia was disappointed and angered by her treatment at the hands of Austria, who had denied her a port on the Adriatic, and was listening to the call of her Slav fellow-countrymen in the Austrian dominions, especially in Bosnia and Hercegovina, which Austria-Hungary had annexed in 1908. Yet her feelings were mild by comparison with the bitterness of Bulgaria. Once again the " Greater "Bulgaria" had been snatched from her, this time after she had performed heroic exploits to deserve it. When war broke out anew she was frankly and cynically in the market, looking out for an ally who would give her what she desired and had lost. On the whole, however, her sympathies were with the Central Powers, partly from hatred of Serbia, partly from gratitude to Austria, who had stood by her when Russia, her old patron, had deserted her. Once again she was looking across to the rich plains of Macedonia and to the Ægean at Salonika, biding her time, but with the fury of thwarted ambition in her heart.

The Struggle between Serbia and Austria in 1914.

Map 1.
Sketch 1.
This history is concerned with the campaign in Macedonia from the moment when Great Britain and France decided to land troops at Salonika in an attempt to succour Serbia. Only an outline of the operations, of 1914, as later of those of October 1915, will therefore be given here.[1] Nor is it necessary to go over again the oft-traversed ground of the murder of Archduke Franz Ferdinand at Sarajevo and the feverish negotiations between that event and the outbreak of hostilities. It suffices for the moment to state that on the declaration of war by Austria-Hungary on Serbia on the 28th July 1914, Italy, Bulgaria, Rumania, Greece, and Turkey decided to remain neutral. Of these Turkey alone came into the war before the end of 1914, though the Austrians in their attacks on Serbia were continually pursuing the will-o'-the-wisp of Bulgarian intervention. Montenegro at once rallied to Serbia's side.

The situation of Serbia was less hopeless than it appeared to the world at large, but had certain grave disadvantages. She had a brave, well-led, and well-trained Army. At Kragujevac she had a good arsenal, though its output was to prove quite insufficient for her needs. Her northern frontier was formed by the rivers Sava, or Save, and Danube, which unite at Belgrade; her western by the Sava's

---

[1] The chief authorities consulted for the summary which follows are, on the Austro-Hungarian side, " Österreich-Ungarns Letzter Krieg," I ; Conrad IV and V, and Schwarte V ; on the Serbian side, Desmazes and Barby.

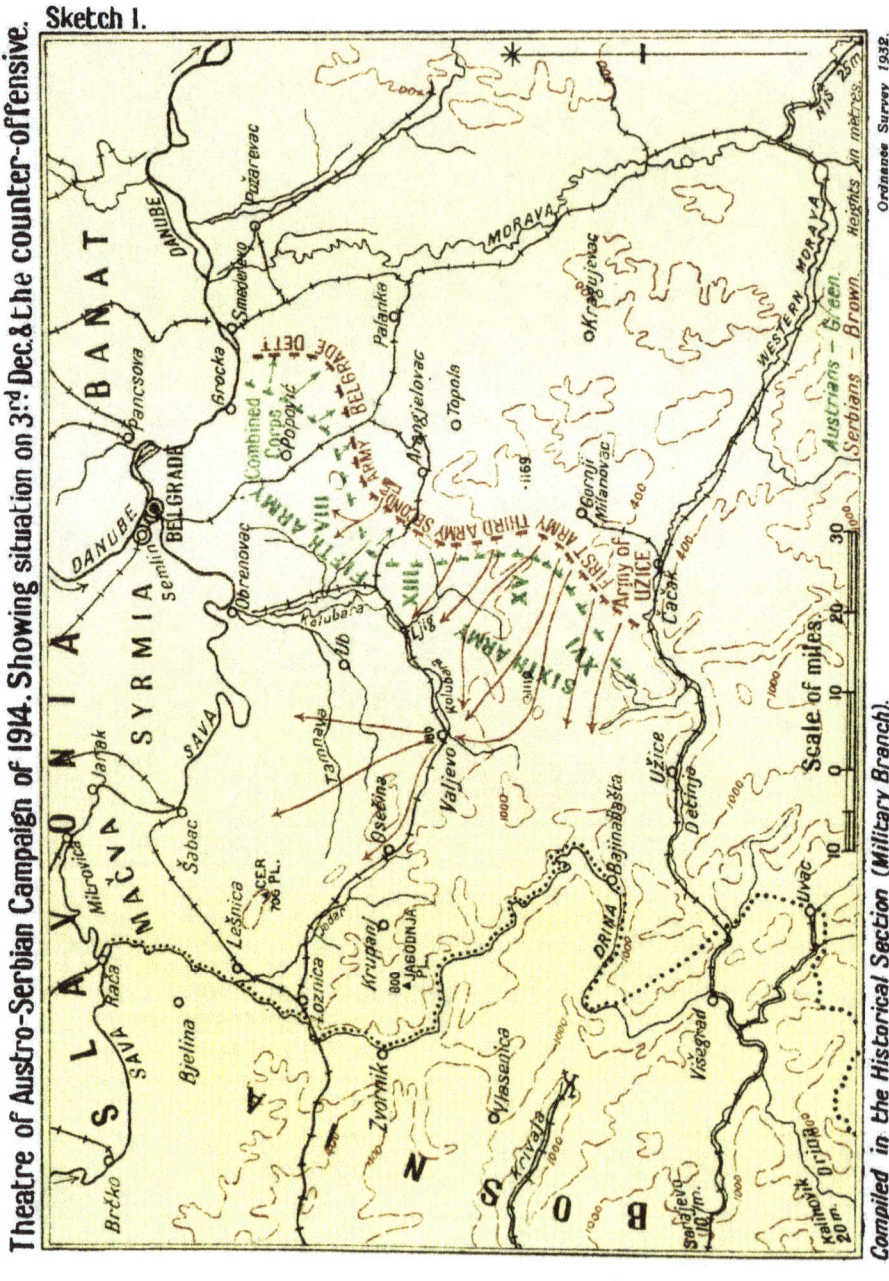

SERBIA'S DANGERS

tributary, the Drina, also a formidable barrier. Montenegro was a small but sturdy ally; no great danger threatened from Albania, and on the south none at all from Greece, if, indeed, help might not be looked for from that quarter. Her eastern frontier with Bulgaria was another matter; and here there was grave risk that her old enemy would attack her, probably waiting until she was deeply engaged with Austria in the north. Her other disadvantages were, first, the inferiority of her equipment and communications by comparison with those of Austria, and, secondly, the fact that her capital and only considerable city lay between the right banks of Sava and Danube, was indefensible, and could be shelled by field guns from Austrian territory. In fact, the Government had to abandon the city at once and retire to Niš, the principal fortress of the country, but a small town of not more than 25,000 inhabitants. There could be no doubt of Austria's power to overwhelm Serbia if Russia did not intervene in the latter's favour. The news of Russia's mobilization was therefore received with great enthusiasm by her fellow-Slavs.

1914.
Aug.

Compelled to leave a proportion of her troops in Macedonia to watch Bulgaria, Serbia managed to concentrate a considerable force to the north to guard against the Austrian menace; but nearly half of it consisted of troops of the " Second Ban " or *Landwehr*. The three principal Armies, the First (four cavalry regiments and 52 battalions), Second (one cavalry regiment and 64 battalions), and Third (about 35 battalions),[1] concentrated south-east, south, and south-west of Belgrade. Learning of a great concentration north of the Sava and Danube, the Serbians expected the main attack from this quarter; but they were stationed in good positions for swinging towards Danube, Sava, or Drina as required. Another so-called Army, the Army of Užice (24 battalions), assembled at the point from which it took its name, on the Niš–Sarajevo railway, prepared to co-operate with the Montenegrins. The supreme command was nominally in the hands of the youthful Regent, Prince Alexander, actually in those of an experienced veteran, the Voivode (Marshal) Putnik.

---

[1] Authorities differ as to the exact number of battalions in the Armies, but the differences appear to be due to " Third Ban " troops being included in some cases and not in others. The approximate figures here given do not include them.

The Austrians had concentrated three Armies, the *Second*, *Fifth*, and *Sixth*. In accordance with the plan worked out long before by the Austrian Chief of the General Staff, General Conrad von Hoetzendorff, the *Fifth* and *Sixth Armies* were to attack eastward across the Drina, thus simultaneously assuring the protection of Bosnia, while the *Second* attacked southward across the Sava and Danube. This plan and the mobilization based upon it had, however, assumed a campaign against Serbia alone— a punitive expedition, as Austria would have considered it. It collapsed at once when it became known that Russia also was about to enter the field. The *Second Army* was now destined for Galicia, but it was found impossible to interrupt the train movements already in progress. The *Second Army* was therefore ordered to complete its mobilization and remain on the Sava and Danube until the northern railway lines were clear, and meanwhile to limit itself to demonstrations. The two remaining Armies, with 140,000 rifles, were inferior in numbers to the Serbians opposed to them, who had some 180,000 rifles of the First and Second Ban. The small Montenegrin Army [1] would have to be contained by the garrison troops of Southern Bosnia and Hercegovina, which numbered some 40,000 men from Sarajevo to Cattaro. The new plan was to cross the Drina and advance by two valleys running east and west, that of the Jadar, a tributary of the Drina, and that of the Detinja, which had its source quite close to the Drina but flowed eastward to the Morava. The supreme command of the two Armies was confided to Feldzeugmeister Potiorek, the commander of the *Sixth*, an energetic officer of high reputation who knew the country well, having been Governor of Bosnia.

The country east of the Drina changes greatly in character from north to south. East of the lower Drina and covering the great bend between it and the Sava is a rich plain known as the Mačva, which becomes swampy in wet weather. Both the Mačva and the banks of the Drina further south are commanded by the Cer Planina, a steep, wooded range, which is in fact a spur connected by a low col with the hills further south. South of the valley

---

[1] Montenegro is believed to have mobilized about 40,000 men, but a considerable portion of these were threatening Cattaro, the harbour of which was shelled from the heights above.

FIRST ROUND TO SERBIA

of the Jadar, which enters the Drina west of the Cer Planina, the heights gradually increase and the country becomes more and more difficult for campaigning. There is, however, one trough cut through it, the valley of the Detinja, continued by that of the Western Morava. But that is the last east-and-west route of any value; further south the country is frankly mountainous, with peaks rising above 6,000 feet, suited only to the movement of lightly-equipped troops with mountain artillery.

1914. Aug.

The fighting which followed the first Austrian attack reminds us of the long-drawn-out combats between Austrians and French on the Rhine in 1796. Then, as now, the passage of a great river was accomplished time after time, to be followed by a counter-stroke which threw the assailant back across it. Then, as now, the dispersion of the opposing forces gave the army attacked at one point opportunity to make a diversion and threaten the attacker's communications at another. The two sides were well matched, the Austrian superiority in artillery and transport being compensated for by the stouter quality of the Serbian infantry in general, which was possibly inferior to the finest Austrian regiments but far more reliable than the disaffected Czech troops in the enemy's Armies.

The battle began on the 12th August, when the Austrian *Sixth* and *Fifth Armies* crossed the Drina at several points between Višegrad and Bjelina. Their advance was fiercely disputed by the Serbian covering troops and their progress was slow, though the *Fifth* reached Krupanj, 15 miles east of the river, on the 16th. The Serbian Second and Third Armies at once advanced westward to meet the threat, and after hot fighting drove the *Fifth Army* back across the Drina on the 20th. The *Sixth Army*, opposed at Višegrad only by the weak Army of Užice, seems to have been brought to a halt rather by its neighbour's lack of success than by the efforts of the Serbians, and its effort was curiously weak. The first round had ended heavily in favour of the Voivode Putnik, who had shown that lack of information is not necessarily fatal to the commander who keeps his head. Ignorant of where the main blow was to fall, and indeed deceived on this point, he had held a mass of manœuvre in a central position until assured of the enemy's intentions, and then struck with all his might. Diversions by both combatants had failed. The Austrian *Second Army* had sent a detachment across the Sava and captured Šabac, but had withdrawn it on the 20th. Away to the south-west the Montenegrins had crossed the frontier into Southern Bosnia, but had been quickly driven out.

It was now the turn of the Serbians to pass to the offensive, urged upon them by Russia and to which they were the more inclined because they had learnt of the departure of almost the whole of the Austrian *Second Army*, and that the Sava and Danube were lightly held. Potiorek had, in fact, been obliged to side-slip his Armies northward, but from the junction of the Sava and Drina his troops were thin on the ground. On the 6th September the Serbian First Army crossed the Sava and entered the rich plain of Syrmia, to be greeted with wild enthusiasm by the inhabitants. At the very beginning a disaster befell its left; for a division which crossed between Jarak and Mitrovica was attacked before it could get its ammunition across and driven back on the bridge, which was broken by the fugitives. Here 5,000 men laid down their arms. To the south-east, in the great loop of the Sava, good progress was made, the limit of the advance, reached on the 11th, being nearly 20 miles from the crossing-place. Prince Alexander entered Semlin, which lies opposite Belgrade, between the Sava and Danube.

Potiorek had meanwhile been making preparations to remedy his first failure. He had been hoping for Bulgarian intervention, but had now received word that this was unlikely. When he heard that the Serbians had crossed the Sava he decided, soundly as it would appear, that his best course was to carry out his already-planned offensive across the Drina, and launched it on the 8th. Affairs, however, went very ill. The *Fifth Army* on the left was repulsed with a loss of 4,000 men. On the right the *Sixth Army* did much better further up the Drina and established its bridgeheads with little loss, but its advance eastward was soon slowed down in this difficult country. On the 11th Potiorek won a considerable success. The *Sixth Army* drove the Serbians off the Jagodnja heights west of Krupanj and thus established itself upon a strong position some eight miles east of the Drina. This came at a very happy moment for him, just as the Serbian advance into Syrmia had reached its high-water mark, and was completely successful in forcing the invaders out of Austrian

SERBIAN ADVANCE INTO BOSNIA

territory. By the 14th the Serbians had evacuated Syrmia. Two of their divisions from the northern flank moved south by forced marches and by the 17th had thrown themselves into the battle to check the progress of the enemy from the west.

1914. Sept.

On the heels of the Serbians retiring from Syrmia the Austrian left wing crossed the Sava at Jarak and invaded the Mačva. Potiorek was hopeful that this threat to the Serbian right would assist his main attack, but the rains had flooded the Mačva and the Austrians made little progress here. East of the Drina attack and counter-attack followed one another in rapid succession amid the wooded hills. Both sides fought with great bravery and—as apparently throughout the campaign—with terrible savagery, and there can have been few bloodier battles in the course of the war. The two Austrian corps most heavily engaged suffered nearly 30,000 casualties between the 8th and 24th September; while in the fighting south of Krupanj one Serbian division had 6,000. The Austrians made practically no progress anywhere, and actually lost the Jagodnja heights. When the Serbians through sheer exhaustion gave up their attempts to drive them back across the river, Potiorek temporarily suspended operations on the lower Drina, glad enough of breathing-time to attend to a critical situation in his right rear.

While the main battle was raging the Serbian Army of Užice had on the 15th suddenly crossed the upper Drina at Bajinabašta and Višegrad, while simultaneously two Montenegrin detachments on its left advanced upon the fortresses of Sarajevo and Kalinovik. The Austrians, having concentrated for their offensive, had left small detachments only on their right flank, and the attack made very swift progress. Potiorek at first hoped that it would be directed mainly against Sarajevo, which he considered impregnable; and indeed the Serbian commander seems to have dallied with the notion of capturing the Bosnian capital for political reasons and to have pictured himself in the rôle of liberator of his fellow-Slavs. If so, a peremptory order from the Voivode Putnik recalled him to realities and directed him to march on Vlasenica, seizing the head of the railway which ran up the Krivaja valley behind the Austrian right. On the 27th Potiorek, who was now beginning to be aware of his danger, struck at the small column from Bajinabašta, forced it back to the Drina, and captured an order which revealed how serious was the threat. Putnik had directed the Army of Užice, after capturing Vlasenica, to press on northward and attack the Austrian *Sixth Army* in rear, while he himself renewed the attack frontally.

Potiorek now acted swiftly and with undeniable vigour. He had received some small reinforcements and was able to spare a couple of brigades from the Drina front. The Serbians, who had occupied Vlasenica on the 28th, found themselves faced with a much sterner resistance and were subjected to heavy attacks. By the 4th October they had been driven back to the railway, where General Bojanović reported to the Voivode that he could not hope to stand. He was indeed dislodged by combined frontal and flank attacks and fell back stubbornly throughout the 8th, 9th, and 10th, while a fresh Austrian column from Sarajevo attacked the Montenegrins on his left. Continuing to press its advantage in very bad weather, the Austrian left reached the Drina at Bajinabašta on the 14th; and by the 25th the Serbian rearguard had crossed to the right bank at Višegrad. The small Serbian force had suffered severely from the haphazard methods and lack of discipline of their Montenegrin allies, brave and dashing soldiers who fought rather by clans than in military formations. The Austrian troops deserve, however, every credit for the energy with which they extricated their comrades lower down the Drina from an ugly situation.

Feldzeugmeister Potiorek had now cleared Bosnia. He had strong bridgeheads over the Drina in enemy territory. Belgrade was not in his hands, but was useless to the Serbians, being under continuous fire from his land batteries and monitors. He certainly had not gained all that his restless and ambitious spirit desired, and the spectacle of his great Empire being thus checked by a small State was humiliating in the eyes of the world. But, considering the numbers of the opposing forces, he had done by no means ill. Possibly he would have now been better advised to content himself with strengthening and deepening his bridgeheads over the Drina, clearing the Mačva to make his left secure, and then calling a halt until the spring. The bad weather was upon him, snow having begun to fall. An advance meant quitting the good roads of Bosnia and Hungary for the bad ones of Serbia. On the other hand,

AUSTRIAN VICTORY ON THE DRINA 15

according to the reports of prisoners and agents, the Serbians were even more weary than his own troops and far less well provided with munitions. He himself had now been freed, to Conrad's disgust, from the control of Austrian G.H.Q., and found himself an independent commander. We cannot say that he was wrong when he decided to renew the offensive.

On the northern front trench warfare, with trench-to-trench attacks, had begun. On the 24th October the Austrian attacks in the Mačva were renewed and by the end of the month the Serbians had been forced out of this salient, the Austrians holding the Šabac–Lešnica railway, which represented its chord. Potiorek was now ready to strike his main blow, having filled up his ammunition dumps along the Drina. On the 5th November he began his artillery preparation and on the following day launched his attack. Now, at last, he began to gather the fruits of his previous labours. The *Sixth Army* in particular made astonishing progress and forced back the opposing Serbian First Army eight miles in two days' fighting, the Third Army on its right being compelled to conform to its retreat. The Voivode Putnik on the 10th decided to break off the action and ordered a withdrawal of the Second Army to Ub and of the Third and First to a semi-circular position eight miles north and west of the important town of Valjevo, in the valley of the upper Kolubara. Valjevo was actually his own former headquarters and a great road junction, which he determined to hold as long as possible. The Battle of the Drina was fought and won.

Potiorek thought he saw his opportunity and ordered an instant pursuit. He now desired above all to get possession of the railway from Obrenovac on the Sava to Valjevo in order to ease the great difficulty which he found in supplying the *Fifth Army*. Time after time the Serbians stood determinedly, but were always forced back. Regretfully the Voivode Putnik was compelled to agree with the commander of his First Army, General Mišić, that it was useless to attempt to stand at Valjevo, and to abandon it. The Austrians entered the town on the 15th. Here, as throughout the retreat, both Putnik and Mišić showed admirable judgment, timing perfectly the successive retirements forced upon them, saving their severely shaken troops from a shock that might have broken them in pieces,

1914.
Oct.

Nov.

but nevertheless subjecting the advancing enemy to the greatest possible loss and fatigue.

Next began a terrible battle on the banks of the Kolubara and its tributary the Ljig. The conditions were of the worst. Snow in the mountains south of Valjevo, rain in the lower lands to the north, fell day after day. The roads were littered with sick, a great proportion of them suffering from frostbite. The Austrians suffered very greatly;[1] their opponents, less well equipped with medical services, even more. To face this merciless weather even the better-furnished Austrian soldiers were in some cases bootless and in rags.

By the 17th the Serbians had been driven over the Ljig. Next day the right of the *Fifth Army* forced its way across the swollen Kolubara just above its confluence with the Ljig.

Now came Potiorek's second opportunity to review his position. He had won an indubitable victory, had taken 8,000 prisoners and 42 guns. But his troops had outrun their supplies and were half starved. The Obrenovac-Valjevo railway, though in his hands, was of no use yet; for it was under heavy fire and he had been unable to repair its broken bridges. "Caution," remarks the Austrian official historian, speaking after the event, " dictated a " withdrawal behind the Kolubara with a bridgehead at " Valjevo, to allow reorganization to be carried out." But could he allow such respite to a beaten enemy? Was it even certain that the Serbian resistance would be any more determined here than it had been in front of Valjevo? He must go on. At once he began the difficult task of getting guns across the Kolubara.

By the 22nd Potiorek was made rudely aware that he was done with rear-guard actions and that another pitched battle had opened. So much the better; he had pinned down the enemy by forcing him into a very ugly position. Behind the Serbians was the valley of the Morava, which bore their one important means of communication, the railway to Niš and Salonika. He ordered his detachment on the extreme right to drive back the Serbians from Užice, the main right wing to press forward on Gornji Milanovac, and the centre to continue its efforts

---

[1] The Austrian *XV Corps* of the *Sixth Army* had in this fighting 5,000 sick to 3,000 battle casualties.

on the Ljig. Once again the Austrians swept forward on the right, meeting with little resistance, while in the centre after bitter fighting they forced the Serbians back from the Ljig.

1914. Nov.

The Serbian command was now faced by the most difficult decision of the whole campaign. The Voivode had realized that his best ally was time. He was in the situation of which Hamley earnestly points out the danger; that is, he was fighting parallel to his lines of communication and risked, if he retreated further, being driven off them. On the other hand, he was reaping the benefit of approaching the railway, while he knew that the Austrians must meet greater difficulties with every step forward. Boldly he took the risk of another big withdrawal, even though that also involved the surrender of Belgrade. The movement was not one of despair, for he hoped that it would provide him with an opportunity to counter-attack; but it was none the less attended with the gravest danger morally and physically. He decided to withdraw his right from the great loop of Sava and Danube, south of Belgrade, and his centre 10 miles east of the Ljig, thus completely abandoning the Valjevo railway to the enemy. The First Army on the left he intended should maintain its position. These orders were not to be carried out unless the retirement was imperative and then only after reference to him.

The fighting of the 27th and 28th solved the problem, the Austrian *Sixth Army* making alarming progress. Not only was Putnik forced to order the withdrawal of his right and centre to begin, but on the left General Mišić, on his own responsibility, fell back about 12 miles along his whole front on the morning of the 29th, his left being then at Takovo, north-west of Gornji Milanovac. The Army of Užice on his left conformed by a very hasty retreat in order to avoid annihilation.

This was Potiorek's opportunity. He had, by the admission of not very friendly or complimentary critics, played " un jeu classique." [1] Another heavy blow, still with its greatest weight from the right, would drive the Serbians off the Salonika railway, force them into the northeastern corner of their territory, with the Danube to the

---

[1] Desmazes, p. 89.

north and north-east and Bulgaria to the east, and so bring about a Serbian Sedan. But he had to give his *Sixth Army*, which had done nearly all the work, a momentary respite, while munitions, clothing, food, and stores were got up to it over the ruined roads. On the 30th he issued orders for the *Sixth Army* to stand fast until the 3rd December, while the *Fifth* improved its position east of the Valjevo railway and made that invaluable means of supply secure. At the same moment the Serbian retreat on the right and centre took place. The Austrian left found nothing in front of it when it began its advance, and pressed forward as rapidly as possible on Belgrade. On approaching the city it was discovered that the Serbians had evacuated it and that an Austrian detachment at Semlin, across the Sava, had already occupied it. Potiorek at once ordered the *Fifth Army* to advance to a line from Popović to Grocka on the Danube. This move had a measure of risk in it, since it greatly increased the frontage of the *Fifth Army*, but it had two compensations: it brought his left well behind the enemy's flank, and it would enable him to base the *Fifth Army* on Belgrade, allotting the Valjevo railway to the *Sixth*. He was now, in fact, attempting to envelop both instead of one of his opponent's flanks.

Men still talk of the "miracle of the Marne," where there is little that is miraculous. There would be more justification in talking of the "miracle of the Kolubara," since the Serbian Armies had been far more roughly handled and far more shaken than had the French in the weeks preceding their counter-offensive. Yet perhaps the solution of the two mysteries is the same. The army pressed back into the heart of its own country may be in grievous moral danger, but materially it is at an advantage by comparison with the aggressor. Its drafts and supplies have an ever shorter distance to travel, those of its opponents a distance ever longer. The soldier and the historian alike think in battalions, and the numbers of the battalions opposing one another in such a battle do not alter. But it is the beaten battalions which become the big ones and the pursuing battalions which become the small ones. Then, if the attacker once for a moment lose his initiative, his momentum, he finds himself in danger, always providing that the defender has been able to preserve or restore the spirit of his troops. The Serbians had to some extent filled up their ranks, and they had received munitions from Britain and France.¹ On the First Army in particular, hardest pressed throughout the retreat, its remarkably able and inspiring commander, General Mišić, seems to have completely restored its fighting spirit. The old King, who had dropped the reins of power in favour of his son, suddenly appeared from retirement, actually entering the trenches with a rifle and fifty rounds of ammunition, and haranguing the troops, in whom he aroused great enthusiasm. When the Serbians turned to the offensive they seemed to have forgotten their fatigue and suffering. The battle had for the moment come to a deadlock; once it began to move westward under the impulse of their ardour the victory was really won, for nothing could now stop the discouraged and exhausted Austrian troops.

1914. Dec.

These material advantages must not blind us to the magnificence of their moral recovery.

The remainder of the battle is eventful enough, but its details need not concern us. On the morning of the 3rd December, while the bells of Belgrade were ringing for the triumphal entry of General Frank, the commander of the *Fifth Army*, Putnik struck his first blow, mainly with the First Army. On the 4th and 5th the attacks of both the First and Third Armies made great progress. Next day there was a panic among the troops of the *Sixth Army* opposing the Serbian First, and the attackers, pressing on down the Gornji Milanovac–Valjevo road, got to within five miles of the Kolubara. Potiorek had one more card to play. The two left corps of his *Fifth Army* were well behind the Serbian right flank, and had meanwhile made considerable progress south-east of Belgrade. He ordered them to press the attack southwards and roll up the Serbian right, at the same time directing that the line of the Kolubara should be held at all costs. These assaults were launched with great resolution and won several important positions, but the progress of the Serbians north of Arangjelovac not only made them unavailing but brought the attackers into serious danger of being cut off from the main body by a Serbian break-through in the centre. At the height of the battle the commander of the Austrian *29th Division*

---

¹ This, despite the action of a band of brigands, led by Bulgarian officers, who crossed the frontier near Strumica and damaged—but fortunately did not destroy—a big bridge carrying the Salonika railway over the Vardar.

on the extreme left received the telegram, heart-breaking in view of the sacrifices made by his troops: "All now " in vain. Make no more efforts. We must back. Orders " follow."

This was on the 9th December. On the same day the Serbians got across the Kolubara at the mouth of the Ljig. Potiorek, realizing that the *Sixth Army* was at its last gasp, decided to break off the battle and ordered the Army to withdraw to a position 20 miles north of the river and approximately half way between it and the Sava, sending back its baggage to Šabac. Next day he directed the transport to cross, and the troops to be withdrawn if necessary. The roads were a dreadful spectacle, blocked with retreating columns of transport and stragglers in wildest confusion; fortunately for Potiorek, the Serbians could follow but slowly. They made no move against the Drina, where the Austrians had only small detachments to hold them. On the 12th the *Sixth Army* began to cross the Sava at Šabac, and was all over by the following morning. The *Fifth Army* was meanwhile holding the loop between Sava and Danube south of Belgrade, where Potiorek at first hoped to maintain it; but on the 13th December Frank informed him that he could not hold his position with the swollen rivers behind him. On the 14th and 15th this Army also crossed, the Austrian monitors checking the Serbians. At 10 a.m. on the 15th the Serbian cavalry entered their capital, and less than an hour afterwards came a roar of explosions as the Austrians blew up the bridges.

Serbia had saved herself and delivered her territory by her bravery and endurance and by the skilful leadership of the old commander to whom her destinies were entrusted. The Serbian Sedan had become a Serbian Marne. The Austrian defeat was indeed catastrophic, and the losses in killed, wounded, and missing numbered more than half the total of troops brought into this theatre from first to last.[1] Potiorek was instantly removed from his command, to be succeeded by the Archduke Eugene, chosen, as a royal prince and a popular soldier, to restore the spirits of the troops.

---

[1] That is, 227,088 out of 450,000. This figure included 76,690 missing, of whom the Serbians claimed only 40,000 prisoners.

EXHAUSTION OF THE VICTORS

And yet the victory of the Kolubara had left the Serbians as exhausted as their enemies. Their losses had also been very heavy, even if not much more than two-thirds of those of the Austrians,[1] and the flower of the race had fallen upon the banks of the river. The claim put forward by the Austrians that their offensive had broken the back of Serbia was exaggerated and designed to make the best case possible for their disastrous campaign; it is none the less true that Serbia had been seriously shaken. The events of the following spring were to remove any hope of Russian aid and to leave her alone, weakened and discouraged, to face a far more terrible onslaught.

1914.
Dec.

---

[1] " Armées Françaises," Tome VIII, Vol. I, Annexes, Vol. II (Report of French Military Attaché). The figure here given is 180,000, but this includes over 16,000 who died in hospital during the first seven months of 1915, of whom at least 10,000 died of sickness. The Serbian battle casualties may therefore be taken to be rather under 170,000.

CHAPTER II.

THE CRUSHING OF SERBIA.

(Maps 1, 3.)

AFTER THE VICTORY.

1915. WHAT, for herself and her Allies, was Serbia to make of her
Jan. victory? For the moment it was clear that she was in a
Map 1. position to pluck none of its fruits. Her Austrian foe might
be forced to send a great proportion of the troops previously
employed against her, exhausted as they were, to the Carpathians and a little later to the Italian front; she could not
take advantage of the opportunity.

In January 1915 the Serbian Armies were in need of
complete reorganization. An epidemic of typhus was
raging through the land, and even as late as April, when the
worst of it was over, there were 48,000 men in hospital.
Nor, had she been readier, would it have been easy for her to
effect anything on her northern front; for, after a season
wetter than the ordinary, the Sava had overflowed its banks
and flooded the whole plain of the Mačva. The one operation she felt herself strong enough to carry out was of little
military value and was dictated solely by political ambitions.
She sent an expedition into Albania, and in June one of
her columns occupied Tirana. Montenegrin forces installed
themselves at Scutari, to the disgust of Italy.

To the Allies it seemed that here was an army standing
idle at a time when its intervention would have been very
useful. The Grand Duke Nicholas, on the eve of his abortive
spring offensive in the Carpathians, requested the Serbians
at least to make a diversion, but found them unwilling
(and, as we have suggested, probably unable) to move.
When Italy entered the war on the side of the Allies, it
was the same. On the 11th May 1915 the British General
Staff asked the Military Attaché at Niš, Lieut.-Colonel
A. P. B. Harrison, whether the Serbians could co-operate
or had made any plans with the Italians, and was informed
that owing to the inundation of the Sava valley and the
lack of forage the projected offensive had been postponed.
Again on the 7th July the representatives of the Allied
Armies, meeting at Chantilly under the presidency of the

French Minister of War, M. Millerand, urged that the Serbians should take the offensive in conjunction with Italy. Still nothing was done, though neither floods, difficulties of supply, nor sickness could now be pleaded as an excuse.

1915. May-Aug.

There were, however, other reasons for inaction, and weighty ones. In the early spring, when Serbia was crippled, the Russian Armies had been established in the Carpathians and holding a great slice of Hungarian territory. Now that she was herself in a better situation, that of the Russians had become deplorably bad. Falkenhayn had on the 2nd May begun the most brilliantly-conceived of all his enterprises—though its parentage has been attributed to the Austrian Conrad—known as the Break-through of Gorlice. Two Armies, consisting of nine German and seven Austrian divisions,[1] with a backing of heavy artillery such as had never yet been employed on the Eastern Front, assembled with great secrecy in Galicia under the orders of General von Mackensen. The frontage of their attack was as admirably chosen as its date, which anticipated Italy's declaration of war on Austria by three weeks; for their flanks were in great part covered by the Vistula to the north and the Beskide range to the south, while any considerable success would completely turn the Russian positions in the Carpathians. So it fell out. By the 6th May the Russians were in full retreat. On the 22nd June Lemberg fell. The threat to Austria was removed and she was able to free troops to meet the Italians. But Falkenhayn was determined to strike the Russians a blow which would put them out of action for that year at least. On the 12th July the Army Detachment of General von Gallwitz broke through north of Warsaw, pressing south-eastward towards the Bug. On the 29th Mackensen's Group broke through in a north-easterly direction, and the whole Russian centre collapsed. By the end of August the Austro-German line had advanced in the centre a distance of 250 miles. Galicia, Poland, and Courland were cleared of the Russians, who had lost three-quarters of a million prisoners and enormous quantities of artillery, stores, and transport, and had been thrown into a state of exhaustion and depression from

---

[1] German *Eleventh Army* of eight German divisions and two Austrian, and Austro-Hungarian *Fourth Army* of five Austrian divisions and one German. One Austrian cavalry division was also included in each Army.

which—despite the Brusilov offensive of the following June —it may fairly be said they never fully recovered.[1]

Long before that date it seemed that the Serbian command had finally decided against any offensive action. In the glow of victory after a defensive battle the Voivode Putnik had not forgotten that his former offensives both in Syrmia and Bosnia had been quite unsuccessful. He had insufficient bridging material to transport large forces over the Sava or Danube with the requisite speed. Serbia was more than ever nervous regarding Bulgaria's intentions. The progress of the British and French since the first landing on the Gallipoli Peninsula on the 25th April had not been rapid enough to reassure her. Lord Kitchener, at least, understood her difficulties and hesitations, and made no comment when Lieut.-Colonel Harrison reported early in July that he had advised the Serbian General Staff not to undertake anything rash, despite the pressure of other military attachés for a vigorous offensive.

Allied to these military considerations was another of a political kind. The general situation in the Balkans had as yet not greatly altered since the outbreak of war. Neither the entry of Turkey on the side of the Central Powers on one flank nor that of Italy on the side of the Entente on the other had so far made much effect upon it. Turkey had been at first fully occupied with her Caucasian campaign and her threat to the Suez Canal, and now had the flower of her Armies pinned down upon the Gallipoli Peninsula. Italy had not even declared war upon Germany; and the nature of her frontier with Austria gave her no great prospects of an important success, even against greatly inferior opposition. Bulgaria, Greece, and Rumania all held fast to their neutrality, though the first-named seemed to be leaning more and more to the cause of Germany. The Russian *débacle* of the summer could not fail to encourage her in this inclination, while proportionately intimidating Rumania, whose sympathies were on the whole with the other side.

From the first it appeared to the Foreign Offices of the Allies that the key to the situation was Bulgaria. She represented from her geographical position a continual threat to Serbia. Had she intervened during Potiorek's

---

[1] Falkenhayn, pp. 78–149.

offensives of 1914, Serbia would have been overrun; next 1914.
time the Austrians would perhaps not attack until her help
was assured. Could she be won over to co-operation or
at least persuaded to remain neutral? Obviously not
without the promise of substantial advantages, which must
be mainly at the expense of Serbia and in a lesser degree
of Greece, though some would come from Turkey. Nothing
could be hoped from her unless she got back what she had
won in the First Balkan War and had had wrung from her
by them in the Second. As early as the 21st August 1914
the British Foreign Office ordered Sir H. Bax-Ironside,
the Minister at Sofia, to sound her on this matter. To
promote a confederation of Balkan States it was realized
that Serbia and Greece would have to " make offers
" sufficiently attractive to Bulgaria." They would get
ample compensation elsewhere if Austria were defeated.
So anxious, in fact, were the Entente Powers not to be
involved in conflicts between the Balkan States that when,
on the 18th August, the Greek Prime Minister, M. Venizelos,
informed their representatives that Greece was prepared
to put the whole of her naval and military forces at their
disposal, they replied that the *separate* entry of Greece
into the war was not desirable. In August and September
there were actual negotiations by Britain, France, and Russia
with Serbia on the subject of concessions to Bulgaria, but
they came to nothing and were based on considerations—
the sympathy for the Central Powers of the Rumanian
Court—which speedily disappeared on the death of King
Charles in October. After Turkey had entered the war and
Serbia had been attacked by the Austrians for the second
time the Allies again approached Bulgaria, on this occasion
asking no more than strict neutrality towards Rumania,
Greece, and Serbia, and promising in return " important
" territorial advantages " at the final settlement. These
advantages would, however, be increased should Bulgaria
attack either Turkey or Austria. Sofia replied with some
coldness on the 9th December that nothing new of a nature
to modify their attitude of neutrality having yet occurred,
the Bulgarian Government had decided not to depart from
it, but would " continue to watch over the interests of the
" country "—which might well be interpreted, " to see
" how the cat jumps."

It appeared then that Bulgaria might be expected to

hold her hand for the time being, but that no help could be obtained from her for Serbia. No better results were obtained from Rumania or Greece, both of whom declared that the Allies' guarantees were useless, since they had no means of controlling Bulgaria. By the middle of December Serbia's immediate danger was over and the defeated Austrian Armies were back in Hungary, but, as we have seen, her position remained one of great danger. Sir Edward Grey, in concert with MM. Delcassé and Sazonov,

1915. Jan. therefore renewed his attempts on the 23rd January 1915. He instructed the Minister at Athens, Sir Francis Elliot, to make the suggestion of territorial concessions to Greece in Asia Minor if she would go to the aid of Serbia. To Serbia he stated, through Sir Charles des Graz, the Minister at Niš, that, according to his information, Bulgaria would at least maintain friendly neutrality if promised territory in Macedonia, which territory would be handed over only when Serbia had realized her own aspirations for a " Greater " Serbia," including part of the Adriatic coast. So far as Greece was concerned, M. Venizelos would not move without the support of Rumania, and whatever scanty hopes there were of his coming to an understanding with Bulgaria were ruined when on the 2nd February the Bulgarian Government secured a large loan from Germany. The Greek Prime Minister, according to a later public statement, thereupon concluded that it was useless to approach Bulgaria, whom he regarded as henceforth tied to the Central Powers. The Entente Ministers at Niš were for their part of opinion that Serbia would cede to Bulgaria no more than the line of the Vardar and that not until the end of the war.

Britain did not so easily abandon hope. Her eyes were just now fixed upon the Balkans, since it was at this moment that Mr. Lloyd George put forward in the War Council his proposal to send an army to Salonika, with the object of bringing in all the Balkan States and overwhelming Austria.[1] Nothing was then decided, except that a number of river monitors for the Danube should be built in sections so that they could be sent up by rail, though before the Gallipoli landings there was a proposal to land the 29th Division and a French division at Salonika. M. Venizelos considered this force insufficient. On the 6th March he

---

[1] Actually at a sub-committee of the War Council, at the War Office, on the 28th January.

resigned after a difference of opinion with King Constantine on the subject of Greek military and naval assistance at the Dardanelles, a project to which Russia objected strongly. Though his successor twice (on the 22nd March and the 14th April) made offers of assistance, nothing came of them, as it appeared to Sir Edward Grey that they were really intended to provoke hostilities with Bulgaria, which he still hoped to avoid. Sir H. Bax-Ironside's reports of how greatly Bulgaria was impressed by the Allies' action at the Dardanelles had, indeed, roused new though ill-founded hopes. Conversations in London and Sofia continued through March and April, and on the 8th May Sir H. Bax-Ironside reported that the Bulgarian Prime Minister had pledged the support of his country, but on the stiffest possible terms. From Serbia he demanded not merely the "Uncontested Zone," that is, the Macedonian territory from north-west of Egri Palanka to Lake Ohrid, which Serbia had been prepared to hand over when she concluded the secret Treaty of Sofia with Bulgaria before the First Balkan War; but also the "Contested Zone," which it had then been decided to submit to the arbitration of the Tsar as between the two States, and which included Kumanovo, Skoplje (Uskub), and Debar. From Greece Bulgaria required the port of Kavalla, with a hinterland including Seres.

These demands were obviously impossible, and to cut matters short, the Entente Powers made a formal offer to Bulgaria, which was presented on the 29th May to M. Radoslavov by Sir H. Bax-Ironside, supported by his French, Italian, and Russian colleagues. If Bulgaria would attack Turkey with all her armed forces the Entente would consent to her immediate occupation of Thrace up to the line Enos–Midia (that of the Treaty of London after the First Balkan War), which would become a Bulgarian possession. After the war they would guarantee to her the "Uncontested Zone" in Macedonia. The conditions were that Serbia should receive "equitable compensation" in Bosnia and Hercegovina, and on the Adriatic coast, and that Bulgaria should make no effort to occupy Macedonian territory before the conclusion of peace. The Allied Powers pledged themselves to use their good offices with Greece regarding the cession of Kavalla when they were in a position to offer Greece compensations in Asia Minor.

The high-handedness of this offer from Serbia's point of view could be excused only by the urgency of buying off Bulgaria. Unfortunately, even supposing Bulgaria to have been sincere, which is doubtful, an affair of this sort could not be decided quickly, and every day it dragged on made the military situation of the Allies appear more unfavourable in the eyes of Tsar Ferdinand of Bulgaria and his Ministers. Serbia at first refused all concessions with indignation. Sir Edward Grey pressed her. What more, he asked in effect, did she want? She was asked to give up now what she had of her own initiative been prepared to give in 1912; in return she was offered Bosnia, Hercegovina, Slavonia, and half Dalmatia. At last, on the 1st September, Sir Charles des Graz reported that, "not without "a long and painful moral struggle" the Serbian Government had agreed to the conditions, subject to certain restrictions.

This very condensed account of the efforts of Allied diplomacy up to the autumn of 1915 is necessary to give the reader a notion of the general situation and also to explain Serbia's unreadiness to take part in any offensive operations. Long before affairs had reached the point up to which we have brought them she had become alarmed, and even seems at one moment to have dreaded that Macedonia would be taken from her by force to be handed over to the Bulgarians. From the first she never had any belief in their good faith, and protested that the Western Powers did not understand their mentality. It must be added that not only Sir Charles des Graz, the British Minister at Niš, but Captain L. S. Amery, who was on a mission to the Near East in June, and the Military Attaché, Lieut.-Colonel Harrison, issued warnings at various times against pressing her too far, the last-named pointing out that as a result of the negotiations she was preparing to send fresh troops into Macedonia.[1] These negotiations we need follow no further, since the affair had already passed beyond the control of diplomacy. On the 2nd August, while they were still in full train, Mr. Hugh O'Beirne, Sir Henry Bax-Ironside's successor at Sofia, informed the Foreign Office that a certain Colonel Gančev had left for Berlin in some secrecy. This officer was, in fact, the emissary sent to arrange with Germany and Austria the convention which was to determine the

---

[1] Lieut.-Colonel Harrison to War Office, 6th August 1915.

FALKENHAYN'S PLANS

exact parts to be played by each in the crushing of Serbia. This was signed by Conrad, Falkenhayn, and himself at Pless on the 6th September. The die was cast. On the 22nd September Tsar Ferdinand ordered a general mobilization.

1915. Sept.

THE CAMPAIGN AGAINST SERBIA.

Occupied as he had been in the spring and summer with putting an end to danger from Russia, while standing on the defensive in France and Belgium,[1] Falkenhayn had all the while had an eye on Serbia. After the Austrian defeat he had sent a few German troops to Syrmia, increasing them to three divisions after Italy had declared war on Austria. There they could rest and refit in a rich and pleasant country, reassure the Austrians, and study on the spot the conditions against the hour when a renewed venture would be possible. Russia more or less off his hands, he gave his full attention to the affair, having now an added spur to endeavour. The destruction of the Serbian Army with the co-operation of Bulgaria would enable munitions to be got through to hard-pressed Turkey by the Danube and the railway through Sofia. Germany would have the right to use the Morava–Maritsa corridor to save her Ally; Bulgaria would win Macedonia and the Vardar corridor. It was " a bargain in valleys." [2] Austria's reward would be the extinction of the South-Slav menace. But there was to be no more muddling. Germany would provide a great proportion of the troops; she must provide as well the leadership, which indeed Bulgaria also demanded as a condition of her co-operation. One German, one Austrian, and one Bulgarian Army were to be placed under the command of Field-Marshal von Mackensen, with General von Seeckt as Chief of the Staff, while a second Bulgarian Army operated directly under the control of the Bulgarian General Staff. The best Army commanders that could be found, the German General von Gallwitz and the Austrian General von Kövess,[3] were selected. The Austro-German

Maps 1, 3.

---

[1] The gas attack of the 22nd April was originally made partly to test the new weapon but mainly to cloak the transportation of troops to Galicia for the Break-through of Gorlice. (Falkenhayn, p. 84.)

[2] Douglas Wilson Johnson, " Battlefields of the World War," p. 583.

[3] Replacing at the last moment General v. Tersztyánszky, who had fallen foul of Count Tisza, Minister-President of Hungary.

attack was this time to be carried out from Syrmia and the Banat, across the Sava and Danube. Despite the difficulty of crossing these great rivers, an attack from this quarter was far preferable to one from the west because of the superiority in communications of Hungary to Bosnia and the easier nature of the country into which the force would advance. For that decision it needed not to recall the hapless Potiorek's words to his successor: "Wenn Sie "Serbien nochmals anzugreifen haben, tun Sie es nur bei "Belgrad."[1] When the Austrians declared that they could not find all the troops required, Falkenhayn did not hesitate to draw upon his scanty reserves to the extent of another German corps of three divisions, which he attached to the Austrian Army. At the last moment he was given a severe fright by the Allies' Champagne–Loos offensive, but it did not cause him to alter his plans.

The Germans and Austrians were superior in numbers to the Serbian forces opposed to them in the north, and the superiority on both fronts would become very great when the Bulgarians joined in on the sixth day.[2] But the superiority in artillery was far greater still, and it was confidently expected that the Serbians would not be able to withstand the fire of massed heavy batteries and trench mortars. Careful reconnaissances had been made during the summer. Battery positions had been prepared, bridging trains brought up in advance, routes of approach and assembly positions selected, all under the direction of that remarkable general-utility officer, Lieut.-Colonel Hentsch of Marne fame, who was attached to the staff of the Field-Marshal when the latter arrived secretly and established his headquarters at Temisoara on the 20th September. The infantry was brought up at the last moment, and "had "practically nothing to do but to march up and proceed "instantly with the crossing."[3] The Austrian *Third Army* was to cross the Sava and Danube between Kupinova

---

[1] Kuhl, I, p. 98.
[2] Falkenhayn's calculation was 330,000 to 190,000 rifles. The German Army consisted of seven divisions, with one Austrian division (the "Fülöpp Group," at Orsova) attached. The Austrians had approximately five Austrian divisions, three German divisions, and six independent brigades. The Bulgarian *First Army* had four very big divisions and the *Second Army* two. The latter was later reinforced by the best part of three more divisions.
[3] Falkenhayn, p. 165.

and Belgrade and advance on Kragujevac, the Serbian G.H.Q. and arsenal. The German *Eleventh Army* was to cross the Danube between Smederevo (Semendria) and Ram, and advance up the valley of the Morava. The Bulgarian *First Army* (General Bojadiev), under Mackensen's orders, was to cross the frontier five days later and march on Niš, while the independent Bulgarian *Second Army* (General Todorov) invaded Macedonia and entered the valley of the Vardar. Conrad, who had the best strategic eye of any soldier of the Central Powers, would have preferred that the Bulgarian *First Army* should attack further south, but was overruled by Falkenhayn, who doubtless desired that Mackensen should be able to exercise over it the fullest possible control.[1]

1915. Sept.

The Serbians had no long warning. On the 20th September Colonel G. F. Phillips, the then Military Attaché, reported to the War Office that there was more than usual movement of troops and trains beyond the rivers, and three days later that there was a "steady increase" in the German and Austrian forces. On the 22nd came the Bulgarian mobilization order. The Voivode Putnik had been long ailing, and the vigorous Sub-chief of the Staff, Lieut.-Colonel Pavlović, who was now virtually in command, instantly bethought him of attacking these new foes before they had mobilized and before the Austro-German force was ready. Both Lord Kitchener and Sir Edward Grey took the grave responsibility of dissuading him from this course. They still had a faint hope that hostilities with Bulgaria might be avoided, and Mr. O'Beirne at Sofia went so far as to suggest to his Serbian colleague that the danger might be averted if Serbia now surrendered the whole of the "Uncontested Zone," for example, by placing it at the disposal of the Tsar of Russia.[2] Lieut.-Colonel Pavlović gave an assurance that Serbia would not make an unprovoked attack, but urged the Allies to realize that rapid action was essential and suggested that they should at once demand of Bulgaria whether it was peace or war. He also pressed that 100,000 Allied troops should be sent to Veles to parry the Bulgarian menace. On the 26th September the War Office informed Colonel Phillips that there was no possibility

---

[1] Kuhl, I, p. 278.
[2] Lord Kitchener to Colonel Phillips, 25th September; Mr. H. J. O'Beirne to Sir E. Grey, 26th September 1915.

of doing this for several weeks, but that it hoped that the arrival of troops then under orders for Salonika would " have a calming effect " on Bulgarian headquarters, and therefore looked with grave concern on the prospect of Serbia's precipitating hostilities. Denied also, as we shall presently see, the Greek support which she had expected, Serbia made preparations to face her danger alone as best she could.

Three small forces, from right to left the Third Army, the Belgrade Detachment, and the First Army, faced the Austro-Germans on the Danube and Sava. The Timok Army and the Second Army covered the valley of the Morava to oppose the advance of the northern Bulgarian columns. All that could be gathered together to cover the Vardar valley at Skoplje and Veles was a detachment of new regiments made up for the most part of recruits, volunteers, and irregulars, which was given the title of " Army of Macedonia." Montenegrin troops held the upper Drina, where a single Austrian division was concentrated at Višegrad. There had been some fortification of the banks of the Danube and Sava, but trench-digging was not congenial to the Serbians, who might have effected here much more in the ample time at their disposal. The trenches and outposts were held by battalions of the Third Ban, the first-line troops being concentrated some distance in rear.

1915. Oct. The bombardment began on the 6th October and the passage of the rivers next day. The Danube in the neighbourhood of Belgrade is over a thousand yards in breadth, the Sava in places about half that. The passage of the rivers was, however, made very much easier by the big islands, whereof one, the Temeziget, on the German front (and already occupied by the attackers) was some 12 miles long with quite a narrow arm of the river between it and the right bank. On the Austrian front was another large island, and though this was not already occupied it proved even more valuable; for the Serbians failed to destroy the bridge on the southern side. The defence was very stout, and some of the attempts to cross failed altogether, but numerous small detachments established themselves on the Serbian side of the rivers. On the 8th troops were pushed over as fast as possible, while the Serbian counter-attacks were broken up by the fire of the land artillery and

THE ATTACK

1915.
Oct.

of the Austrian monitors. Belgrade was captured by the Austrians on the 9th. The next three days were occupied in winning elbow-room to get the main bodies across and were marked by fierce but in the main unsuccessful counter-attacks. On the 15th Mackensen issued orders for a general advance. Gallwitz immediately went to see the Field-Marshal and pointed out that this was impossible, as he had not got his horses over. The general attack was therefore postponed until the 18th. At first it gained little ground, but on the 19th the Germans went forward with a rush. By the 24th the *Eleventh Army* had advanced 25 miles up the Morava, and the Austrians on its right were in front of Arangjelovac. Thereafter the two armies advanced steadily but slowly into the heart of Serbia. Mackensen had hoped to fight the decisive battle and destroy his opponent in front of Kragujevac, but it was not to be. The Serbians broke off the fight and blew up their arsenal before retiring, and the pursuing forces could never get to grips with their main body owing to the state of the roads and the already wintry weather. It is, indeed, clear that the Serbians, if forced to abandon their territory, could easily have kept their Armies in being if they had had to do with the Germans and Austrians alone. Their worst danger was now from the east and south.

Bulgaria was late, but when she did move she did so decisively. She declared war on the 13th October and marched next day. It is true that her *First Army*, advancing on Niš, made very slow progress in face of a stubborn resistance. The *Second Army*, however, captured Kumanovo by the 19th. The Salonika–Niš railway was thus cut behind the backs of the retreating Serbians. Meanwhile the Austrian division at Višegrad had contrived to cross the Drina and was pressing their left flank.

The Serbian command had now no hope left unless the Allied troops which had landed at Salonika during the first days of October and had advanced up the Vardar as far as Krivolak in the latter part of the month could establish contact with its troops at Veles. And that hope had to be abandoned. We shall turn again to the operations of the French on the Vardar and Crna ; here it need only be said that the Bulgarians forced their way right across the rear of the Serbians and cut them off from their allies ; and that the French fell back across the Crna on the morning of the 21st November, and on the 23rd began their preparations for retreat towards Salonika.

1915. Nov. The Serbian Armies from the north and east were meanwhile falling back to the Kosovo Polje, the fatal " Plain " of the Blackbirds " which had seen the overthrow of their race in the year 1389. Two divisions made a heroic defence of the Kačanik defile, the deep pass between the Crna Gora or Kara Dagh and the Šar Planina, against the Bulgarian columns advancing northward from Skopjle, and thus saved their comrades from complete encirclement and destruction. For a moment it was hoped that this defence might even permit the main Serbian forces to escape southwards by the cart-track from Prizren to Tetovo and thence down the road to Monastir, the only route by which they could join the French now that the Vardar valley was barred.[1] That hope, too, was shattered. On the morning of the 19th November word came that the Bulgarians, attempting to turn the Kačanik defile since they could not force it, were at Tetovo. To the north the Austro-German columns were approaching Novi Pazar and Mitrovica; to the east a Bulgarian column was pressing up the arm of the Morava which runs along the northern slopes of the Crna Gora. The last chance of safety lay in a march to the Adriatic across the craggy and inhospitable hills of Albania.

Now began the Calvary of the Serbian Army. Leaving behind the thousands of women and children who had accompanied them hitherto, but whow ere now dying in great numbers and could go no further, the troops followed three routes—one cannot call them roads. The northern was in Montenegrin territory and ran through Peč and Podgorica, thence southward to Scutari, and was perhaps the best, though even it was scarcely fit for wheeled traffic. The centre followed the White Drin from Prizren, then crossed the watershed in two forks leading to Scutari and Alessio. It was by this that the Voivode Putnik was carried in a sort of Sedan chair, taking ten days on the journey. The southernmost route was by way of Debar to Tirana. The tracks were deep in snow; the cold was bitter; the unfriendly Albanians of the poor and scattered villages had hidden what provisions they had, and money being

---

[1] Feyler, I, p. 110.

well-nigh useless to them, would produce a morsel of their wretched food only in exchange for clothes. Officers and soldiers, their teeth chattering with cold, stood half naked holding out their shirts to the villagers. Slowly this army of misery drifted to the coast, bestrewing the tracks as it went with frozen corpses.

1915. Dec.

In scattered bands, without discipline or order, often without arms, the remnant arrived at Scutari during the month of December. Its numbers were at first estimated to be about 100,000, but day by day stragglers drifted in, until finally half as many again were concentrated in the neighbourhood. The losses of the Serbians cannot be computed with certainty, but it is stated that the total ration strength before the offensive, including all auxiliary services, was 420,000.[1] The Austrians, Germans, and Bulgarians took 170,000 prisoners and some 900 guns. On the other hand, the retreating Serbians contrived to bring out 24,000 Austrian prisoners captured in 1914. There was for the time being no pursuit. The Austrians crossed the Montenegrin frontier, but halted at Peć, while small columns of Bulgarians occupied Debar, Ohrid, and Monastir.

The sufferings and dangers of the Serbians were by no means at an end. Albania was at this date in a state of chaos. The Government of Prince William of Wied ("the "Mpret of Albania") which had only just been set up at the outbreak of war, had collapsed, and the country was under no central control. The only administration with any power was that of Essad Pasha, an Albanian ally of the Turks against the Montenegrins and Serbians in the First Balkan War. Essad was helpful, but his authority did not extend far from his capital of Durazzo. At Durazzo and further down the coast at Valona the Italians had landed detachments. Where Montenegro was concerned it was well known that she had never had much heart in the war, was now in any case helpless, and would crumple up at once if the Austrians chose to advance.

San Giovanni di Medua, the port of Scutari, was not only very small but was too close to the Austrian fleet at Cattaro to be used for the embarkation of the Serbians. It was dangerous enough as a landing-place for their most

---

[1] Feyler, I, p. 114.

pressing necessities, as was proved when the Austrians raided it on the 5th December and sank most of the shipping in the harbour. It was therefore decided by the British and French authorities that the Serbians must move south to Durazzo and Valona after supplies sufficient to enable them to make the march had been put ashore at San Giovanni di Medua.

The War Office had in mid-November sent out a mission to the Serbian Army, subsequently known as the British Adriatic Mission, on the assumption that a proportion of the Serbian forces might be compelled to fall back through Montenegro and would require to be supplied from the Adriatic. The first officers of this mission reached Scutari on the 24th, four days before the arrival of the Serbian General Headquarters. A party of Royal Engineers under Lieut.-Colonel A. C. Macdonald was despatched a little later for the construction and repair of roads. When it was realized that measures of a nature quite different to those originally contemplated were now required, a senior officer of the A.S.C., Br.-General F. P. S. Taylor, was sent out at the end of November to take command of the mission. Simultaneously the French had despatched a mission under the orders of General de Mondésir, the object of which was the reorganization of the Serbians, whilst that of the British Adriatic Mission was the very necessary preliminary of preventing them from dying of starvation. The two missions had no knowledge of each other's existence until they met; but they speedily arranged to co-operate and to overcome the reluctance of the Italians to allow the Serbians to move south into their zone. The British engineers did very valuable service in improving the ferries across the streams between Medua and Durazzo—service in default of which the Serbians would never have escaped. For the Austrians advanced at the beginning of January, scattered the Montenegrins at the first attack, overran the whole country, and entered Scutari on the 21st, not long after the last of the Serbians had quitted it. Fortunately, there were no Montenegrins to be rescued, as their Army desired nothing better than to go home.

After marches which were a veritable torture in view of their weakness and fatigue, the Serbians reached Durazzo and Valona, whence they were taken off in British, French, and Italian ships, the great bulk to the Greek island of

GALLIPOLI OR SALONIKA

Corfu, which had been occupied by the French Navy, and a comparatively small number to Bizerta. French supplies also were now arriving in quantities, and were sent on to Corfu. Here the reorganization and re-equipment of the Serbian Army was taken in hand by General de Mondésir. Br.-General Taylor now returned to England, but Major W. C. Garsia, his staff officer, remained at the head of the British Adriatic Mission under the orders of General de Mondésir. Falkenhayn believed that he had destroyed the Serbian Army. He had, indeed, dealt it a terrible blow, but by the end of the following May he was to find 125,000 men, re-equipped, restored in health and spirit, eager for revenge, confronting his German troops and their Bulgarian Allies in Macedonia.

1916. Jan.-Feb.

The Landing of the Allies at Salonika.

It cannot be said that the Allies had been short of time for discussion of the Serbian question, since from the very beginning of 1915 the project of sending troops to Salonika had been in the air. They were, however, surprised by the speed and secrecy of the German preparations, and did not decide to intervene until too late. It was actually only as an afterthought that the troops which they had made up their minds to despatch to the Mediterranean went to Salonika instead of to the Gallipoli Peninsula or the neighbouring Asiatic shore.

1915. July.

In July the commander of the French Third Army, General Sarrail, was superseded and ordered to report at the Ministry of War, where he was told that he was to succeed General Gouraud, commanding the Corps Expéditionnaire d'Orient at Gallipoli, who had been severely wounded at the end of the previous month. After some discussion he informed the Minister of War, M. Millerand, on the 3rd August, that he would accept on the following conditions: that an " Armée d'Orient " should be constituted; that he should not, like his predecessor, be placed under the orders of Sir Ian Hamilton; and that he should go out with reinforcements.[1] Asked to make an appreciation of the situation, he put forward some considerations in favour of capturing the Turkish batteries on the Asiatic

Aug.

---

[1] Sarrail, p. viii.

1915. shore, and of a landing at Alexandretta. Finally, he
Sept. touched upon the possibility of a landing at Salonika.
After long delays he was informed on the 28th September
that his destination was Salonika, not the Dardanelles,
that he would be accompanied by a mixed brigade, and that
other troops would follow. Finally, on the 7th October—
the date of the Austro-German attack—he embarked at
Toulon.

British policy in the Near East was meanwhile in a
state of uncertainty and flux. On the 3rd September
Lord Kitchener told the Dardanelles Committee that
M. Millerand had informed him of the projected despatch
of four divisions for employment against Turkey and had
asked that the two French divisions at Cape Helles should
be relieved. He added that he would have to send out two
British divisions for this purpose. He gave the Committee
no information as to the French scheme, which was still
apparently a landing on the Asiatic shore of the Dardanelles.
On the 11th Lord Kitchener met M. Millerand, Field-Marshal
Sir John French, and Generals Joffre and Sarrail at Calais,
when it was decided that no troops could be sent to the
Mediterranean until the results of the Champagne–Artois
offensives, to begin on the 25th, could be estimated.[1]

The Bulgarian mobilization turned the scale in favour
of Salonika. M. Venizelos was now again in power at
Athens. After his resignation the King had dissolved the
Chamber, doubtless hoping that the Liberals would be beaten
at the polls. They had, however, returned victorious from
the elections in June, though, owing to the King's illness,
there had been no change of Ministry till August. M.
Venizelos at once, on the 23rd September, persuaded King
Constantine to order mobilization likewise. He had already
sent for the Ministers of Great Britain, France, and Russia,
and pointed out to them the urgency of the question and
the difficulties in which he found himself. Greece was
bound to Serbia by a military convention accompanying
a treaty between the two States, in which it was provided
that " in the event of war between one of the Allied Powers
" and a third Power breaking out in the circumstances
" foreseen by the Treaty of Alliance between Greece and
" Serbia, or in the event of a sudden attack by considerable

---

[1] " France and Belgium, 1915," II, p. 405.

" forces—two divisions at least of the Bulgarian Army [1]— 1915.
" against the Greek or the Serbian Army, the two States, Sept.
" Greece and Serbia, promise each other mutual military
" support, Greece with her whole force by land and sea,
" Serbia with her whole force by land." Greece pledged
herself to provide an army of 90,000, and Serbia an army of
150,000 men in these circumstances, to be concentrated in
positions designated in the convention. This convention
was, it will be seen, somewhat vague, and it had not appeared
in 1914 that the Austrian attack was of a nature " foreseen
" by the Treaty of Alliance." The convention, in fact,
obviously envisaged Bulgaria. M. Venizelos found, however, so he told the Ministers, that the King and the General
Staff still considered that the case was outside the terms of
the convention, because Serbia, faced by attack from the
north, was unable to fulfil one of its terms ; that is, she
could not furnish 150,000 men to operate against Bulgaria.
He himself admitted that Greece alone could not affront
the danger without an equivalent reinforcement. On the
22nd he asked the Ministers of France and Britain whether
their Governments could supply the 150,000 men. In
reply Sir Edward Grey asked what number of troops would
be required at Salonika " to induce Greece to give her full
" support to Serbia if Bulgaria attacks Serbia," adding that
it would take some time to land 150,000 men but that a
small force could be landed quickly. The French Government, without going into details or stating what share they
would take, replied that they were ready to furnish the
troops. On the 25th Sir Francis Elliot wired that the King
did not wish the Allied troops to be sent for the present, but
that M. Venizelos hoped that all preparations for their
despatch would be made. When a final application to
land them was made it might be necessary, to save King
Constantine's face with the Germans, for Greece to make a
formal protest.

The British Government objected strongly to these
diplomatic methods and protested against them, but made
preparations as requested. The tide of political and military
opinion was now flowing against the Gallipoli Campaign,
which appeared to have reached an impasse, and Lord
Kitchener suggested to the Dardanelles Committee on the

---

[1] *I.e.* about two corps, as regards infantry at least, by the standard of western formations.

24th that the Suvla Bay positions should be abandoned and two divisions, the 10th and 11th, despatched to Salonika. During the meeting he read out an appreciation by the General Staff in which it was urged that the rôle of the Allied troops to be sent to Salonika should be, in the first instance, restricted to assisting the Greek Army to protect the Serbian flank and the communications with Serbia. On the 25th September he informed Sir Ian Hamilton that France and Britain had promised to send the force asked for by Greece, that the question of reinforcements from the Western Front was in abeyance until the offensive was over, and that two British divisions, the 10th and 11th, were required. The French also required a brigade or a division from Cape Helles.

There was then some crossing of messages. On the 25th Sir Ian Hamilton telegraphed that the French commander, General Bailloud, had been ordered to send away a division. He himself still desired to retain the Suvla position, and declared on the 26th that he could just spare two divisions and a French brigade without abandoning it.[1] This did not meet the case, as General Bailloud received urgent and repeated orders from Paris to embark forthwith a whole division, reconstituted so as to contain European troops only. Eventually it was decided that the French division and the British 10th Division should sail as soon as possible. Br.-General A. B. Hamilton and other staff officers were sent to Salonika to make preparations for the landing and arrived on the 1st October.

1915.
Oct.
Now came a wholly unforeseen interruption of the slow-moving plan. On the 1st October the Allied Ministers at Athens found M. Venizelos in a state of indignation aroused by a speech made in the House of Commons on the 28th September by Sir Edward Grey, in the course of which the Foreign Secretary had spoken of the traditional warm feelings of sympathy for Bulgaria in Great Britain, and had stated that British policy was to promote agreement between the Balkan States, to secure which " the legitimate aspirations " of all Balkan States must find satisfaction." Probably M. Venizelos had seen only a summary of the speech ; for Sir Edward Grey had also stated that if the Bulgarian mobilization resulted in Bulgaria's assuming an aggressive

---

[1] These divisions would have been the 10th and, in place of the 11th, which would have remained at Suvla, the 53rd.

MISUNDERSTANDING AND DELAY

attitude on the side of our enemies we were prepared to give our friends in the Balkans all the support in our power, without reserve and without qualification.[1] It seems that the phrase quoted above thoroughly alarmed M. Venizelos; at all events he declared to the Ministers that the Allied troops could not be allowed to land unless assurances were given that they should not be used to extort concessions for Bulgaria at the expense of Greece and Serbia. He urgently requested the French Minister to stop the French transports, five of which were actually at sea; and this was done. The sailing of those carrying the 10th Division, which should have taken place next morning, and the netting of the harbour, which Admiral de Robeck had ordered to begin, were likewise cancelled. Next day, however, on the two Governments' informing M. Venizelos that all offers made to Sofia had now lapsed, he asked that the troops should be sent at once. He read out his formal protest, but it was addressed only to France, who had apparently not objected to its being made. Once more the ships were ordered to sail. The first British and French troops landed on the 5th October, but, actually before they were ashore, M. Venizelos, finding that his policy was so far at variance with that of the King and the General Staff that there was in his view a risk of civil war if he remained in office, once more resigned.

Here, then, was a situation which would have been ludicrous had it been less tragic. Britain was sending troops only to help Greece fulfil her obligations; and now it was almost certain that Greece did not intend to fulfil them. It had been agreed that no force which the Allies could spare would suffice without Greek co-operation; and now it appeared that the troops could hope for no more than neutrality and might have to face hostility from the Greek forces. To crown all, it was probable that the landing had in any case been made too late to save Serbia.

1915.
Oct.

---

[1] *The Times*, 29th September 1915.

CHAPTER III.

THE EXPEDITION INTO SERBIA.

(Maps A, 4.)

THE CAMPAIGN UNDER DISCUSSION.

Maps A, 4. THE French division from the Dardanelles, which was commanded by General Bailloud and was now to be numbered the 156th, began its landing at Salonika on the 5th October, all the fighting troops being ashore within 48 hours, though the regimental transport arrived only gradually. On the same day the headquarters and two battalions of the British 29th Brigade disembarked and moved to a camp on the Seres road. Then came yet another delay, which this time affected the British only and adversely influenced their situation for some time to come; since it put the French ahead in the choice of camps, the hire of buildings, and the control of the railways—all matters difficult enough to arrange now that the Greek mobilization was in progress.

On the 5th October Lord Kitchener and Mr. Balfour had a conference with MM. Millerand and Augagneur, the Ministers of War and the Marine, at Calais, at which the Secretary of State for War promised to send three more divisions from France to Salonika and the First Lord of the Admiralty agreed to assist the French in the transport of their troops, which it was then intended should consist of two more infantry divisions and two cavalry divisions.[1] Immediately afterwards Lord Kitchener learnt of the fall of M. Venizelos. To go on without the backing of that statesman appeared to him dangerous; and he at once cancelled the move of the 10th Division, even directing that its commander, Lieut.-General Sir Bryan Mahon, should return to Mudros if he had already started.[2] The

---

[1] " Armées Françaises," Tome VIII, Vol. I, p. 153.
[2] From Secretary of State for War to General Sir Ian Hamilton.
No. 8580, cipher.   6th October 1915; 10.30 a.m.
   Venizelos, as you probably know, has resigned, and the whole question of landing troops at Salonika is very doubtful.
   Until the situation is cleared up I am asking Admiralty to stop the troops going which have not yet started.
   If Mahon has not started for Salonika he should remain at Mudros until orders are sent, and if he has started he should return to Mudros.

FURTHER DELAY

General had, in fact, sailed in a destroyer, and had been about two hours at sea when he was recalled by wireless. Lieut.-General Sir John Maxwell, commanding in Egypt, who had formed a composite Yeomanry regiment from the details of the Mediterranean Expeditionary Force in that country, was also instructed to hold it back. Next day Lord Kitchener was instructed by the Dardanelles Committee to allow the troops from Mudros and Alexandria to proceed.

1915.
Oct.

The Government, however, did not yet hold themselves committed to a campaign in Macedonia. The spectre of danger to the Suez Canal, and even to Britain's position in the Mohammedan world, had been raised by the possibility of Germany's forcing a way through to Constantinople and making the front on the Gallipoli Peninsula untenable. On the 11th Lord Kitchener asked Sir Ian Hamilton for his estimate of the losses that would be incurred if it were necessary to abandon the Peninsula. On the same day the Dardanelles Committee decided that a strong force should be despatched as soon as possible to Egypt, "without "prejudice to its ultimate destination," and that an experienced general officer should be sent out to report on the situation in the Mediterranean, and particularly on the Gallipoli Peninsula. On the 14th it decided to recall Sir Ian Hamilton and replace him by General Sir Charles Monro, who was to furnish a report as to whether it was desirable to evacuate the Peninsula.

Affairs were now extremely complicated. General Sarrail landed at Salonika on the 12th October and immediately despatched up-country a regiment of infantry and a field artillery group to cover the railway in the Vardar valley between the Greek frontier and Strumica Station. Lieut.-General Mahon was not under his orders and had instructions not to move, though Britain declared war on Bulgaria on the 14th. The British troops about to be despatched to the Near East were not necessarily intended for Salonika at all, and there were difficulties and delays regarding their relief in France. On the 25th October Lord Kitchener informed the Dardanelles Committee that the French Military Attaché had brought him a strong Note, asking that these troops should be sent, not to Alexandria, but to Salonika, "to prevent the destruction of the Serbian "Army." The Secretary of State declared that he, and the General Staff with him, thought it was too late to save

Serbia; the French apparently did not. It was then decided to confer with General Joffre regarding the military expediency of a campaign in Serbia and to inform Sir John French that four British divisions, in addition to the two already under orders for Marseilles, should be disengaged from the line in France for service in the East.

The conference with General Joffre was held at 10 Downing Street on the 29th.[1] The French Commander-in-Chief came to urge the importance of pursuing the operations begun in Serbia and preserving the Serbian Army from destruction He considered that if the Central Powers could be held up for a time Greece might still be brought in on the side of the Allies. All he now asked of the British was that they should assure the safety of Salonika and the railway as far as Krivolak, eight miles east of the confluence of the Vardar and Crna. He was optimistic about the capacity of the port, declaring that 2,000 tons a day could be landed when the piers which the French Navy were putting up were finished. The representatives of the British Admiralty, on the other hand, were unduly pessimistic, putting the figure at 500 tons, owing to the congestion which was reported on the quays. General Joffre let it be understood that his position as Commander-in-Chief and even the cordiality of the Alliance depended upon the answer of the British Government.

This was serious enough. Not only was the General looked upon with affection and respect in this country, but he seemed to represent the only stable and unchanging element in France, where the Ministry had fallen that very day. When the Committee met on the 30th, therefore, though the C.I.G.S., Lieut.-General Sir Archibald Murray, declared that the General Staff was utterly opposed to the Serbian enterprise, it was decided to make a concession, while maintaining the general British point of view. A written reply was prepared, given the approval of the Cabinet, and handed to General Joffre that same day. In view of the French assurances regarding the capacity of the port and railways (for which the British General Staff took no responsibility) and of the limited task required of the

---

[1] Present: the Prime Minister, Lord Kitchener, Mr. Balfour, Lieut.-General Sir W. R. Robertson (representing Field-Marshal Sir John French). Admiral Sir H. B. Jackson, Colonel Pont (accompanying General Joffre), and an interpreter.

British, namely, to ensure the railway to Krivolak while the French undertook that of protecting the line between Krivolak and Veles, the British Government were prepared to co-operate. But it was to be understood that if communication with the Serbian Army could not be opened and maintained the Allied forces would be withdrawn.[1]

1915.
Oct.

That apparently settled the matter, but in reality this was far from being the case. The question being so closely entwined with the other problems of the Near and Middle East, it is necessary, in order that it shall be understood, to outline all of them and their inter-relations up to the end of 1915 before turning to consider what was happening at Salonika meanwhile.

On the 31st October Sir C. Monro telegraphed that he was in favour of the evacuation of the Gallipoli Peninsula. To Lord Kitchener the decision was repugnant. He was deeply impressed by an interview with Commodore Roger Keyes, R.N., who had prepared a plan for a renewed naval attempt to force the Straits. At all events he refused to sign orders for evacuation until he had viewed the situation with his own eyes.[2] At the first meeting of the reconstituted War Council, henceforth known as the War Committee,[3] on the 3rd November, it was decided that he should at once go out to the Eastern Mediterranean. Before leaving London he had a telegram from Sir John Maxwell, who pointed out the moral and material dangers of an abandonment of the Peninsula and suggested a landing in the Gulf of Iskanderun to counterbalance it. By cutting Turkey's main communication with Syria and Mesopotamia, this would have the double advantage of assisting the British advance on Baghdad, to which the Government were now committed, and assuring the defence of Egypt. The scheme, which he had himself previously considered, greatly attracted Lord Kitchener now, and when he reached Mudros he found General Monro and Admiral de Robeck equally in favour of it. He proposed to the Government that two first-class divisions (the 27th and 28th) under orders for Salonika, should be kept in Egypt to make the first landing in Ayas Bay, on the western shore of the Gulf, and that their places at Salonika should be taken by three weak and weary

Nov.

---

[1] The reply is given in full in Note I at end of Chapter.
[2] "Gallipoli," II, p. 408.
[3] "France and Belgium, 1915," II, p. 406.

divisions from Gallipoli.¹ The War Office therefore temporarily cancelled the move to Salonika of the 28th Division, which had already reached Egypt. However, the criticisms of the General Staff, the opposition of the Admiralty, which was aghast at the prospect of having to provide for a new campaign before either Gallipoli or Salonika was liquidated, and the political objections of the French, put forward at a conference held in Paris on the 17th, killed the project.²

Visiting Salonika on the 17th, Lord Kitchener found a most disquieting situation. The bulk of the three French divisions which had now landed and—Lieut.-General Mahon having meanwhile been given permission to advance —the British 10th Division were across the Serbian frontier. Between them and Salonika were two Greek corps. The authorities had refused to allow the Allies to create defensive positions at Salonika, and if the Greek forces became hostile General Sarrail did not think that the French and British troops would be able to re-embark.

Now, as the British Government knew, there was a possibility that the Greeks would become hostile. While M. Zaimis, the successor of M. Venizelos, was in office there had been no such danger. M. Zaimis had repulsed Sir Edward Grey's urgent plea that Greece should fulfil her treaty obligations, and had refused the offer of Cyprus, which had been made as an inducement to her to do so. He had, however, declared on the 20th October that, though Greece would not take action, as both he and the King thought that this would bring disaster upon her, her neutrality would be benevolent. A fortnight later M. Zaimis had resigned, to be succeeded by M. Skouloudis, who, probably under German pressure, assumed a different attitude and announced on the 10th November that it would be the duty of Greece to disarm the Allied troops if they fell back across the frontier. The British Government had promptly ordered all ships with supplies for Greece at Malta and in Egyptian harbours to be held up, cancelled the issue of export licences to that country, and made

---

¹ Lord Kitchener to the Prime Minister, 10th November 1915.
² The details and discussion of this question are given at greater length in "Egypt and Palestine," I, pp. 76–83. It is, however, there stated that Lord Kitchener was informed of the decision on the 19th. He actually learnt of it at Salonika on the 17th.

preparations to co-operate with the French in a naval demonstration off Piræus. No ultimatum was actually sent to Greece, but it was arranged that one should be delivered in the event of her committing any hostile act, that if an unfavourable reply were received an Allied squadron should be prepared for immediate action at Piræus, and that the naval force at Salonika should be strengthened when the reply was due.[1] Meanwhile, on the 12th November, Sir Francis Elliot called on M. Skouloudis and informed him that, "if a single soldier were touched "with a view to disarmament," there would be serious consequences.

1915. Nov.

To reinforce this pressure Lord Kitchener went on from Salonika to Athens, and on the 20th had an interview with King Constantine, at which the King pledged his word that the Allied troops should not be interned or disarmed if they recrossed the frontier into Greece. He protested strongly against the action of Britain and France, but vowed that he was at heart anti-German and was prevented from attacking the Bulgarians only because that would involve the destruction of his country. The personal views and motives of the King of Greece do not concern us here; nor need we take note of the polemics—intemperate and tendentious like most concerning Balkan questions—which his actions and those of the Allies have since aroused. We may recognize that he was between the hammer and the anvil. He seemed at that moment half disposed to protect his frontier against the Bulgarians, but Germany had threatened that intervention against them would be considered by her an act of war. He complained that he would be in an impossible situation if the Bulgarians attacked the Allies while the latter were in the act of crossing the frontier. The Allies were in an uglier situation still and could not afford to chop logic with him. On the 26th November M. Guillemin, the French Minister, supported by his British colleague, demanded the following concessions:—withdrawal of Greek troops from Salonika, control of the railways to the frontier, permission to establish defences round the city and across the peninsula of Khalkidike, and the right of the Allied naval forces to search merchant

---

[1] On the 21st November it consisted of three French and two British battleships, two French armoured cruisers, three British monitors, four French destroyers with some trawlers, and four British torpedo-boats.

shipping and destroy enemy submarine bases if found in Greek territorial waters.

On the 28th the Greek Minister in London informed Sir Edward Grey that these demands had been accepted. There was, however, some misapprehension on this point, and the Greek reply was not categorical. The French Minister was actually informed by the Greek Government that they would despatch a military representative to discuss with General Sarrail how best the demands could be met " within the limits imposed by the independence of Greece, " by the maintenance of her neutrality, and by the essential " requirements of her mobilized Armies."[1] This communication was followed, after some delay, by the despatch to Salonika of Lieut.-Colonel Pallis.[2]

At least the Greek reply indicated that no hostile action would be taken. The immediate danger was thus averted. But the whole fate of the expedition was still in doubt, and the Government were growing impatient because no reply came from the French to their representation that it was futile. On his return to London, Lord Kitchener told the War Committee on the 1st December that the official French view seemed to be that Britain could not now draw back. Not for a moment would the Committee accept this argument. It was decided that the Prime Minister, the First Lord, and the Secretary of State for War, with their naval and military advisers, should meet their French colleagues holding the same posts at Calais on the 4th December, for a full discussion.[3]

The conference took place at a moment of gloom and uncertainty. The advance on Baghdad had failed, and Major-General Townshend had fallen back with the remnant of his force to Kut. The Serbians were streaming across the Albanian mountains, and General Sarrail was slowly falling back towards Salonika. On the other hand, the Keyes plan for the forcing of the Dardanelles had for a brief moment come under serious consideration, so that the British Government were anxious to know if their troops at Salonika

---

[1] " Armées Françaises," Tome VIII, Vol. I, p. 388.
[2] The visit of this officer is described in Chapter V.
[3] The French ministers were now M. Briand (Prime Minister and Minister of Foreign Affairs), General Galliéni (War), and Admiral Lacaze (Marine).
In " Naval Operations," III, p. 215, it is erroneously stated that the conference was held on the 5th.

THE CALAIS CONFERENCE 49

or in process of arrival would be available on the Peninsula for a renewed offensive in co-operation with the fleet.[1] The three Cabinet Ministers were all equally opposed to the retention of troops at Salonika, and the General Staff had " no hesitation in urging that Salonika should be " vacated, and as soon as possible."

1915. Dec.

At Calais all the extraordinary persuasiveness of M. Briand was without avail. The British refused to be moved. Finally Mr. Asquith read out a statement embodying their views. They could not agree to the continued retention of the troops at Salonika, as they thought it likely to lead to a great disaster, and were of opinion that preparations should be made without delay for evacuation. The French representatives agreed.[2]

Thus on the 30th October it had been decided that if communication could not be opened up and maintained with the Serbian Armies the Allied Forces should be withdrawn;[3] and it had now been decided that they were to be withdrawn. Yet the British Government were to be forced to go back upon their resolve. On the 6th December Sir A. Murray, attending a military council at Chantilly, found himself alone in opposition to the French, Russian, Italian, and Serbian representatives in regard to evacuation; and on the same day Mr. Lloyd George was informed by M. Albert Thomas that French sentiment on the Calais decision was one of consternation. The Alliance was without doubt being subjected to the severest strain that had fallen upon it since the beginning of the war. What was to be done? The War Committee, impressed by the danger of this deadlock, instructed Sir Edward Grey and Lord Kitchener to cross to Paris with *carte blanche* to reach a settlement.

They found on their arrival on the 9th an attitude of annoyance and mistrust, which had to be dissipated, and therefore decided not to discuss the broad question of remaining at Salonika, but only how the British troops could best be employed to secure the safety of the whole force there. Lord Kitchener was able to report to the War Committee on the 13th that good feeling was restored and

---

[1] " Naval Operations," III, pp. 213–215.
[2] The Prime Minister's statement is given in Note II at end of Chapter.
[3] See p. 45.

that defensive positions around Salonika were being prepared.

The evacuation of Suvla and Anzac had been ordered on the 8th, though the naval commander at the Dardanelles, Rear-Admiral R. E. Wemyss, was still fighting vigorously against it.[1] But if there was any life still in the Keyes plan, the decision regarding Salonika snuffed out that last spark. To add to British anxieties, Major-General Townshend was now besieged in Kut, the Grand Senussi was attacking Egypt from the west, and the Suez Canal on the other side of Egypt was thought to be in the gravest danger once Turkey was freed from pressure at the Dardanelles. In the midst of all this we were committed to the defence of Salonika for an indefinite time. For it was no good buoying ourselves up with the saving clause of "without prejudice." It was going to be harder now to come away than it had been to land. Step by step, disputing every step but dragged irresistibly forward, we had engaged ourselves, probably "for the duration," in a venture which at the moment had scarcely a friend among our statesmen, our soldiers, or our sailors. A stranger story were not easy to find in the annals of military policy.

The Advance into Serbia.

The 10th Division had been hastily shipped from the Gallipoli Peninsula to Mudros harbour, where the troops almost immediately again went aboard their transports for Salonika. The division was very weak, battalions averaging not more than five hundred. Its first-line transport, left in the United Kingdom, was made up from that of the 13th Division in animals and vehicles, and the personnel was to rejoin at Salonika. Its artillery consisted of what could most conveniently be allotted to it: the divisional artillery headquarters, the LXVII and the LXVIII Brigades R.F.A. of the 13th Division, from Alexandria; and its own LIV Brigade R.F.A. from Mudros. Not a single howitzer battery was at that time included. As it was to be an independent force, it required various detachments of auxiliary services in addition to the normal ones; of these the majority were to go to Salonika from Egypt, while

---

[1] Lord Wester-Wemyss: "The Navy in the Dardanelles Campaign," pp. 224–228.

others were taken from Lemnos and Imbros.[1] Serge clothing, two blankets per man, and tents were issued to the division at Mudros, but the issue cannot have been complete, since there are many reports of troops wearing drill uniform and " shorts." As to greatcoats, an examination of the evidence seems to show that a number were issued at Salonika, and that the numerous drafts which joined the division there for the most part had them, but that a large proportion of the infantry went up into Serbia without them.

1915. Oct.

The embarkation was hurried and not very orderly, the ships being loaded as quickly as possible without much regard to the suitability of their cargoes. Thus, when the first detachment, consisting of headquarters of the 29th Brigade, the 6/R. Irish Rifles, and the 6/Leinster, landed at Salonika on the 5th October it had great difficulty in carrying its tents up to the camp owing to the lack of transport. On the 6th the 10/Hampshire, the 5/Royal Irish (Pioneers), and part of the 5/Connaught Rangers arrived, having sailed just before orders were received to cancel the moves.[2] Next day came 500 transport animals from Mudros, with few nosebags and no picketing pegs or ropes. This gave the Army mule one of those opportunities to display his variability of temperament of which he never failed to take advantage.

Meanwhile at Mudros the remaining troops who had embarked were close-packed in their ships; and for the sake of their health and comfort some of them were put ashore again during the period of waiting. Having got permission for the move to continue, Lieut.-General Mahon sailed in a destroyer on the morning of the 8th and arrived at 5 p.m. By the 17th all his troops, including the composite Yeomanry regiment from Egypt and a considerable number of infantry drafts from the United Kingdom, had arrived.

The first days were not pleasant. There was heavy rain, and the camps quickly became a quagmire. The people of Salonika showed complete indifference to the arrival of the troops, but the merchants and shopkeepers

---

[1] One ammunition park, one supply column, one reserve horse park, two field bakeries, two field butcheries, one ordnance detachment, one casualty clearing station, one stationary hospital, one base depot medical stores, one sanitary section, one veterinary hospital.

[2] See p. 41.

were far from indifferent to their official and private purchasing-power, and immediately sent prices soaring up. Not far from the British camp was one containing Greek refugees, who sold the men all too potent liquor and tempted them, when their money was gone, to barter articles of their kit, with results which were disastrous when they moved into Serbia.

The French troops destined to support the 156th Division arrived quickly: a mixed brigade of the 57th Division between the 12th and 16th October, the remainder of that division between the 20th and 23rd, and the 122nd Division between the 1st and 8th November. The French had speedily decided that two cavalry divisions would be useless in Macedonia and landed only two regiments of Chasseurs d'Afrique, with an additional regiment of Zouaves.[1] For reasons which have already been given, no other British troops arrived until the 5th November, when the 22nd Division began to disembark. As previously stated, General Sarrail, on taking over command of the French troops already on the spot, sent up by train to Strumica Station a detachment of three battalions and artillery, which on the 15th October took up a position covering the railway. It had on its right a couple of Serbian battalions likewise guarding the railway, while five others lay more or less at right angles to it, facing north-east towards the Bulgarian frontier. On the 16th another French regiment reached Gevgeli,[2] the first station in Serbia, and Strumica Station,[3] but was for the moment tied down to the railway line, as its transport was not yet ready to follow it.

It was, in fact, difficult for troops without pack transport to act at any distance from the railway owing to the roughness of the hills and the absence of roads suitable for wheeled traffic on either bank of the Vardar. It is an

---

[1] "Armées Françaises," Tome VIII, Vol. I, pp. 156–157.
[2] For once the usual practice of transliterating Serbian names in Serbian territory according to the scientific method has been abandoned here, " Gjevgjelija " being too trying. " Gevgeli " is the Turkish form.
[3] It is important not to confuse the stations with the towns from which they take their names. Strumica was a Bulgarian town (though it is included in modern Yugoslavia), 11 miles from Strumica Station, on the Salonika–Belgrade line, and connected with it by a bad road through a mountain pass, the station being in New Serbia. The station was also known as Hudova, from a neighbouring small town. Dojran town was in New Serbia, and Dojran Station, on the Salonika–Constantinople railway, in Greece.

unfortunate habit in the Balkans, once a railway is built, to let the road which has hitherto followed the same course fall into disrepair and gradually disappear; and now in the Vardar valley, one of the great highways of history, there were only bridle-paths or the most primitive cart-tracks. There were no bridges over the river in Serbian territory up to Veles except those of the railway, and they were of steel, with the rails bolted to the traverses and no footway. The ferries were few and the boats small. The line under its present management could provide only six short trains a day in either direction, and the officials on the Greek section were unaccommodating.

1915. Oct.

On the 17th October the Serbian detachment was summoned northward to Veles in view of the progress made by the Bulgarians; and General Sarrail relieved it, pushing forward a detachment to cover the Strumica–Dojran road. General Bailloud, whose third regiment was coming up, took over command on the 20th. Incredible as it may appear, the Bulgarians were unaware that the French had moved up the Vardar until the 21st, when the Bulgarian *14th Regiment*, moving down from Strumica with the object of destroying the railway bridge near Strumica Station, came in contact with them and was repulsed.[1] Following up, the French drove the enemy out of Rabrovo, seven miles east of the railway.

All that France could do for Serbia was to secure for her communication with the sea and her Allies; other demands she had perforce to refuse. She was now holding about 30 miles of railway up to Demir Kapija Station. Anxious to give the Serbians more assistance, General Sarrail next despatched the leading brigade of the 57th Division up the line to Krivolak, 20 miles south-east of Veles. Once again the enemy was taken by surprise; for the road to Veles was open. On the other hand, it would have been a bold step on the part of the French to advance further, owing to the paucity of their numbers and the length of the railway behind them which had to be defended. Moreover, the road bridge on the Negotino–Štip road was discovered to have been down since 1912. With only a wretched Turkish ferry-boat at its disposal, the brigade was at first unable even to push a detachment across to the east

---

[1] Lon, p. 61, gives the date as the 22nd, but a fairly sharp engagement took place the previous day.

bank for the purpose of seizing the high ground north of Krivolak. Veles and Kumanovo had fallen, and by the 24th the Bulgarian *Second Army* had completely cut off the main Serbian forces from the French.

General Sarrail had not ceased to press the British commander to give him assistance. General Mahon was, however, forbidden to move from Salonika until the 22nd, and even then was instructed not to cross the frontier. The British Government were clinging to their formula that the troops had been sent to enable Greece to fulfil her obligations and for no other purpose. The 30th Brigade (Br.-General L. L. Nicol), with the LXVII Brigade R.F.A., half the 66th Field Company R.E., and the 31st Field Ambulance, had been got ready, though its transport could be completed only by borrowing from the 29th Brigade. It was General Mahon's intention to send it up by the Constantinople railway to camp inside the Greek frontier but within easy reach of the French on the other side. On the day its move was to have begun, the 25th October, and after all arrangements had been made with the railway officials, the Greek Government, which had assumed control of all the lines in Greek Macedonia to facilitate mobilization, suddenly refused to allow the troops to camp close to the frontier. They must either cross it or stay where they were.

On the 26th Lord Kitchener telegraphed to General Mahon that, whatever happened, he must not fail the French. If it was necessary to cross the frontier in order to support them, he was authorized to do so and was trusted not to make any move of a rash or merely quixotic nature. The Greeks refused the use of Dojran Station for the troops, who were therefore to entrain to Gevgeli on the Belgrade line; it was, however, arranged that they should be supplied by the Dojran line, up which the supply company of the divisional train was to be sent. Again at the last moment the Greeks changed their minds and refused permission for any use of the Dojran line, presumably because they required it for their own troops on the frontier. The decision was subsequently reversed, but to begin with the British supplies had to be sent by the hard-worked and inconveniently situated Belgrade line. The writer of the General Staff war diary had reason for his annoyance when he recorded: " The Greeks are always doing this sort of " thing and are certainly very difficult people to deal with."

The 30th Brigade Group began its move to Gevgeli on the 29th. On the 31st two of its battalions relieved two French battalions in reserve at Hasanli and Čausli, northwest of Lake Dojran, and on the 2nd November another battalion moved up to Tatarli. The transport had great difficulty in making its way from Gevgeli, and later from Dojran, when the Constantinople railway was brought into use, and it was at once apparent that the four-wheeled G.S. wagons were quite unsuited to country of this nature. General Mahon asked for a new establishment for the transport of all troops in the country or on their way, and received permission to begin the reorganization of that of the 10th Division with the aid of a remounts depot already landed. At the same time the War Office decided to reorganize the transport of the 26th Division, which had not yet left France, before it embarked. The alterations made were quite small—far smaller than General Mahon had suggested. In the establishment of the first-line transport of an infantry battalion the chief changes were the substitution of pack-mules for the Maltese carts and water-carts, and of limbered wagons for the four travelling kitchens; in the second-line (train wagons for baggage, etc.) twelve limbered wagons were substituted for six G.S. four-wheeled wagons. In the divisional train and divisional ammunition column few changes were made with regard to vehicles, but the number of animals was increased, four draught mules replacing each pair of heavy draught horses in the train, and six draught horses each team of four in the divisional ammunition column.

There were conflicting instructions and uncertainty with regard to the command. On the 12th November Lieut.-General Sir H. F. M. Wilson and the staff of the XII Corps landed at Salonika. General Wilson had commanded the corps in France, but he was only a temporary lieutenant-general and therefore junior to General Mahon; and the only troops of his command which had yet landed were those of the 22nd Division. Two days later orders were received that General Sir C. Monro was to take over the command with the staff of the XII Corps. General Monro never did so, though for several days the War Office thought he had, until on the 19th November Lord Kitchener, on his way from Salonika to Athens, telegraphed from Mudros that he had brought him back there with a badly

1915. Nov.

sprained ankle, and that he intended to place him in command of all the Mediterranean forces outside Egypt, leaving General Birdwood in command at Gallipoli and General Mahon at Salonika until a decision was reached regarding the future of the forces there. The War Office objected to this arrangement and did not recognize it while Lord Kitchener was away from England, preferring in the meantime to deal with Generals Birdwood and Mahon direct. General Mahon, having decided to send up-country the whole 10th Division, having already got the 22nd Division ashore, and having been informed that three more were shortly arriving,[1] on the 15th November formed a new headquarters from the staff of the XII Corps (B.G.G.S., Br.-General P. Howell; D.A. and Q.M.G., Br.-General Travers Clarke) under the title of "G.H.Q., Salonika Army." He appointed Br.-General Nicol to the temporary command of the 10th Division and sent the staff up to Dojran. His own headquarters began work under extraordinary inconveniences. The start which the French had got with the authorities and their financial influence had procured them fairly good accommodation, but the British were applying for more just at the moment when relations with Greece were most strained, and were met by deliberate procrastination or blank refusal. For over three weeks the administrative branch of the staff had only one room and a verandah for its office work, while the officers whose duties forced them to remain in the town had to pay five times the normal rates for bedrooms. It was not until the 22nd November that the Greek authorities gave their sanction for the hire of suitable houses by G.H.Q.

The very complicated and interesting operations of the French troops from the last week of October to the beginning of December can only be shortly recounted here.[2] The first

---

[1] General Mahon cannot have known yet that these were to be the 26th, 27th, and 28th, because the decision against the landing in Ayas Bay, for which the 27th and 28th Divisions were earmarked, had not yet been taken. It was actually on the 17th November that orders were sent for the 28th Division to move from Alexandria to Salonika and that the Admiralty was asked to divert the ships carrying the 26th, then at sea. The 27th did not begin to leave Marseilles until the following day.

[2] The student will find this little-known phase of the war described with great skill and fairness in the French official history, "Armées Françaises," Tome VIII, Vol. I. The account of the fighting and of the retreat from Serbia fills a space equal to half the present volume and is illustrated by some thirty maps. It will therefore readily be understood

mission of the troops sent up into Serbia was defensive. The whole of the 57th Division (General Leblois) had gone up the line by the 27th October, but it had to cover a front of 15 miles between Gradec and Krivolak, and had still only the ferry for crossing the Vardar at the latter point. In the early days of November this difficulty was to some extent overcome by throwing two flying bridges, one French and one British,[1] at Krivolak, and the French were enabled to establish a strong semi-circular bridgehead east of the Vardar, having for its centre the high ground at Karahojali. Even before the flying bridges were complete a detachment was established here, which beat off with heavy loss an attack on the 3rd, catching the Bulgarians in the open and mowing them down. The enemy had, in fact, despatched two brigades of the *11th Division* from Štip to reinforce the brigade of the *7th* already on the spot,[2] and the French were now opposed to 24 Bulgarian battalions.

At Vozarci on the Crna, eight miles S.S.W. of its confluence with the Vardar, the bridge was standing, and a second bridgehead was established here. The French now held comparatively high ground, with the Vardar and Crna protecting their flanks, and were in an almost impregnable position unless the enemy contrived to cross the Crna behind them. Of this there was no immediate danger, the left flank being covered to a great extent by a Serbian detachment which had been driven back from Veles but had behind it a very strong position in the Babuna Pass on the Veles–Prilep road.

---

that the account here given is only the barest summary. The Bulgarian side is given in some detail by Lieut.-Colonel Lon.

[1] The British flying bridge was constructed by a temporary bridging detachment of the 10th Division under Major B. Borradaile, which was sent up to Krivolak with six pontoons and six trestles on the 2nd November. Great difficulties were encountered owing to the speed of the current and the eddies of the turbulent river; stone had to be tipped in to protect the landing stages; and the detachment had to cut its own timber for the raft which was to be anchored in midstream and on which the flying bridge was to swing. The bridge was ready on the 9th, though minor adjustments had to be made thereafter, and on the 15th Major Borradaile returned to his division, leaving a small party under Lieutenant J. E. Gill to work the bridge. Lieutenant Gill got his pontoons removed by train when the French abandoned their advanced positions, and in the course of the retreat constructed another bridge with the aid of a French working-party on the 7th December. On his return to Salonika he was sent for by General Sarrail, who personally thanked him for his services.

[2] Lon, p. 64. The losses of the Bulgarian *11th Division* in this attack were over 3,000. This division, previously known as the "Macedonian Legion," had not previously been engaged and was not fully trained.

On the 31st October General Sarrail had a message from the Voivode Putnik that he was about to make an attempt to recover Skoplje with two divisions and desired the French to attack from the south. On the same date the French commander learnt also of the agreement reached between General Joffre and the British Government in London on the 29th, that General Mahon would protect the railway as far north as Krivolak. He knew that the British were not yet in a position to do so much for him, but at least they could take over a portion of the defensive position of the French 156th Division north-west of Lake Dojran. General Sarrail considered he would then be in a position to strike two considerable blows in aid of the Serbians. He would first of all clear the country between the positions he already occupied north-west of Lake Dojran and the frontier crest (the Belašica Planina), and occupy as much of that crest as possible. This would enable him to look down upon the Strumica valley and the town of Strumica behind the crest, and by alarming the Bulgarians for the safety of their own territory would probably attract enemy troops to this area to the advantage of the Serbians further north. He was, as we shall presently see, more than sufficiently successful in attracting the Bulgarians to this quarter. His second stroke would be made westward across the Crna against the flank of the Bulgarian columns which were following up the Serbians from the direction of Veles.

The operations of the 156th Division were on the whole successful, though unfortunately the demands which they made upon the railway rendered it impossible for the two remaining brigades of the British 10th Division to be sent up as soon as General Sarrail desired. On the 3rd November the 156th Division captured the villages of Dorlobos and Kajali. On the 6th, after two days of thick fog, it launched an attack on the "Fortin Bulgare" and Hill 526 on the slopes south of Kosturino. This attack failed, and Dorlobos was also lost to a counter-attack. On the 11th, however, the division established itself on the crest, taking the Fortin Bulgare and Hill 526, and forcing the Bulgarian batteries on the Kosturino–Strumica road to retire. Next day it carried out a big advance east of the road, capturing the "Dorsale des Cinq Arbres" and reaching the outskirts of Ormanli and Kosturino. The troops, who like those of the 10th Division had come from the Gallipoli Peninsula, were, however, fatigued, and their difficulties of supply were considerable. The Bulgarians had been reinforced, though not to a very great extent, on the Belašica Planina.[1] General Sarrail therefore ordered the offensive movement to cease for the time being. The remainder of the British 10th Division having come up,[2] the 30th and 31st Brigades relieved the French from Kosturino to Lake Dojran on the night of the 20th, when the headquarters of the 10th Division moved to Dedeli.

1915. Nov.

The troops higher up the Vardar and on the Crna, which consisted at first of the 57th Division and later of the 122nd Division also, had meanwhile acted with boldness considering that they had to defend the line behind them as far as Gradec. General Leblois, finding that the tracks leading westward from the valley of the Crna to that of the Desna Babuna were impracticable for field artillery, while his mountain batteries were tied down to the Karahojali bridgehead, got General Sarrail's permission to advance instead up the Vardar towards Veles; that is, to strike at the rear of the Bulgarian columns instead of their flank. While awaiting this permission he occupied Kamendol and Debrišta, on the left bank of the Crna, and Gradsko Station, north of the confluence of the two rivers, on the 5th November. On the 6th and 7th he was held up in front of a very strong position, the Monastery of Archangel, perched upon a hill-top. On the 8th General de Lardemelle, commanding the 122nd Division, came up and, as the bulk of the troops available for offensive action were by this time those of his own division, was ordered by General Sarrail to take over the direction of operations. General de Lardemelle to a great extent returned to General Sarrail's own scheme of attacking the Bulgarian flank between the Crna and the Desna Babuna. He was, however, too late. The whole situation was changed; for the Bulgarians had lost interest in the fate of the Serbians in the Babuna Pass

---

[1] The *14th Regiment* had been at Strumica since the opening of the campaign, and had, as we have seen, come into action on the 21st October. On the 28th the *44th Regiment* of the *2nd Division*, which had been watching the Greek frontier in the neighbourhood of Petrić, was moved up to Strumica. It at once advanced to Kosturino and dug itself in. (Lon, p. 62.)

[2] The 31st Brigade moved to Gevgeli between the 7th and 10th. When the time came for the 29th to be sent up permission was given to use the line to Dojran, where the brigade arrived between the 13th and 15th.

and were now about to concentrate their main effort against the French. The true drama of what was in effect an encounter battle was just opening.

On the 9th the French occupied the villages of Kruševica and Sirkovo, both about two and a half miles west of the Crna. General de Lardemelle had decided next day to capture the heights beyond Kamendol, Mrzen, Sirkovo, and Kruševica, and also the Monastery of Archangel, on the other side of a fairly deep valley. He would then, he thought, be in a position to crush the Bulgarian forces west of the Crna, which would be caught between his troops on these heights and the Serbian detachment on the Veles–Prilep road. When that was accomplished it would be time enough to advance northward on Veles. The scheme was a good one, and might well have succeeded a few days earlier. The old adage to the effect that he who will not when he may is not likely to get another opportunity was to be proved true, as it has so often been in war.

The general situation of the opposing forces may be shortly summarized. On the French right was the 156th Division, facing the Belašica Planina and covering the valley of the Vardar to Gradec. Two regiments of the 57th Division covered the railway and the Vardar from Gradec to Karahojali. The 122nd Division with two regiments of the 57th held the Vardar and Crna from Gradsko Station to the bridgehead of Vozarci, the advanced troops, facing westward, being between two and three miles beyond the left bank of the Crna. In face of these troops there were two Bulgarian regiments on the Belašica Planina, and along the Vardar and Crna three brigades, making another six regiments.

At the very moment when General de Lardemelle was making his plans for the 10th, the commander of the Bulgarian *Second Army*, General Todorov, was entrusting to his artillery commander, Colonel Bogdanov, the task of clearing up the situation and bringing the French advance to a halt. For this purpose he placed him in command of the two Bulgarian regiments (the *3rd* and *53rd*) west of the Crna, and handed over to him also the *49th Regiment* of the *5th Division*, which had just reached Veles.[1] Colonel Bogdanov's orders were simply to " stop the enemy's

---

[1] Lon, pp. 64 *et seq*. The *5th Division* was on the move from the Rumanian frontier, where it had hitherto been stationed.

"advance." What he actually did was to launch first the two regiments already on the ground, and then the *49th Regiment*, which he had overtaken as he rode down from Veles, into a general attack.

1915. Nov.

Thus both sides moved forward almost simultaneously on the 10th. On the part of the Bulgarians the attack was half-hearted and never really developed, but it completely paralysed the attempt of two French battalions against Archangel. Nothing more was accomplished on this flank by the French than the occupation of Dolnje (Lower) Čičevo, on the slopes of the hill whereon the monastery stood. On the 11th the state of affairs was much the same. The Bulgarians refused to leave their trenches, despite the orders and haranguings of Colonel Bogdanov, who finally gave way and ordered them to dig in where they stood. On the other hand, the French did not get a footing in Gornji Čičevo until late in the evening, and even then the monastery, though only a thousand yards to the north-west, defied them. This was perhaps the crisis of the action. Had General de Lardemelle known how weary and demoralized was the enemy he would doubtless have continued to press on, but the troubles of the Bulgarians were hidden in the fog of war. During the night the French evacuated the two Čičevos.

Meanwhile the fire-eating Bogdanov had ordered a general attack to be carried out on the morning of the 12th, directing one regiment on Gradsko, one on the Čičevos (which he believed still to be held by the French), and one on Mrzen. This time his troops responded to his appeal and went forward all along the front. The *3rd Regiment* succeeded in entering Gradsko Station, and the *53rd* late in the afternoon reached Kruševica.[1] On the 13th the attacks were renewed, but after the Bulgarians had made some progress on both flanks, they got orders to hold what they had gained. Two more brigades of the *5th Division* had been despatched by General Todorov, who did not desire a renewal of the attack until they were ready to take part in it. The situation of the French was likely to be an exceedingly difficult one during the next few days, especially in view of the fact that the *11th Division*, east of the Vardar, had

---

[1] The French claim to have lost no ground on this date. If that is so, they had certainly abandoned the station by the 13th.

now been licking its wounds for ten days and might be expected to attack again soon.

The French Government had meanwhile become aware of the desperate pass which the Serbians had reached and alarmed for the safety of their own troops, in view not only of their exposed position but of the hostility of the Greeks behind them. They warned General Sarrail on the 12th of his danger, practically ordered him to bring his offensive to an end, and gave him little or no backing when he demanded that British troops should be sent to Monastir to support the Serbian detachment now falling back upon that town. His request being refused, by instruction from the War Office, on the 17th, he directed Generals de Lardemelle and Leblois to begin their preliminary arrangements for retreat. Since the 14th the front had been quiet; on the 20th the Bulgarians struck again. One of the newly-arrived brigades of the *5th Division* moved up the Prilep–Vozarci road and installed itself on high ground commanding the Vozarci bridgehead. The French fell back at one or two points, and General de Lardemelle, coming upon the scene in person, ordered the withdrawal of all troops across the Crna. Though General Sarrail was contemplating retreat, he was deeply angered by this retirement. On hearing of it, however, he decided that no other course was open to him than to order the destruction of the bridges over the Crna. On the 22nd he learnt that the Serbian offensive against Skoplje, the main *raison d'être* of his own advance, had failed, and immediately ordered preparations for retreat to be begun by the evacuation of the great quantities of material which had been accumulated between the Vardar and the Crna.

NOTE I.

REPLY HANDED TO GENERAL JOFFRE ON THE 30TH OCTOBER 1915.

In view of the French Staff statement dated the 28th October 1915, including definite calculations of the capacity of the Port of Salonika and of the carrying power of the railways into Serbia (for which the British Headquarters Staff do not make themselves responsible), and in view of the strictly limited rôle that General Joffre and the French General Staff desire British troops to fulfil, viz., to ensure the position of Salonika to Krivolak inclusive, in order to support the French Army, which assumes the duty of protecting the railway between Krivolak and Veles and of ensuring communications with the Serbian Army (the whole operations not to be conducted beyond the line Monastir–Uskub–Stip–Salonika,

MR. ASQUITH'S STATEMENT

and solely with the purpose of maintaining communication with the Serbian Army), and with the full understanding that if communication with the Serbian Army cannot be opened and maintained the whole Allied forces will be withdrawn, to be used as circumstances may require, the British Government are prepared to co-operate energetically in the manner proposed by the French Government.

KITCHENER.

NOTE II.

MR. ASQUITH'S STATEMENT AT THE CALAIS CONFERENCE, 4TH DECEMBER 1915.

We give no opinion as to what new operations may be undertaken in the future in the Balkans or elsewhere, and we agree that there are questions which should be considered in concert by the Allies. But in the opinion of the military advisers of the British Government, the retention of the present force of 150,000 at Salonika is from a military point of view dangerous and likely to lead to a great disaster. They cannot therefore agree to its continued retention, and are of opinion that preparations should be made without delay for evacuation.

In regard to the method of carrying out the retirement, the Greek Government should be informed that military necessities compel the Allies without delay to occupy and prepare for defence such tactical positions as the General on the spot may consider necessary for the security of our troops. They should at the same time be assured that these measures are not in contravention of our expressed intention not to infringe the independence and sovereign rights of Greece.

CHAPTER IV.

THE RETREAT FROM SERBIA.

(Maps A, 5 ; Sketch 2.)

THE ACTIONS OF KOSTURINO.

Maps A, 5. Sketch 2. THE front taken over by the 10th Division on the night of the 10th November was in savage, almost trackless country, broken up by steep hills and ridges, whereon scant scrub or a few dwarf oaks found an almost miraculous sustenance amid huge outcrops of rock. There was little to be seen of the Bulgarians, except for a number of deserters who declared that reinforcements were expected at Strumica. A sudden change in the weather proved for the time being far more deadly than the enemy. On the 26th rain began to fall, soon turning to snow and rendering the tracks impassable. An intense frost accompanied by a high wind followed—the great storm, the effects of which on the Gallipoli Peninsula are so well known—and in the course of a few days played havoc with the troops, especially those on the hill-tops. The men were soaked to the skin by the rain and snow, and the bitter frost then froze their clothing on them. Greatcoats were frozen so stiff that when taken off they stood unsupported, and split like boards if an attempt was made to beat the frost out of them; and, as has been stated, some of the troops had actually none, the sentries wearing horse-blankets. The officers had to prevent their men from lying down during the coldest nights, keeping them on the move to stave off the coma which appeared to be creeping over them.

The nights of the 29th and 30th in particular were terrible, upwards of 600 men of the 30th and 31st Brigades having to be evacuated, many of them in a state of collapse. The strain would have been unbearable even had the constitutions of many of the men not been undermined by their experiences on the Gallipoli Peninsula, while among the drafts were others invalided home from France, sent out to the East as more likely to stand the climate there, and now diverted to Salonika. The administrative staff of the Army began to purchase underclothes, waistcoats, and charcoal to send up, but the contractors and tradesmen did not always

SUFFERINGS OF 10TH DIVISION

1915.
Nov.

carry out their bargains, and there was considerable delay. Fortunately the weather took a turn for the better about the 3rd December and the temperature rose to well above freezing-point. In all 23 officers and 1,663 men of the division were evacuated to Salonika on account of complete collapse, frost-bite, or general debility.

Br.-General Nicol, becoming alarmed for the safety of his line owing to its depletion by sickness, telegraphed to General Mahon on the 29th November that he could not guarantee to hold it unless another brigade were sent up. General Mahon had by now no shortage of troops. The whole of the 22nd Division was ashore and the 26th, 27th, and 28th were disembarking. Only the 22nd was complete as to fighting troops, and it had not all its transport; but its presence and that of troops of the other three relieved Generals Mahon and Sarrail of their worst anxieties regarding Salonika itself. The British commander was, however, not inclined to send up any more troops than necessary now that withdrawal had been decided upon, seeing how difficult it was to keep those already in Serbia supplied. Moreover, General Sarrail assured him that there was no great concentration of the enemy in the Strumica valley; and the French commander was in the better position to know, as he now had a squadron of aeroplanes at his disposal, and General Mahon had none.[1] It was therefore decided to send up only the pioneer battalion of the 22nd Division, the 9/Border Regiment, instead of the brigade which had been demanded. The work done by this battalion in draining and repairing roads within the next few days was of great value. Br.-General Nicol had the 6/R. Munster Fusiliers and 7/R. Dublin Fusiliers of the 30th Brigade, the heaviest sufferers, replaced by the 10/Hampshire and 5/Connaught Rangers of the 29th.

Dec.

The situation of the 10th Division on the morning of the 6th December may be described from left to right, because the left was the exposed flank, the right being thrown back in echelon and far from any contact with the enemy. The left was in touch with the French at the head of the Kajali ravine, about half a mile south of Kosturino, this defile being held by a single company of the 7/R. Dublin Fusiliers. The line of the 30th Brigade (Lieut.-Colonel

---

[1] On the 30th November the French put two machines at Dojran at the disposal of the 10th Division.

P. G. A. Cox) ran thence south-eastward along the Kosturino Ridge to beyond the Serbian Frontier House : 7/R. Munster Fusiliers on the left, 5/Connaught Rangers in the centre, 10/Hampshire on the right. The 7/R. Dublin Fusiliers, less one company, was in reserve north of Kajali. On the right of the 30th was the 31st Brigade (Br.-General J. G. King-King), holding a front of over two miles, which ran nearly south, by the villages of Memešli and Prsten, to the Kozli Dere [1] stream : 5/R. Irish Fusiliers on the left, with one company in an outpost position known as " Rocky Peak," which was separated from the main line by a deep valley and stood several hundred feet above it ; 5/R. Inniskilling Fusiliers in the centre, 6/R. Irish Fusiliers on the right, and 6/R. Inniskilling Fusiliers in reserve. South of the Kozli Dere the right flank was held by the two remaining battalions of the 29th Brigade (Br.-General R. S. Vandeleur) along the Kara Bail ridge to the shore of Lake Dojran, with the 5/Royal Irish (Pioneers) in reserve at Hasanli. The 6/R. Dublin and 6/R. Munster Fusiliers were in divisional reserve at Tatarli, and the 9/Border Regiment (Pioneers) of the 22nd Division was south of the lake. In support there were twelve four-gun 18-pdr. batteries of the LIV, LXVII, and LXVIII Brigades R.F.A., the first-named being in the neighbourhood of Hasanli, covering the right flank, and so far away from the left that throughout the 7th it knew nothing of the Bulgarian attack. Two of the other batteries, C/LXVII at Kajali and B/LXVII west of Prsten, were in dangerously exposed positions. Being without mountain artillery, Br.-General Nicol had no choice but to take this risk if he was to give the infantry any support, and even now the support was slight enough. The lack of 4·5-inch howitzers, which could have dropped shells into the deep ravines, was also felt.

The front line on the left taken over from the French was not well sited, being exposed to the enemy's view from his higher ground and for the most part lacking a good field of fire to compensate for this defect. On that of the 10/Hampshire it was some way down the forward slope,

---

[1] " Kozli Dere " and " Bajimia Dere " are Turkish names of the upper and lower reaches respectively of a river for which the Serbian name is " Anska." The Turkish forms are retained, as the other would be quite unknown to British participants in the campaign. For the same reason " Kara Bail " (below) is preferred to " Boskija."

but likewise exposed to view. Owing to the rocky nature of the ground and the stoppage of work by frost, the defences were even now not good. The troops were, as has been explained, in an exhausted state, even though they had not yet been in action, and this was particularly the case with the 30th Brigade. The fact that nearly half the strength of several battalions consisted of recently-arrived and unassimilated drafts from various regiments still further lowered their efficiency. The infantry was, in the words of an officer who joined the division at this period, " a con-" glomeration of officers and men from all over the British " Army."

1915. Dec.

The French retreat down the Vardar had been in progress since the 3rd December. The period between the 22nd November and that date had been spent in preparations ; for only rigid method and orderliness could save the force in the Vardar–Crna loop from the risk of a grave disaster. Stores, transport, and a proportion of the artillery had been evacuated, and two strong intermediate positions had been fortified. The retreat had been begun just in time, for the Bulgarians had been strongly reinforced. According to General Sarrail's information, they intended to launch five of their huge divisions, numbering 120 battalions, against the 50 which the Allies had in Serbia. The case was not really anything like so bad as this, but the enemy—freed from any anxieties previously felt regarding the conduct of Greece—moved two brigades of his *2nd Division*, previously posted in the Struma valley, to the Strumica area. With the two fresh brigades of the *5th Division* already mentioned and another brigade of the *11th*, he had now on the ground 10 brigades or 80 battalions : on the Crna two of the *7th*, one of the *5th*, and one of the *11th Divisions;* on the Vardar to Gradec two of the *11th* and one of the *5th;* and from this point to the village of Ormanli on the Belašica Planina three of the *2nd*.[1] He was, in fact, now only too eager to attack, but he was to be foiled by the skill with which the French slipped away from the Vardar–Crna loop and subsequently covered up their withdrawal down the Vardar.

The retreat was, in fact, conducted by General Leblois (who had been placed in command of the two divisions)

---

[1] Lon, p. 75.

strictly in accordance with the programme laid down by General Sarrail and with remarkable coolness. Owing to the small number of trains which could be run, the troops had in the main to be withdrawn by march route. The transport was for the most part sent down by rail, and after reaching the first intermediate position at Demir Kapija Station the infantry had for a period the support of five mountain batteries only, as it was necessary to entrain the field artillery. The Bulgarians, with commendable promptitude, had thrown trestle bridges across the Crna by the morning of the 4th, and followed up in four columns. On this flank they did not really come into touch with the French until the 6th, but thereafter their pressure was severe. On the left bank of the Vardar their attacks were fortunately pushed with less resolution. The risk was, however, very great, even though the danger that the Greeks would attempt to intern the Allies as they crossed the frontier had been removed.

General Sarrail had offered to help the Serbian Monastir detachment to fall back with his own troops to Salonika, but its commander preferred to make for the Adriatic in order to rejoin the forces of his own country, and was now out of touch. The Bulgarian cavalry had, in fact, occupied Monastir on the 4th. On the morning of the 6th the French were holding the first intermediate position at Demir Kapija. Their 57th Division was to withdraw that night through the 122nd, which was in the second intermediate position round Gradec Station, in touch with the 156th Division in its original position on the left of the British 10th Division. The withdrawal of the two last was not to begin until the 14th December, but the British had already begun, in anticipation of an earlier retirement, for which General Mahon had strongly pressed, to send down the line stores and baggage.

During the 4th and 5th considerable artillery fire had been directed upon the Kosturino ridge. At 2.30 p.m. on the 6th the enemy began a heavier bombardment, particularly on the front held by the Connaught Rangers and on Rocky Peak, and from 3 p.m. onwards small bodies of Bulgarians were seen making their way down the ridge in front of the position. The Rangers drove them to ground, though not until they were within 60 yards of the wire. At Rocky Peak the Bulgarians effected a lodgment in the

[*Photographie Boissonnas.*

The Vardar entering the Demir Kapija Defile.
(On the right bank, a railway tunnel.)

ATTACK ON 10TH DIVISION

position held by the company of the Royal Irish Fusiliers **1915.**
but were driven out with the bayonet. At dusk orders were **6 Dec.**
issued to reinforce this position by another half company
and a machine gun; the 6/R. Dublin Fusiliers from general
reserve was moved up to the neighbourhood of Kajali, and
three companies of the 9/Border to that of Hasanli, at the
north-west corner of Lake Dojran. Br.-General Nicol
sent a message to Br.-General King-King that, if the Rocky
Peak outpost position was lost, the line from Memešli to
the right of the 30th Brigade must be held at all costs and
that it was to be strengthened during the night. General
Mahon, somewhat disquieted for the safety of the 10th
Division, had come up to see Br.-General Nicol, and now
telegraphed to Salonika that another brigade should stand
by ready to entrain if called for in the morning.

Before dawn on the 7th, in dense fog, the Bulgarians **7 Dec.**
suddenly attacked Rocky Peak, creeping up the gullies
and attacking with the bayonet. The bayonet also was
the only weapon of the garrison, unable to distinguish
friend from foe in their very similar uniforms until the last
moment. The remnant fought its way back down the
rearward slope. Then the enemy's artillery opened on the
front of the 30th Brigade and several machine guns, which
had been brought up on to Rocky Peak, swept its line in
enfilade. A little later a mountain battery came into
action at this point. Between 9 a.m. and 10 a.m. masses
of the enemy were reported to have closed up on the front
of the Connaught Rangers, but this attack was held in
check by the rapid fire of the defenders.[1] The situation
was a serious one, but, though casualties were heavy, there
was no sign of the Bulgarians breaking through. The
troops seemed to be in good heart and responded readily
to the demands of their officers. An attack on the French
front had been repulsed.

About 2 p.m. the first breach was made in the line.
The evidence as to the exact order of events and the times
at which they occurred is conflicting, but there is little
doubt as to what happened, or that the main cause of the
collapse of the front was the enemy's capture of Rocky
Peak. Coming under enfilade fire from this quarter and being also heavily shelled, the right-centre of the four Hampshire

---

[1] The main attack against the 30th Brigade was carried out by two regiments, the *14th* and *28th*. (Lon, p. 79.)

companies in line fell back and could not be rallied until it reached Crête Simonet, the previously selected second line of defence. The left company of the Hampshire maintained its position until about 3.30 p.m., but it was not actually visible from the line of the Connaught Rangers, who, seeing the retirement of a few individual men, thought their right was turned. The Bulgarians followed up a devastating bombardment with an attack in overwhelming numbers on the Connaught Rangers. They were received with rapid fire, but, showing complete contempt for their heavy losses, charged in with the bayonet, and after a fierce hand to hand struggle forced their way through. This was about 2.30 p.m., though even now the centre company of the battalion maintained its position for over an hour longer. The battalion was then rallied by Lieut.-Colonel H. F. N. Jourdain in the ravine behind the position. The commanding officer had orders to take up a position on Crête Simonet, to which the whole of the Hampshire eventually withdrew, but found it impossible to scale this hill, which was very steep on his side. Finally he was ordered to lead the remnants of his battalion back to Dedeli, and to hold the pass there. The line of the Munsters on the left was assaulted in less strength, and the battalion's fire kept the enemy in check. On receiving a report that the Bulgarians were in the Connaught Rangers' trenches, Lieut.-Colonel G. Drage swung his right company back to cover his flank. At 3.40 p.m. he received orders to retire, and did so company by company. This battalion also received orders to withdraw to Dedeli.

The enemy made no very vigorous attempt to follow up, but unfortunately the first company of the Hampshire to retire had fallen back in some confusion through the guns of C/LXVII near Kajali, and the detachment, thinking that the whole front had caved in, abandoned the guns after removing the breech-blocks and dial-sights. These guns could hardly have been saved, even if teams could have been brought up to them, as they had been hauled up a hillside with ropes in order to give them a field of fire.

Meanwhile Lieut.-Colonel Cox had taken up a position on Crête Simonet with the 6th and 7th R. Dublin Fusiliers, soon afterwards joined by the 10/Hampshire. On the front of the 31st Brigade the whole line, with the exception of the 6/R. Irish Fusiliers about Prsten, had been withdrawn and

had taken up a position on the right of Crête Simonet, on 1915.
the high ground north of Tatarli. The battery near Prsten 7 Dec.
had likewise been abandoned, again in the belief that the
whole front had collapsed. In this case an attempt was
made next day to bring the guns out, but was frustrated
by a second withdrawal of the infantry. General Mahon,
who had spent the previous night with the headquarters
of the 10th Division, had, immediately he learnt of the
serious situation, telegraphed to Salonika for another
brigade to be despatched as quickly as possible. The
leading battalion of the 65th Brigade, 22nd Division, reached
Dojran that night.

Br.-General Nicol was hopeful that the Bulgarian
advance would be checked on the new position, which he
ordered should be held at all costs, as any further withdrawal would imperil the French line. He informed General
Bailloud of the situation, whereupon the latter ordered a
welcome reinforcement of a mountain battery and two
battalions to Tatarli. The leading French battalion came
into the line between Crête Simonet and the Kajali ravine
at 1 a.m. on the 8th.

The Retreat into Greece.

The night passed quietly, the fog having partially 8 Dec.
dispersed, and the troops consolidated Crête Simonet—
on which sangars had already been built by both French
and British—as best they could with their entrenching
tools. On the morning of the 8th Lieut.-Colonel Cox,
finding that Crête Rivet,[1] the hill in front of his position,
was not occupied by the enemy, sent up two companies of
the 6/R. Dublin Fusiliers to hold it and a French company
to prolong their left to the Kajali ravine and make contact
with the line of the French 156th Division.

At the point of junction the French mountain artillery
completely broke up a Bulgarian attack, but by 11 a.m. the
enemy had massed in front and on the flanks of Crête Rivet
and opened heavy rifle fire upon it. For the tired, hungry
defenders it was a nerve-racking action. The fog was again
so thick that only the tops of Crête Rivet and Crête Simonet
emerged from eddying whorls of mist, out of which came

---

[1] This was the " Hill 526 " referred to on p. 58.

the rattle of musketry and machine-gun fire: the only indication of the enemy's movements, though once, for a fleeting moment, there was a view of the Dorsale des Cinq Arbres, black with troops. A determined attack was beaten off before noon, but at about 1 p.m. the French company was withdrawn. Orders were then sent to the British companies to fall back if heavily attacked. Heavily attacked they were at 2 p.m., the enemy rushing the hill in great numbers, under cover of machine-gun fire. The two companies of the Dublins fought their way back to Crête Simonet, losing 64 men, of whom 54 were wounded. However, Crête Rivet being only an outpost, the work of the Bulgarians was still in front of them.

Then came a bolt from the blue. At 3.30 p.m. Br.-General Nicol received a report that the Bulgarians had likewise massed on the front of the 31st Brigade and were working their way down the Memešli–Prsten–Čalkali ravine, in an endeavour to turn the right flank of the division. Half an hour later he was told by his signal officer that the brigade was about to retire. On telephoning to Br.-General King-King he learnt that the latter had actually issued orders for retirement, as he believed that the brigade was in danger of being surrounded. The enemy had not only worked round its right, but also penetrated between the 6/R. Irish Fusiliers on the right and the 5/R. Inniskilling Fusiliers in the centre. Br.-General Nicol sent the 7/R. Munster Fusiliers to his support and told General Bailloud that he would be forced to uncover the French right. At 5 p.m., hearing that the 31st Brigade had begun to retire on Čaušli, he ordered the 30th to fall back on Dedeli. After the withdrawal had begun, at 5.45 p.m., the Bulgarians charged Crête Simonet, but five rounds rapid drove them back in discomfiture into the fog. Again, while the rear guard was scrambling and slipping down the back of the hill in the darkness, the enemy rushed up the forward slope, cheering, blowing bugles, and sending up flares. On the top, however, he stopped, as if his duty for that day were done, and neither the 30th nor the 31st Brigade was pressed in its retirement.

At night the line of the 10th Division ran from the shore of Lake Dojran along the Kara Bail Ridge, which was held to north-east of Čaušli by the 29th Brigade—6/R. Irish Rifles, 6/Leinster, and 5/Royal Irish (Pioneers), with the

A RESPITE

9/Border Regiment attached in reserve—and thence across the mouth of the Dedeli Pass, which was held by a detachment under Lieut.-Colonel Fair, C.R.E. of the division, consisting of the 5/Connaught Rangers, the 7/R. Munster Fusiliers, and the divisional cyclist company. The remainder of the 30th Brigade bivouacked in the pass, while the 31st, after halting for the night at Pazarli, was withdrawn into reserve on the morning of the 9th. Two battalions of the 65th Brigade, the 9/King's Own and the 14th King's (Liverpool) Regiment, had reached Čaušli and come under the orders of Br.-General Vandeleur.

1915.
9 Dec.

On the left the French did not begin to withdraw behind the Bajimia Dere until 2 a.m. on the 9th. The Kosturino–Dojran road, which was used by the bulk of their infantry and probably all their transport, rose sharply to the Dedeli pass from the Bajimia, and was open to the view of the enemy as soon as he had occupied the high ground north of the valley on the former British front. The French transport moved with painful slowness and many halts on the steeper parts of the hill, so that when day broke a large proportion of the column had not yet reached the pass. By good luck, however, it was veiled in thick fog until midday, by which time the last vehicle was through it. In anticipation of the retreat, the 66th Field Company R.E. had prepared for demolition the culverts which carried the road over a series of watercourses, and as the rear guard retired up the pass these culverts were blown up successively.

On the 9th, after a quiet night, the new British position was divided into three sectors : Lake Dojran to the Pazarli–Dorutli track, under Br.-General Vandeleur ; from this track to the neighbourhood of Čaušli, the 65th Brigade (Br.-General L. N. Herbert), which had now all arrived; thence to the Dedeli pass the 30th Brigade and 10/Hampshire, the pass itself being still held by Lieut.-Colonel Fair's detachment, from which the Munster battalion had been withdrawn. The 31st Brigade was in reserve on the Dojran road. The enemy did not attack during the day, or in the course of the 10th, when General Mahon came up with Major-General the Hon. F. Gordon, commanding the 22nd Division, whom he placed in command of all British troops in Serbia. It must be confessed that this only added another link to the chain of command, which had enough of them already, since General Bailloud had been empowered to issue orders to the British troops during the retirement. It would have been open to General Mahon to supersede Br.-General Nicol if he had lost confidence in his ability to extricate the troops, but this was not the case. Major-General Gordon, who knew nothing of the country or the conditions, was in a difficult situation.

The French retreat had been hastened by the events of the 7th and 8th on the British front and also by strong pressure on their own, the Bulgarians having handled their rear guards roughly on both banks of the Vardar. During the 9th troops of the 57th Division began to move across towards Lake Dojran in order to take up on the morrow a position from Kara-Ular, near the western shore, through Černište, to Furka, behind the British and through which they were to be withdrawn. A second line was to be organized, entirely in Greek territory, from the southern shore of the lake and running thence roughly south-west across the Vardar, and through this line the final retirement was to be carried out on the nights of the 11th and 12th. General Sarrail had reason to suppose that the Bulgarians would not violate Greek territory, though of this he could not be sure. He would not listen to the demands of his subordinates to hasten the retreat, being determined to evacuate the stores at Gevgeli Station before he abandoned it.

1915.
10 Dec. The fog which had served him so well on the 9th was renewed on the 10th rather to his disadvantage, and with the enterprise of the enemy upset his plans. All day long small parties of Bulgarians were pushing up the gullies south of the Bajimia, and General Bailloud was growing more and more alarmed by their progress. General Sarrail authorized him to make a slight withdrawal at night and take up a new line from Borlova Kurbeleri, west of the Vardar, to Dedeli, in touch with the British. As regards the left flank there was no difficulty, but east of the Vardar bodies of the enemy were already far across this line. Between 8 p.m. and 9 p.m. General Bailloud therefore ordered his troops to fall back on the Grčitše–Furka road, Furka being over three miles south of Dedeli, where General Sarrail had directed him to establish his right flank. At 8.55 p.m. he telephoned to Major-General Gordon, whose headquarters were in Dojran village, informing him of what he was about to do and ordering him to withdraw south of the lake all British troops except for one brigade,

which was to hold a very short front on the French right between Kara-Ular and the lake.

Major-General Gordon communicated these orders to Br.-General Nicol, who, in accordance with the plan already arranged between them, ordered the 31st Brigade to take up a position at Pataros, in Greek territory, to cover Dojran Station from the east; the 29th to follow and bivouac south of the station; the 30th to follow at 4 a.m.; and the 65th, with the 9/Border Regiment and the LIV Brigade R.F.A. (less one battery) to prolong the right of the French 113th Brigade from Kara-Ular to the lake. Battalions in the line were each to leave one officer and 20 men to deceive the enemy. The withdrawal was a matter of great difficulty, but the enemy did not follow it up, and not until after daylight, when the fog cleared slightly and temporarily, did the little detachments left behind become engaged with his scouts.

Once more on the 11th the retreat was hastened by the bold action of the enemy. West of the Vardar two of his columns advanced down the valleys of the Sermenli and Kojnska streams, which entered the Vardar just north of the frontier. East of that river he won a far more important success, forcing his way down the valley of the Furka Dere and capturing Bogdanci at 1 p.m. His action here was, in fact, a good example of his enterprising spirit. Colonel Ruef, commanding the 312th Brigade at this point, was first aware of it when his ammunition wagons were captured in the fog. At first he could not believe that more than a reconnoitring detachment was in Bogdanci, but he soon discovered that the place was held by a strong column with mountain guns.[1] The enemy had also cut his telephone line to General Bailloud, so that he had not received the order sent him to take up a new position in rear. Judging the situation critical, he ordered his troops to fall back on Dojran. General de Clermont-Tonnerre, commanding the 113th Brigade on his right, thus found himself in the air, and likewise withdrew, in three columns, one on Dojran Station, one on Büyükli, and one on Dautli, all of which were inside the Greek frontier. Unfortunately he neglected or was unable to send word of his retirement to the British,

---

[1] This was, in fact, the leading regiment of the *11th Division*. The Bulgarians claim also to have captured a gun and a number of prisoners. (Lon, p. 83.)

who found themselves in a very awkward predicament that night.

As a preliminary to the next stage of the retirement the 113th Brigade was to relieve the British 65th Brigade from Lake Dojran to Kara-Ular during the evening. This brigade had three battalions in line, the 12/Lancashire Fusiliers on the right, the 9/East Lancashire in the centre, and the 9/King's Own (R. Lancaster) on the left, with the 14/King's (Liverpool) in reserve. The Bulgarians had not approached the position but there had been some long-range shelling by their artillery, and the British batteries had found distant targets on the forward slopes of the recently evacuated Kara Bail Ridge. About 2 p.m. General de Clermont-Tonnerre himself, with several regimental officers, had come to reconnoitre the position, and the relief had begun at 5 p.m.

At 8.30 p.m. Br.-General Nicol, who was in bivouac between Dojran and the station, was told by a French regimental commander that the headquarters and the whole division would have to withdraw at once, as " everybody " was retiring " and he had orders to clear the roads of transport. When the brigadier expressed doubt, the French officer formally cautioned him that he had been warned.

Br.-General Nicol wrote a warning order for all troops to be prepared to move at shortest notice on Kilinder, but held it back until he had communicated with Major-General Gordon, then at Dojran Station. Major-General Gordon was for the moment disposed to doubt the news, and with some cause ; for it was at once followed by a message from the 65th Brigade that it had been relieved and that all was quiet. However, a solid stream of French troops and guns marching down the road speedily proved that the report was correct ; and Br.-General Nicol was thereupon instructed to move the division into Greek territory.

The mystery regarding the relief is explained by the fact that the French troops which carried it out got their orders to withdraw while it was actually taking place. It was, in fact, not carried out completely, a French officer galloping up to Lieut.-Colonel A. C. Gabbett, commanding the 12/Lancashire Fusiliers on the right, and telling him that the French were not taking over that part of the front but were retiring. On the front of the left battalion, the 9/King's Own, the French officers, who had thoroughly reconnoitred the ground, moved straight to the positions they were to take up without passing by battalion headquarters. One French company relieved one of the two British front-line companies, but the second apparently took up a position at some distance from the trench held by the other. At 6.30 p.m. three companies of the King's Own formed up at battalion headquarters and after some delay, as the fourth did not appear, marched off, leaving an officer to await the fourth and direct it to follow. That it was in any danger occurred to no one, for there had been no intimation that the French also were withdrawing. This does not, however, excuse the officer left to await it for his action in handing over the task to two or three brigade signallers, who in turn left their post.

It appears that the company commander, doubtless under the influence of the trench-warfare training he had received during his short service in France—where the 22nd Division had remained scarcely two months—repeatedly refused to withdraw until he had been formally relieved, despite the urging of his subordinates, who pointed out that all other British troops were gone and later that there were no French either to be seen. He did not actually move until 12.45 a.m. on the 12th, and three-quarters of an hour later came upon a whole battalion of the enemy resting by the roadside. It was at first uncertain whether they were French or Bulgarians, and an officer who went forward to reconnoitre could not make sure until he was within a few yards of them, his approach unfortunately giving the alarm. The company, which had meanwhile deployed, then fired a volley and charged with the bayonet. A desperate struggle followed, but as the British were outnumbered by five to one and were opposed to troops who had no superiors in close fighting, it could have but one end. Seventeen individual men broke away and crossed the frontier, the remainder, two officers and 120 other ranks, being all killed or captured. The rest of the brigade withdrew without molestation south of Dojran Station, but had great fortune in doing so. The troops in rear, especially the 12/Lancashire Fusiliers, were mixed up with the French, and that on a road from which deployment was very difficult, since there was a rocky wall on one side and a steep drop to the lake on the other. Had the enemy brought to bear on the road a single gun, perhaps even a

1915.
11 Dec.

single machine-gun from a boat on the lake, he could have turned it into shambles.

**1915.
12 Dec.**
At midnight on the 11th Major-General Gordon sent for Br.-General Vandeleur, commanding the 29th Brigade, who made his way to the station through a congested mass of French transport and found the commander of the force with Br.-General Nicol in a railway carriage. Major-General Gordon told him of the withdrawal, and that there was nothing to stop the Bulgars pressing on into Greece if they had a mind to, and ordered him at once to take up a position on the Greek side of the frontier from the lake on the right to a point about a mile and a half south-west of it. The brigadier returned to his brigade, now made up of its own four battalions, and got it in motion at 1 a.m. on the 12th. The road—and it was the only one—was completely blocked by French transport, the retiring columns having halted for the night, and was encumbered on either side by troops in bivouac. Occasional bands of refugees and herds of livestock, which the French were taking out, added to the congestion. The night was dark and again foggy. Br.-General Vandeleur took his brigade across country by compass-bearing, marching on the Greek frontier-stone on the Dojran road, which the head of the column reached at 2.30 a.m. After a quick reconnaissance, he put the 6/Leinster in position on the hill above and afterwards moved the remaining battalions up on its left, though he had no notion how his line was sited owing to the density of the fog. "A" Battery, LXVIII Brigade R.F.A., and a troop of the Composite Yeomanry regiment were put at Br.-General Vandeleur's disposal.

Thus the whole British force which had entered Serbia was back in Greece by the early hours of the 12th December. The French were not all across the frontier until late that day, and in the evening their 57th and 122nd Divisions held a line through Büyükli, Seideli, Smol, and on the right bank of the Vardar, Drevenon. Up to the last the affair was marked by the fantastical touches by which it had throughout been accompanied. The instructions given to the Greek posts were evidently not uniform. West of the Vardar they showed themselves sympathetic and gave French officers information as to the tracks. One of their officers actually stated that they had orders to oppose the Bulgarians if the latter attempted to cross the frontier.

South-east of Lake Dojran the patrols of a recently arrived French cavalry regiment which General Sarrail had sent up to cover the withdrawal were prevented by them from reconnoitring the neighbouring villages.

1915.
12 Dec.

The Retreat in Greek Territory.

General Sarrail's belief that the enemy would respect the Greek frontier was confirmed by information through Chantilly from a secret Bulgarian source on the 12th December.[1] Yet the French commander dared not stand as soon as he himself had crossed into Greek territory. Even if the chance of the enemy following him up was only one in a hundred, he could not take this risk for his exhausted troops in an unfavourable position; besides, the enemy might at any moment change his mind. The general was anxious to get the troops back as soon as possible upon a position for the defence of Salonika which he had been reconnoitring and regarding which he came to an understanding with General Mahon on the 14th. Yet he still showed his old deliberation and determination to evacuate all material before he moved, leaving over half the total force which had entered Serbia on the frontier while the roads and railways in rear were cleared. Withdrawing the 156th Division to the neighbourhood of Amatovon Station—about half way between the frontier and Salonika on the Belgrade line—he left the other two, under the command of General Leblois,[2] on the rear-guard position running south-west from the southern shore of Lake Dojran to Drevenon, west of the Vardar. He had put at the disposal of General Leblois a French cavalry regiment south-east of the lake, and, by arrangement with General Mahon, two British infantry brigades.

Maps A, 5.

The British 30th Brigade entrained at Dojran Station during the night of the 11th and reached Salonika the following afternoon. The divisional artillery, less the LXVIII Brigade R.F.A., marched from the neighbourhood

---

[1] "Armées Françaises," Tome VIII, Vol. I, p. 372, and Annexes there referred to. The message stated that the Bulgarians would halt on a line two kilometres short of the frontier, except in the region of Dojran.

[2] The 122nd Division was now commanded by General Gérôme, General Sarrail having superseded General de Lardemelle in consequence of his unauthorized withdrawal across the Crna on the 20th November.

of Dojran Station in the early hours of the 12th and, after moving all the morning at a crawl along the still congested road, got clear of the traffic and bivouacked north of Kilkis (Kukush), prepared to continue its withdrawal by march route on the morrow. The 65th Brigade, 9/Border Regiment, two batteries LXVIII Brigade R.F.A., and certain other troops of the 10th Division marched to Kilinder Station, where orders were received for the troops to begin entraining that night, all guns, vehicles, and animals marching. Major-General Gordon and Br.-General Nicol both returned with their staffs to Salonika by train.

This left only the 29th and 31st Brigades, each with a battery of the LXVIII Brigade R.F.A. attached, under the orders of General Leblois; and the 31st was ordered by him to march to Kilinder on the afternoon of the 12th. The 29th Brigade had, it will be recalled, taken up in the fog a position just south of the frontier. On the morning of the 13th, when the fog cleared, it was found that this position was better sited than could have been hoped and required little adjustment to bring it into line with the French 113th Brigade, which was discovered digging in on its left. An order was received from General Leblois that the frontier was to be very carefully watched but not recrossed, even by patrols. If the Bulgars violated it they were of course to be fired on, but not otherwise. General Leblois also sent a warning order for the conduct of the retreat on Salonika when he authorized it to begin. In the column east of the Dojran railway, which alone concerns us, the 29th Brigade was to form the leading portion of the main body, the remainder consisting of two regiments under General de Clermont-Tonnerre, with a rear guard consisting of the cavalry and the 2nd *bis* Regiment of Zouaves.

1915.
13 Dec.

14 Dec.
The night passed quietly. At 10.30 a.m. on the 14th General Leblois came round to brigade headquarters, much upset by a cipher message from Major-General Gordon which stated that General Sarrail was sending him (Leblois) orders to withdraw the 29th Brigade. Br.-General Vandeleur reassured him, telling him that as the brigade had been placed under his orders he might rely on its not moving until he gave his consent. At 11 p.m. orders were received from General Leblois for the retreat on the morrow, the 29th Brigade withdrawing under cover of darkness at 4 a.m., so that its head should reach Kilinder by 8.15 a.m.

END OF THE RETREAT

This movement was carried out without event, other than the difficulty experienced by the troops in making their way in the dark over bad tracks and A/LXVIII Battery becoming bogged at one point. The Bulgarians had, it was now conclusively proved, received orders not to follow into Greek territory. A few men were seen by the cavalry troop, which covered the withdrawal, actually to cross the frontier and enter the vacated position, but they carried their rifles slung. The 10/Hampshire and 5/Connaught Rangers were entrained at Kilinder for Salonika, the rest of the column setting out to march. These troops had a weary road to follow, through rain and mud, not reaching Sarigöl Station, only 15 miles from their position on the shore of Lake Dojran, until the morning of the 17th. Here they received orders to entrain. The 31st Brigade reached a camp outside Salonika the same day, having marched all the way. The troops were completely exhausted, and some of the men could not even eat the hot food which had been prepared for them. Their one desire was to sleep.

1915.
15 Dec.

During the 15th General Sarrail left two small rear guards to cover the retreat : one across the Constantinople railway with its main body at Kilinder, the other between Lake Arjan and the Vardar. He then issued orders to his three divisions to fall back upon the line selected for the defence of Salonika, between the two railways (that is, between the Galiko and Vardar) from Naresh to Kara Oghlu, which was prolonged eastward to Lake Langaza by the British troops not hitherto engaged. The rear guards were ordered to maintain their present positions as outposts. West of the Vardar a detachment of 1,500 Serbians (railway defence troops of the Third Ban, who had retired with the French) took over the task of covering the marshy ground between Vardar and Vistritsa. The last French division was in its place by the 18th December.

* * * * *

Thus ended the expedition into Serbia. It had failed in its main purpose, but it had undoubtedly taken a good deal of weight off the Serbians and made their retreat easier. By containing the Bulgarian *Second Army* it may well have saved them from complete encirclement and destruction. Its cost had not been inconsiderable. The total casualties of the French amounted to 143 officers and 4,822 rank and file; those of the British 33 officers and 1,176 rank and file.[1] On the other hand, by the testimony of friend and foe alike, the losses of the enemy were vastly greater.[2] Little material had been lost, and the withdrawal had been conducted largely in accordance with the will of the French commander, who halted and moved again when he had made up his mind to do so. The most important exceptions were due to the rupture of the 10th Division's front on the 7th December and that of the French on the 11th. The whole retreat had, indeed, in the words of an observer not biased in favour of the French, been " capably directed and " marvellously well executed."[3]

In the expedition the British had taken a subsidiary part. It was not of their conception and had been condemned in advance by their General Staff at home, which was left with the unprofitable and melancholy satisfaction of seeing its prophecy come true. And yet, as we look back upon this stage of the campaign, we must admit that it cannot be so easily dismissed. In war, plans which succeed do not always owe their success to their being the best

---

[1]

	KILLED	WOUNDED	MISSING
Officers	1	20	12
Other Ranks	98	366	712

These are the figures given by Army headquarters, which agree with those given by the headquarters of the 10th Division. All the casualties were in this division, with the exception of two officers and 125 men of the 65th Brigade missing. On the other hand, " Medical Services: Casualties and Medical Statistics," gives the total number of wounded admitted to hospital in 1915 as 34 officers and 481 rank and file. It is difficult to account for this difference, unless some of those reported " missing " were evacuated through French dressing-stations. A second and more probable supposition is that among the thousands evacuated sick there were a number who were also wounded but were not included under that category by the divisional headquarters. To swell the figures given by the medical authorities, there may also have been wounded from the troopship *Marquette*, sunk by a submarine in the Gulf of Salonika on the 23rd October with considerable loss of life, but this is not recorded.

Out of the 1,209 casualties given above, just over half were suffered by the 5/Connaught Rangers and 10/Hampshire.

[2] Lieut.-Colonel Lon gives figures of casualties on three occasions only. In the first attack on the French in the Vardar–Crna loop the Bulgarians had 4,333 casualties; in the general attack of the 13th November they had 1,544; and in an attack on the French on the 9th December one regiment had 400 *killed*. These figures amount in sum to 6,277, more than the French and British losses combined for the whole period.

Lieut.-Colonel Lon states that the Bulgarians captured 1,234 prisoners, 14 guns (of which 8 would be British), and 62 artillery wagons.

[3] Lon, p. 84.

REVIEW OF THE EXPEDITION 83

possible, but often rather to their being undertaken at a favourable moment and prosecuted with unlimited energy and determination. The converse is equally true. Hesitation, divided counsels, half measures, and delays may well have been far more damaging to the Salonika plan than any unsoundness inherent in itself. If France and Britain, fully forewarned as they were, could have decided to send to Salonika some three months earlier [1] the troops which they had landed by the early days of January, the move might not have been an ideal one, but there is no reason to suppose that it would not have prevented the envelopment of the Serbians by the Bulgarians. Nor must it be forgotten that the appearance of five or six Allied divisions in October would have made upon the Greeks an impression very different from that caused by the landing of two obviously weary and ill-found divisions from the Dardanelles.

With regard to the communications, their deficiencies were emphasized in many reports and appreciations; but, after all, for a Near Eastern port, Salonika, with its good harbour easily made secure against submarines, with three broad-gauge railways—that to Constantinople *via* Dojran, that to Belgrade, and that to Monastir—radiating from it, must be admitted to have been unusually favourable to a great military enterprise. The carrying-power of the railways was low, but, according to the estimate of the British General Staff, it could have been greatly increased under British or French control; it was indeed considered that the six trains a day in each direction on the Belgrade line could have been at least doubled if an understanding had been reached with Greece at an early stage. The road communication with and in New Serbia was very much worse than that of the railways, but that again could have been bettered; the French, in fact, greatly improved the roads in the neighbourhood of the Vardar valley with the aid of local labour during the period that they held the Vardar–Crna loop, and the British did some useful work of the same kind in the Dojran area.

These considerations are put forward not in advocacy of the landing at Salonika, which was at best risky and doubtful, and would, if carried out as suggested above, have

---

[1] Shipping would then have been ample for the transfer, as it would have preceded the evacuation of Gallipoli and the move of the Indian Corps to Mesopotamia.

made impossible the Champagne–Loos offensive. (If it be argued that that would have been all to the credit of Salonika, it can only be retorted that the offensive seemed promising; that, in Champagne at least, it scared the German command; and that it represented the first serious attempt by the Allies to end the deadlock on the Western Front.) The object of advancing these arguments is merely to ensure that the reader does not condemn the venture out of hand. In fine, early co-ordinated and determined action by the Allies might, at the least, have frightened Bulgaria out of her engagements, brought Greece into the field, and further limited the extent of the Serbian disaster. Failure was due above all to the clash of policies, Britain hankering after a renewed attempt to force the Dardanelles or a landing in the Gulf of Iskanderun, while France had decided that Salonika was the goal.

CHAPTER V.

THE ENTRENCHED CAMP OF SALONIKA.
(Maps A, 2, 6, 6A.)

THE FORMATION OF THE ENTRENCHED CAMP.

THE last two chapters contained an account of the expedition into southern Serbia. By the time that expedition had ended, the greater part of four British divisions, in addition to the 10th, had been landed at Salonika. Their arrival has so far only been mentioned in passing, in order not to interrupt the narrative of the operations. Maps A, 2.

All four divisions came from the Western Front. The 22nd (Major-General the Hon. F. Gordon) began entraining for Marseilles on the 25th October. Divisional headquarters sailed for Alexandria on the 30th, receiving orders at sea that its destination was Salonika, and landed on the 6th November. The disembarkation of the infantry was completed on the 10th, but there was then some delay, the CI Brigade R.F.A. not reaching Salonika until the 11th December. The division was, however, transported more quickly than those which succeeded it. The 26th Division (Major-General E. C. W. Mackenzie-Kennedy) began entrainment at Longueau on the 9th November and embarkation at Marseilles on the 13th. One battalion actually reached Alexandria (on the 18th) before the move to Egypt was countermanded, and the first troops reached Salonika on the 23rd. In most cases the transport did not accompany the units but came on in later ships; so that when the troops already landed were exposed to the bad weather at the end of November they suffered very severely. The troop-carrier *Norseman*, carrying the divisional train, was torpedoed on the 22nd January 1916 in the Gulf of Salonika. The ship was, however, beached, all the personnel and half the thousand mules aboard being saved. The ammunition column did not disembark until the 8th February. The 27th Division (Major-General G. F. Milne) began entrainment on the 15th November. One infantry brigade sailed on the 18th and 19th, and the other two on the 28th, their voyage being lengthened because they had to put in to Toulon to await their escort. Orders were then received that the Indian Corps, on its way to Basra, should have precedence over the troops for Salonika in the ships available. As a result, the rest of the division,[1] including its transport, remained in camp near Marseilles all December.[2] Sailings were resumed at the beginning of January and continued throughout that month. The three infantry brigades had a long and weary journey. Two battalions of the 80th went to Alexandria and remained some days there without disembarking, while both the 81st and 82nd were kept aboard their ships for about a week in Salonika harbour.

The 28th Division (Major-General C. J. Briggs) was the first to start, but was held up in Egypt owing to the discussion regarding a landing in the Gulf of Iskanderun. It began its entrainment on the 21st October, and its first troops reached Alexandria on the 29th. On the 22nd November, by which time the division was complete in Egypt but for two artillery brigades which sailed direct from Marseilles, divisional headquarters embarked for Salonika. Here disembarkation was slow, partly owing to the congestion of the quays, partly to its being discontinued for two days (the 8th and 9th December) at the moment when the Government were disposed to evacuate Salonika altogether. The period in Egypt had been of great value to Major-General Briggs for training and reorganizing the division after its losses at Loos.

The trans-shipment of these five divisions must be ranked as one of the most remarkable of Britain's maritime achievements in the course of the war, when it is remembered that, more or less simultaneously, British transports were lent to the French to assist them in moving their three divisions, the Indian Corps was despatched from Marseilles to Basra, the Gallipoli Peninsula was evacuated and the troops shipped to Egypt, two other divisions, the 31st from home and the 46th from France, were also carried to Egypt, and vast quantities of warlike stores were shipped both to Salonika and Egypt. Criticism of its methods would therefore be unfair; but the results showed the desirability of

---

[1] Only the personnel of the three field ambulances had accompanied the infantry brigades.

[2] Some detachments embarked in the middle of the month, but they were ordered to disembark two days later, as the ships were required for the Lahore Division.

THE DIVISIONS FROM FRANCE

putting the transport of troops by sea under the military authorities, except as regards the provision and timetables of the ships, which was obviously not the Army's affair. Troops were landed in winter, in a bleak and inhospitable country, sometimes without tents, sometimes with tents but no tent-poles,[1] generally without transport vehicles, and almost always without transport animals. They were immobile from the point of view of offence, little less helpless from that of defence, and scarcely able to feed themselves in camp. In those anxious days Sir Bryan Mahon would far sooner have seen single battalions and single batteries with their transport than the whole brigades of infantry which actually arrived without horses or vehicles.

The 22nd and 26th were divisions of the New Armies, having both been formed in September 1914 and sent to France a year later. Neither had yet taken part in a battle, but both were composed of good, well-trained young troops. The 27th and 28th were Regular divisions. Both had been heavily engaged at "Second Ypres," in which the 28th was almost destroyed; and the 28th had just taken part in the Battle of Loos. These two divisions were still, however, far above the average in quality; and in the force as a whole the general standard of discipline, training, and military experience was higher than that of the divisions successively landed on the Gallipoli Peninsula. The 10th Division was in a very different condition to the other four and required steady training, rest when that should become possible, and above all time to throw off the effects of its recent experiences and to absorb its large drafts. On its return to the neighbourhood of Salonika, Br.-General J. R. Longley, formerly commanding the 82nd Brigade, 27th Division, was appointed to the command, Br.-General Nicol resuming that of the 30th Brigade;[2] Br.-General King-King, who was sick, was replaced by Lieut.-Colonel E. M. Morris in command of the 31st Brigade; many senior officers, including all those of the artillery, were gradually replaced, and the staff was almost entirely changed.

The chief weaknesses of the force were in artillery and

---

[1] On at least one occasion a ship had to go on to Egypt without being able to disembark the poles, which were at the bottom of her hold.

[2] Br.-General Nicol had been recommended for permanent command of the division by General Mahon, but General Monro had directed that the post should be given to a serving officer, whereas Br.-General Nicol had retired before the war.

mechanical transport. Three 60-pdr. batteries (the 13th, 18th, and 20th) and one section 6-inch guns (43rd Siege Battery) constituted the only heavy artillery between November and the end of January. Then Vice-Admiral de Robeck provided nine naval guns from the defences of Mudros and Alexandria—not the most suitable weapons for the support of an entrenched line, but very welcome.[1] The 2nd, 5th, and 7th Mountain Batteries disembarked on the 28th December. The force was without aircraft and, until the end of January, anti-aircraft artillery; it then received three guns from Mudros. It had only 350 motor lorries, which were insufficient to keep the quays clear during the busy period of disembarkation, especially as 25 per cent of them were always out of action owing to over-work on bad roads.

1915.
Dec.
Maps 2, 6.

General Sarrail had been warned by his Government on the 25th November that he should set about the fortification of Salonika; but he had been unable to accomplish anything, even reconnaissance, owing to the objections of the Greek authorities. It was as a result of the pressure exercised by Sir Francis Elliot and M. Guillemin at Athens that a Greek staff officer, Lieut.-Colonel Pallis,[2] was despatched to Salonika, where he had an interview with Generals Sarrail and Mahon on the 9th December. General Sarrail's demands were similar to those already made through diplomatic channels: that the Allies should be allowed to fortify a position for the defence of Salonika; that the Greek troops should evacuate the city; that a neutral zone should be established south of Dojran on either flank of the Allied line of retreat; and that the Greeks should hand over Fort Kara Burun and the battery at the mouth of the Vardar, which covered the entrance to the roads of Salonika. These claims were forwarded by Lieut.-Colonel Pallis to Athens. So far as reconnaissance went the Allies, in their desperate situation, were unable to await the reply. General Sarrail ordered reconnoitring parties to be sent out on the morrow, and General Monro,[3] who was then

---

[1] Four 6-inch Mark XI and two 4·7-inch guns were manned by personnel of the 84th Siege Battery from Alexandria, and took that number. One 6-inch Mark VII and two 4-inch guns were manned by naval ratings.

[2] See p. 48.

[3] The position of General Monro at this time is described later in this chapter.

THE LINE OF DEFENCE

at Salonika, directed General Mahon to do likewise. The reply, which came on the 11th, was moderately satisfactory. The Greek troops would not offer armed resistance to the construction of field works, and the Greek V Corps had been ordered to move eastward out of the area required by the Allies for defensive purposes, but a strong protest would be made; if the Allies by their movements drew the enemy across the frontier all Greek forces in the neighbourhood would withdraw and leave the field clear; Greek troops would not evacuate Salonika; the King would not hear of the Allied occupation of the forts, but he ordered work upon them to cease and the garrisons to be reduced by one half; the staffs of the railways were to remain Greek, but were to be increased to meet the needs of the Allies. Lieut.-Colonel Pallis had from the first made it clear that, unless the Allies expressed their intention of quitting Salonika as soon as possible, the Greeks would in no case oppose the advance of the Bulgarians.

The French and British commanders were now free to prepare defensive positions, though General Sarrail had practically no troops for the purpose, as all the French contingent save a single regiment was up-country, and General Mahon's units could move only with great difficulty owing to the shortage of transport. Reconnaissance was hindered by the fog, but the line of defence was decided upon, after some hesitation in regard to minor detail, on the 14th December. It ran from the village of Tumba, on the south-western shore of Lake Langaza, through Aivatli, Balcha, Dautli, and Naresh to the Vardar about Kara Oghlu, and thence down the left bank to the bridge which carried the Monastir road over the river.

Salonika, to add to its other not inconsiderable advantages as a base, was very well situated from the point of view of defence from the landward, the country round it constituting wonderfully good natural fortifications for the purposes of modern warfare. The line just mentioned may be called the inner perimeter, and runs along the forward slope of a sharp ridge, which has in front of it a fosse in the form of a wide, gently-curving basin. The ridge is connected south of Lake Langaza with the mountainous peninsula of Khalkidike, while the fosse is continued eastward—but now as a very deep and rugged gorge—by Lake Langaza itself, by the Eiri Dere valley between that lake and Lake

Beshik, by Lake Beshik, and by the Rendina Gorge running down to the Gulf of Orfano. To the west is a veritable moat, the wide and swift-flowing Vardar. The marshy right bank of the Vardar would not require to be strongly held, but the Eiri Dere valley and the Rendina Gorge would need strong detachments.

The natural outer perimeter of the fortress could not at this period be occupied by the Allies, but as it was to be their main position at a later date it may also be described here. From the Gulf of Orfano to Lake Dojran it consists again of a mountain ridge—the Beshik Dagh rising out of the gulf, continued to the northwest by the Krusha Ridge—again fronted by a great fosse: first Lake Tahinos, then the valley of the Struma, then Lake Butkovo and the river of the same name, then the Hoja, running westward into Lake Dojran. West of Lake Dojran Nature has not so generously collaborated with the military engineer, but even here her work has not from his point of view been ill done. The obvious line of defence runs across a plateau from the lake to the Vardar. Thence it can be traced, in accordance with the numbers of the available garrison, either in semicircular form through Vodena to the Vistritsa or nearly due westward to Lake Prespa.

Maps 6, 6A. Directly he received the Greek reply through Lieut.-Colonel Pallis, even before he had decided upon the precise manner in which his own portion of the line should be sited, Sir Bryan Mahon issued orders to the 22nd, 26th, 27th, and 28th Divisions to be prepared to begin work and to make the moves necessary. The 26th was to hold the right flank from Tumba to Aivatli, the 28th thence to the neighbourhood of Balcha, and the 22nd to the junction with the French at Dautli. The three brigades of the 27th were to be in reserve at Lembet, on the Seres road, where they were now in camp or on the point of arriving, and two of them were to work on the track to Akbunar, which was essential for the purpose of supply. As the headquarters had not arrived, Br.-General S. W. Hare, who had been sent from Mudros to succeed Br.-General Longley in command of the 82nd Brigade, temporarily took over command of the division with the brigade staff. The 66th Brigade of the 22nd Division was to march to Naresh on the Dojran railway and work on the section of the line to which the French were

THE WORK OF FORTIFICATION

falling back.[1] The 10th Division was to be concentrated as soon as possible at Kapujilar, south-east of Salonika.

1915. Dec.

Work had begun all along the British line by the 16th and made good progress, though hindered by the difficulty of getting up engineer stores. Great quantities of barbed wire had been shipped to Salonika, some of it from Mudros.[2] The general system of defence was a chain of mutually supporting strong points upon the line mentioned above, which was to form the first and principal line of resistance. The posts were in general connected by communication trenches, which were usually so sited and dug as to form a fire-trench in emergency. Sir Bryan Mahon, however, laid it down that a continuous front-line trench, necessitating a large garrison, was not required. In the course of his frequent inspections of the work in progress he found that in some cases it had been too strongly influenced by the conditions of the Western Front, which had here no parallel. He pointed out that the fortification was not being carried out in contact with the enemy, that there would be ample warning of the approach of the Bulgarians, and that after they had been repulsed (as he was convinced they would be) they must be immediately pursued. Detachments of all arms (a battalion, a battery, a squadron of Yeomanry and the divisional cyclists) were pushed forward by the 26th Division to the village of Lankados (Langaza), north of the lake of that name, and by the 28th to Güvezne on the Seres road. These detachments were not nearly so far advanced as the French outposts, since the former were on bad roads and the latter on the railways. They were withdrawn early in January.

---

[1] This brigade moved on the 12th, reaching the neighbourhood of Naresh next day, and some of the other moves also took place before the line mentioned above was decided upon on the 14th. The 80th Brigade of the 27th Division began work on the 13th upon an advanced position, the line Palaiokhora (Gnoina)–Yeniköi–Rahmanli, which General Mahon afterwards decided to abandon, at least for the time being, and moved back to Balcha on the 15th.

[2] By the 12th January the C.R.E. of the 26th Division, Lieut.-Colonel C. G. W. Hunter, calculated that his division had put out 245 miles of wire, and that he would require ten times that amount if three lines of defence were to be prepared and the redoubts were to be wired all round in accordance with the original plan. This was, however, never carried out. The supply of engineering stores for the entrenched camp is a remarkable feat to the credit of British administration, because at the same time far greater quantities were being sent to Egypt, where the fortification of the Suez Canal on a grand scale was being undertaken. (See "Egypt and Palestine," I, pp. 89–96.)

In rear, the second line of defence, through Stanovon, close to Tumba at the south-west corner of Lake Langaza, Stena Galikou on the Dojran railway, and Vathylakkos (Kaziköi), running thence southward parallel to the Vardar, followed the crest of the ridge. This line was traced by General de Castelnau, who arrived at Salonika on the 19th December. The Armée d'Orient, from the time of its constitution in October until the 2nd December, had been directly subordinated to the Minister of War. On this date it came under the orders of General Joffre, now nominated Commander-in-Chief of the French Armies, who formed at Chantilly a " General Staff of the French Armies " under General de Castelnau, with a section devoted to forces in the Mediterranean.[1] Seeing that there was at Salonika no unified command, it behoved the Allies to ensure that the system of defence was uniform. Lord Kitchener had agreed with General Joffre that the position and experience of General de Castelnau made him the most suitable choice for a visit of inspection. General de Castelnau found no fault with the first line of defence, but suggested that the Dremiglava ridge—actually the portion which General Mahon had been in two minds whether to hold or not and on which the 80th Brigade had begun work —should be occupied later. In addition to tracing the line along the crest, he urged the importance of preventing the infiltration of enemy troops along the valleys separating the spurs. For this purpose an intermediate line, or chain of posts, was constructed, on the right quite close to the first line and near the foot of the slope, on the left half-way down it.

While General de Castelnau was at Salonika General Mahon began to take measures for the defence of the line of Lakes Langaza and Beshik, which had been impossible until the 10th Division was ready. Even as it was, the division was by no means fully re-equipped when it was ordered to move. One brigade, with a battery of artillery, a field company R.E., and two troops of Yeomanry was to defend the Rendina Gorge between Lake Beshik and the sea; a second, with similar detachments of cavalry and engineers, but with a whole brigade of field artillery, was to hold the gap between the two lakes; the remainder of

---

[1] " Armées Françaises," Tome VIII, Vol. I, p. 561.

THE WORK OF FORTIFICATION 93

the division was to be held in reserve on the high ground five miles south of Lake Langaza.

1915. Dec.

On the 20th and 21st the 30th Brigade Group marched to Lankadikia (Langavuk), south of the Eiri Dere valley between the two lakes. These marches were not long, but were very trying, since the troops had had only three days' rest at Kapujilar after the retreat, and rain had made the roads deep and heavy. On the 28th December the 29th Brigade, less artillery and transport, was sent by sea round the peninsula of Khalkidike in four troop-carriers, with store-ships and lighters, arriving in the Gulf of Orfano next day. The landing at the mouth of the Rendina Gorge could not begin until a five-mile anti-submarine net had been laid across the bay. Headquarters was established in the inn of the little fishing-village of Skala Stavros, the troops bivouacking along the valley. The artillery and transport marched all the way from Kapujilar.

Both in the Eiri Dere valley and the Rendina Gorge defensive work was begun. In the former case the entrenchments were along the ridge south of the valley, through the villages of Langavuk and Gomonich, and were virtually as strong as those west of Lake Langaza. In the Rendina Gorge they consisted of isolated works, protected by wire, upon the craggy hills north of the river. The Navy made arrangements to support this position by fire from the sea upon the flat and exposed strip of land between the hills and the shore. Lake Beshik was patrolled by a party in a fishing-boat; but, that method proving unsatisfactory, two motor-boats were procured from Mudros and carried in pontoon wagons with big teams supplied by the heavy artillery batteries, one to Lake Langaza, where it arrived on the 10th January, and the other to Lake Beshik, arriving on the 15th. Later in the month the Navy brought another boat from Mudros direct to Skala Stavros and launched it on Lake Beshik.

By the early days of January the British and French defences between Lake Langaza and the Vardar had made such good progress that the danger of a Bulgarian attack on this part of the line had greatly diminished. General de Castelnau had decided that the Allied Armies at Salonika did not require reinforcement for the purpose of defence, though both Generals Sarrail and Mahon were asking for more troops. The Bulgarians had still not crossed the

1916. Jan.

Greek frontier, though on the 7th German aeroplanes carried out a bombing raid on Salonika which caused 18 casualties. In any event an advance by the enemy against the Entrenched Camp would have been a difficult undertaking; for it was reported that he had by no means succeeded in repairing all the damage done to the railway in Serbia by the retreating French. To add to these difficulties General Sarrail, on the advice of General de Castelnau, blew up the Demir Hisar bridge, which bore the Constantinople railway over the Struma, bridges at Kilinder and Khirsova on the same line south of Lake Dojran, and others on the Kilinder-Karasuli branch line on the 13th. General Mahon, however, received information that the enemy was showing increased activity in the Struma valley and near Xanthi, which he thought might indicate an intention to attack his long and weakly-held right flank. The detachment in the Rendina Gorge was dangerously isolated. It had to be supplied almost entirely by sea, and the tracks across the peninsula were so bad in the wintry weather then prevailing that when General Mahon visited it he preferred to ride all the way, using relays of horses. It was arranged that a brigade of the Royal Naval Division, now released from the Gallipoli Peninsula and at the disposal of the Admiralty, should be sent over from Mudros in case of emergency; but a landing under fire at Stavros on the little sandbag pier made by the Navy would probably have been impossible.

General Mahon therefore issued orders on the 13th that, to complete the defences of the Eiri Dere valley and the Rendina Gorge, one brigade of the 27th Division should be sent to each point, to reinforce the brigades of the 10th Division already there. This would leave him with a very small general reserve, and he was anxious that, as soon as the two necks were fortified strongly enough to be held by a single division, the 27th should take them over, so that the 10th could be withdrawn for a much needed rest. The moves had to be put off for some days owing to heavy snow making the tracks impassable, but were then carried out, the Rendina detachment this time moving by march route. On the 26th the 80th Brigade took over half the 29th Brigade's front at Stavros, which had naval support in the shape of a cruiser and later a monitor in the Gulf of Orfano.

Digging, wiring, and road-making were to continue for over four months. The formation of the Entrenched Camp was a hard and bitter task, owing to the rocky nature of the ground and the exposure of the troops engaged in the work or camped in tents in the neighbourhood of the defences they were to man in the event of a Bulgarian advance. In the early weeks, especially, they suffered severely. There were several heavy falls of snow, and every few weeks the "Vardar Wind" blew from the north with almost the force of a gale, icy cold and chilling to the bone even men wearing the goatskin jackets which had been issued in large numbers. Yet the troops not only worked hard but remained cheerful.

Command and Administration.

It has been recorded that Lord Kitchener, during his visit in November, had designed to place General Monro in command of all forces in the Mediterranean outside Egypt and that the War Office disapproved of the arrangement.[1] On Lord Kitchener's return to London it nevertheless came into force. General Monro established at Mudros a headquarters known as "Headquarters Mediterranean Expedi-"tionary Force." That of General Birdwood, commanding the troops on the Gallipoli Peninsula, was at Imbros, and was called "Headquarters Dardanelles Army." General Monro exercised a real supervision at Salonika, which he visited for several days in December.

1915.
Dec.
Maps A, 6.

On the 14th December the War Office sanctioned the formation of two corps headquarters. That of the XII Corps was to be re-formed under the orders of Lieut.-General Sir H. F. M. Wilson, who had been waiting for a month in Salonika without employment. That of the XVI Corps was to be formed under the orders of Major-General G. F. Milne, commanding the 27th Division, when he arrived. The XII Corps headquarters (B.G.G.S., Br.-General C. J. Perceval;[2] D.A. and Q.M.G., Br.-General G. S. Richardson) was formed on the 28th December, and took over the 22nd, 26th, and 28th Divisions. Major-General Milne did not arrive until the 8th January. General Mahon then suggested that he should postpone the formation of the XVI Corps headquarters, as it would have only two

---

[1] See p. 55.
[2] Br.-General Perceval was invalided home on the 21st January and succeeded by Br.-General F. G. Fuller.

divisions under it, of which one, the 27th, was then in general reserve and at the direct disposal of Army headquarters. General Monro, however, sent a peremptory reply that the corps must be formed at once and that the letter and spirit of War Office instructions must be complied with. As a fact, the War Office showed by a subsequent message that it would have been glad not to have had to provide for the headquarters of another higher formation at this moment. The headquarters of the XVI Corps (B.G.G.S., Br.-General G. N. Cory; D.A. and Q.M.G., Br.-General H. J. Everett) was established at Asvestokhorion (Kirech-köi) on the 17th, by which date, as has been explained, the 27th Division, less one brigade, was under orders to reinforce the 10th between Lake Langaza and the Gulf of Orfano. Major-General W. R. Marshall succeeded General Milne in the command of the 27th Division.

Meanwhile there had been a reorganization of command in the Mediterranean, in part due to the appointment of General Sir Douglas Haig to be British Commander-in-Chief in France and of General Sir William Robertson to be Chief of the Imperial General Staff. After the evacuation of the Anzac and Suvla positions on the Gallipoli Peninsula, which was completed on the morning of the 20th December, General Sir Charles Monro was informed that he was to return to France and to take command of the First Army in succession to Sir Douglas Haig. He was to be succeeded by the late C.I.G.S., General Sir Archibald Murray, who was to establish his headquarters in Egypt and to be in command of the troops from the Dardanelles and the United Kingdom then assembling for the defence of the Suez Canal. General Maxwell was to remain responsible for internal order in Egypt and for the defence of the country against attack from the west. The force under General Murray's command was to be regarded as the "Imperial Strategic Reserve." Its first duty was to be the fortification of the Suez Canal; but as soon as the situation in the Near East was clearer the Government hoped to transport the greater part of it to France, which the War Committee had decided was "the main theatre of war." General Murray was also informed that he was to be in command of the Levant Base, the great military depot established at Alexandria for the supply of the forces in the Near East, and that he was to "supervise the operations at Salonika." However, the day after he took over command from General Monro, the 11th January, instructions were received that the British Salonika Army was to come under the control of General Sarrail, and that General Mahon was to comply with his instructions " regarding military operations for the defence " of the town and harbour of Salonika." The Gallipoli Campaign was by this time wiped off the slate, Cape Helles having been evacuated by the morning of the 9th.

1916. Jan.

There could be no doubt that a single command was necessary at Salonika, and it was agreed by the two Governments that the particular interests of France justified placing that command in the hands of a French general, even though the British contingent was the larger.[1] General Mahon was to remain under General Murray's orders in respect of administration and was to communicate through him with the War Office on all matters of principle. With regard to intelligence, the progress of events on his front, and administrative detail, he was authorized to communicate with the War Office direct.[2] General Sarrail took over command of all forces at Salonika, including the Serbian detachment already mentioned,[3] which was now about 3,000 strong, on the 16th January. Thus was instituted, at a moment when the British Government had not finally decided whether their troops were to remain at Salonika, the unified command in French hands which was to endure until the end of the war.

In the case of this theatre of war it is necessary, as in few others, to discuss the personality of an Allied commander, because that of the French Commander-in-Chief had here an influence so important not only on operations but also

---

[1] It must be noted, however, that the French contingent was stronger than the British in artillery and cavalry, and that it possessed aircraft, which the latter did not. General Sarrail was also expecting a fourth division, the 17th Colonial. This was the division which had been left at Helles under the orders of General Brulard, and was now at Lemnos and Mitylene. The delay in transporting it to Salonika was due, first, to shortage of shipping, secondly, to its need of rest and reorganization, and, thirdly, to the fact that its two Senegalese regiments, unfitted to withstand the winter climate of Macedonia, were to be replaced by two Colonial regiments from France. (" Armées Françaises," Tome VII, Vol. I, Annexes, Vol. III, pp. 366–367.)

[2] The text of this telegram is given in Note at end of Chapter. The method of communication with the War Office was impracticable, and its only effect was that General Mahon addressed his messages simultaneously to London and Egypt.

[3] See p. 81.

on the relations between the French headquarters and the British. The demands neither of expediency nor of good taste forbid it ; for the matter has frequently been debated in print. If until the end of 1917 the unified command in Macedonia produced friction it was through no fault inherent in the principle. At the Dardanelles, where four French commanders in succession, Generals d'Amade, Gouraud, Bailloud, and Brulard, had been subordinated to General Sir Ian Hamilton, there had always been the friendliest and most loyal co-operation ; at Salonika itself in the year 1918, when General Milne was under the orders, first of General Guillaumat, then of General Franchet d'Espèrey, the case was the same.

General Sarrail started with many advantages, though the most notable, the record of his magnificent defence of Verdun in 1914, was probably at that time little known to any but soldiers of his own people. An attractive presence and great charm of manner in private intercourse, a fine physique, a soldierly bearing, an obvious forcefulness of character: these were all the outward marks of a man fitted to direct the troops of different nations, who were even more likely to be influenced by them in a foreign commander than in one of their own race. His expedition into Serbia might have been open to criticism on the ground of rashness ; but that was over now, and the chief impression left by it was of the extraordinary skill with which he had extricated his troops. His very deliberation and stubborn refusal to abandon the stores accumulated at various points along the railway, which had caused anxiety at the time, had now to be judged in the light of its success.

These happy auspices were to prove misleading. The Commander-in-Chief showed himself secretive in his plans to an extent which caused the gravest embarrassment to the commanders of the British, Serbian, and Italian contingents. This secretiveness was the more resented by them because on occasion it was found to cover designs for which there did not seem to be full warrant in the instructions he had received from Chantilly or Paris, and the more unfortunate because French and British policies were often different. Necessarily detained at Salonika and involved in political affairs, he showed a zest for Near Eastern politics which appeared neither desirable nor dignified in a soldier. His treatment of the Greek Royalists was, in the eyes of the

ARREST OF ENEMY CONSULS

British commanders and of the British Ministry at Athens, needlessly harsh, humiliating, and from the most material point of view unprofitable. Still more unhappy was it that in strictly military matters his judgment deteriorated and his natural impulsiveness grew upon him, causing him to embark on schemes, sound in principle, without proper preparation, and to brush aside with angry impatience the objections of his collaborators and subordinates.

The first unfortunate incident occurred before the unified command had been established, and concerned political affairs. The presence in Salonika of the Consulates of four hostile Powers was intolerable. The most exact and detailed information about the numbers and dispositions of the Allies was known to be telegraphed regularly to Berlin, Vienna, Sofia, and Constantinople. The city was swarming with spies, whose connection with the Consulates could easily be traced. Some of the agents did not even trouble to adopt the methods implied by the word " spy " ; they stood on the water-front and recorded openly in their note-books the numbers and regimental badges of the troops as they disembarked. General Mahon's intelligence service had been weaving a net in which he hoped to take all the spies at one sweep ; this had been submitted to General Sarrail, who had given no verdict upon it. At 2.40 p.m. on the 30th December General Mahon received a message that General Sarrail was going to seize the Consuls at 3 p.m. and invited him to co-operate. To give an air of unity to the proceedings a small British party was hurriedly gathered up and sent to take part in the arrests. General Mahon was put out because he feared that the incident gave warning to some of the agents he had been watching ; he was also, being himself the soul of frankness, astonished that he should have had no more warning of the execution of a scheme contrary to his own. At a meeting next morning General Sarrail expressed regret that his action (which caused a strong protest from Greece) appeared to be an independent measure ; and the two commanders made plans to round up the remaining agents, some of whom had been arrested actually in the Consulates. " The incident," telegraphed General Mahon, " is therefore closed, and our " good relations with the French are in no way impaired ; " but I much hope that there will not again be independent " French action, and that Sarrail will keep me as frankly

"informed of his intentions as I always endeavour to keep
"him informed of mine."

The second incident was due to direct orders received by General Sarrail from France, though here again he gave General Mahon little time to consider his orders. General Mahon had strongly advised that for the sake of Greek susceptibilities the question of Fort Kara Burun and the Vardar Battery should not be reopened, particularly as he had reason to hope that the Greeks would shortly evacuate them of their own accord. At 6 p.m. on the 27th January he was informed that twelve hours later Kara Burun was to be occupied by a French battalion and two batteries under the guns of French warships. No warning was to be given to the garrison, and, if it resisted, the fort was to be taken by assault. The British were called upon to place two battalions east of Salonika to resist any attempt of Greek troops in the city to march towards the fort. "I greatly "regret this step and particularly the methods about to "be employed," General Mahon telegraphed to London. "They are in opposition to the spirit of your instructions "to me in W.O. 12312 of 21st; but I have not been con-"sulted, and the measures are now too far advanced to "attempt to modify them." He went on to suggest that some conciliatory action should be taken at Athens.

Happily the occupation of the fort passed off quietly, and there was no serious excitement in Salonika.[1] Nevertheless, General Mahon found it was very bitterly resented by the senior Greek officers, who pointed out that this action, following upon the destruction of the bridges, had had the effect of rallying all military opinion, even that most favourable to the Allies, to the side of King Constantine. General Mahon also stated that the destruction of the bridges had caused a considerable withdrawal of Greek troops from the northern frontier and thus deprived him of the valuable information regarding the enemy's movements which came through them.

While the control of operations, at least so far as the defence of Salonika was concerned, was in the hands of the French Commander-in-Chief, on the administrative side the British Salonika Army was under a British command a

---

[1] The torpedoing of the *Norseman* was the immediate cause of the French Government's decision. ("Armées Françaises," Tome VIII, Vol. I, p. 412.)

thousand miles away. To increase the difficulties inevitable in this arrangement, there was for some three months a measure of divided responsibility in Egypt, so that, while demands from Salonika for normal requirements or those already approved were made on the Levant Base, those in any way out of the common had to be addressed to G.H.Q. at Ismaillia. The War Office was often brought into the correspondence, and it is not hard to imagine that confusion resulted. Demands would be repeatedly addressed to one office, and at the end of weeks or even months there would come a telegram from another, blandly enquiring what was wanted. Some of the most essential requirements of the force, especially Ordnance stores such as pack-saddlery, were not met without long delay, due as much to misunderstandings of this sort as to the difficulty of providing them. Warm underclothing, for example, ordered for the first winter, began to arrive at the end of March, when the hot weather was approaching.

Again, it was obvious that under this system the claims of Egypt would come first. Ships with stores from home consigned to Salonika sometimes went to Alexandria first, and it was not unheard of for these stores to be unloaded there and taken over on the ground that they were urgently needed by the E.E.F. It sometimes appeared that there was an impression in Egypt that the Salonika campaign would shortly fizzle out. At all events, the British force had in the early days to live from hand to mouth, and its administrative services were then at a grave disadvantage as compared with those of the French. The Director of Ordnance Services, Br.-General C. M. Mathew, records in his private diary a visit which he paid to the French Artillery Park on the 13th March 1916, when he was painfully struck by the contrast between its equipment and his own. The French had everything the British lacked: good permanent buildings, plenty of room, a full staff, and highly-trained artificers with a supply of machine tools which enabled them to undertake practically any work. His own demands were constantly met by queries which seemed to him vexatious, and which at least showed that the situation at Salonika was not understood.[1]

---

[1] Thus, to a demand for fire-extinguishers, the reply was received: " Why are fire-extinguishers required ? " Their need at any base was obvious enough, but in a Near Eastern port, with a hot, dry summer climate and a poor water supply, it was pressing, as was to be proved.

Egypt held the purse-strings, but Egypt's efforts to avoid expense often resulted in waste of money in the long run, as well as in still more serious evils. Thus, the demand for sun-helmets for the coming hot weather, made as early as February 1916, was opposed by the Director of Medical Services in Egypt. It was first considered that even in the hottest weather neck-covers fitted to the service caps would give sufficient protection. Next it was decided that slouch hats, similar to those worn by Australian troops, were necessary; and these were issued. Finally, on the 18th June, the then Army commander at Salonika had to insist that the estimate of the Macedonian summer climate made by Egypt was incorrect, and that sun-helmets were urgently required. Similarly, the authorities in Egypt at first cut down the scale of summer hospital requisites put in in February 1916, even as to mosquito netting, though it was already known at Salonika that Macedonia in summer was a very malarial country. Though ample warning of this was given, the supply of netting for the first summer was quite inadequate, until after the damage against which it was required as a protective measure had been done.

It may here be mentioned that, though matters improved very greatly when the Salonika Army was administered direct by the War Office, this difficulty respecting mosquito netting recurred, and that even for the second summer of the campaign the supply was late.

Army headquarters moved on the 7th January to better accommodation in Queen Olga Avenue, in Kalamaria, the south-eastern suburb of the city. Despite the difficulties which have been mentioned, there was already an improvement in conditions. Laundries and hot baths were organized. Supply became more regular, and the improvement of the roads with the aid of Greek labour ensured that rations reached the troops in full quantity and up to time. The detachment in the Rendina Gorge remained dependent on local purchase for fresh meat and vegetables, and there was some delay before this could be arranged with the Greek authorities. Wells were sunk in the neighbourhood of the camps along the defensive positions. Generally speaking, the Army had by the end of January settled down and made itself rather more comfortable in the new and curious conditions wherein it found itself.

INSTRUCTIONS AS TO COMMAND

NOTE.

INSTRUCTIONS WITH REGARD TO THE COMMAND AT SALONIKA.

From—Chief of the Imperial General Staff,
To—Lieut.-General Sir B. Mahon.
No. 11939, cipher.   10th January 1916, 7.30 p.m.

You will comply with the instructions of General Sarrail regarding military operations for the defence of the town and harbour of Salonika, on receipt by General Sarrail from his Government of instructions corresponding to these.

The Secretary of State for War has been informed by the Secretary of State for Foreign Affairs that the French Ambassador has been charged by his Government to express its high satisfaction with and gratitude for the co-operation you have afforded General Sarrail, and to say that the only considerations which have led the two Governments to recognize the necessity for placing their forces under the control of General Sarrail are the military situation and the special interests of France in the Salonika affair.

You will continue to be under the Commander-in-Chief of the Mediterranean Expeditionary Force as regards administration. You are authorized to report direct to the War Office as regards information of the enemy, the progress of events on your front, and questions of administrative detail. All questions of principle should be forwarded through the Commander-in-Chief Mediterranean Expeditionary Force.

CHAPTER VI.

THE ADVANCE FROM THE ENTRENCHED CAMP.
(Maps A, 2; Sketch 3.)

GENERAL SARRAIL'S PROJECTS.

Maps A, 2. LIFE at Salonika was uneventful, but not without its interesting and even its amusing side. The longer the war lasted the better pleased were the citizens. When it finished the troops would go, and the magnificent custom they had brought would be no more than a golden memory, to be recalled for the benefit of half-incredulous children and grandchildren. The only inconvenience was an occasional air raid, apparently in retaliation for a very successful French bombing-attack on Monastir. One attack by a Zeppelin on the 1st February caused a certain amount of damage and a fairly serious fire; another, by aeroplanes, on the 27th March detonated a store of high explosives in the French engineer park and did even more destruction. There were, however, few civilian casualties, and the danger was not great enough to daunt the inhabitants in their sedulous pursuit of gain. The humbler folk both of Salonika and the neighbouring villages who were not engaged in trade found labour on the roads or in military workshops profitable; the shopkeepers reaped a golden harvest; the manufacturers and contractors had a still better return for their industry; the providers of food, drink, and entertainment in general had their full share of the spoils.

Here, however, it may be well to strike one more blow at an old slander in case any life should remain in it. If this entertainment was neither very striking nor very edifying, it afforded the troops on rare leave from up-country some relief from a monotonous existence and recreation after work. To the educated there was interest in the memorable history of the place, its ancient buildings, its blend of East and West. Those who had to live and carry out their duties there came to detest the deafening noise of the traffic, the seething polyglot streets of what was now one of the most over-crowded cities in Europe, the mud in winter, and, when summer appeared, the sweltering heat and the flies. There were several indifferent but lively music-halls, filled each night with an audience which kept up such a din as to make its title a mockery; and, for the officers especially, cafés and restaurants, though the prices were exorbitant. The French *Cercle Militaire*, open to all Allied officers, was not established till 1917, but then its well-cooked food and good wine-list proved a great boon. In its tawdry fashion Salonika undoubtedly was gay, but the tawdriness was more notable than the gaiety; the very women of pleasure were the last reserves of the Army of Aphrodite. The legend of the Salonika Army as an army sitting in cafés is, however, ludicrously false. Salonika, in fact, was a base, which happened also to be the only convenient situation for the headquarters of the chief contingents, the British and French. The British troops to be seen there belonged to Army headquarters or came from the neighbouring base camps. After the advance from the Entrenched Camp, leave to visit the place was granted sparingly to officers and in still smaller measure to the rank and file. In any case, hard work and exposure to heat, dust, mosquitoes, and flies, or to bitter cold and searching winds, according to the season; a sick-rate higher than in any other major theatre of the war; very little leave home; very poor prospects until the end of three long years of a decisive victory—these were the conditions of the Macedonian campaign, for which the attractions of an occasional visit to Salonika were no great recompense.

1916. Feb.

It was only in the air that the enemy crossed the frontier; and by the beginning of February he no longer appeared to contemplate an attack on the Entrenched Camp. It was known that a considerable portion of the German *Eleventh Army* had been withdrawn and that there were only two divisions and the *Alpine Corps* (the equivalent of a third) in Macedonia. The troops of the Austrian *Third Army* were for the most part in Montenegro and Albania. Almost the whole weight of an offensive would therefore fall on the shoulders of Bulgaria, who was probably not only unequal to bearing it alone but also unenthusiastic about the task. Apart from information about the enemy, the strength of the defences furnished a strong argument. Their wiring, which was to earn for the position the title of " The Birdcage," now surpassed in depth and thickness any within the experience of officers who had served on the Western Front. A Greek general who saw them during the month declared publicly that he considered them impregnable. As General Mahon reported to the War Office on the 26th, this information was certain to reach the Bulgarians and " further reduce our hopes of being attacked " here, already at vanishing point."

General Mahon was correct in his view that an offensive by the army was unlikely. Falkenhayn seems virtually to have given up all intention of attacking after the complete evacuation of the Gallipoli Peninsula in January, though he did not come to a final decision until March.[1] Whether the Germans and their Bulgarian allies lost a great opportunity is a question which will always be debated but can never be settled with certainty. Falkenhayn has been strongly criticized by more than one German writer in this matter. The weightiest critic, by reason of his intellectual power and eye for strategy, is Major-General Max Hoffmann. But Hoffmann does not argue the case; he simply declares, basing his verdict upon the reports of the Director of Railways, General Groener, that Falkenhayn's plea of insuperable technical difficulties is false.[2] On the other hand, General von Gallwitz, one of the most confident and resolute of German commanders, thought the venture hopeless.[3]

In fact, the decision to halt upon the Greek frontier was a perfect example of Falkenhayn's strategical conceptions, and must stand or fall with them. "No nebulous " war-aims ! " was the motto by which he defended them. When he had to deal with any opponents but Britain or France—with Russia, Serbia, or Italy—his aim was to cripple them, to put it beyond their power to harm him or interfere with his plans, at least for a long time to come. Russia he now looked upon as sufficiently beaten; he had actually foreseen the revolution, though he did not expect it to be so overwhelming as was the case. Serbia he had overrun, and almost destroyed her Army. Italy

---

[1] Falkenhayn, p. 257.
[2] Hoffmann, " Der Krieg der Versäumten Gelegenheiten," p. 126.
[3] Gallwitz, p. 490. " Behind in the offices they are always urging " us to push on, but here up in front are the difficulties and hard work." Again, hearing on the 11th March that the offensive was cancelled, he writes (p. 514) : " I could only say to Voelckers that I had reached this " conclusion months ago."

he did not fear. He was now eager for a trial of strength in 1916.
the West. Had he seen the chance of an easy victory at Feb.
Salonika he would, of course, have seized it with both
hands ; but he did not see it. When the Allies re-entered
Greek territory the German troops were far to the north,
and by the time they could be brought south the fortification
of the Entrenched Camp had made great progress. Then
there was the factor of Greek neutrality. Greece had
promised to remain neutral if he held back the Bulgarians
from her territory, and Germany had foes enough without
making new ones. So he decided upon the defensive,
confident that in their very strong positions the Bulgarians
would be able to hold their own with the aid of a sprinkling
of German troops. Looking back, it would seem that the
only chance of success would have been to let the four
Bulgarian divisions follow the retreating Allies across the
frontier and risk the consequences. Once the British had
got their guns and transport ashore and had entrenched, the
prospects of a successful attack became doubtful in the
extreme. By the time the Entrenched Camp was completed
they had vanished.

Meanwhile the Allies had been further reinforced. On
the 6th February began the arrival of the 7th Mounted
Brigade [1] from Egypt, which absorbed the Composite
Yeomanry Regiment (made up of squadrons from its own
three regiments) and took over the outpost work, with two
regiments at Langaza and one at Güvezne. On the 21st a
brigade of the Royal Naval Division disembarked at
Stavros ; but this was not a permanent reinforcement, as
the brigade was sent only to make itself acquainted with
the ground.[2] The 10th Division had been relieved on the
8th February by the 27th Division in the Eiri Dere valley
and the Rendina Gorge, and withdrawn into reserve on the
Khortiates (Ortach) plateau. General Mahon had now
decided that the defences were far enough advanced for

---

[1] This brigade, like some other Yeomanry formations, had several titles, official and unofficial. Originally the 2nd N. Midland Mounted Brigade, it appears in orders while on the Gallipoli Peninsula as the 3rd Mounted Brigade. It was described by G.H.Q. Salonika by this title until June 1916, though it is referred to in its own records as the 7th Mounted Brigade in February.

[2] Its re-embarkation began at the end of March ; and early in May the Admiralty decided to withdraw the whole division from the Mediterranean.

two days a week to be devoted to training, an allowance which he subsequently extended. Brigades in turn carried out manœuvres lasting two or three days, practising attacks with artillery—a happy relief from all the trench-digging and road-making. During the latter part of the month the 17th Colonial Division joined General Sarrail.

It was but natural that with so strong a force at Salonika and the prospect of this force's being greatly increased in the near future by the arrival of the Serbian troops from Corfu, General Sarrail should begin to consider what steps he could take to exert pressure upon the enemy. General Joffre had ordered him on the 28th January to show such activity as would lead the Germans and Bulgarians to expect an offensive operation.[1] He had four French divisions including the 17th Colonial, and five British, and the Serbian forces when reorganized would amount to six; that is, a total of 15. For a real offensive General Joffre thought he would require 28, while he himself put forward a modified plan of attack with 21 divisions. His own Government did not feel themselves in a position to reinforce him. The French were, however, much concerned over the apparently excessive number of British divisions then in Egypt and hoped that some of these would be sent to Salonika. They met with a refusal from the British C.I.G.S.; nor were their approaches to Italy any more fruitful.

The British Government had not, in fact, developed any increased enthusiasm for the Salonika venture, and they looked with distrust upon any proposals for an offensive from that quarter. Their forces were under the orders of General Sarrail for the defence of the city, but for that purpose only; as regards the future they kept an open mind. It appeared to them that General Sarrail in his conversations with General Mahon was inclined to go beyond his instructions from Chantilly. Whether this was actually the case or whether the French commander created a false impression by over-secretive methods is not clear; at all events the impression was created. On the 19th February he informed General Mahon that the British Government were considering the question of adapting the organization of their force to the conditions of the country with a view

---

[1] " Armées Françaises," Tome VIII, Vol. I, p. 420.

to active operations. He then left for Athens, where he had a fairly satisfactory interview with King Constantine,[1] General Mahon having the honour of commanding the Allied forces during the three days of his absence. While he was away the C.I.G.S. telegraphed, in answer to General Mahon's account of the interview, that British policy regarding Salonika was unchanged and that the question of undertaking offensive operations was not under consideration. On the 24th, however, evidently as a result of the great German offensive at Verdun, which had been launched three days before, he telegraphed that, though no operations on a large scale were contemplated, a portion of the British forces would be given transport suitable for offensive action. That he was not prepared to allow the British troops to be seriously engaged was proved by a subsequent message in which he stated that he hoped eventually to withdraw some of them.[2]

1916.
Feb.

A little later the question cropped up again. General Mahon telegraphed on the 5th March that General Sarrail had received orders from France to take the offensive. General Mahon pointed out that only by withdrawing transport from all the other divisions could he hope to make as many as two fully mobile, and added that in his opinion an offensive with the present force had no reasonable prospect of success. After further discussion with General Sarrail he telegraphed next day that it appeared as if no more than bluff were contemplated and on that he was not inclined to look favourably. The C.I.G.S. declared himself unable to understand the receipt by General Sarrail of any such orders, which in fact could not justifiably be sent without the concurrence of the two Governments, and did not believe that a demonstration would have any permanent value. Finally he sent a copy of a telegram from Br.-General Yarde-Buller, the Military Attaché in

March.

---

[1] "Armées Françaises," Tome VIII, Vol. I, Annexes, Vol. III, p. 446.

[2] From—Chief London.
To—General Mahon.
13817, cipher.   Secret, Personal.   27th February 1916.
Glad to receive your telegram G.C.43 and to learn that you are devoting further time to training, as I hope eventually to employ some of your troops elsewhere more usefully than at present. The heavy German attack about Verdun may have the effect of proving the futility of keeping large forces idle when main decision is being fought out on Western Front.

Paris, who had gone to Chantilly and seen all the correspondence, to the effect that General Sarrail had quite misunderstood his instructions and that there was no intention of taking the offensive from Salonika. General Joffre afterwards wrote to General Robertson stating that he had merely called for an appreciation of the possibilities.[1]

At a conference held at Chantilly on the 12th March the question of operations in the Balkans was fully discussed. Agreement was reached that for the moment it was impossible either to reinforce or to withdraw troops from the Armée d'Orient. Reinforcement was out of the question owing to the very severe pressure which the Germans were then exercising at Verdun; withdrawal equally so, because all available shipping was required for the British divisions now hurrying from Egypt to France and for the Serbian divisions about to be transferred from Corfu to Salonika. General Joffre asked General Porro, the Italian representative in France, whether Italy could effect anything from Valona, which she still held, though she had evacuated northern Albania after the Austrian advance.[2] General Porro replied that, though Italy had the equivalent of three divisions at Valona and might send a fourth, the mountainous nature of the country made an offensive impossible. General Robertson declared that the whole question of Salonika would have to be reopened at a later date, and pointed out that, while Britain was being urged to make mobile her troops there, France, Italy, and Russia were making calls upon her shipping, without which the mules required for that purpose and for the needs of her Armies in France could not be procured from South America. The conference decided that the Allies should embark upon a general offensive in the summer of 1916; that meanwhile the Armée d'Orient should be as far as possible reorganized for mountain warfare; and that both it and the Italian forces at Valona should threaten the enemy with an immediate attack in order to prevent him from detaching troops to other fronts. With this end in view General

---

[1] "Armées Françaises," Tome VIII, Vol I, Annexes, Vol. III, p. 486. General Joffre had pointed out (*Ibid.*, p. 464) that the Germans had withdrawn troops from Russia and three divisions from Macedonia to France. He called upon General Sarrail to "study in detail and as a matter of "urgency" how the Armée d'Orient could advance from its lines and act against the enemy forces in such a manner as at least to pin them down.

[2] See p. 36.

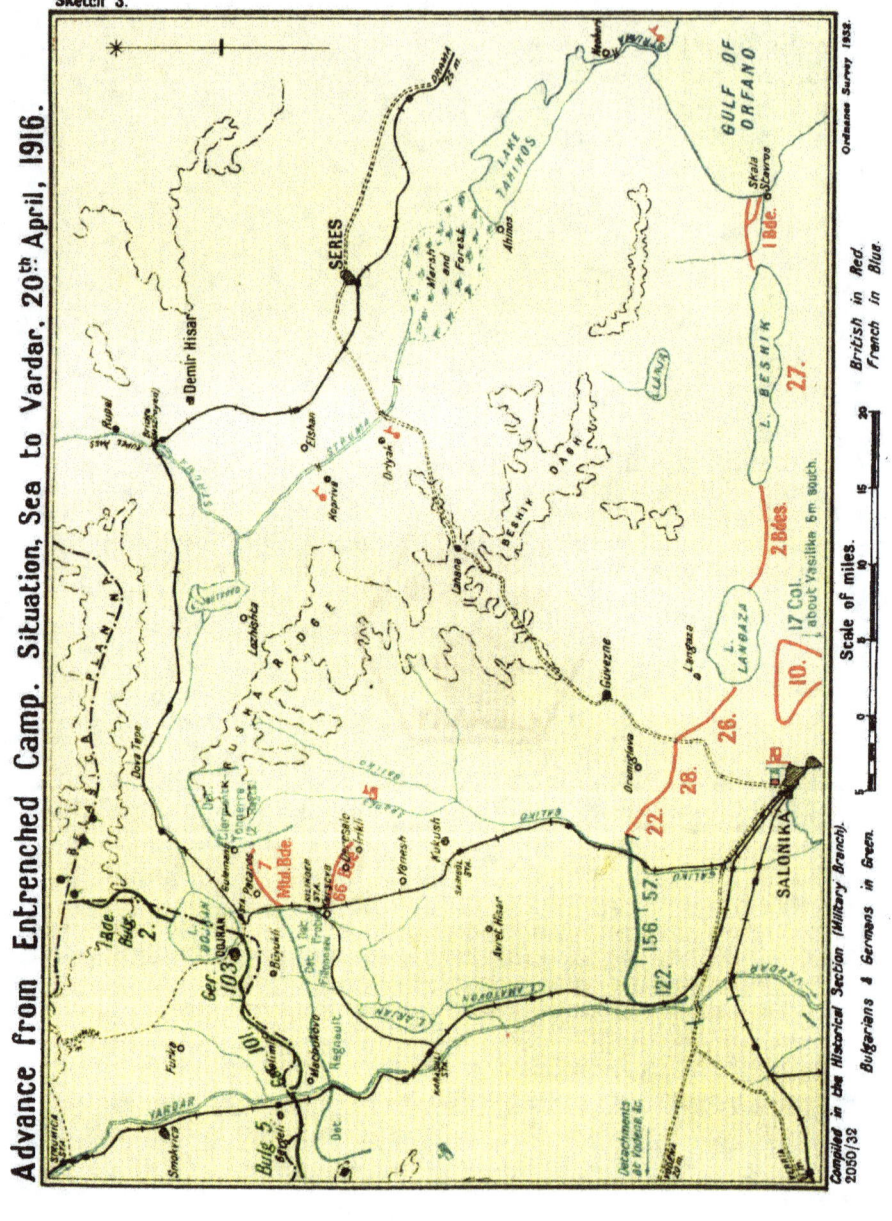

Joffre gave his approval to proposals made by General 1916.
Sarrail to advance from the Entrenched Camp up the Vardar March.
and to move a division up the Seres road as a threat against
the valley of the Struma.¹

The Advance to the Frontier.

By the beginning of March the enemy had crossed the Maps A, 2.
frontier at several points, though only to occupy favourable Sketch 3.
observation posts just beyond it or to deny these to the
French. The arrival in front line between Lake Dojran
and the Vardar of two German divisions had been signalized
by increased activity on his part. On the 11th General
Sarrail ordered the 243rd Brigade, with mountain and horse
artillery, to move out from the lines and advance up the
Vardar. On the 16th the brigade drove a German patrol
out of the village of Machukovo, on the left bank of the
river and two miles south of the frontier. On the 19th
another brigade group moved out to Avret Hisar, half-
way between Salonika and Dojran, to improve the roads
leading towards the frontier, and was followed by a regiment
which moved to Sarigöl Station. At General Sarrail's
request General Mahon issued orders for the divisional
Yeomanry squadrons of the XII Corps to take over on the
26th the immediate protection of the corps front, and for
the 7th Mounted Brigade, thus relieved, to concentrate at
Kukush, north-east of Sarigöl Station, in order to take over
from the French cavalry some of its heavy patrol work.
General Sarrail then further reinforced his 243rd Brigade,
and sent forward the divisional commander, General
Regnault, to take command. This force, which constituted
the most direct threat to the enemy, now held a definite
sector from Lake Arjan to Mayadagh, but had orders to
retire if heavily attacked. On its right front, south of
Lake Dojran, was a brigade of cavalry under General
Frotiée in touch with the British 7th Mounted Brigade.

General Mahon had been given no hint of General April.
Sarrail's intentions, though he had naturally divined that
these movements had been made for purposes of demonstration. On the 1st April a telegram from General Robertson
revealed to him that steps were at last to be taken to meet

---

¹ " Armées Françaises," Tome VIII, Vol. I, Annexes, Vol. III, p. 512.

the wishes of the French and make his force mobile. He was informed that, as there was still no prospect of any troops being withdrawn from Salonika, circumstances might justify a departure from a purely defensive policy and the adoption of a limited offensive, and was asked for an estimate of his requirements in transport and mountain artillery. He replied at once that for active warfare in this country a division would require two cavalry squadrons instead of one, and a brigade of six-gun mountain batteries in place of two of 18-pdrs. The divisional artillery would then consist of one three-battery mountain brigade, one four-battery 18-pdr. brigade, and one four-battery howitzer brigade. Each division would require 1,676 pack animals and 1,232 drivers (of whom a proportion could be hired locally) in excess of the present scale. The question of transport for rearward services he did not think he could usefully discuss until he knew what operations were contemplated. He was informed by General Robertson that no more cavalry could be spared, but that as soon as shipping was available sufficient mules would be sent to equip two divisions on the scale he recommended, and later on a consignment for a third. It was suggested that if one or two divisions could be based on the railway or a good road all five might thus be made sufficiently mobile. The mountain artillery already at Salonika would suffice for one division. A second mountain brigade might possibly be equipped from Egypt, but there was little likelihood of more mountain guns coming from the manufacturers before July. The French, who had already some 12,000 mules at Salonika, were now in course of reorganizing all their divisions with pack transport.[1]

On the 10th April a troop of Sherwood Rangers ambushed two troops of German cavalry in a nullah near Pataros, south-east of Dojran Station, and caused some loss to men and horses, this being the first occasion since the retreat that British troops had been in close contact with the enemy, though the Yeomanry had previously driven back some of his patrols. On the 15th General Mahon, after obtaining the approval of the C.I.G.S., ordered General Wilson, commanding the XII Corps, to detail a group of an infantry brigade, a brigade of 18-pdrs., a field

---

[1] " Armées Françaises," Tome VIII, Vol. I, Annexes, Vol. III, p. 541.

BRITISH ADVANCE BEGINS

company R.E., and a field ambulance to move by the 18th to Yanesh, four miles N.N.W. of Kukush, in support of the 7th Mounted Brigade. The 66th Brigade (Br.-General H. O. D. Hickman) of the 22nd Division was selected, and by the 20th April had taken up positions well north of Yanesh, holding a line from the village of Herakleia (Irikli) to the railway at Khirsova. On the 24th the C.I.G.S. informed General Mahon that though the general policy was defensive, this did not preclude preparations for pinning down the enemy by the threat of an attack. He was therefore authorized to move troops, at General Sarrail's request, up to but not over the frontier. General Mahon then issued orders for the XII Corps to despatch a second brigade group to join the 66th Brigade by the 1st May. The 65th Brigade reached Kukush on that date, and at the same time Major-General the Hon. F. Gordon moved to the village with his staff and took over command of all the advanced troops, including the 7th Mounted Brigade. The detachment was, for tactical purposes, directly under Army headquarters. Its mission was to resist hostile incursions into Greek territory but, if the enemy advanced in force, to avoid becoming so deeply engaged as to be unable to withdraw.

1916. April.

By this time all the four French divisions had moved out from their lines. On the right the 17th Colonial had its outposts in the Struma valley, holding the bridges and ferries from Lake Tahinos to Kopriva, whilst its main body was at work repairing the Salonika–Seres road. Then came the 57th, holding the Krusha Ridge, with outposts on the Constantinople railway in the Butkovo valley. Next came the British 22nd Division between Dereselo and Khirsova, and on its left the 156th and 122nd Divisions covering the two railways and the Vardar valley. The French cavalry covered the flanks.[1] By agreement with the Greek authorities General Sarrail had sent small detachments along the Monastir railway to guard the bridges, a duty which for the moment they shared in amity with Greek troops.[2] The Greeks were still to some extent intermingled with the Allies, but had withdrawn from the main front between Dova Tepe and the Vardar, and, except for small detachments, were in two groups on the flanks. On the

---
[1] " Armées Françaises," Tome VIII, Vol. I, pp. 433–4.
[2] *Ibid.*, p. 428.

right their IV Corps had five of its six divisions between the Struma and the Mesta, holding Kavalla, Drama, Seres, and Demir Hisar, with one division south of Lake Tahinos, and was thus between the Allies and the enemy. On the left their III Corps of three divisions was on the line Salonika–Vodena–Florina.

1916. May. On the 5th May the Allied warships in the harbour met a Zeppelin attack with triumphant success. The airship was caught by a searchlight of the *Agamemnon* and evidently hit, for she dropped no bombs and drifted at a low altitude over the boom defences, when a British torpedo-boat on duty there fired three shells into her and brought her down near the mouth of the Vardar. The survivors of her crew scattered in the marshes, where apparently all of them were rounded up by French cavalry, though there were camp rumours that some of them had escaped.

On the same date General Sarrail informed General Mahon that the rôle of the advanced troops was now to hold their present positions as a line of resistance. The British commander had some temporary anxiety for his small section of the front, as the force was not yet entrenched and he did not consider its position tactically a strong one. He informed Major-General Gordon that he might now move up to Kukush as much more of his division as he could maintain. Major-General Gordon then issued orders that between the 9th and 11th the bulk of his remaining artillery and the 9/Border Regiment (Pioneers) should move up.

On the 10th May Army headquarters, in accordance with the desire of General Sarrail, directed that the position of Major-General Gordon's force between Dereselo and Khirsova should be held as the line of resistance. As soon as the necessary arrangements could be made, the third brigade of the 22nd Division was to join Major-General Gordon, leaving only one battalion in the division's old position, on which no further work was to be begun.

The Armée d'Orient was now upon its new front and had occupied a great proportion of what has been described as the outer perimeter of the fortress of Salonika.

The Change in Command.

The last order mentioned above was issued by a new Army commander. On the 4th May a message was received

A NEW BRITISH ARMY COMMANDER 115

from Egypt, sending on a War Office telegram to General Murray, which stated that, "in view of General Mahon's "knowledge of Egypt and special qualifications it is con- "sidered that he would be of more use to succeed Peyton "in command of your western front [1] than in his present "appointment." General Murray was therefore directed to appoint him to the command of the Egyptian Western Frontier Force and to replace him in command at Salonika by Lieut.-General G. F. Milne, the commander of the XVI Corps. General Mahon handed over command on the 9th and on the same date sailed for Egypt. He held his new appointment for a few days only. Arriving in Egypt when the temperature was above 100 degrees in the shade at noon, he was taken to hospital with sunstroke, narrowly escaped with his life, and had to be invalided home. In the following November he was appointed Commander-in-Chief in Ireland.

Sir Bryan Mahon was not superseded for any failure or omission. He had accomplished all that was possible in a difficult and trying situation, which he faced with good sense and tact, and had shown energy in the fortification of the Entrenched Camp. His appointment to the command had, however, been largely a matter of accident and due to his seniority, he being, when he landed at Salonika, probably the only substantive lieutenant-general in the British Army in command of so small a formation as a division. Sir Charles Monro, when in command of the M.E.F., had reported that he was suffering from strain and seemed in need of a rest, adding that the excellent service he had accomplished at Salonika merited further employment in the future. Yet the deciding factor with the British Government was the conviction that, at a moment when the Allies were once more in touch with the enemy, when offensive operations might shortly be resumed, and when proof had appeared of a wide cleavage of opinion between France and Britain, a British commander of great experience in the present war and of altogether exceptional firmness and strength of will was needed at Salonika.

1916. May.

---

[1] The reference is to the defence of the Nile valley and the Mediterranean coast west of Alexandria against the forces of the Senussi and his Turkish allies (see "Egypt and Palestine," I, Chapters VII–IX). The command was at this moment a considerable one, even if smaller than that which General Mahon was relinquishing, but was soon afterwards greatly reduced in numbers and importance.

This proof consisted of a letter from General Joffre to the C.I.G.S., dated the 25th April, in which the French Commander-in-Chief for the first time definitely expressed himself in favour of an offensive in Macedonia.[1] He pointed out that, when the Serbian troops had arrived, the fifteen French, British, and Serbian divisions would be on a numerical equality with the enemy, and might even have considerable superiority if a proportion of the Bulgarian forces were called to the Danube frontier by an attack, or the threat of one, on the part of Russia and Rumania. He therefore considered that no other mission could be assigned to the Armée d'Orient than " to attack the enemy " with all its forces on the Greek frontier immediately it " had received the reinforcement of the Serbian Army."

If this attack succeeded in bringing in Rumania (and through her Greece also) the most favourable results were to be anticipated. The Austrians and Germans would be obliged to leave the Bulgarians to their own resources, and the situation in the Balkans would turn to the advantage of the Allies.

If neither Greece nor Rumania came in, the Allies would still have forces sufficient to win, by themselves, important successes, and these successes would have a tremendous effect upon a country already weary of war.

Finally, to take the least favourable case, if no striking success could be won, considerable enemy forces would be pinned down in this theatre, or even attracted to it, to the profit of the projected offensives on the main fronts.

General Joffre therefore urged that the British divisions should be equipped for mountain warfare as quickly as possible, and stated that he would request the Italians to attack simultaneously from Valona. It was to the interest of all the Allies to cut short the period during which France had to bear alone, at Verdun, the full weight of the German onslaught, so that she should not emerge from this battle completely worn out and therefore incapable of taking part in the general offensive projected by them.

The British Government took time to consider their reply, which was made in the form of a long memorandum by the War Committee on the 17th May. The arguments of General Joffre were considered one by one.

---

[1] " Armées Françaises," Tome VIII, Vol. I, Annexes, Vol. III, p. 585.

FRENCH AND BRITISH VIEWS 117

With regard to the first, it did not appear that the intervention of Greece and Rumania on the side of the Allies was sufficiently probable to justify the adoption of offensive operations in the Balkans. Unless the attack were followed by a victorious advance on Sofia and accompanied by a successful offensive on the Russian southern front, it would not have the effect of bringing Rumania into the war. The Greek Army was ill-equipped, and to make it fit to take the field would require munitions and stores of all kinds, which would cause new demands to be made on British shipping.

1916.
May.

With regard to the second, the Bulgarians might be weary of the war, but they were renowned as good fighters and would fight for Macedonia as for their own country. On the other hand the Serbian forces had just been re-equipped and had to acquire confidence in their new arms; and the British were deficient in animal transport, heavy artillery, and mountain guns. It was known that the approaches from the Greek frontier to Sofia were strongly entrenched and could not be captured unless the Allies possessed a large superiority both in troops and heavy artillery. At the best the operations would resolve themselves into a deadlock similar to that on other European fronts, while a failure would give the increased prestige, put forward as one object of the operations, to the enemy.

As to the third argument, the Bulgarians required no detaining in Macedonia. They would stay there of their own choice in order to hold the country.[1] They were not likely to go north or fight the Russians, still less to go to the Western Front.

The Committee considered it better to do nothing at Salonika than to attempt an enterprise which could lead to no really good result and must prove costly. The demands of a great offensive would cause undue strain upon British shipping, on which the financial position of all the Allies so much depended. The general policy in the Balkans must be defensive, and the Allied troops there should be reduced to the number required for the defence of Salonika. The War Committee was therefore definitely

---

[1] It is notable how closely these opinions coincide with those of Falkenhayn. He realized that the Bulgarians would not fight on other fronts, and the development of trench warfare in the Balkans, disliked by Austria-Hungary and Bulgaria, had no terrors for him. (Falkenhayn, p. 190.)

and unanimously opposed to any offensive operations from Salonika.

We have seen, then, during the last four months of Sir Bryan Mahon's command a growing divergence of French and British opinion. It was still the view of the British General Staff that " strategically the right course was " to bring the whole of the troops away." [1] That course was for the moment out of the question. Not only would the French Government refuse to agree to it, but the confession of another failure after the evacuation of the Gallipoli Peninsula, and still more after the surrender of Kut on the 29th April, would be dangerously humiliating. All that could be done therefore was to mark time, and later on attempt to withdraw the British contingent.[2] The Government, if perhaps not going so far as this, would not agree to an offensive, and let it be known that the British troops were not available for the purpose. They were at Salonika for the defence of the city and harbour, which must not be allowed to fall; but even before the Serbians arrived the War Committee considered that the Allied forces were in excess of the numbers needed for that. Nor was the policy of exercising pressure on the enemy by the advance to the frontier looked upon with enthusiasm. As France demanded that insistently, and as neither its danger nor its cost seemed to be considerable, the British Government could hardly refuse, in view of what France was suffering at that moment. Further they could not go, however much France desired it. We shall see that this disagreement was not one that could be easily or quickly ended.

---

[1] " Soldiers and Statesmen," II, p. 104.
[2] *Ibid.*

CHAPTER VII.

EVENTS LEADING TO THE INTERVENTION OF RUMANIA.

(Maps A, 1, 2.)

THE GENERAL SITUATION: FORT RUPEL.

ON the 11th April the transport of the Serbian Army to Salonika began. The Serbians, thanks to the devoted work of the British and French hospitals at Corfu and to their own powers of recuperation, had made a remarkable physical recovery. When they first arrived on the island many of them were so terribly emaciated that it was not uncommon to see a woman nurse carrying a tall man from his bed to the operating ward. Between the 29th January and the end of April 5,400 died at Corfu;[1] but the great majority of the remainder swiftly regained strength. In fact, as the survivors of a nation in arms, they were salted against disease and the effects of exposure, and their sick rate was found to be far lower than that of any other troops in Macedonia. Nevertheless, the men bore signs of what they had endured, above all the marks of hunger, those lines which are never wholly effaced. Their march discipline was poor, and they gave an impression of slowness and clumsiness, all the more so because a large number of them were over thirty-five years of age. For a moment British observers doubted whether they had either the mental and physical energy needed for an offensive campaign or the patience to endure without abandoning hope the present stagnant warfare. That view was to be proved incorrect by the Battle of Monastir. The Serbians then showed that their high merits could not be truly assessed by Western European standards and that their efficiency in mountain warfare was worthy of the traditions of their race.

1916.
April.
Map 1.

The sea-route from Corfu to Salonika round the southern shores of Greece being long and dangerously exposed to submarine attack, especially in the area of the Cyclades, the French and British Governments considered the possibility of sending the Serbian troops overland by railway from Patras, but were met on the 3rd April by an indignant

---

[1] "Armées Françaises," Tome VIII, Vol. I, p. 471, fn.

refusal of permission from Greece. There was then some thought of using the Corinth Canal to shorten the voyage; but as it would not admit vessels with a draught of over 20 feet it was decided to take the risks of the longer route. The transport was effected slowly, on account of the shortage of shipping, and was not completed until the end of May. Thanks to the secrecy observed and the careful measures taken for the protection of the troop-ships,[1] it was carried out without any loss whatsoever. On arrival the Serbians were accommodated in six camps, each holding a division, in the valley of the Vasilika Deresi, some 10 miles south-east of Salonika. Here they were to complete their training and receive the rest of their equipment.[2] Prince Alexander and the Serbian War Ministry (established at Corfu with the other Government offices) moved to Salonika in July.

The Serbian divisions bore the old territorial titles, Danube, Drina, Šumadija, Timok, and Morava, with one new one, Vardar, added; but whereas before the Austro-German offensive there had been two divisions—one of the First Ban and one of the Second—bearing each title, there were now, owing to the reduction in numbers, six only in all. The titles of the former Armies—First, Second, and Third—were retained, though as each consisted of only two divisions they were, according to Western nomenclature, only small army corps. General (afterwards Voivode) Bojović had succeeded the ailing Voivode Putnik as Chief of the Staff in January. With the 3,000 Serbians already on the spot,[3] the force numbered 120,000, while 25,000, including sick, wounded, recruits, and surplus officers, were left at Corfu or in Northern Africa. The six divisions were equipped for mountain warfare, France having supplied the great bulk of their arms and stores, though Britain contributed clothing, and later on transport animals and lorries. When they reached Salonika they were, however, by no means complete in transport or artillery. General de Mondésir returned to a command in France, but French and British officers of the Allied missions remained with the Serbians for liaison duties.

---

[1] The story of the passage, as well as the whole record of the rescue and reorganization of the Serbian Army, is well told by Lieut.-Colonel de Ripert d'Alauzier in " Un Drame Historique : La Résurrection de l'Armée Serbe, Albanie–Corfou 1915–1916."

[2] " Armées Françaises," Tome VIII, Vol. I, pp. 476–478.

[3] See p. 97.

THE GENERAL SITUATION

In addition to the Serbians, 1,700 Bosnians, who had served with the Montenegrin forces, were also transported to Salonika, having been formed into a battalion under French officers. It is in connection with this battalion that we first meet in the military records the word "Yugo-"slav" (South Slav), long in use in Serbia to describe the nation's ideals and aspirations.

1916. May.

The detached critic, considering the situation in the Balkans at the end of May, after the arrival of the Serbians, may well find the British attitude harder to comprehend than the French. Here, one can fancy his saying, is the situation in a nutshell. There are now 15 Allied divisions at Salonika, or 300,000 Allied troops, opposed to perhaps 260,000 Bulgarians, who can hardly be reinforced from the north unless Bulgaria's anxieties regarding Rumania are set at rest. They still lack sufficient aircraft and both heavy and mountain artillery, and have not yet a transport system suited to the country; but these wants are surely not beyond the resources of Britain and France to supply. The formidable German troops are nearly all gone [1] and occupied elsewhere, while Austria now has her hands full on her Italian as well as her Russian front. The general situation in the world struggle calls for activity in the Balkans. Italy is hard pressed by the Austrian offensive in the Trentino, and the Battle of Verdun is still raging; on the other hand, Russia is preparing to attack, and in the Western theatre the moment for the Somme offensive is drawing nigh. Rumania, it seems, only awaits a favourable moment to stake her fortunes upon the arms of the Entente. Any fresh blow or even serious threat directed against the Central Powers or their Allies will hasten her decision. Is it not therefore strange that Britain should constantly balk her Ally in the latter's projects for exerting pressure upon the Bulgarian forces from the Salonika base, that she should prefer to see 300,000 men idle rather than allow them to be employed in any offensive action, limited or unlimited?

In truth this attitude may seem strange, but it is not inexplicable. Britain had been brought into the Salonika venture largely against her will and could not now, certainly not at this moment, escape from it. Being committed to

Maps A, 2.

---

[1] By this time only one division, the *101st*, remained.

it, she had to consider the following problems. Pressure can be exerted in many ways against an enemy in the field; but before any one of them is adopted it has to be calculated, first, how far existing resources suffice to exert enough pressure to give an adequate return for the cost of the effort; secondly, if they seem insufficient, how far the deficiencies can be filled. The first question was easily answered: there were not nearly troops enough to embark upon any large-scale offensive with distant objectives. The whole of the enemy's position between the Struma northeast of Lake Butkovo and the valley of the Crna was of extraordinary strength, and upon it the work of the engineer had powerfully reinforced that of Nature. On the eastern half, up to the Serbian frontier north of Lake Dojran, attacking troops would have to scale the great wall of the Belašica Planina, with a crest-line of some 4,000 feet, crossed by no routes but bridlepaths or the most primitive cart-tracks. Between the "Frontier of the Three Nations" and the valley of the Vardar there were indeed two fair passes leading into the Strumica valley by which an invasion of Bulgaria might have been practicable; but access to them was denied by the enemy's advanced position between Lake Dojran and the Vardar, amid tumbled hills forming a barrier of immense strength, even though they were of no great height as mountains go in Macedonia. Then, west of the Vardar valley, the Serbian frontier followed a well-defined ridge running generally south-west to the great bend of the Crna below Monastir. Here, as everywhere, the actual frontier-line on the map had great strategic importance, because it was traced along the highest crests and because it was upon the frontier that the Bulgarians had halted. Only on the two flanks, in the Struma valley on the east and the Crna valley on the west, was the ground in the least favourable to offensive action; and from Demir Hisar on the Struma to the Crna bend at Brod was a distance of 96 miles. The only other feasible operation was an advance up the valley of the Vardar. It seemed certain that on a hundred-mile front of this nature nothing more than a local success could be gained with the force and, above all, the ammunition at the disposal of the Allies. Even that would be costly, and an attempt to achieve more might well be disastrously so.

As to the force required for a major operation, General

[*Imperial War Museum Photograph.*]

The Belašica Planina across the valley of the Hoja. (Peak in centre is Point 1843—Map 10.)

Sarrail had, we have seen, stated in March that 21 divisions would be necessary, while General Joffre had put the figure at 28.[1] General Mahon, on the 31st October 1915, had estimated that 20 divisions would be required for an advance on Sofia.[2] There were at that time various conditions not now prevailing which perhaps more or less cancelled themselves out—German and Austrian troops in large numbers being on the scene but still contained by the Serbian Army, the frontiers of Serbia and Bulgaria being still unfortified and the French being established in the Vardar–Crna loop. General Milne was not, apparently, called upon when he took over the command to give his opinion on the subject; but in October 1916 he stated that "with 24 good divisions " and adequate artillery" there was a reasonable prospect that the Bulgarian forces on the Macedonian front could be forced back, though he considered 29 divisions necessary to provide a safe margin.

1916. May.

To find even six more divisions and to equip them with the necessary pack transport and artillery was at this time out of the question. Britain had not yet produced transport and artillery enough for the troops already in the theatre, and she could spare no more divisions without weakening the effort she was preparing to make on the Somme. France could not at the moment send another man. Italy had refused to send any troops, though she soon afterwards consented to despatch a reinforced division. Russia had promised only a brigade.

Such, generally speaking, was the attitude of Britain towards the Salonika campaign. When the General Staff came to study the plan put forward by General Sarrail in May it was much disquieted. He proposed to attack rather as the nature of the ground than his resources seemed to dictate. The Serbians were to be employed in an advance against Monastir, the bend of the Crna, and the passes in the frontier-chain further east; the British were to attack between the Vardar and Lake Dojran, mainly as a demonstration and to pin down the enemy upon this part of the front; four French divisions were to debouch north-east of Lake Dojran (where there was a gap between the lake

---

[1] See p. 108.
[2] These would, of course, have been additional to the Serbian Army in the field, whereas in the other estimates six Serbian divisions are included.

and the Krusha Ridge) and attempt to scale the Belašica Planina; the French cavalry and Zouaves were to make a demonstration up the Struma valley; and one British division was to hold the lower Struma. These were only the preliminary measures,[1] but it is hardly necessary to consider those projected after the rupture of the enemy's front. No detailed criticism of the plan was called for from the General Staff, because British objections to it were fully covered by the War Committee's memorandum of the 17th May.[2] General Milne was, nevertheless, instructed by the C.I.G.S. to make it clear to General Sarrail that the British Government had not agreed to any offensive operations, however limited.

That message was sent to Salonika on the 28th May. Two days earlier there had occurred an event which had great importance from the political point of view. Hitherto, as has been stated, the enemy had crossed the Greek frontier only to obtain observation posts just beyond it. On the 26th a force of Bulgarians and Germans suddenly advanced down the Struma towards Fort Rupel. The Greek garrison opened fire, whereupon the column retired without casualties. In the afternoon the Greek troops received orders from Athens not to oppose the advance, the Greek divisional commander at Seres being forbidden to inform the French or British of what was happening. Next day the enemy, in strength about a division, occupied not only Fort Rupel but the villages of Radova, Vetrina, and Ramna, on a line some ten miles south of the frontier, thus covering the mouth of the pass and blocking the chief gateway to Bulgarian territory from the Struma valley. Thereafter he made no appreciable further advance. The effect of this move upon the relations of the Allies with the Greeks must be considered a little later; from the military point of view it was also of importance, since the Bulgarians had now closed the pass against invasion, and were also free to make any further advance with the certainty that it would not be opposed by the Greeks. Meanwhile Br.-General Howell, General Mahon's chief General Staff officer, who had been replaced by Br.-General W. Gillman from the staff in Egypt after General Milne had taken over command at Salonika, had reached London and had explained to General Robert-

---

[1] "Armées Françaises," Tome VIII, Vol. I, Annexes, Vol. III, p. 601.
[2] See p. 116.

NEW BRITISH DISPOSITIONS 125

son in detail the French dispositions. The C.I.G.S. took a view of the situation even graver than before, warned General Milne on the 3rd June not to be drawn into any offensive, and on the same day induced the Government to make a further communication to Paris, pointing out that the instructions which the British commander had received in January to comply with General Sarrail's instructions for the defence of Salonika did not apply to operations of any other kind or to movements of British troops likely to lead to other operations.

1916. June.

In the first week of June General Milne had made considerable alterations in his dispositions, mainly with a view to supporting the advanced line of his own 22nd Division and the two French divisions on its left astride the Vardar.[1] The 10th Division from reserve relieved the 26th in the right sector of the XII Corps line between Tumba and Aivatli, which sector was then transferred to the XVI, in the command of which Major-General C. J. Briggs had succeeded General Milne. The 26th moved west and took over the left sector, previously held by the 22nd and now in the hands of a maintenance detachment. The division was to act as Army reserve, but was to be at the disposal of the XII Corps for road construction. At the same time the 28th Division evacuated the former centre sector of the XII Corps front between Aivatli and Balcha, and moved north to the area between Lake Arjan and the Dojran railway, with its head at Yeniköi, to act as reserve to the advanced force.

On the 6th and again on the 8th, while these moves were in progress, General Milne had very difficult interviews with General Sarrail. The French Commander-in-Chief informed him that he had definite orders to attack, and that he would do so with or without British support. General Milne was fearful that a situation would arise in which the British Army would either be forced to support the French or have put upon it the stigma of leaving them unsupported in an emergency. He saw no other solution of the difficulty than to disengage the British troops from contact with the French, and therefore requested that he should be given a definite zone of operations, which would also facilitate his supply arrangements. General Sarrail

---

[1] See p. 113.

agreed, and on the 8th General Milne issued orders for the new dispositions to be taken up. The British Army was now allotted the zone south and east of a line drawn from Lake Butkovo along the Bahisli river to Sariköi, three miles east of the Dojran railway at Yanesh, and the boundary between the two British corps was to be the Salonika–Seres road. The French cavalry and 17th Colonial Division, which were in the British zone, were to move north-west as quickly as possible, the defence of the Struma devolving on the British from the evening of the 9th. The XVI Corps was to despatch the 29th Brigade Group of the 10th Division, which was working on the Seres road, to relieve the 17th Colonial Division between Lakes Tahinos and Butkovo, while the Sherwood Rangers of the 7th Mounted Brigade relieved the French cavalry. This was a temporary measure, to give the XII Corps time to move its 28th Division (which had now two brigades between the Dojran railway and Lake Arjan) eastward to the Struma to take over the front allotted to the corps between Orlyak and Lake Butkovo. The 22nd Division, on the advanced line south of Lake Dojran, and the 7th Mounted Brigade were to be relieved by the French about the 16th.[1] General Sarrail stated that he did not intend at present to prolong his right flank beyond Radile, seven miles west of Lake Butkovo, leaving this gap to be watched by a regiment of his own cavalry and a second regiment (the South Notts Hussars) of the 7th Mounted Brigade. The arrangement was accepted readily enough by General Milne, since it lessened the prospect of his being drawn into operations which he had been forbidden to undertake and which were contrary to his own judgment.

The movements necessary to bring this new division of the front into force were very complicated, especially as those which preceded them had not been completed when the orders were issued. It would be fruitless to detail them here, since they did not result in any active operations. It will suffice that by the 27th the dispositions were as follows. On the front of the XVI Corps the 27th Division was holding the Rendina Gorge between Lake Beshik and the sea, with the 2/Shropshire Light Infantry pushed forward round the Gulf of Rendina to a point five

---

[1] The relief did not actually take place until the 20th.

miles west of the mouth of the Struma, and the 82nd Brigade in reserve on the Ortach plateau; on the left the 10th Division had the 29th Brigade on the Struma from the north-western edge of Lake Tahinos to Orlyak bridge, the 30th Brigade in rear spread out along the Salonika–Seres road, upon which it was working, and the 31st Brigade in the old Salonika defence line between Tumba and Aivatli.[1] On the front of the XII Corps the 28th Division had its 85th and 84th Brigades holding the Struma between Orlyak and Lake Butkovo, with the 83rd Brigade in rear about Lahana on the Seres road; the 22nd and 26th Divisions were nominally holding the two left sectors of the old defences between Dautli and Aivatli, but the troops were actually accommodated in camps in this neighbourhood. The 7th Mounted Brigade (less the Sherwood Rangers, at the disposal of the XVI Corps) was under the orders of Major-General H. L. Croker, who had succeeded General Briggs in the command of the 28th Division on the latter's promotion.[2]

1916. June.

It must be added that the unavoidable marching and counter-marching of June subjected the troops and the administrative services to great strain. For the first time the heat had become excessive, the thermometer approaching 100 degrees more than once in the course of the month. A fire which broke out in the forage store of the main supply depot on the 3rd June would have been unfortunate at any moment but was a calamity at this. Over 2,000 tons of hay, as much tibben, and 1,500 tons of grain were destroyed, and it became necessary to put the animals on half rations just when big exertions were being demanded of them. A number of them were also affected by the sun. The troops did not suffer so severely from this cause, though there were some cases of sunstroke and much discomfort from the occasional hot winds; but, directly the brigades of the 10th and 28th Divisions reached the valley of the

---

[1] The artillery at the disposal of the XVI Corps consisted of the 24th Anti-Aircraft Section; a group under the orders of the headquarters XX Heavy Artillery Group, consisting of the 32nd Anti-Aircraft Section, the 84th Siege Battery, and one battery 10th Divisional Artillery; and the XXXVII Heavy Artillery Group (18th and 20th Heavy Batteries). There were also two naval guns in the Stavros defences.

[2] The heavy artillery attached to the XII Corps consisted only of the 13th Heavy Battery and the 43rd Siege Battery, of which the former was transferred to the XVI Corps a week later.

Struma, malaria began to make its appearance among them. Wooden platforms were built for the troops near the river, so that they should sleep well above the ground, near which the mosquitoes were thickest. Mosquito netting was issued, but at first, owing to the shortage of the supply from Egypt, in pieces so small as to be practically useless; and not until the end of June were there available 3,000 nets of the hospital pattern for issue to the 10th Division in the most infested quarter. Major-General Longley also considered the food unsuited to the climate and obtained the issue of an extra quarter-pound of bread in place of a proportion of the meat ration. Wells and streams were running dry, and the Struma itself was so muddy that horses would not drink from it. About Salonika the city's water supply had been tapped for so many camps, hospitals, and stores that it was exhausted to a dangerous extent both from the point of view of drinking and from that of fighting outbreaks of fire.

These moves, too, far from contact with the enemy as they were, proved that neither the British transport nor the communications were in a state to permit of active operations. The one main road, that from Salonika to Seres, was cut up by the heavy traffic to such an extent that all the work of the troops, aided by a body of about a thousand Greek labourers under semi-military discipline, hardly kept pace with the damage done. The secondary roads had been well developed in the neighbourhood of the old Salonika defences, but in the new forward area that work was all to do. The number of lorries for the rearward services was inadequate, and the fighting troops had not yet been equipped with pack transport. Though mules were now arriving in considerable numbers, upwards of 4,000 having been landed during the month of May, these were hardly sufficient to make up the casualties from sickness. An Indian transport company, with the little mule-carts which can travel on the roughest tracks—often where no track exists—had arrived in April, and proved very useful beyond lorry-head; but its carrying-power was limited. Had an engagement involving heavy expenditure of ammunition broken out on the Struma it would have been impossible to keep up the supply. In fact, for the 84th Brigade of the 28th Division, two stages had to be made between the Seres road and Hamzali, south-east of Lake Butkovo, and

INTERNAL AFFAIRS OF GREECE

1916. June.

for this purpose the wagons of the small-arms ammunition column had to be used, its ammunition being dumped.

Signal communications were also a matter of difficulty owing to the shortage of wireless sections—both wagon and pack—and the great distances which had to be covered by hastily reeled out telephone wire when the troops moved forward to the Struma and the region of Lake Butkovo. The Greek telegraph system was, of course, employed as far as possible; but it was found that the wires were heavy and slack and the poles often rotten.

Many of the obstacles with which the force had to struggle during the month of June were happily about to be removed. Steam-rollers were shortly to be sent from Egypt, and later others from Great Britain, which by binding the metal laid upon the roads enabled twice as much value as heretofore to be got from the work done upon them. Stone-crushers were subsequently sent. Almost as valuable as the new tools was to be the recognition that the upkeep of the roads and the undertaking of fresh road-making needed more thorough organization and more forethought than had yet been given to these tasks. Light-railway material had been promised. Mechanical and pack transport were soon to be supplemented, and muleteers were even now being recruited in Cyprus. At the worst, the recent marches had proved the soundness of the views held by the British regarding their present capacity for the offensive and shown them exactly where their deficiencies lay.

GREECE AND THE ALLIES.

After an understanding had been reached in December 1915, by the Greek authorities on the one hand and the British and French on the other, regarding the fortification of Salonika and the control of the railways, the relations between Greece and her invited but unwelcome guests had somewhat improved. Yet the improvement did not last long. The country was now governed by a Ministry which was in no sense representative. After the resignation of M. Zaimis the King had, for the second time that year, dissolved the Chamber. On this occasion M. Venizelos had indignantly boycotted the elections, and a purely Conservative Parliament had been returned in December.

M. Skouloudis had continued in office, without an opposition. He had for some time been, as was afterwards discovered, in negotiation with Germany for a loan. In March Greece obtained a credit of forty million marks; but that was at once swallowed up by the mobilized Army and the throngs of refugees from Turkey and Macedonia, and she soon had to call for more. In April, as mentioned, she refused with indignation the request that the troops of her forsaken ally, Serbia, should be transported by rail to Salonika. A little later there was formed a military league against "native traitors (*i.e.* M. Venizelos and his adherents) and "foreign intriguers," which threatened to oppose any landing of the Serbians by force. On this matter the Allies at once gave way, but without forgetting.

The surrender of Fort Rupel was a much more serious incident. No one expected Greece to pit herself against Bulgaria, backed by Germany, for the defence of the gateway into Bulgarian territory from the Struma valley. But it was strongly suspected—as it was subsequently proved by the publication of the Greek "White Book" in 1917—that there had been long negotiations regarding its occupation, and that the Greek Government were in no way surprised by it. Not only had they kept any hint of these negotiations from reaching the Allies; they had actually, as has been recorded, forbidden the Greek divisional commander at Seres to telegraph the news to Salonika.

Their action, though it might conceivably be held to be within their rights as neutrals, played into the hands of General Sarrail, who was more in love with a policy of repression and coercion than were either General Milne, the French Admiral Dartige du Fournet, or the Allied Governments in Paris and London. The Commander-in-Chief had been eager to proclaim a state of siege at Salonika, but had hitherto been prevented from doing so by the veto of General Joffre. Directly they heard of the surrender of Fort Rupel the French Government changed their view on this matter and gave General Sarrail permission to take any steps he thought necessary for the safety of the Allied forces,[1] while on the 1st June M. Guillemin warned M. Skouloudis that if the Bulgarian advance

---

[1] "Armées Françaises," Tome VIII, Vol. I, p. 491.

in Eastern Macedonia continued without opposition from the Greek Army the consequences for Greece would be very serious.

1916. June.

General Milne found himself without instructions as to how to act in this emergency. The French Commander-in-Chief had decided not only to proclaim a state of siege in Salonika on the 3rd, but to prohibit a torch-light procession planned for that same evening in honour of King Constantine's name-day. General Milne disliked both measures, considering the first unwarranted by the military situation and the second injudicious.[1] Having no time to receive a reply to his enquiry as to the course he should take, he put some military police at the disposal of the French, thus formally acquiescing in their action. That he had rightly interpreted General Robertson's wishes was proved by a telegram received that afternoon after all was over. General Sarrail's measures included the complete control of the post and telegraph offices, the railways, and the Salonika Press. The day passed quietly.

Meanwhile at Athens the celebrations had degenerated into a demonstration against the Allies. The German Minister was greeted with great applause, apparently started by order, and the King conferred the Grand Cross of the Order of the Redeemer upon a member of the Government who had a few days previously made a violent attack upon France and Britain.[2]

The next steps of the Allies were the institution of a partial blockade of the Greek coasts—for one reason, because food could not be allowed to go to Kavalla, which might at any moment be occupied by the Bulgarians—and to make preparations for a naval demonstration before Athens. Curiously enough, although the demonstration was organized by the French and British naval authorities in concert and British as well as French warships were to take part in it,[3] though General Sarrail embarked a brigade to accompany it, no communication was made on the subject

---

[1] There is, however, little ground for the accusation which has been made against General Sarrail that he deliberately chose the King's name-day for the proclamation of a state of siege. He got permission for the proclamation on the 1st and acted as quickly as he well could, on the 3rd. ("Armées Françaises," Tome VIII, Vol. I, p. 491.)

[2] Sir F. Elliot to Sir E. Grey, 4th June 1916. "Armées Françaises," Tome VIII, Vol. I, p. 492.

[3] "Naval Operations," IV, pp. 133–134.

to the British War Office,[1] and General Milne learnt of it only from Sir Francis Elliot and unofficially from the French naval Commander-in-Chief.

On the 9th June Sir Edward Grey instructed Sir Francis Elliot to make to the Greek Government a communication identic with one which had been drawn up by the French Foreign Minister, explaining the reasons for the measures taken by the Allies and setting forth their demands. The Note actually presented was, however, stronger in terms than the version proposed by the two Foreign Offices, and was, in fact, drawn up by the Ministers of the three Protecting Powers, Sir Francis Elliot, M. Guillemin, and Prince Demidov, and afterwards submitted to the Governments for approval.

It began with the statement that the Protecting Powers did not ask Greece to abandon her neutrality, but that they had good cause for suspicion regarding the Greek Government, which had shown favour to foreigners endeavouring to ensnare Greek public opinion and create on Greek soil hostile organizations, to the danger of the Allies' military and naval forces.[2] It went on to speak of the surrender of Fort Rupel " with the connivance of the Government," of the violation of the constitution—the Chamber having been dissolved twice in one year against the will of the people—and of the violence of the police directed against the party of M. Venizelos. In these circumstances, it declared, France, Great Britain, and Russia, the guarantors of Greek liberties, had the right and duty to protest. Finally, it formulated the four following demands :—

The Army was to be totally demobilized and reduced to a peace footing ; the Ministry was to be replaced by a " Business Ministry " without political tendencies ; the Chamber was to be dissolved and new elections held ; certain police officials, " inspired by foreign influences," who had

---

[1] From—Chief of the Imperial General Staff
To—Headquarters Salonika Army.
No. 18062, cipher.   19th June 1916.
Your No. G.C. 202. The French authorities have not made any communication to us on the subject, and you are not expected to take any part in the demonstration until you receive instructions from me. Report the object of the demonstration and any details you have as to Sarrail's intentions in making it.

[2] The individual chiefly aimed at in this phrase was Baron Schenck, the director of German propaganda, who was known to have spent large sums on the corruption of the Press.

facilitated insults to the Legations, were to be relieved of their posts.[1]

1916. June.

It was intended that the presentation of the Note should coincide with the fleet's arrival in Phalerum Bay, but the commander, the French Vice-Admiral Moreau, refused to take the bigger warships there until the entrance had been netted, and the fleet was in the bay of Milos, an island of the Cyclades, when the Note was delivered on the 21st. Meanwhile M. Skouloudis had resigned. M. Zaimis undertook to form a Ministry on the lines laid down by the Protecting Powers and to execute all their demands. From the 23rd Greek ships from British ports were allowed to proceed to all Greek ports but Kavalla.

So ended this much-disputed incident. There is the clearest proof that Greece had foreknowledge of the occupation of Fort Rupel and that she made no protest until it had actually taken place. She concealed her information from the Allies. On the other hand, there is no proof that the occupation was carried out with her " connivance " in any sense other than this. Whether, as a neutral, she had any justification for the course she pursued may be still a matter for argument. But, from her own point of view, the surrender by her Government was probably as needless as it was shameful ; for Falkenhayn can scarcely have changed his views, within three months, of the danger of bringing another enemy into the field. The comment of M. Venizelos is unanswerable. " If we had told them " decidedly that we would not surrender our forts to the " very enemy against whom we had built them, who will " believe that they would have pushed matters to the " point of war only for the sake of occupying Rupel ? "

The Prospect of Rumanian Intervention.

The long-drawn-out negotiations between Great Britain, France, and Russia on the one hand, and Rumania on the other, which had been in progress since the earliest stage of the war, are not our concern here. In brief, Rumania

Map 1.

---

[1] While Sir Francis Elliot was in consultation with Sir Edward Grey regarding the terms of the Note, there was a review at Athens, after which the newspaper offices of the Venizelist party were stoned by the crowd, the police looking on inactive, or, as the British Minister suspected, instigating the attack by means of secret agents. Afterwards there was hooting outside the British Legation.

had, since the death of King Charles in October 1914, been inclined by the sympathies of her Court, of her political and military authorities, and of the predominant section of her public opinion to the cause of the Entente. Naturally, however, there was an anti-war, though hardly a pro-German party. The strife of party and still more the fluctuations of the world struggle had caused uncertainty in her counsels. Always, just as she grew hot, the chill wind of a Russian reverse cooled her ardour and withered her resolutions.

For their part, the Germans had never been under any illusions as to the sympathies of the country or the risk that a nation which could put nearly 400,000 men into the field would enter the war against them. It seemed to them, indeed, that a settlement with Rumania was in the end inevitable; but they decided not to precipitate it even when the military situation was more or less favourable at the end of the summer of 1915.[1] The Serbian plan then took precedence of it; and, besides, there were considerations other than those of a purely military order. Rumania was immensely rich in two products of which Germany was becoming urgently in need, namely, corn and oil. So long as she would sell, it was better and even cheaper to buy than to go and take the spoils. Sell she would—though she also sold grain to Great Britain in January 1916—and purchases from her, in fact, went far towards averting a famine in Turkey in the early part of 1916, besides meeting Germany's most pressing needs.

Rumania had not yet made up her mind; she was merely awaiting a sign. At the beginning of June it came in the form of one of the most astonishing and spectacular episodes of the whole world war. On the 4th June the Russians launched on their southern front, from the great eastward buckle of the Styr in Volhynia to the Rumanian frontier, the "Brusilov Offensive." Here there was only one German Army, the *Southern*, with three Austro-Hungarian Armies to the north of it and one to the south. The attack was made after a short but heavy artillery preparation and met with astonishing success on the two flanks. On the right at Lutsk a gap 30 miles broad was created in the first onrush. On the left, under the eyes of Rumania, an even

---

[1] Falkenhayn, p. 204.

greater success was achieved. Here the Russians covered some 20 miles between the Dniester and the Pruth in the first six days, overflowed the Bukovina, and reached the foot of the Carpathians by mid-July, their rate of progress being checked rather by their own transport difficulties than by the resistance of the Austrians.

1916. June.

Rumania was convinced that here was an advantageous occasion such as might never recur. In this she was right, and it had been well if she had seized it at once. Yet she did not realize the true significance of the Russian victory: that it was in part due to the half-heartedness, if not the treachery, of some of the corps belonging to the subject races of the Austrian Empire, and so might well be nullified once sounder troops had been brought to the scene of action. That no other Russian offensive coincided with that of Brusilov, that the later attacks at Baranovici and further north were repulsed by the Germans with almost contemptuous ease even while they were denuding their front to check Brusilov, did not appear ominous to her. Prisoners reported by the hundred thousand, her frontier with the Bukovina covered, the prospect that Russian troops would now be able to cross the Carpathians side by side with her own and pour down into Hungary: that, naturally, was the picture which most appealed to her. On the 4th July, after the Somme offensive had also been launched and the Italian counter-attacks in the Trentino had made their weight felt, the Rumanian Prime Minister informed the French Minister at Bucharest that he was ready to sign a military convention on certain conditions, one of which was that Rumania should be protected against Bulgaria either by Russian troops or by an offensive from Salonika.

The Allied Army based on Salonika thus assumed a position of greater importance than before. If, since it failed in its first mission of saving the Serbians, it had had any object beyond the defence of the harbour, that object had been to bring Rumania and Greece, or one of them, into the war. Now that Rumania was on the brink of hostilities with Austria it was natural that the British attitude towards offensive operations from Salonika should be in some degree modified.

In the interval since the 17th May [1] discussions between

---
[1] See p. 116.

Britain and France had, as can well be imagined, not ceased. On the 9th June an Anglo-French conference had been held in London, after which a memorandum had been addressed to the French Government to the effect that an offensive could not then be taken with any prospect of success. In the two final paragraphs it was stated that the British Government would " not refuse at a future date " to examine the question of an offensive from Salonika " as soon as circumstances and the condition of the troops " allow," and that they would hasten the necessary equipment of their Army there.

These last paragraphs obviously gave the French advocates of an offensive a loophole, since it appeared that the British Government now condemned it, not on general principles, but for temporary technical reasons.[1] In an endeavour to strengthen their position, the Government despatched a further memorandum on the 21st in which they stated that, pending the result of the Somme offensive, Allied policy in the Balkans must be defensive, and that they could not agree to make any preparations there which would deprive the British Armies in France of any part of the resources required by them. After the Somme offensive had taken place they would not refuse to reconsider the question of offensive operations in the Balkans. They would fulfil their promises regarding the preparation of their Salonika Army for an active campaign, but saw little prospect that it would be fully equipped for mountain warfare before September or that the necessary heavy artillery would be ready before November.

Right they might well be in principle ; in argument they were less happy. General Joffre, in a letter to M. Briand which has since seen the light,[2] handled the whole correspondence in a manner very damaging to the logic of the British case ; but the French Government in their formal reply on the 30th June contented themselves with pointing out that the situation had been altered by the extent of the Russian victory and by the Italian counter-offensive. The Somme offensive had begun (*i.e.* by the time the letter reached the British Government). To speak of a possible offensive from Salonika *after* the Somme offensive was an entirely new suggestion, against which the French generals

---

[1] " Soldiers and Statesmen," II, pp. 114–117.
[2] " Armées Françaises," Tome VIII, Vol. I, Annexes, Vol. III, p. 694.

and ministers protested. It was *during* the attack on the Somme that Allied action in the Balkans would be most efficacious. They went on to argue that there had never been a moment more favourable to the entry of Rumania into the war.

1916. July.

The War Committee did not consider this communication until the 6th July, by which date Sir George Barclay, the Minister at Bucharest, had reported that Rumania was ready to conclude a military convention. Sir Edward Grey was therefore instructed to draft a reply, handed to M. Cambon on the 10th, in which it was stated that, though the Government could not agree that a new situation had yet arisen to cause them to modify their former conclusions, nevertheless, if Rumania definitely intervened, they would be prepared to co-operate in an offensive from Salonika, with the object of holding the largest possible proportion of the Bulgarian Army on the Greek frontier, " on a scale " commensurate with the strength and equipment of their " force."

After some further discussion, the War Committee decided on the 18th July that a conference of the Allied military representatives should be held in Paris regarding the entry of Rumania into the war and the measures to be taken in co-operation. At the same time the Committee determined that, in view of the new situation, there must be a change in the agreement as to the relationship between General Sarrail and the British Army commander, dated the 10th January.[1] On the 19th July Lord Hardinge, the Permanent Under-Secretary of State for Foreign Affairs, handed to M. de Fleuriau, the Chargé d'Affaires at the French Embassy, the following memorandum :—

" With regard to the question of command, His " Majesty's Government are unable to deprive themselves " entirely of control over their troops when engaged in " offensive operations, but, in the event of such operations " being undertaken from Salonika, General Milne will be " placed upon the same footing with regard to General " Sarrail as that of Sir Douglas Haig in regard to General " Joffre, that is to say, General Milne will be instructed to " support and co-operate with the other Allied forces against " our common enemy in the execution of such a plan of

---

[1] See p. 103.

"operations as may be agreed upon by the French and "British Higher Commands."

This was a political formula, not precise enough for military purposes. A military formula, drawn up by General Joffre and agreed to by the British General Staff, was telegraphed to General Milne on the 25th. It was to the effect [1] that the French Commander-in-Chief would consult the British Army commander as to the employment he proposed to make of the British forces. With that reservation, the Commander-in-Chief would decide the missions, the objectives, the boundaries, and the dates on which each action was to commence. At the same time it was laid down that the rôle of the Allied Armies was, first, to cover the mobilization of Rumania by containing the maximum number of Bulgarian troops, and, secondly, when Rumania should have begun operations south of the Danube, to combine their action with the Russo-Rumanian Army and direct their efforts towards the destruction of the enemy forces. The first part of the mission would, it was stated, probably begin on the 1st August.

Meanwhile Rumania had been endangering a golden chance by hesitation and bargaining, and had come to a decision which still further damaged her prospects. To the dismay of the Allies, it became evident that she had no intention of declaring war against any Power but Austria-Hungary, and that the hoped-for attack across the Danube against Bulgaria would not take place. General Alexiev, Chief of the General Staff of the Russian Armies, tried hard to convince the Rumanian Government of their error, but without avail.[2] At the military conference in Paris on the 23rd July her resolution was found to be unalterable, and on the 28th the War Committee therefore instructed Lord Grey to telegraph to Paris that until Rumania was at war with Bulgaria the rôle of the Salonika forces would be merely to observe and contain the Bulgarian forces on the Greek frontier. There were also delays over the terms of the military convention with Rumania, which in turn caused the date when General Sarrail was to begin his offensive to be deferred. Political and military conventions between Great Britain, France, Italy, Russia, and Rumania were actually signed at Bucharest on the 17th August, the

---

[1] See Note at end of Chapter.
[2] "Armées Françaises," Tome VIII, Vol. I, Annexes, Vol. III, p. 777.

Military Attachés [1] of the four Allied Powers putting their signatures to the military convention, which was signed on behalf of Rumania by M. Bratianu, Prime Minister and Minister for War. The convention contained seventeen articles, of which only the following [2] are of importance from the present point of view :—

1916.
Aug.

"*Article I.*—Following on the Treaty of Alliance
" concluded on the 4th/17th August 1916 between France,.
" Great Britain, Italy, Russia, and Rumania, Rumania
" undertakes to mobilize all her forces by land and sea
" and to attack Austria-Hungary at latest on the 15th/28th
" August 1916 (eight days after the offensive from Salonika).
" The offensive operations of the Rumanian Army will
" begin on the same day as the declaration of war.

"*Article III.*—Russia undertakes at the moment of
" the mobilization of the Rumanian Army to send into the
" Dobruja two divisions of infantry and one division of
" cavalry to co-operate with the Rumanian Army against
" the Bulgarian Army.

" The Allies undertake that a definite offensive [3] from
" Salonika shall precede by at least eight days the entry of
" Rumania into the war, in order to facilitate the mobiliza-
" tion and concentration of all the Rumanian military
" forces. This offensive will begin on the 7th/20th August
" 1916. . . .

"*Article IX.* . . . Rumanian action will be generally
" directed, so far as the military situation south of the
" Danube permits, through Transylvania on Budapest. . . ."

Rumania did actually declare war on Austria-Hungary on the 27th August, the day before Italy declared war on Germany ; Germany declared war on Rumania on the 28th, Turkey did so on the 30th, and Bulgaria on the 1st September. Rumania took the field when the situation was far less favourable than it had been a month earlier. The Russian southern advance had been brought to a halt and the other offensives north of the Pripet marshes had been completely defeated. As had happened so often on

---

[1] The British Military Attaché was Lieut.-Colonel C. B. Thomson, afterwards Lord Thomson of Cardington, who met his death in the destruction of the airship *R.101* in 1930.

[2] The extracts are here translated from the French original.

[3] "*Offensive affirmée*" in the original.

Preparations for an Offensive.

the side of the Entente, the decisive step had been too long delayed.

The British Salonika Army was being slowly prepared for active operations. On the 11th July the War Office approved of a pack-transport establishment, based upon the proposals first put forward by General Mahon but a good deal larger, and authorized General Milne to begin the organization of units on a pack scale so far as his means allowed. This, at the moment, was not very far. Ten thousand mules were required, exclusive of those which would be needed if any 18-pdr. brigades were converted into mountain artillery brigades, and without counting the necessary 10 per cent reserve to meet wastage.[1] Moreover, an undertaking (which the French regarded as a definite promise and the British War Office as a pious aspiration to be fulfilled at some future date) had been given that Great Britain would supply 4,000 mules to the Serbian Army. Finding that the demands of the British Army were much higher than originally anticipated, the War Office decided that the deficiency still existing after 6,500 animals from Egypt and 2,500 from the United Kingdom, for which they had arranged, had been handed over, should be made up by 2,000 purchased in Cyprus and intended for the Serbians. To this General Milne demurred, since he had given the Serbians a promise that at least 2,000 mules would be available by the end of the month, and considered the Cypriot mules small for the British needs. Eventually the Egyptian command—which had a great quantity of horses and mules to spare now that the reconquest of Sinai was being carried out with camel transport—increased its consignments, and more mules were obtained from America. The required establishment was not attained until the autumn, partly owing to the shortage of drivers. By mid-August, however, all battalions, except those of the 80th Brigade at Stavros and the Pioneers, had been equipped on a pack scale.

The question of " drivers "—actually the men to lead the pack mules—has been mentioned as one cause of delay.

---

[1] As a result of the arrival of new units and successive revisions in an upward direction by General Milne's staff, the numbers eventually reached 15,000.

It was necessary, for first-line transport with fighting units, to employ soldiers, and even though for second-line transport permission was given for the enlistment of Cypriots, Macedonians, and later Cretans, a proportion of British N.C.O.'s and men had to be found for their supervision. After A.S.C. drivers in existing units with wheeled transport had been replaced by native drivers and allotted to this work, the balance was made up from the United Kingdom.

1916. July.

Under the new establishments all units, such as field companies R.E., infantry battalions, and machine-gun companies, which could be equipped in this manner, were to be placed entirely on a pack basis, without any wheeled vehicles whatever. In the case of the field companies the pontoon and trestle wagons were to be parked under corps arrangements for use if required. In the case of the divisional trains a proportion of the vehicles had to be retained. Each brigade company had a pack echelon without any vehicles, and a wheeled echelon consisting entirely of wheeled vehicles, with the exception of two water-mules.[1]

Rearward transport deficiencies were also to be remedied by the despatch of three reserve parks,[2] which were embarked in July. There were already two at Salonika, so that there was now one for each division, each capable of carrying two days' rations and forage. One hundred extra lorries were despatched in mid-July; and, as General Milne considered that he required a mechanical transport supply column and ammunition park for each division, the War Office agreed to send sufficient lorries for the purpose in August and September.

If the War Office, in part from necessity, in part perhaps from anxiety as to how the troops were to be employed, had been slow in the equipment of the Salonika Army to meet the needs of the country, it had also been thorough, and had with the aid of Sir Archibald Murray in Egypt done its utmost to meet General Milne's requirements. Certainly by the autumn of 1916, so far from being

---

[1] In Appendix 4 are given the establishments for a S.A. section ammunition column, a field company R.E., an infantry battalion, a machine-gun company, and a divisional train. In all but the last case the establishments existing before the reorganization are given for purposes of comparison in parallel columns.

[2] The reserve park consisted of a horse-transport company A.S.C. with 144 wagons for supplies.

(as was previously the case) behind the French, it was the best-found force in the theatre of war.

In July the artillery of the five divisions was regrouped as in other theatres of war by breaking up the howitzer brigades and distributing the batteries among the other brigades. The 22nd Division then had four brigades, each of three 18-pdr. batteries and one 4·5-inch howitzer battery, all of four guns; the other four divisions had three brigades of three 18-pdr. batteries and one howitzer battery, and a fourth brigade of three 18-pdr. batteries only. General Milne at that time contemplated converting these 18-pdr. batteries into mountain batteries when more mountain artillery became available. He had already been promised the IV Highland Mountain Brigade, consisting of only two batteries (Argyll, and Ross & Cromarty), each of four 2·75-inch guns, which arrived from Egypt on the 10th August. The Bute battery was promised from England to bring the brigade up to a strength of three, but was not sent until November. The 2nd, 5th, and 7th Mountain Batteries (each of six 2·75-inch guns), already in the country, had been formed into a brigade.

Welcome reinforcements in heavy artillery had now been promised, consisting of the 143rd and 153rd Heavy Batteries (60-pdrs.), and the 127th, 130th, 132nd, 134th, and 138th Siege Batteries (6-inch howitzers). Hitherto the Army had been wretchedly equipped with this arm, being without a single heavy howitzer. These batteries did not begin embarkation in England until late July, and the howitzers only arrived gradually after active operations had begun. Two more anti-aircraft sections, Nos. 73 and 74, of which the Army was also sadly in need, arrived on the 6th August. By this date there were also under orders for Salonika two pioneer battalions for divisions which were without them, two Army Troops companies R.E., and two garrison battalions. Six machine-gun companies arrived during July for the 22nd and 26th Divisions, those for the other divisions having previously been formed in the country.

An equally serious weakness, the lack of aircraft, was also remedied. Hitherto the French had put machines at the disposal of the British and had trained British officers as observers; but when the Serbians were ready to take the field these machines were withdrawn for attachment

ARRIVAL OF AIRCRAFT

to them. No. 17 Squadron R.F.C. was sent from Egypt in July. General Milne represented the need of a second squadron but did not receive one until September, the personnel of No. 47 Squadron reaching Salonika from England on the 19th. At the same time No. 17 Balloon Section landed, and the three units were formed into the 16th Wing, under the orders of the Middle East Brigade, which had its headquarters in Egypt. There were already British aircraft in the neighbourhood, though not based on Salonika or at the disposal of the Army. These were six machines of the R.N.A.S. which had been formed in May into a composite force with a French flight on the island of Thasos, and were employed in July in dropping incendiary bombs amid the ripening crops in southern Bulgaria. A small detachment of infantry from Salonika was employed for the protection of the aerodrome. "D" Squadron R.N.A.S. was subsequently based on Stavros to spot for the warships covering the Allied right flank in the bay, and after the occupation of the lower Struma by the Army also worked with the troops holding that line.

In consequence of the advance from the Entrenched Camp and the far greater area now within the British zone, it was decided that an Inspector-General of Communications was necessary. Major-General F. W. B. Koe, from Egypt, was appointed to the post, and on the 10th August the area under his control was defined as all the country south of a line drawn through Sarigöl, on the Dojran line 23 miles N.N.W. of Salonika, through Likovan on the Salonika–Seres road, to Stavros.

On the medical side, the Army, which had had no casualties to speak of other than those from sickness since the expedition in Serbia, was fully equipped, having in July on land or on the way five casualty clearing stations, four motor ambulance convoys, seven general hospitals, and four stationary hospitals. Apart from malaria—and that was not severely felt outside the Struma valley before the end of July—the health of the troops was good. Work was limited to six hours a day, and, as the heat increased, was carried out in the mornings and evenings. The summer dress of the troops consisted of shirts and " shorts," though the latter were not permitted to be worn by mounted men on account of the danger of blood-poisoning from sweating horses. The question of headgear has already been discussed.¹ On the 12th July 120,000 sunhelmets arrived from Egypt and were issued as quickly as possible. Steel shrapnel helmets were also issued in August, but at first only in quantities sufficient for use as trench stores.

As July drew on General Milne became concerned by the growing incidence of malaria, the sick rate in the 10th Division alone having risen to a hundred a day and being still on the increase.² The cavalry was suffering as severely, and at the end of the month the South Notts Hussars had to be formed into a composite regiment with two squadrons of the Derbyshire Yeomanry.³ The Army commander ordered General Briggs to withdraw all his troops from the Struma between Orlyak bridge and Lake Tahinos to the higher ground, with the exception of small posts at the bridges.

The problem of malaria was never satisfactorily solved. Southern Macedonia is probably the most malarial country in Europe, and it is one in which, owing to the vast area of marsh and lake and the countless streams feeding the great rivers, such as the Vardar and Struma, a campaign against the mosquito is almost fruitless. The anopheles is by no means confined to the low-lying country; in fact, one of the two predominating types found in Macedonia is essentially a hill mosquito. The valleys were far worse than the hills, but only because the breeding season there was considerably longer and the mosquitoes were more numerous. In 1916 anti-mosquito measures were limited, but they were subsequently extended, and by 1918 were carried out on a vast scale, every known method of combating the breeding of mosquitoes being adopted. But the area covered by the troops was too large for these methods to be effective, and it is now the considered view of the medical

---

[1] See p. 102.
[2] In the Medical History of the War, " Diseases of the War," I, p. 230, it is stated that the admissions for malaria for " one division " from June to October were for the successive five months 4, 1,300, 2,500, 1,600, and 1,100. Probably this was the 10th Division; but it must be noted that the figures represented only the admissions to *hospital*, not the numbers treated in the field ambulances. By the 27th July the sick rate in this division had risen to 150 a day. The 28th Division suffered almost as much.
[3] At the end of August another composite regiment was formed from the headquarters, the machine-gun section, and one squadron of the Derbyshire Yeomanry, and two squadrons of the Lothians and Border Horse, the divisional cavalry of the 22nd and 26th Divisions.

authorities that the work was in great part wasted. The mosquito's range of flight being probably two or three miles —instead of half a mile, as was then believed—these pests flew in from outside the cleared areas, in some districts from within the enemy's lines. The very fact that an area was cleared meant that there were numerous troops in it and thus made it a centre of attraction. The mortality rate from malaria in 1916 was 1 per cent of admissions to hospital, exceptionally high for this disease, but during the two following summers improved treatment reduced it to about ·3 per cent.[1]

1916. July.

The troops carried out a great deal of training during July, together with road work and, in the case of the XVI Corps, work on the defences of the Struma bridges at Orlyak and Komarjan. The Greek troops were demobilizing, in accordance with the agreement reached with the Allies, and embarking at Kavalla for transport to Old Greece. A certain number, whose homes were in Salonika or the peninsula of Khalkidike, were allowed to cross the Struma above Lake Tahinos.

* * * * *

Meanwhile General Sarrail was pushing on his preparations. On the 15th July General Joffre called for his plan of operations for covering the mobilization of the Rumanian Army and afterwards co-operating with the Russo-Rumanian Army south of the Danube. It was in general similar to that put forward in May. The principal effort was to be made by the Serbian forces, which on the 17th July began to move out from the Entrenched Camp and to take over the front between Kupa (12 miles west of the Vardar and five miles south of the Serbian frontier at Huma) and Florina, hitherto merely watched by a French detachment of four battalions and a few squadrons. The main Serbian attack was to be made in the direction of Huma, presumably because there was a fairly good road from that place to the Vardar, which would enable the attackers, if they broke through, to turn the fortifications along the frontier in the Vardar valley. The Russian brigade which he was expecting and at least one French brigade would operate between the Serbians and the Vardar. General Milne having still

Maps A, 2.

---

[1] Medical History, "Diseases of the War," I, pp. 227–246.

not received permission to attack, the Commander-in-Chief desired to place British troops upon the "more or less "defensive or demonstrative front" between the Vardar and Lake Dojran. Along the railway in the zone of Dova Tepe the French troops would remain on the defensive. In the Struma valley, on account of the malaria reported by General Milne, there would be only a demonstration in the direction of Rupel. With the French troops relieved by the British, General Sarrail would "operate either in "the zone of Lake Dojran (presumably on the south- "western shore of the lake) or against Machukovo," on the left bank of the Vardar. He hoped thus to pin down the maximum Bulgarian forces and to obtain a local success either west of Lake Dojran, at Machukovo, or Huma, which would "orient his manœuvre" and permit him to march in the direction of the Rumanian advance.[1]

On paper these plans looked excellent, and any misgivings they aroused in British breasts were on the score of transport, especially for the Serbians on the left flank. It was proved before operations began that there was some justification for these misgivings, since none of the troops west of the Vardar were in their places by the 1st August, the date originally fixed for the attack.

General Sarrail had all this time, in addition to exercising a limited command over the British, had directly under his orders four French divisions and many other units. Now he had the Serbians (who had agreed upon a formula somewhat similar to the British with regard to command), and was expecting a Russian brigade and an Italian division. In July, therefore, General Joffre decided to send General Cordonnier to command the French divisions, which took the name of "Armée Française d'Orient." General Cordonnier took over his command on the 11th August.[2] The new link in the French chain had, however, no effect upon the relationship between Generals Sarrail and Milne.[3] By this time both the Russian and Italian troops had arrived, the Russian brigade having landed on the 1st August and the Italian 35th Division begun disembarkation on the

---

[1] "Armées Françaises," Tome VIII, Vol. I, pp. 511–512, and Annexes there referred to.
[2] "Armées Françaises," Tome VIII, Vol. I, p. 525.
[3] See Note at end of Chapter, telegrams of 10th and 11th August.

11th. Both contingents, and especially the Italian, were 1916. valuable acquisitions, having been specially chosen to uphold July. their countries' prestige in this theatre. The Russian troops were men of magnificent physique. The Italian division had a fine record and had been brought up to strengh and admirably equipped, though its artillery consisted only of 32 mountain guns. It was joined during the autumn by a third infantry brigade, which brought its strength up to 18 battalions.

Immediately his plan had been given the approval of General Joffre, General Sarrail requested General Milne to relieve the French troops (the 156th Division and part of the 17th Colonial) on the line Gola–Chaushitsa, south of Lake Dojran. On the 24th July General Milne ordered General Wilson, commanding the XII Corps, to send up two divisions for the purpose, and directed General Briggs to concentrate the 10th and 27th Divisions of the XVI Corps, less a brigade at Stavros, on the Ortach plateau. He also placed the 7th Mounted Brigade and 28th Division at General Briggs's disposal to take over the line of the Struma. Hitherto this had been held only as far down as the point where it entered Lake Tahinos. Partly in consequence of the Greek demobilization, General Milne now decided to hold the short stretch between the lake and the sea and to patrol the south-western shore of the lake with his mounted troops. Learning that the Greeks were willing to hand over the important Neohori bridge, the only one over the river between Lake Tahinos and the sea, if they could plead that the demand for its possession was backed by superior numbers, he ordered General Briggs to occupy it. On the 28th the bridge was handed over by the Greeks to the squadron of Surrey Yeomanry, divisional cavalry of the 27th Division, which was relieved later in the day by a company of the 80th Brigade ; and on the 30th that brigade began its march from Stavros to occupy the mouth of the Struma.

By the morning of the 3rd August the new dispositions Aug. had been taken up. On the right, in the area of the XVI Corps, the 80th Brigade of the 27th Division was defending the lower Struma and constructing works to cover the Neohori bridge, the other two brigades being on the Ortach plateau, east of Salonika, with two battalions carrying out the duties of town guards. From Ahinos, on the southern shore of Lake Tahinos,[1] to Lozhishta, south of Lake Butkovo, on a frontage of 32 miles, was the 28th Division. In front of it, on the left bank of the Struma a French force under General Frotiée, consisting of three regiments of Chasseurs d'Afrique, and the 2nd *bis* Regiment of Zouaves, with some horse artillery, was to demonstrate in the direction of the Rupel Pass and was now moving up from Salonika. The 7th Mounted Brigade, under the orders of the 28th Division, was also patrolling on the west bank. The 10th Division was in reserve, with two brigades training about Dremiglava, and the 31st working on the Salonika–Seres road.

On the left of the XVI Corps the French 57th Division held from Lake Butkovo to Gulemenli, six miles east of Dojran Station. Then came the 17th Colonial Division, facing north-west and with its left on Kilinder, in touch with the British XII Corps.

The two divisions of the XII Corps held the front from Kilinder, on the Dojran railway, to Chaushitsa, north of Lake Arjan. On the right the 22nd Division had the 65th Brigade in line from Kilinder to Hill 420, just east of the village of Büyükli (three miles S.S.W. of Dojran town). The 66th Brigade was in rear of the 17th Division, and the 67th at Yeniköi, in support to the 65th. On the left, to the shore of Lake Arjan at Chaushitsa Station the 26th Division had two brigades in line, the 78th on the right and 79th on the left, the 77th being in reserve between the Dojran railway and Lake Arjan. The French 156th Division, having been relieved by the British, was moving down the Vardar to Amatovon Station, where it was to be in reserve.

On the British left the French 122nd Division was astride the Vardar from Chaushitsa to Lyumnitsa. On the left of that the Serbian First Army, sadly hampered by the conditions of the roads and its shortage of transport, was moving slowly up into line. The other two Armies were in position facing the frontier, their line running through Strupino to just north of Lake Ostrovo, and thence, as a mere skeleton, to Lake Prespa, with one small detachment

---

[1] On the indifferent 1/250,000 map of this area the lake is shown as extending to a point 10 miles north-west of Ahinos. In fact, this area is a marsh, comparatively dry in summer, through which the Struma runs in three channels, and Ahinos is at the head of the lake proper. The reason why the general map (Map A) in this volume is taken from the 1/250,000 map is because it contains almost all the names mentioned in the text.

BULGARIAN DISPOSITIONS

1916.
Aug.

actually at Koritsa, 40 miles from the nearest point on the Monastir railway and 115 miles from Salonika.

The total length of the Salonika front, if this detachment be included, was at this moment, in fact, 170 miles as the crow flies, or nearly twice that of the British front in France and Belgium when at its longest, on the 21st March 1918.

The dispositions of the enemy, as known to General Sarrail, were as follows:—On the right from west of Lake Prespa to Sovich, 20 miles east of Monastir, the *8th Division*; thence along the frontier crest to the Duditsa Mountain the *3rd Division* and a regiment of the *9th*; thence to the Vardar the *5th Division*. East of the Vardar, from north of Machukovo to north-west of Krastali, the French Intelligence believed there was a mixed division, made up of troops of the German *101st Division*—representing the only German infantry remaining on the front—and the Bulgarian *9th Division*. Then came the *2nd Division* holding the hills west of Lake Dojran, and also from the north shore of the lake to near the " Frontier of the Three Nations " ; then the *11th Division* on the Belašica Planina almost up to the Rupel Pass ; then the *7th Division* with a brigade of the *2nd* astride the Struma, with its left at Krushevo. In the coast area of Southern Bulgaria was the *10th Division* at Pashmakli, Xanthi, and Dedeagach. Against the 201 battalions and 1,025 guns of the Allies (counting the Russian and Italian detachments, of which the former had landed and the latter was embarking at Taranto) General Sarrail estimated that the enemy had 172 battalions and 900 guns.[1]

---

[1] " Armées Françaises," Tome VIII, Vol. I, p. 519. There were some errors here. On the right of the *8th Division* there were actually three brigades (24 battalions) of different divisions ; and the total number of battalions between Lake Prespa and the Duditsa Mountain was 65. (" Herbstschlacht in Macedonien," p. 23.) The only foundation for the reported " mixed division " was the fact that one regiment of the German *101st Division* had been relieved by Bulgarian troops and withdrawn into reserve. On the outbreak of war with Rumania this regiment (the *45th*) was despatched to the Dobruja. (" Das Infanterie—Regiment [8 Ostpreussisches] Nr. 45," p. 134.) The command, of which General Sarrail as yet apparently knew nothing, was exercised as follows :—Lake Prespa to the Duditsa Mountain, Bulgarian *First Army*; Duditsa Mountain to Lake Dojran, German *Eleventh Army*; Struma Front, Bulgarian *Second Army*.

NOTE.

TELEGRAMS BETWEEN GENERAL MILNE AND THE C.I.G.S.

From—C.I.G.S., War Office.
To—G.O.C., A.H.Q., Salonika.
19962 cipher.   25th July 1916.

Reference my personal unnumbered telegram from Paris of the 23rd inst., the text of Joffre's instructions to Sarrail is as follows:—
" The English and French High Commands, after an examination of
" the question of the command at Salonika, of the mission of the Allied
" Armies, and of the plan of operations, have agreed on taking the following
" decisions :—

" A. *The question of the command is settled by the following formula :*
" The instructions relating to the initial offensive, as well as to the
" general directions [1] required for the later development of the operations,
" will be settled by agreement between the French and British High
" Commands.

" In the execution of these instructions, the Commander of the English
" forces will give to the Commander of the French forces support and
" co-operation proportionate to the numbers and equipment of the troops
" under his orders; he will in addition be responsible to the British
" Government for the employment of his forces.

" The Commander of the French forces will consult the English
" Commander as to the employment he proposes to make of the British
" forces; with this reservation he will have, as Commander-in-Chief,
" latitude to decide on the missions, the objectives to be gained, the zones
" of action, and the dates on which every operation is to commence.

" B. *Mission of the Allied Armies.*
" *At first,*[2] the mission to be fulfilled by the Allied Armies at Salonika
" is the following : In order to cover the mobilization of the Rumanian
" Army, as well as its action against Austria-Hungary, from an enemy
" offensive on its southern front, the Allied Armies at Salonika will under-
" take their offensive operations at a date which will be settled later
" (probably 1st August) with a view to containing the maximum number
" of Bulgarian troops.

" *Afterwards,*[2] when Rumania shall have begun her operations south
" of the Danube, the Allied Armies at Salonika, combining their action
" with the Russo-Rumanian Army, will direct all their efforts towards the
" destruction of the enemy forces."

(The remainder of the telegram contains a summary of the plan of operations then contemplated and some remarks by Sir W. Robertson.)

From—A.H.Q., Salonika.
To—Chief, London.
G.C. 416.   10th August 1916.

General Cordonnier, lately commanding VIII Corps in France, has arrived here to command French Army in place of Sarrail, who is, I understand, assuming position of Commander-in-Chief of the Group of Armies of the East. I have as yet received no official intimation of this change, which I presume does not affect British Army.

---

[1] " *Directives* " in the original French version.
[2] " *Initialement* " and " *ultérieurement* " in the original French version.

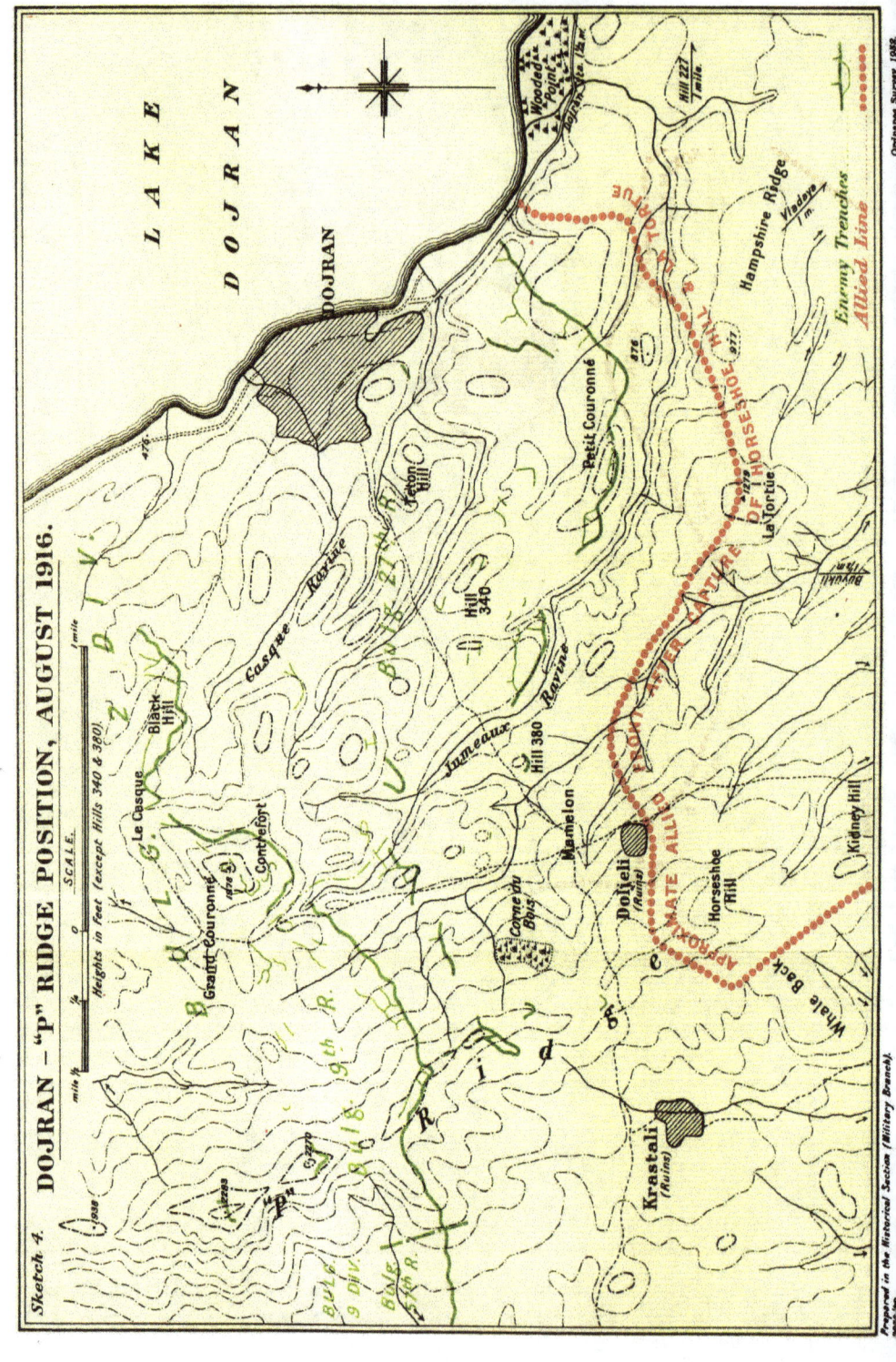

From—Chief, London.
To—A.H.Q., Salonika.
21466 cipher.   11th August 1916.

Your G.C. 416. The change in Sarrail's status does not affect your responsibility and position in any way ; it remains as defined in my 19962 of 25/7. Joffre may probably have made the change so that Sarrail might be in a better position to exercise general command over the French, Russians, Italians, and Serbians. I think that he contemplated taking this step some time ago.

CHAPTER VIII.

THE DOJRAN AND STRUMA OPERATIONS, 9TH AUGUST TO 23RD SEPTEMBER 1916.

(Maps A, 7; Sketches A, 4, 5, 6.)

THE DOJRAN OPERATIONS AND THE BULGARIAN ADVANCE ON THE FLANKS.

Map A. GENERAL WILSON, commanding the XII Corps, learnt that
Sketches the French 17th Colonial Division had been ordered to
A, 4. attack in a north-westerly direction towards the line Dojran–Doljeli. This attack was to be carried out in two phases, the first being the occupation of Hill 227, south of Dojran Station, and the village of Vladaya; and the second that of the Petit Couronné, a very steep-faced hill south of Dojran town, and La Tortue, a flatter hill separated from the Petit Couronné by the deep Jumeaux Ravine.

The rôle of the British XII Corps was to secure the left flank of the attack by occupying the low hills west of Vladaya when the French had captured the village, and to support the right by placing a brigade on the ridge between Gola and Kilinder after the French had moved forward from this ground. Both these tasks were to be carried out by the 22nd Division, which was also to be prepared to send a brigade of field artillery to the neighbourhood of Vladaya with the object of giving artillery support to the 17th Division in its further advance. The heavy artillery of the XII Corps (XXXVII Heavy Group and 43rd Siege Battery, under the orders of Br.-General H. E. T. Kelly, acting G.O.C.R.A.) was to co-operate by engaging the enemy's artillery and observation posts on the Grand Couronné and " P. " Ridge, its targets having been indicated by General Dauvé, the French artillery commander. The 17th Squadron R.F.C. was to have its first serious task in preventing the enemy's aircraft from observing the fire of his artillery, and in reporting the positions of his guns in action. The XII Corps Signals had only two days to establish telephone lines from XII Corps headquarters at Kirech to the French 17th Division's command post at Hill 540, north-east of Gola (16 miles); to the artillery command post on The Commandant (11 miles); and to the battle headquarters of the 22nd and 26th Divisions at

FRENCH ATTACK AT DOJRAN

Yeniköi and Chugunsi (5½ and 7 miles). These two villages were, like so many in this neighbourhood, bombarded and burnt-out relics of the Balkan Wars, with hardly a roof intact. The two British divisions in this area were now supplied by rail, railhead for the 22nd being at Yanesh, on the Dojran railway (later advanced to near Khirsova), and that for the 26th and the heavy artillery south of Kalinova, on the Karasuli–Kilinder branch line. The French 17th Division on the right was able to avail itself of a light railway recently constructed from Sarigöl Station, through Kukush and up the valley of the Spants to Snevche.

1916. Aug.

General Sarrail had intended to begin his attack on the 1st August and had postponed it until the 4th because his troops were not ready. Now he had to make another postponement, as there was still no news regarding the signature of the military convention with Rumania, of which he was expecting from day to day to hear. As has been stated, the convention was not signed until the 17th. Before the Allies had moved and while the Serbians on the left flank were still struggling into their positions, the Bulgarians, on the morning of the 5th, crossed the Greek frontier on the railway south of Monastir and occupied Negochani, pushing on to Rahmanli, which was evacuated by the Greeks, on the 7th. General Sarrail then ordered the demonstrative action of the 17th Colonial Division to begin at once.

At 5.25 a.m.[1] on the 9th a very heavy bombardment [2] of the enemy's positions south and west of Lake Dojran began. The artillery of the 22nd Division took as yet no part, since it had to be ready to move at the shortest notice. At nightfall the troops of the 17th Colonial Division, discovering that the Bulgarians, as a result of their heavy punishment, had abandoned both Hill 227 and Vladaya, moved forward and occupied the objective of the first phase and also Dojran Station. The British XCIX Brigade R.F.A. promptly went into action south of Vladaya, while the 66th Infantry Brigade occupied the Gola–Kilinder ridge on the French right before dawn.

---

[1] The Allies were now working to Eastern European time, clocks having been put forward 26 minutes on the 27th July.

[2] There were five groups of French heavy artillery, the British siege battery and three heavy batteries, the divisional artillery of the French 17th and 156th Divisions, and an armoured train. ("Armées Françaises," Tome VIII, Vol. I, p. 515.)

On the morning of the 10th General Gérôme, commanding the 17th Colonial Division, requested General Wilson to co-operate in the second phase by attacking the western half of La Tortue and thence the westernmost works of the Petit Couronné, and said he would postpone his own attack until a reply was received from the British Army commander. General Milne was in a difficult position. There was now no question of " marching in the direction " of the Rumanian advance," [1] because it was clear that there would be none and that the Rumanians would not attack south of the Danube. He had been informed by General Robertson that only if the Entente Powers accepted the Rumanian proposals, and only after the British Government were satisfied that Rumania had definitely entered the war and would make an effective attack on Austria-Hungary, was he to co-operate with General Sarrail for the purpose of holding the Bulgarian forces on the Greek frontier.[2] Anxious as he was to help, he considered that an attack of this scope would be beyond his instructions and therefore had to refuse his assent to it.

During the night of the 10th the XCVIII and CI Brigades R.F.A. of the 22nd Division relieved the French artillery behind the Gola–Kilinder ridge. On the 11th the French, working up the eastern shore of the lake, occupied the village of Brest. Gradually pushing forward their left, the French seized La Tortue in the early hours of the 15th, but were driven off it again. On the 16th, after a heavy bombardment, in which some of the British batteries took part, the 17th Colonial Division carried La Tortue and Doljeli. On the former it maintained itself, but was driven out of the village. Next day it again seized Doljeli, but was shelled out of it at noon. Its casualties had so far been over 1,100.[3] The French left, just south of the village, was now 1,200 yards in advance of the right British post (a company of the 7/R. Berkshire, 78th Brigade) on Kidney Hill. This hill was at the toe of the " P." Ridge, which rose abruptly to the northward to Horseshoe Hill, whence the enemy looked right down into Doljeli. Br.-General J. Duncan, commanding the 78th Brigade, had already prepared an operation for the capture of Horseshoe

---

[1] See p. 146.
[2] See Note at end of Chapter.
[3] " Historique des Troupes Coloniales," p. 63.

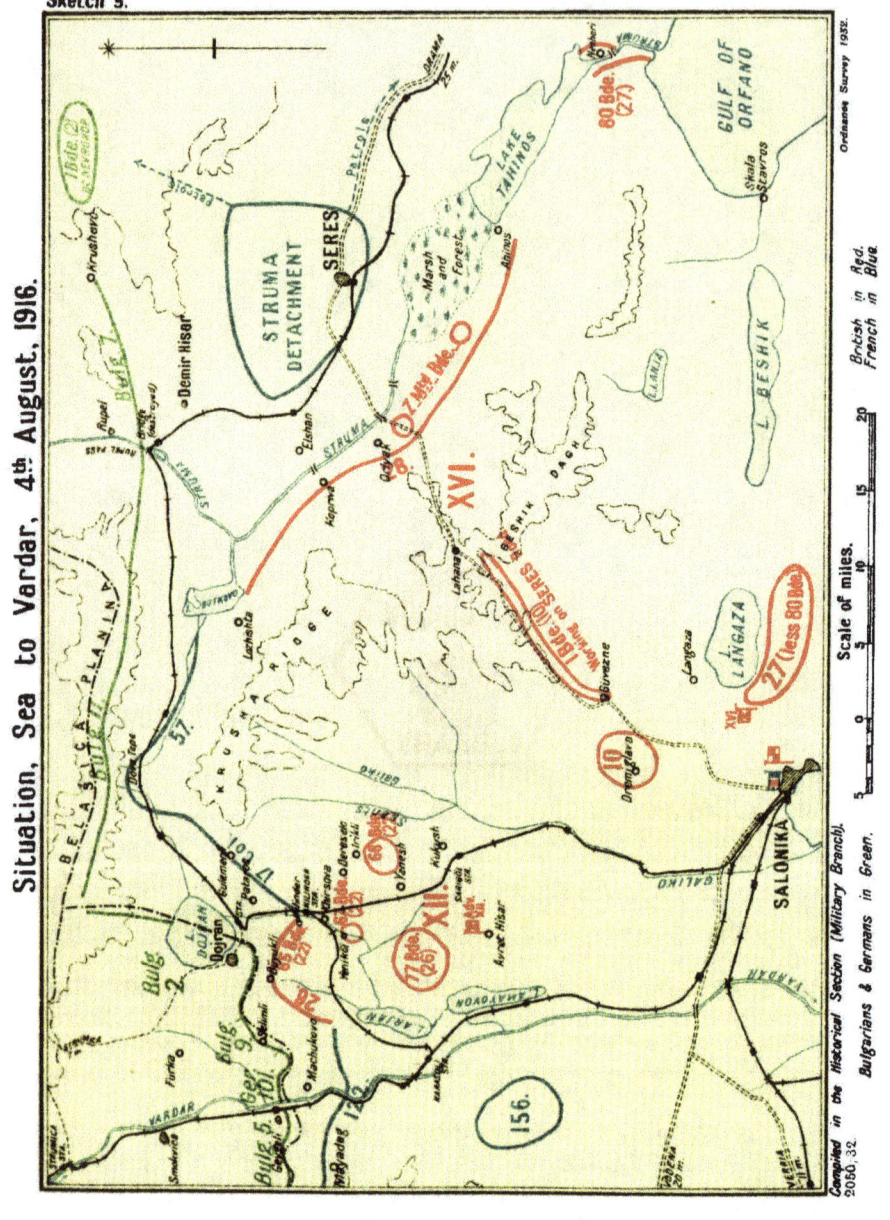

Hill to assist the French in their advance from La Tortue against the Petit Couronné. This was now sanctioned by General Milne; and General Wilson ordered it to be carried out during the night of the 17th, as the French attack was to be continued next morning.

1916.
17 Aug.

The attack was entrusted to the 7/Oxford and Bucks Light Infantry, to which were attached four guns of the 78th Machine-Gun Company and two sections of the 131st Field Company R.E. with wiring material. Two companies of the battalion were lightly equipped, to act as carriers and in support, and had orders to return to their bivouac before morning light. The force assembled in the nullah west of Büyükli, about $2\frac{1}{2}$ miles from its objective, at 8.15 p.m., and 15 minutes later began its deployment at the head of the nullah, east of The Commandant. It was followed by its first-line transport, for which there would be ample cover in the ravine south of Horsehoe Hill when that was captured. As the works on the hill—known as " C.1," " C.2," and " C.3 "—appeared to have been practically destroyed already, it was decided not to give the enemy warning by any unusually heavy artillery fire previous to the assault.

The force advanced in two columns, the right under the second-in-command, Major F. Debenham, against C.3 on the eastern side of the horseshoe, the left, under the commanding officer, Lieut.-Colonel A. T. Robinson, moving across Kidney Hill against C.1 on the western.[1] The fighting companies of each were subsequently to capture C.2 in the centre. The two flank positions were captured at 10.40 p.m., but there was fierce resistance with bomb and rifle from C.2, where the enemy was more strongly entrenched than had appeared, and the attack here was beaten off. Having ascertained the situation, Lieut.-Colonel Robinson accepted Br.-General Duncan's offer of artillery assistance, and it was arranged that the CXV Brigade R.F.A. should bombard C.2 while a renewed attack, with the assistance of another company, was prepared. This time the assault was succcessful, though the enemy defended himself stoutly before making off in the darkness. Horseshoe Hill was

---

[1] Right Column :—" B " Company (fully equipped), regimental transport escorted by half " C " Company, battalion Lewis guns, 4 machine guns, 2 sections R.E.; Left Column :—" A " Company (fully equipped), " D " and half " C " Company (in fighting order and carrying tools).

heavily shelled during the following day, and two counter-attacks—the second a very determined one—were made against C.2 in the early hours of the 19th. When the battalion was relieved that night it had suffered 105 casualties. The French attack on the Petit Couronné was postponed.

Sketch 5.   Meanwhile, during the period that negotiations between Rumania and the Allies had dragged on, General Sarrail had directed General Cordonnier, who had now assumed command of the Armée Française d'Orient, to make demonstrations on other parts of the front, especially in face of the Belašica Planina. Here the 57th Division occupied several of the villages north of the railway line and beat off a counter-attack on Gornje Poröi. On the left bank of the Struma the detachment of General Frotiée, which had concentrated about Seres, pushed out mounted reconnaissances towards Drama.[1] West of the Vardar the troops were still behindhand with their preparations, but were making some progress. It was General Sarrail's intention that the 17th Colonial Division should continue its attacks and capture the Petit Couronné.

General Milne had still not been shown a way out of his perplexities. He had carried out the little affair at Horseshoe Hill because he could not leave the French left in the air, but it was evident that he was shortly to be called upon by General Sarrail to attempt much more serious enterprises, which were prohibited by his instructions from Whitehall. The fact of the matter was that General Joffre and General Robertson were at odds as to the interpretation to be put upon the formula: " The immediate objective of the " Salonika forces will be to contain the Bulgarian forces " so as to facilitate the action of the Rumanian Army " against Austria-Hungary." The British General Staff was determined that no action should be taken until Rumania was definitely committed to the war ; when she was committed the British Salonika Army would be allowed to co-operate with the French in containing the Bulgarian forces on the frontier ; but what amount of pressure would be necessary for that purpose it was left to General Milne to decide in consultation with General Sarrail. As he had a shrewd notion that General Sarrail's solution of the problem

---

[1] " Armées Françaises," Tome VIII, Vol. I, p. 532.

ALLIED FLANKS FORCED BACK 157

would not be acceptable to the British General Staff, his predicament was an awkward one.[1] The action of the enemy and General Sarrail's consequent change of plan were, as it happened, to make his path clearer.

1916.
17 Aug.

On the afternoon of the 18th August General Sarrail learnt that the military convention with Rumania had been signed and that by its terms the Allies were required to begin offensive action on the 20th. When, however, he received this information, he was considering another piece of news much less welcome. On the 17th the Bulgarian *First Army* made a swift advance along the Monastir-Salonika railway, driving in the Serbian posts. Next day part of the Serbian Danube Division counter-attacked in the neighbourhood of Banitsa, but encountered greatly superior Bulgarian forces and was driven back. On the same night the Bulgarian *Second Army* moved down the Constantinople railway from the direction of the Rupel Pass, surrounded Demir Hisar, and reached the outskirts of Bairakli Jum'a. The detachment of General Frotiée fell hurriedly back across the Struma, and patrols of the 7th Mounted Brigade, beyond Seres, were fortunate in being able to regain their lines. The Greeks made no resistance, and were perhaps incapable of doing so owing to their formations having been reduced to a peace footing and the serious deterioration of their troops, which General Mahon had noticed several months before and which had increased of late.

Map 7.

The advance of the Bulgarians on the flanks was undoubtedly a brilliant stroke. On the east there was every prospect that they would obtain their objective—the line of the Struma—without great trouble, and occupy eastern Greek Macedonia, which they desired as greatly as Serbian Macedonia. On the west they had already shortened their front; but here it was plain that they would not rest content with their gains. Both advances had the effect of interfering with the plans of General Sarrail, which they had more or less divined and which they knew had been framed with a view to Rumania's entry into the war.

For the moment, however, General Sarrail would not abandon his original projects. He ordered up the Vardar Division to reinforce the Serbian Third Army on the extreme

---

[1] See Note at end of Chapter.

left and instructed both the Serbian Chief of the Staff and General Cordonnier to carry out on the 20th the operations already planned.[1] The attack of the 17th Colonial Division on the Petit Couronné was, according to British information, to take place on the 21st. Meanwhile General Briggs, commanding the XVI Corps, had, in view of the weakness of his line on the Struma, ordered the 10th Division to concentrate in the neighbourhood of Lahana on the Seres road.

1916.
20 Aug.
On the 20th, however, affairs went badly on the flanks. General Frotiée, seriously ill with malaria, had been succeeded by Colonel Descoins, under whose orders the French detachment on the Struma recrossed the river. The French encountered greatly superior numbers of the enemy on the railway and fell back across the river at Orlyak in some confusion with a loss of about 300. Three squadrons of the 7th Mounted Brigade, which had crossed on the 19th, found Kumli and Bairakli Jum'a strongly held, and the Sherwood Rangers ran some risk of being cut off from Kopriva bridge by a body of the enemy who fired on the led horses at Ormanli. The detachment likewise withdrew across the Struma after dark, having had 24 casualties. On the other flank the Serbian Danube Division was heavily attacked at Banitsa on the afternoon of the 19th, and by the following evening had fallen back to the ridge west of Lake Ostrovo.[2]

In view of this situation General Sarrail summoned General Milne and the other Allied commanders to a conference on the 20th, and placed before them a new plan. He would now stand upon the defensive on the Struma and Vardar fronts, while attacking on the left flank. For this purpose he proposed to relieve his 57th Division by the Italian 35th Division and to despatch both the 57th and the Russian brigade to the extreme left, to assist the Serbians in holding up the enemy's advance and eventually to take part with them in an offensive. The commander of the Serbian Third Army, General Jurišić-Šturm, a veteran who had fought on the German side in 1870, was relieved of his post.

The first essential was to make secure the line of the Struma. It appeared that so far the Bulgarians had no more than advanced posts on the Constantinople railway

---

[1] " Armées Françaises," Tome VIII, Vol. I, p. 533.
[2] *Ibid.*, p. 535.

south-west of Drama, and it was therefore decided to make a bold attempt on the front of the 80th Brigade to destroy two railway bridges over the Angista River. For this purpose a party of six officers and 77 other ranks drawn from the divisional squadron of Surrey Yeomanry, the cyclists, and the 17th Field Company R.E., under the command of Captain G. F. Hall, R.E., moved out from Neohori bridge on the afternoon of the 20th, and at 6 a.m. the next morning blew up the railway bridge beyond Angista Station. Almost immediately afterwards a body of about 60 Bulgarians advanced on the station. It was, indeed, remarkable that the enemy was not actually guarding the bridge; for, though the British orders had been issued verbally, a large crowd of civilians had been found waiting to see the show. The Yeomanry and cyclists opened fire, while Captain Hall rode back to the other bridge south-west of the station and ordered the charges already placed in it to be fired. Unfortunately some of them did not explode; but a girder was cut sufficiently to prevent the passage of a train. The party then retired without pursuit, having had one officer and one sapper slightly wounded.

1916.
21 Aug.

This was satisfactory so far as it went, but General Milne desired that road bridges also should be destroyed. He telegraphed direct to the 80th Brigade to that effect, leaving it to the judgment of Br.-General A. C. Roberts whether the attempt should be made. This time a raid on a bigger scale was decided upon. A mixed force was formed under Major A. F. C. Maclachlan, 3/K.R.R.C., consisting of a troop of Surrey Yeomanry, four sections of mounted infantry (each of one officer and 20 men, drawn from each of the four battalions), two platoons of cyclists, and a demolition party of the 17th Field Company R.E. under Captain Hall. In support was a covering force under Lieut.-Colonel W. J. Long, 3/K.R.R.C., consisting of that battalion and two guns of the 99th Battery R.F.A., which was to take up a position at Zdravik, about half way between Neohori and Angista. Beginning with three wooden road bridges over the Angista River near Zdravik, the mixed force was then to destroy another at Vulchista. It had originally been intended then to complete the work begun at Angista, if that were possible, but the project had been abandoned, as the place was now occupied and surprise was impossible.

Marching out from Neohori bridge at 3 a.m. on the

1916.
23 Aug.
23rd, both forces reached Zdravik at 7.30 a.m. The " New " bridge and Kozaki bridge were burnt simultaneously, but the party engaged in the latter task came under machine-gun fire. The enemy had crossed the river at Vulchista, and another body of at least two battalions with two guns was seen moving out of Rahovo. It therefore appeared impossible to press on to the bridge at Vulchista. However, while the enemy was engaged at Zdravik, a demolition party with an escort of mounted infantry slipped off unobserved and completely destroyed the " Old " bridge, downstream from the two already dealt with. The whole force returned that evening to Neohori, having had only two casualties.

Meanwhile General Milne had despatched the 143rd and 153rd Heavy Batteries from the Vardar front to the Struma, and the 31st Brigade of the 10th Division had moved to Paprat, eight miles north-west of Lahana, being placed under the orders of the 28th Division and prepared to support its line on the Struma if necessary. General Sarrail desired that the Zouaves of the detachment of Colonel Descoins (now on the Struma between Ahinos and Sakavcha) should be relieved for employment on the left flank. On the night of the 26th, therefore, the 29th and 30th Brigades of the 10th Division—of which the 29th, owing to sickness, had been reduced to a composite battalion —relieved the French on the important part of the front between Gudeli bridge and Sakavcha. This left the French, now consisting of two regiments of cavalry, one battery, and an Annamite battalion, covering the marshy area between Ahinos and Gudeli bridge. The 31st Brigade was returned to Major-General Longley and moved into reserve behind his front.[1] The 81st Brigade (less two battalions) and the I Brigade R.F.A. formed the corps reserve on the Seres road, the other two battalions being at the disposal of the 28th Division. The 82nd Brigade was in Army reserve, with two battalions on the Ortach plateau and two at Güvezne. The 7th Mounted Brigade was at Kopazi, south-west of Gudeli bridge.

---

[1] The front of the XVI Corps was now therefore held as follows :—From the sea to Ahinos, 80th Brigade of 27th Division ; Ahinos to Gudeli, detachment of Colonel Descoins ; Gudeli to Sakavcha, 29th and 30th Brigades of 10th Division ; Sakavcha to Butkovo village, 84th, 83rd, and 85th Brigades of 28th Division.

END OF THE ADVANCE

On this flank the Bulgarians were inactive. On the Struma above Lake Tahinos their advanced troops began to dig in close to the left bank. Below the lake they moved in leisurely fashion down towards the coast, occupying on the 24th the villages of Provishta and Semaltos, where they were bombarded by the monitor *Sir Thomas Picton*. Further east they advanced to Kavalla. They did not at first occupy the town, but on the 24th the Greek commander, Colonel Hadzapoulos, handed over to them all the northern forts, having first removed the breech-blocks of the guns.

1916. Aug.

Between the British XVI and XII Corps the Italians relieved the French 57th Division by the 27th August. To set free another French division for employment west of the Vardar, General Milne ordered the XII Corps to extend its left to the river. For this purpose the 22nd Division evacuated the Gola–Kilinder ridge on the night of the 27th; and on the 29th its 67th Brigade relieved the troops of the French 122nd Division (on the left of the British 26th Division) to the left bank of the Vardar southwest of Machukovo.[1] The 65th Brigade was placed in divisional reserve further down the Vardar at Oreovitsa, and the 66th Brigade in corps reserve at Mihalova, behind the point of junction of the two divisions.

Out on the left flank in the neighbourhood of Florina the situation had by the end of August been stabilized. The first onrush of the Bulgarians had undoubtedly taken the Serbians by surprise, and the result had for the moment been disquieting. News of a " great Bulgarian victory " had, as was natural, been flashed over Europe, and had caused a good deal of anxiety and misapprehension at Bucharest. It was satisfactory, therefore, to find that the morale of the Serbians was quite sound and that as soon as infantry and artillery in sufficient numbers could be brought up they repulsed their old enemy coolly and without trouble. Evidently there was no more to be feared in this quarter.

---

[1] The front from the left of the XVI Corps to the Vardar was thus held as follows:—From Butkovo to the shore of Lake Dojran, Italian 35th Division; round the southern shore of the lake to La Tortue, 17th Colonial Division; from Horseshoe Hill to near the Piton Boisé (northwest of Reseli), 26th Division; from the Piton Boisé to the Vardar, 22nd Division.

BRITISH HOLDING OPERATIONS—THE ACTION OF
MACHUKOVO.

Maps A, 7.   General Milne had received the reinforcements in heavy artillery which he had been promised and distributed them between his two corps.[1] He was now ready to do what he could to assist the offensive on the left flank, which General Sarrail was preparing to undertake with Serbian, French, and Russian troops. First of all, on the 5th September, to enable another French brigade to be sent west of the Vardar, he ordered the XII Corps to extend its front half a mile to the east.[2] On the same day he ordered General Briggs, commanding the XVI Corps, to make preparations for vigorous demonstrations on the Struma front with the object of preventing the withdrawal thence of Bulgarian troops.

Now began a long period of British pressure upon the enemy, on both Dojran and Struma fronts, effected by operations ranging from quite small raids or mere feints to attacks made by a whole division and with the object of holding the ground won. They did not wholly succeed in their object of pinning down all the Bulgarian troops on the British fronts and preventing any from being transferred to the Monastir area; nor did they fully satisfy General Sarrail. So far as could be judged, however, they prevented a much larger transfer from being carried out and inflicted heavy loss upon the enemy. In any case they represented all that the British Army commander felt to be justified by his resources and instructions. Some of them were costly in proportion to their size, and the total casualty

---

[1] When moves ordered on the 3rd and 6th September had been completed, the heavy artillery was distributed as follows:—XII Corps: XXXVII Heavy Artillery Group, consisting of the 130th, 132nd, 134th, and 138th Siege Batteries and one section 127th Siege Battery (all 6-inch howitzer); and LXI Heavy Artillery Group, consisting of the 13th, 18th, and 20th Heavy Batteries (60-pdr.) and 43rd Siege Battery (three 6-inch guns). XVI Corps: XX Heavy Artillery Group, consisting of the 143rd and 153rd Heavy Batteries (60-pdr.) and 127th Siege Battery, less one section (6-inch howitzer). The 60-pdrs. were horse-drawn, the 6-inch howitzers had mechanical wheel transport, and the 6-inch guns were tractor-drawn, with mechanical wheel transport for ammunition.

[2] General Sarrail had hitherto left one brigade of the French 57th Division in reserve to the Italians, who had relieved that division in the line. He now desired to move this brigade west of the Vardar and replace it by one of the 17th Colonial Division, the front of which it was therefore necessary to shorten. The additional frontage was taken over by the 26th Division.

list incurred in them was high. All were carried out with difficulty. Unfortunately the XVI Corps, which was not faced by strong entrenchments and had room to manœuvre, had to depend for communications on the Seres road—except for a very small proportion of its troops at the mouth of the Struma—and the distance from Salonika to Orlyak was 44 miles. On the other hand, the XII Corps, which had the Dojran railway for its supplies, was faced by almost impregnable positions between Lake Dojran and the Vardar.

1916. Sept.

During the first few days of September there were only minor affairs of patrols on the fronts of both corps, but the artillery on both sides was active in the neighbourhood of Lake Dojran. Learning on the 6th from General Sarrail that the offensive on the left flank would probably begin on the 12th, and two days later, that the Bulgarians had gained a success in Southern Rumania, General Milne ordered General Wilson to commence a slow bombardment at once and on the 11th to bombard systematically the Machukovo salient on the left bank of the Vardar. He told General Briggs that the series of demonstrations would have to begin on the 10th and urged him to make his action as energetic as possible.

The operation conceived by General Briggs was in the nature of a series of raids on a very large scale. The chief effort was to be made above Lake Tahinos, where the 10th Division was to capture the villages of Karajaköi Bala, Karajaköi Zir, and Yeniköi; and the 28th Division Nevolyen. The 27th Division on the lower Struma was ordered to carry out a similar attack with naval support, the choice of objectives being left to Major-General Marshall. Between them the 7th Mounted Brigade and the detachment of Colonel Descoins [1] were also to cross the river. The infantry was in each case to be withdrawn across the Struma after dark.

10 Sept.

On the front of the 27th Division, the 80th Brigade

---

[1] There had been a slight readjustment of the line, the frontage of the detachment of Colonel Descoins having been shortened owing to the withdrawal from him of further troops, and he had been relieved by the 82nd Brigade (less two battalions) west of Ahinos. The 27th Division now held from the mouth of the Struma to the ford at Bairaktar (three miles beyond its old left flank at Ahinos), Colonel Descoins thence to Suhabanya, and the 7th Mounted Brigade thence to Gudeli, where it was in touch with the 10th Division.

pushed out two battalions from the Neohori bridgehead; but the enemy, who had on this part of the front only small posts in the forward zone, fled so hastily that, though the British troops advanced over a mile from their wire, it was impossible to make contact with him. The 82nd Brigade despatched a patrol across the ford at Bairaktar, which drove back an enemy post and burnt the hamlet of Kara Orman in the midst of the marsh. The French crossed opposite Fitoki and reached the outskirts of Yeni Mahale, two miles from the bank. On their left the 7th Mounted Brigade put a dismounted party across in boats and rafts, which drove back small posts of the enemy encountered in the scrub and reached Kato Gudeli. This party suffered only a single casualty, though, owing to a raft breaking adrift, some of the yeomen had on their return to swim the river, under fire from Bulgarians who had followed up under cover of the scrub.

On the front of the 10th Division the whole of the 31st Brigade (Br.-General E. M. Morris), with the exception of two companies of the 5/R. Irish Fusiliers, crossed the Struma by a hastily-thrown footbridge, ferries, and fords, and by 2.30 p.m. was established in a wood on the left bank, covered by three battalions of the 30th Brigade, which had crossed without opposition the previous night and dug themselves in. The advance began at 3 p.m., one battalion attacking each village, and was supported by four batteries of the 10th Divisional Artillery, as well as by the heavy artillery and certain batteries of the neighbouring 28th Division. All three battalions were held up short of their objectives by heavy fire, and were withdrawn to the fords after dark, unobserved by the enemy, having suffered 129 casualties. This was the first test of the reorganized 10th Division, and, so far as the battalions engaged were concerned, gave satisfactory proof of steadiness and discipline.

The operation against Nevolyen by the 2/Northumberland Fusiliers of the 84th Brigade (Br.-General G. A. Weir) was more successful. This battalion, under the command of Lieut.-Colonel A. C. L. Hardman-Jones, began its crossing below Turbes Island at 11.30 a.m. The troops for the most part waded over, two rafts prepared by the 1/7th Hampshire Field Company R.E. being chiefly intended for bringing back the wounded. At 2.45 p.m. the crossing had been completed unseen, and a company of the 2/Cheshire

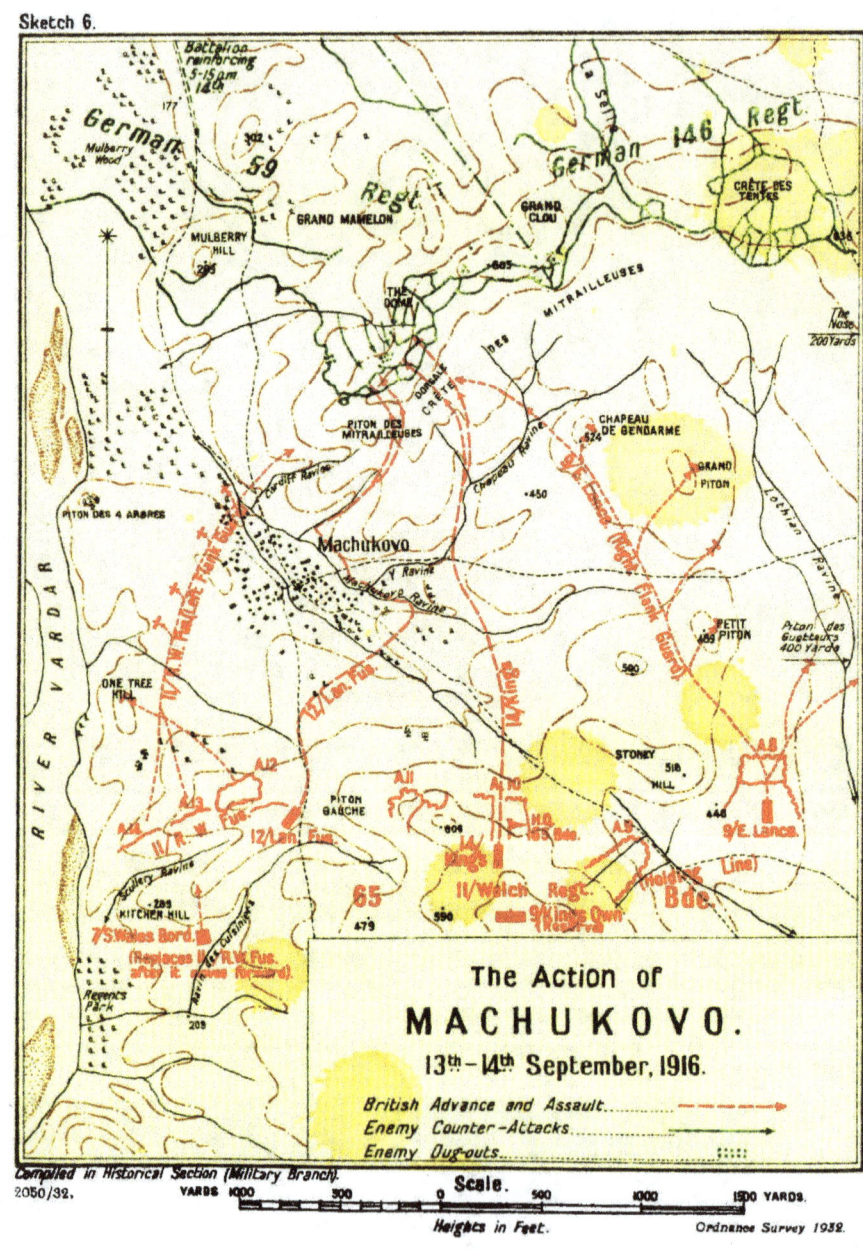

had crossed above the island to protect the flank. Nevolyen lay 2,000 yards from the river, but the ground for the first thousand yards was under a crop of high-growing maize, through which the troops moved without drawing fire. Faced by the remaining stretch of perfectly open ground, the battalion signalled at 4.15 p.m. for artillery fire to be opened. Batteries of the 28th Divisional Artillery at once opened fire on Nevolyen, while the heavy artillery engaged batteries of the enemy which had now come into action. The battalion advanced with admirable steadiness, its attack being clearly visible to Generals Milne and Briggs from the hills overlooking the valley. The centre of the village was reached just before 5 p.m., 30 prisoners being captured and sent back over the Struma, while the rest of the garrison abandoned its trenches and made off. Within half an hour a Bulgarian counter-attack against the southeast end of the village developed, and a few minutes later two battalions were seen moving down from the direction of Kalendra. By 6 p.m. the enemy was in the northern part of Nevolyen, where some close fighting took place and the Northumberland Fusiliers had a number of men captured. The battalion then fell back, and the artillery, giving it time to get clear, opened so accurate a fire on the enemy when he attempted to pursue that he was driven back into the village. The withdrawal across the Struma began at 7.40 p.m. and was carried out without interruption from the Bulgarians. The total casualties, of which all but five were in the Northumberland Fusiliers, were 124, including four officers (all known to be wounded) and 37 rank and file missing. It was thought, however, that the enemy, who was frequently caught in the open by the British artillery, had suffered more heavily.

If any evidence was wanted that the fighting qualities of the Bulgarians were not to be lightly estimated, it had been provided here. The attack on Nevolyen had been timed to give them the shortest possible warning and to make it difficult for them to organize a serious counter-attack before the fall of darkness. They had organized their counter-attack and they had pressed it resolutely in face of heavy fire. On the wooded and roadless parts of their line on the Struma they might allow raiding parties to penetrate a considerable distance beyond the bank; but it was clear that any enterprise in the neighbourhood of Orlyak bridge, where the Seres road crossed the river, would meet with determined opposition.

On the 11th September the artillery of the XII Corps began its bombardment. On the 12th General Sarrail began his offensive on the left flank. On the 15th a series of demonstrations across the Struma above Lake Tahinos was carried out by the XVI Corps. Small detachments of the 2/R. Irish Fusiliers (82nd Brigade) and French troops crossed at Bairaktar ford and advanced on Kara Orman and Yeni Mahale, respectively. The 7th Mounted Brigade sent its temporary composite regiment of Derbyshire Yeomanry and Lothians and Border Horse,[1] dismounted, across at Gudeli ferry, and with very little opposition reached the hamlets of Ano and Kato Gudeli, both of which were destroyed. Two and a half companies of the composite battalion of the 29th Brigade,[2] under the orders of Major W. C. Garsia, crossed at Chasseur Island and carried the village of Jami Mahale after some fighting, suffering 14 casualties. The remainder of the battalion, under Lieut.-Colonel J. D. M. Beckett, captured Komaryan, with 25 prisoners, assisted by a small demonstration by the 30th Brigade on the left. The 84th Brigade constructed a dummy bridge opposite Nevolyen, which drew some fire. The casualty list was only 28. A similar demonstration on the 23rd met with rather more resistance, the British casualties being exactly one hundred. On this occasion, however, the Bulgarians appeared to have suffered far greater loss, and 16 prisoners were taken by the French detachment.

During the same period raids were made by the Italians, who had some heavy fighting and from whom the Bulgarians claim to have captured 87 prisoners on the 12th.

Sketch 6. On the front of the British XII Corps the 65th Brigade (Br.-General L. N. Herbert) carried out an important operation on the night of the 13th against the Piton des Mitrailleuses and the Dorsale, north of Machukovo. It was on this occasion intended to hold the ground won. The 22nd Divisional Artillery had begun wire-cutting on the afternoon of the 12th, and on the 13th an artillery preparation had been carried out all day, including further wire-cutting, fire on the enemy's works by 4·5-inch and

---

[1] See p. 144.   [2] See p. 160.

THE ACTION OF MACHUKOVO 167

6-inch howitzers, and counter-battery fire by the LXI Heavy Group near Kalinova and French heavy artillery from the other bank of the Vardar. The 12/Lancashire Fusiliers and 14/King's, under the orders of Lieut.-Colonel W. J. Lambert of the latter battalion, moved out from the British wire at 7.30 p.m. and assembled in a gully at the south-east corner of Machukovo. The 9/East Lancashire, acting as right flank guard, moved out two hours later to take up a position from the British post on the Piton des Guetteurs to the Chapeau de Gendarme, which was subsequently to be consolidated and to form the new front line. The 11/R. Welch Fusiliers (detached from the 67th Brigade), detailed to cover and prolong the left flank in similar fashion, established itself from the northern outskirts of the village to One Tree Hill, overlooking the Vardar. The 9/King's Own was held in reserve and was to provide carrying parties.

1916.
13 Sept.

Having sent forward strong patrols to ascertain that the enemy's wire was well cut, the 14/King's advanced to the assault of the Dorsale and the 12/Lancashire Fusiliers to that of the Piton des Mitrailleuses, the artillery lifting off the objective at 2 a.m. on the 14th. There was some resistance, but the position was quickly carried, and parties of bombers dashed through the trenches, summoning forth the occupants of the dugouts and throwing bombs in when they refused to obey. About 7 a.m. the enemy opened heavy artillery fire on his lost position from three sides. As the day wore on, machine-gunners on the Dome, whom not all the efforts of the British heavy artillery could drive off it, also galled the attackers with enfilade fire. Just after 2 p.m. a determined counter-attack was launched. It was beaten off ; but the losses of the 14/King's on the right were too heavy to be endured, and the battalion was withdrawn at 3.20 p.m. to the lower slopes of the Dorsale. The Fusiliers temporarily lost the Piton, but retook it by a counter-attack, and succeeded in blocking the trenches leading to the Dorsale. At 4 p.m., however, the battalion also withdrew to the south-west side of the hill ; and, recognizing that the enemy's enfilade fire made the whole position untenable, Major-General Gordon at 4.35 p.m. ordered a withdrawal to the original line to commence at dusk.

14 Sept.

Br.-General Herbert had previously, at 3.20 p.m., ordered the 9/East Lancashire to reinforce the right on the

Dorsale, and that battalion began to move forward at almost the same moment as the order to abandon the position was received by the brigade. Its advance in artillery formation, over open ground and in face of heavy fire, was carried out with the steadiness of a movement on the parade ground, and it rendered invaluable service by supporting the King's and then covering the withdrawal.

Before, however, that withdrawal had taken place, one of the 18-pdr. batteries was given an opportunity of an extraordinary kind, the quick seizure of which may well have been of vital importance to the infantry. Major C. T. Lawrence, commanding A/XCIX, had been ordered to watch the approaches down the Vardar valley. At 5.15 p.m. he suddenly saw through his glasses a Bulgarian battalion marching in fours into Mulberry Wood. Opening rapid fire at 4,000 yards, he dispersed the leading company, and then, when the rest of the battalion had lain down, raked it backwards and forwards with low-bursting shrapnel. A French 75-mm. battery from beyond the Vardar presently joined in, and at the end of 15 minutes the three rear companies of the battalion appeared to have been completely destroyed, not a man being seen to run back.

The artillery also covered the infantry withdrawal with great effect. The enemy made an attempt to follow up, but so fierce was the British barrage laid on the crest—from which the Lancashire Fusiliers and King's had retired a bare 50 yards—that the Germans who had lined it were at once driven to ground.[1] The remnants of the two British battalions were back in their own lines by 10 p.m.

About 70 prisoners,[2] all belonging to the German *59th Regiment*, and nine machine guns were captured, and a number of trench mortars were destroyed. Considerable numbers of the enemy were killed with bomb and rifle in the trenches, and his casualties from artillery fire must also have been heavy. But the losses of the attackers were also severe in all battalions except the Welch Fusiliers, the total being 586. The seriousness of this loss can be realized only if the weakness of the battalions owing to malaria

---

[1] There is an excellent account of the action from the artillery point of view, and especially of the incident recorded concerning A/XCIX Battery, in *The Gunner*, I, No. 2, the article being entitled "Lorenzo's Coup."

[2] Forty-three unwounded prisoners were brought in; the exact number of wounded is not recorded, but it was between 25 and 30.

be taken into account. The other three battalions must have had about 50 per cent of the numbers engaged— about 350 each—put out of action. The enterprise had been well planned, well led, and gallantly executed. The artillery had done its wire-cutting work thoroughly, though it had had little effect upon the excellent dugouts constructed by the Germans. After this experience it would have been over-sanguine to expect that any large operation upon this heavily-fortified front could be carried out without very heavy losses. While keeping up pressure by means of bombardments, raids, and demonstrations, General Milne made for a long time to come no further call upon the XII Corps for any operation of this scope. The Struma front might be costly enough; it was unlikely to be so expensive as this.

1916.
14 Sept.

NOTE.

TELEGRAMS BETWEEN GENERAL MILNE AND THE C.I.G.S.

From—C.I.G.S.
To—A.H.Q., Salonika.
21254 cipher.   5th August 1916.

The question of Rumania's intervention has not yet been settled, but apparently she will not at present declare war against any Power except Austria-Hungary. The Entente Powers are now more or less prepared to accept this, and if it is finally accepted and after we are satisfied that Rumania has definitely entered the war and will make an effective attack on Austria-Hungary, your rôle will be to co-operate with Sarrail for the sole purpose of holding the Bulgarian forces on the Greek frontier. A counter-draft prepared by Rumania has replaced the Paris draft Military Convention of the 23rd July referred to in my telegram from Paris of the same date. We have not yet seen the Rumanian draft, but the point indicated in the first sentence above is apparently the main point affecting us.

From—A.H.Q., Salonika.
To—C.I.G.S.
G.C. 444.   14th August 1916.

From what I gather from Sarrail, he intends, if Rumania declares war even on Austria-Hungary, to attack the Bulgarians on our front. This action seems in excess of that laid down in the instructions contained in 20095 cipher, though it appears more in accordance with General Joffre's instructions to Sarrail, where, in order to fulfil the first mission of the Allied Armies, *viz*, to cover mobilization of Rumanian Army, it is laid down that the English Army will not confine itself to demonstrations but will attack in the zone allotted to it. This Army therefore seems to be under obligation to attack in order to hold Bulgarians, even should Rumania not cross the Danube, though unfortunately the heavy howitzers have not yet arrived. Pending further instructions, I am guarding against being committed to anything serious, but as the French are pressing on it is difficult to hang back, and Sarrail is anxious to settle plan to-morrow, Tuesday, if possible. Trust that if convention is signed I may have early instructions as basis of discussion with Sarrail. Reference 21427 cipher, am not clear what underlies the necessity of operations commencing three days after the signing of the Convention.

From—Chief, London.
To—A.H.Q., Salonika.
21621 cipher.   15th August 1916.

Your G.C. 444. Approval is not and never has been given by H.M's. Government to our troops' being committed to offensive action until they are satisfied that Rumania has definitely joined the Entente. I will at once inform you when they are so satisfied, but you are not to commit your troops to offensive action meanwhile. There is no probability, as you have already been informed, of Rumania declaring war except against Austria-Hungary, and it has been decided therefore, *vide* my 21427 of 10th instant, that the Salonika forces will have for their immediate objective the containing of the Bulgarian forces so as to facilitate the action against Austria-Hungary of the Rumanian Army. This would be without prejudice to any further objectives which may present themselves for consideration later, having regard to available resources, including transport. The reason why operations are commenced three days after Convention is to ensure that pressure on Bulgarians opposing Salonika forces is brought to bear in sufficient time to prevent Rumania being interfered with by Bulgaria before she is ready. The amount of force required to achieve the immediate objective above mentioned and the action to be taken is a matter for agreement between Sarrail and you.

From—A.H.Q., Salonika.
To—Chief, London.
G.C. 456.   16th August 1916.

French on our right have advanced this morning, and now hold from Point 238 [otherwise known as Hill 227] south of Dojran Lake to Doljeli village inclusive, their left at Doljeli being reported about 1,200 yards in front of our advanced post referred to in my G.C. 437 of 12th August [Kidney Hill]. They intend to push forward their right and centre to-morrow, and in order not to leave their left in the air I feel I must push forward to maintain connection. I impressed upon Sarrail yesterday the advisability of going slowly, but their successful advance to-day was unexpected, casualties being only six.
Your 21621 cipher received, and I have explained to Sarrail the limits of my instructions. Milne.

From—C.I.G.S.
To—A.H.Q., Salonika.
21697 cipher.   17th August 1916.

It is reported by the British Minister Bucharest that the Military and Political Conventions with Rumania will be signed on August 18th. The Salonika offensive is to begin on August 20th according to Military Convention, and on August 28th Rumania will declare war on Austria. As soon as I hear that the Convention has been signed I will let you know at once.

From—C.I.G.S.
To—Headquarters Salonika Army.
No. 21758.   19th August 1916.

My 21697 of 17th August. Political and Military Conventions have now been signed by Rumania, and latter will declare war on 28th August on Austria-Hungary, but not on any other Power. As stated in my telegram

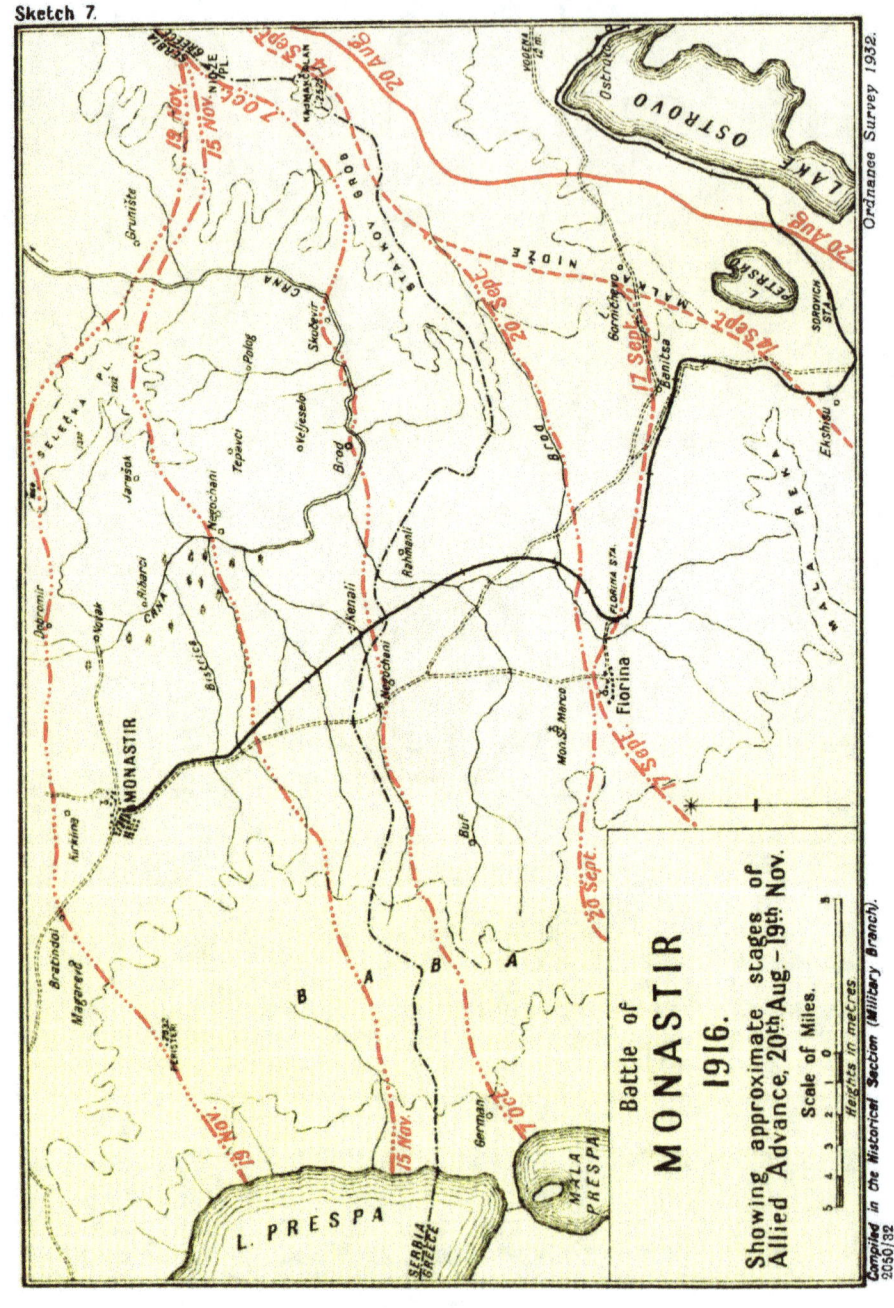

No. 21621 of 15th August and as agreed between the British and French Governments, the immediate objective of all Allied forces at Salonika will be to contain the Bulgarian forces so as to facilitate the action of the Rumanian Army against Austria-Hungary, without prejudice to any further objectives which may present themselves for consideration later, having regard to available resources, including transport. Your mission will be to support and co-operate with General Sarrail in gaining the above objective, the amount of force required and the action to be taken being a matter of arrangement between you and him. My 19962 of 25th July [1] defined your status with reference to General Sarrail, and this remains unchanged.

---

[1] See p. 150.

CHAPTER IX.

THE MONASTIR OFFENSIVE AND THE RUMANIAN CAMPAIGN.

(Maps A, 1, 2, 8; Sketches 6, 7, 8, 9.)

THE ACTION OF THE KARAJAKÖIS AND CAPTURE OF YENIKÖI.

Maps A, 2. ONE result of the more active operations in which the British were now engaged was the decision to sever the last tie between Egypt and Salonika. On the 21st September the War Office telegraphed that in future the British Salonika Army should not be under the control of the Commander-in-Chief in Egypt for administrative purposes. Alexandria was, however, to remain the principal base for the forces in the Mediterranean, and demands were to be made through General Headquarters in Egypt in order to avoid reference to the War Office if possible. So far as the organization of shipping permitted, reinforcements, munitions, and stores provided from sources outside Egypt would be sent direct to Salonika. The change was welcome to General Milne. When questions so complicated as the change-over to a pack-transport basis, for example, were being discussed, it was obviously impossible for a staff in another theatre of war to master all their details. Such business had in the end to be thrashed out between Whitehall and Salonika, and the intervention of Egypt could mean little more than that the telegrams on the subject were duplicated. The other defects of that system have already been discussed.

News from the battle-front in the neighbourhood of Florina soon compelled General Milne to call upon the XVI Corps for another effort. On the 26th September he telegraphed that Bulgarian troops had been withdrawn from its front, as well as that of the XII Corps, to oppose the French and Serbians, and that every endeavour must be made to prevent the continuance of this movement. He therefore directed General Briggs to prepare for an early offensive, and suggested an attack in the direction of Seres, any ground won being retained. To achieve the result desired the operation would have to be protracted but continuous. He promised to send the XXXVII Heavy

THE ENEMY REINFORCES HIS RIGHT 173

Artillery Group, with three 6-inch howitzer batteries,[1] to the Struma valley.

1916. Sept.

The French and British Intelligence Services had, indeed, discovered an important movement westward of Bulgarian troops. Three regiments of the *2nd Division* (the *21st, 27th,* and *43rd*) and two of the *9th Division* (the *33rd* and *58th*) had apparently been identified west of the Vardar, and their transfer was subsequently proved to have taken place. There was even some likelihood that the *17th* and *57th Regiments* of the *9th Division* had moved in the same direction; but this was happily found not to be the case. The German *45th Regiment* and some regiments of the Bulgarian *6th Division* had gone to the Dobruja immediately after Rumania's declaration of war. General Milne could not know, though he had reason to fear, that other German troops were about to be transferred from the Dojran to the Monastir front. As a fact, two battalions of the *146th Regiment* began to move on the 10th October, leaving only four German battalions, one of the *146th* and three of the *59th*, between Lake Dojran and the Vardar.[2]

General Briggs decided to begin his operations by capturing and holding the villages of Karajaköi Bala and Karajaköi Zir. Owing to the weakness of the 10th Division, due mainly to malaria but also in some measure to the lack of recruits from Ireland, he entrusted the task to the 27th Division, to which he lent the 29th Infantry Brigade and two field artillery brigades of the 10th Division,[3] and the Argyll Mountain Battery. He also returned to the 27th Division the 81st Infantry Brigade, from corps reserve. The 27th Division was now commanded by Major-General H. S. L. Ravenshaw, formerly commanding the 83rd Brigade of the 28th Division, Major-General Marshall having left on the 14th September on appointment to the command of

---

[1] One section of the 127th Siege Battery was already present, so actually two and a half batteries were sent. The only other heavy artillery available consisted of the 143rd and 153rd Heavy Batteries.

[2] " Das 1. Masurische Infanterie-Regiment Nr. 146," p. 163.

[3] The LIV and LXVIII Brigades R.F.A., grouped under the command of Lieut.-Colonel A. R. Hudson of the LXVIII, were allotted to the attack on Karajaköi Bala. As the attack was carried out on the frontage covered by the 10th Division, the other two brigades were available to support it also, the LVII to cover the left and the subsequent advance on Karajaköi Zir, and the LXVII to watch the right. For the same reason the 27th Division had only one field artillery brigade, the I, available. The 28th Divisional Artillery was not to take part in the preliminary bombardment, but was to be prepared to protect the left of the attack.

an army corps in Mesopotamia. Major-General Ravenshaw decided to carry out the main attack with the 81st Brigade (Br.-General B. F. Widdrington). The 82nd Brigade (Br.-General C. R. I. Brooke), less two battalions, was to act as a reserve under Br.-General Widdrington's orders. The 29th Brigade (Br.-General R. S. Vandeleur) was to protect both flanks.[1]

The orders came at an awkward moment for the 27th Division, which was in process of transferring its advanced headquarters from the Rendina Gorge (behind the front of the 80th Brigade on the lower Struma) to the Seres road, where the XVI Corps also had an advanced headquarters. Moreover, the C.R.A., C.R.E., and the O.C. Signals were engaged in tours of inspection on the lower Struma, and on this enormous front it was impossible to get them back in time to make the necessary preparations, though they arrived before the attack was launched. The orders were actually communicated verbally by General Briggs to Br.-General Widdrington, and the latter had made his arrangements before the formal divisional order to which reference is made had been received. Major-General Ravenshaw hurriedly established a report centre near the advanced headquarters of the XVI Corps and asked for outside assistance. The XVI Corps provided signals personnel, and the 10th Division lent the services of its C.R.A. (Br.-General W. E. Emery) and C.R.E. (Lieut.-Colonel E. M. S. Charles), the former of whom commanded all the artillery placed under Major-General Ravenshaw's orders. As the crossing was to be carried out on the 10th Division's front, which these officers knew well, and as a large proportion of the force to be engaged belonged to that division, the temporary arrangement had its advantages.

Again, the 82nd Brigade, which was to be employed in reserve, had recently relieved the detachment of Colonel Descoins between Ahinos and Bairaktar. It now had to hand back this part of the front in some haste to the French, who had recently been reinforced by a Greek battalion, formed at Salonika by the adherents of M. Venizelos to assist the Allies and in opposition to the policy of the King of Greece. Two battalions, the 1/Royal Irish and 1/Leinster, were in Army reserve nearly 30 miles away, behind the

---

[1] 27th Division Order No. 40 is given in Appendix 6.

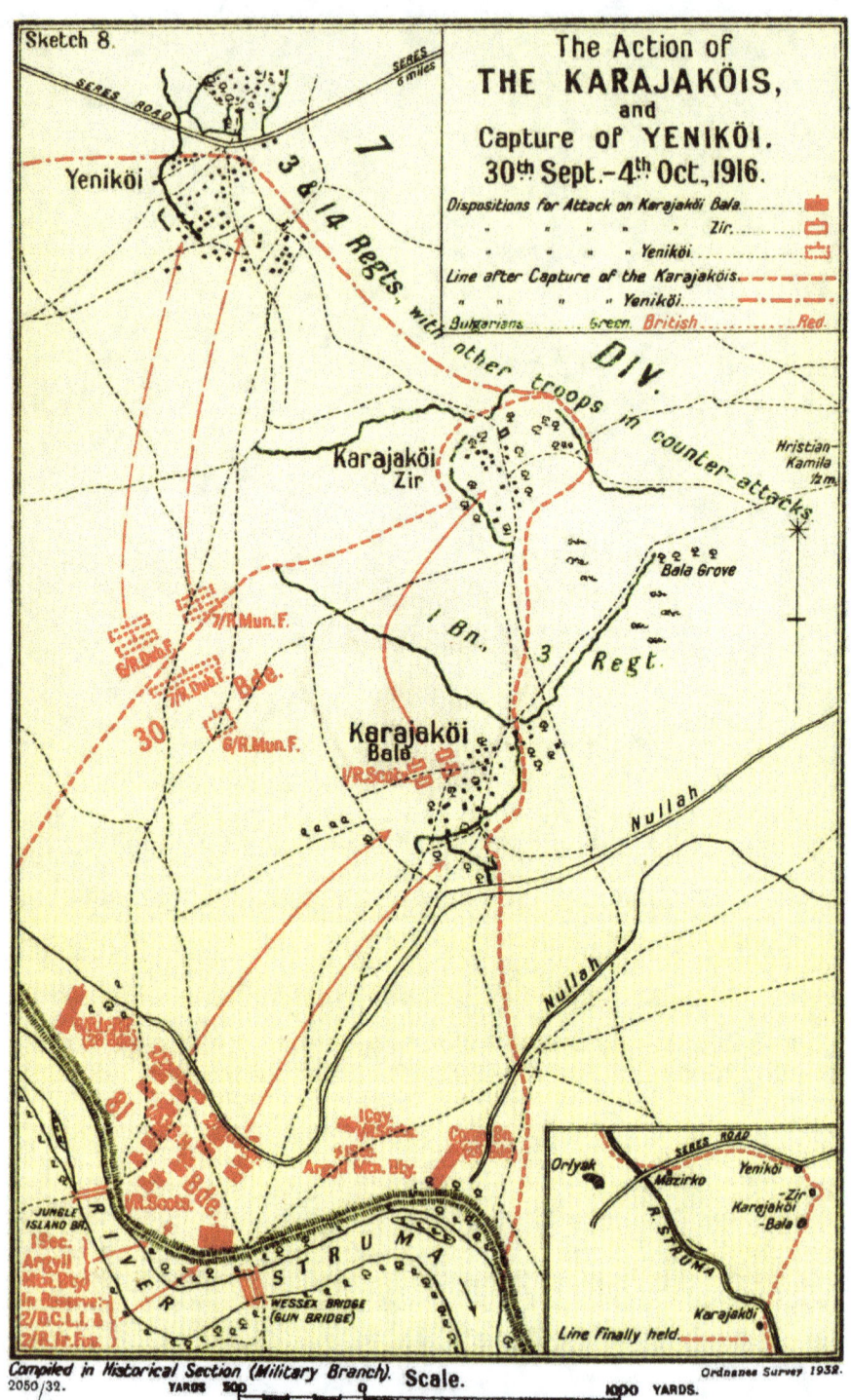

front of the XII Corps, and though General Milne gave permission for them to rejoin there was no possibility of their arrival during the early stages of the operation. The battalions of all the brigades varied greatly in strength, according to the incidence of malaria and the number of drafts they had recently received, but some could not muster more than about 250 rifles for the attack. The 29th Brigade had only two battalions, its original composite battalion and another made up of the 6/R. Irish Rifles and two companies of the 6/Leinster; but they were fairly strong.

1916. 30 Sept.

The field artillery belonging or attached to the 27th Division took up positions between Sakavcha and Orlyak bridge, the batteries being from 100 to 800 yards from the bank. Behind were the 6-inch howitzers of the XXXVII Heavy Group, on the lower slopes of the foot-hills west of Orlyak. Three bridges were constructed by the Royal Engineers of the 10th Division, one to take field artillery[1] and two footbridges. A gun-raft and ferries were also provided.

Map 8. Sketch 8.

During the foggy night of the 29th the 81st Brigade crossed the river, by the gun-bridge and one of the foot-bridges, and at 5.15 a.m. on the 30th had reached its position of deployment. The two battalions of the 29th Brigade followed, the composite battalion by the gun-bridge and the 6/R. Irish Rifles by the second footbridge, upstream at Jungle Island. The 81st Brigade formed up on a frontage of a thousand yards, 2/Gloucester on the right, 2/Cameron Highlanders on the left, 1/Argyll and Sutherland Highlanders in support, and 1/Royal Scots behind that battalion, with the exception of one company which was to act on the far side of an unfordable pond or nullah on the right flank, filled with rain-water. Each battalion was in four lines, the distance between the lines being 50 yards. The fourth line of the leading battalions carried picks and shovels. One section of the 81st Machine-Gun Company was attached to each of the four battalions except the 2/Cameron

---

[1] This was a good piece of work by the 66th Field Company. The company had at noon on the 27th finished a trestle footbridge 540 feet long. By noon on the 29th this had been converted to an artillery bridge, having been decked and strengthened; each trestle was now anchored on the upstream side to a wire cable, the transoms being dogged to the legs and chocks nailed under them. A screen of maize on each side hid movement on the bridge.

Highlanders, the fourth section being with the company of the 1/R. Scots which was to move on the far side of the nullah. To this company also was attached one section of the Argyll Mountain Battery, the rôle of this force being to take up a position on the south side of the nullah and bring enfilade fire to bear on Karajaköi Bala.

The valley of the Struma is here a flat stretch of black cotton soil, some nine miles broad. Apart from a few ditches, the villages, which generally contained groves of trees, represented almost the only cover. There had recently been standing crops, but these had now been in great part cut and removed, or in some cases left in stooks.

At 5.45 a.m. the bombardment began, that of the field artillery being directed against trenches on the southern and south-western outskirts of Karajaköi Bala, and thence along a line running north-westward; that of the heavy artillery over the whole front, its targets being trenches, dugouts, and buildings. At 6.20 a.m. the line went forward. The Gloucesters were checked by enfilade machine-gun fire, and halted until the artillery had been turned on to works on their right from which it was coming; meanwhile, after some delay, the half of the barrage in front of the Camerons was lifted, and at 7.50 a.m. this battalion entered the northern end of the village. Shortly afterwards the Gloucesters entered the southern part and the place was then quickly cleared. Wiring parties of the Royal Engineers, who had been standing by at the bridge with their carrying parties, at once went forward to consolidate this objective. The 2/R. Irish Fusiliers of the 82nd Brigade, which had remained at the bridge, was also ordered up to reinforce and assist in reversing the captured trenches. All had gone well so far, 87 prisoners having been captured and the British casualty list being small; but the hardest task was obviously ahead. Reports from the air showed that the enemy's reserves were astir; it appeared, in fact, that about six battalions were moving out from the villages of Kalendra and Prosenik on the railway line.

Br.-General Widdrington then ordered the 1/Argyll and Sutherland Highlanders, supported by the 1/Royal Scots, to attack Karajaköi Zir at 11.30 a.m. after a quarter of an hour's bombardment. Two companies of the Argylls debouched from the north-east corner of the village and carried a trench on their front, but soon afterwards came under heavy fire from an unlocated trench, concealed by crops, on their right flank. An attempt to capture this trench was made by the right company, but it came under enfilade fire, this time from Karajaköi Zir, as it faced to the flank, suffered heavy loss, and fell back to the shelter of the houses to reorganize. All efforts to continue the advance, whether across the open or by crawling up the sunken road connecting the two villages, were stopped by heavy machine-gun fire and were eventually abandoned.

1916.
30 Sept.

Major-General Ravenshaw now telephoned to Br.-General Widdrington and gave him the choice of continuing the attack that evening or carrying it out next morning. The brigadier chose the former alternative. He was at first of a mind to employ the Camerons, but, finding that this battalion could not be withdrawn in time from the position it had taken up for the defence of Karajaköi Bala, ordered the Royal Scots to take its place. Meanwhile every effort had been made to locate the trench on the right flank which had caused the failure of the first attack. Two forward observing officers got sight of it from the church steeple. It was then too late to register the guns, but six field batteries were directed on to it and ordered to search and sweep. Certain 6-inch howitzers also picked it up. All these guns were ordered to open intense fire at 4 p.m. and continue until ordered to stop. All other batteries available were ordered to concentrate their fire on Karajaköi Zir at the same hour, and to lift at 4.15 p.m. This bombardment was renewed at 5 p.m., as it was found necessary to postpone the attack for an hour.

At 5.15 p.m. the Royal Scots moved out from the sunken road leading south-westward from Karajaköi Bala, in four waves, each of a company, the pipers marching with the first wave and playing throughout the attack. The precision and steadiness of this advance over ground as flat as a table, visible as it was to so many eyes, brought back the spirit of earlier forms of warfare ; and one officer who was an onlooker has declared that the attack served " all who were privileged to witness it as a model for " emulation." The battalion at once came under rifle fire from a trench on its front—actually a continuation of that captured by the Argylls in the first attack—but kept on, crossed this trench, where 83 Bulgarians surrendered, wheeled right-handed, and entered Karajaköi Zir a quarter of an hour later. One company of the Camerons advanced simultaneously with the Royal Scots, on their right, and captured the north-east corner of the village. The remainder of the Camerons, who had been ordered to support the attack, followed shortly afterwards.

The enemy immediately launched a small counter-attack from the north-west, but was driven back without any difficulty. Five minutes later, about 5.50 p.m., a much heavier attack developed from the east, but was likewise broken up by artillery, machine-gun, and rifle fire, the Bulgarians being caught in the open and apparently suffering heavy loss. By 6.15 p.m. the enemy's fire had greatly diminished and it was possible to begin the consolidation of the position. For this purpose a dump of engineer stores had already been formed at Karajaköi Bala and carrying parties had been organized to bring them forward.

In the course of the night a wire entanglement was put up from the river bank to the nullah by two sections of the 66th Field Company R.E. of the 10th Division, and continued round Karajaköi Bala and in front of the sunken road between the villages by the 1/Wessex Field Company of the 27th Division. The remaining two sections of the 66th Field Company wired Karajaköi Zir, and the 65th Field Company put up some 4,000 yards of wire between the village and the Struma. The position was held by the 29th Composite Battalion from the river to the nullah, by the 2/Gloucester thence to the church of Karajaköi Bala, by the 1/Argyll and Sutherland Highlanders to the road fork half a mile north of the village, by the 2/Camerons to the outskirts of Karajaköi Zir, that village by the 1/Royal Scots, with one company of the Camerons in the north-east corner and one of the Argylls in the south-west; and by the 6/R. Irish Rifles to the river. The 2/R. Irish Fusiliers of the 82nd Brigade was in support to the 2/Gloucester, and the 2/D.C.L.I. remained in reserve at the bridge.

About 250 prisoners had been captured, with three machine guns. The casualties of the 81st Brigade were 364, there being so far few among the other infantry or the engineers.

It was a very dark night, and to reorganize the battalions, which were, as has been explained, somewhat mixed up at Karajaköi Zir, was inadvisable in face of the probability of a heavy counter-attack before morning. Companies therefore began to dig in as they stood. In fact, between 1 a.m. and 2 a.m. on the morning of the 1st October, only a few minutes after the wire fence had been completed, the enemy launched an attack on the whole front between the two villages. The Bulgarians showed great determination, coming on again and again in face of well-directed rifle and machine-gun fire and of an artillery barrage which was dropped 300 yards in front of the half-dug trenches. Nowhere did they penetrate the wire, and they presently gave up the attempt. The rest of the night was fairly quiet, with only intermittent shelling.

1916.
1 Oct.

About 9 a.m. the enemy's artillery fire increased, but beyond an attempt by a party to reach the wire by crawling through the bushes and crops, which was easily frustrated, there was no attack. The defenders meanwhile dug themselves in deeper, strengthened their wire, and got up ammunition and bombs, well knowing that their stubborn foe had not yet resigned himself to the loss of his position.

At 1.30 a.m. on the 2nd a much stronger counter-attack by several battalions, preceded by heavy shelling, was launched against the two villages and practically the whole of the line between them. The assault was repulsed at 2.15 a.m., but was renewed with even more determination about an hour later. The British Lewis guns were in many cases rendered useless by sand. The attack was heaviest against the little salient held by the company of the Camerons in Karajaköi Zir, and here the Bulgarians got a footing in some of the houses, but were driven out again at once. They drew off again at daybreak, leaving great numbers of dead on the ground, 80 being counted on the front of the Cameron company mentioned above. About 50 prisoners, for the most part wounded, were brought in. The 2/R. Irish Fusiliers, hardly 150 strong, had been sent to the support of the Camerons and arrived in time to help them repulse the last counter-attack. The 2/D.C.L.I. had been employed bringing up bombs and ammunition, one company carrying them to the Cameron post in the most exposed corner of Karajaköi Zir, when the bombardment and counter-attacks were at their heaviest. Two companies were sent up to support the Royal Scots, but the infantry action was over when they arrived. The two battalions of the 29th Brigade on the flanks were not attacked.

2 Oct.

General Briggs had to bear in mind his instructions that the action was to be continuous. In any case the ground already won represented an acute salient. The enemy so far had only butted his head against its strongly-held apex; he might next attempt to drive in the lightly-held flanks. Such an operation would probably be impossible in daylight owing to the proximity of the British batteries; but the Bulgarians knew the ground well and had a fondness for night work. General Briggs therefore issued orders late on the night of the 1st October for the advance to be continued on the 3rd with the object of capturing Yeniköi, on the main Seres road. The houses of this village stretched for nearly half a mile south of the Seres road, and the southernmost were a thousand yards from Karajaköi Zir.

For the purpose of the attack General Briggs placed the 30th Brigade of the 10th Division under Major-General Ravenshaw's orders. He directed the 28th Division to occupy Mazirko, the first village beyond the Struma on the Seres road, and to join hands with the 30th Brigade.

Major-General Ravenshaw ordered the 30th Brigade (at present commanded by Colonel A. D. Macpherson, owing to the absence on leave of Br.-General Nicol) to cross the Struma by Jungle Island bridge during the night of the 2nd, deploy from the position held by the 6/R. Irish Rifles south of Karajaköi Zir, and advance to the attack on Yeniköi at 5.30 a.m. on the 3rd. The 81st Brigade was to protect the right flank by means of bombing parties and machine guns moving along the sunken road from Karajaköi Zir to Yeniköi. It was to relieve during the night preceding the attack the 29th Composite Battalion on the right flank, which was then to be at the disposal of the 30th Brigade. The 6/R. Irish Rifles was also to come under the 30th Brigade after the attack had passed through its line. Colonel Macpherson only learnt, from General Briggs in person, that he was to undertake the capture of Yeniköi at 10 a.m. on the 2nd.

Presumably General Briggs telephoned to Major-General Croker, commanding the 28th Division, that he desired Mazirko to be occupied; for the village was actually seized without opposition by the 1/Suffolk of the 84th Brigade before the XVI Corps order was issued. Three companies, with two of the 23/Welch (Pioneers) and the

CAPTURE OF YENIKÖI

Hampshire Field Company R.E. worked all night to establish strong defences round the village, and at dawn all except one company of the Suffolk were withdrawn to the bridgehead defences at Orlyak bridge.

Between 3 a.m. and 4 a.m. on the morning of the 3rd the 30th Brigade crossed the Struma. The two leading battalions, 7/R. Munster Fusiliers and 6/R. Dublin Fusiliers, both under the orders of Lieut.-Colonel P. G. A. Cox of the Dublins, deployed upon the position held by the 6/R. Irish Rifles, and at 5.45 a.m., after half an hour's bombardment, advanced to the attack. Yeniköi was evidently lightly held, and small parties had been observed by the troops of the 28th Division hastily retiring northwards. There was little opposition, and before 7 a.m. the whole village was captured with very small casualties. Each man of the rear platoons of the two attacking battalions, and every man of the 7/R. Dublin Fusiliers in support and the 6/R. Munster Fusiliers in reserve carried a pick or shovel strapped on his back, and wire had been dumped on the left bank of the river both at Mazirko and near Jungle Island bridge. Consolidation of the position therefore began very quickly. On the right the 2/R. Irish Fusiliers, 2/D.C.L.I., and 1/Royal Scots had advanced along the road from Karajaköi Zir, found touch with the 7/Munster at the south-east corner of Yeniköi, and begun a line of defence between the two villages. On the left two companies of the 1/Suffolk and the cars of the 6th Armoured Motor Battery [1] had advanced up the Seres road and found touch with the 30th Brigade at the 79th kilometre stone, half-way between Mazirko and Yeniköi.

Now began the inevitable counter-attacks. At 8.15 a.m. three or four battalions of the enemy were seen moving southward from Topalova, and his artillery began to shell Yeniköi and the line thence to Karajaköi Zir. To General Briggs and the artillery observers on the hills south-west of Orlyak this and the subsequent counter-attacks presented extraordinary spectacles, as rare in modern warfare as the advance of the Royal Scots had been. The Bulgarians could be seen forming up, deploying, and advancing in extended order across the flat bottom of the

---

[1] This unit, consisting of four cars with machine guns, had been at Salonika for some time, the first two cars, without personnel, having been landed at the end of January.

valley. They made good use of what little cover there was in the shape of slight folds in the ground, and also of the numerous gullies, so that the infantry in Yeniköi could see little of them; but as they came into the zone of the field artillery the shrapnel played havoc with them. At first they continued to advance with great resolution, but eventually could no longer face the fire, and were driven to ground or turned back in confusion. After the first attack had thus been stopped there was comparative quiet for some three hours. Then, at 12.45 p.m., an intense bombardment was directed on Yeniköi, under cover of which the Bulgarians again advanced in force, led by an officer on a white charger. The British artillery was less successful in neutralizing the enemy's batteries than in stopping his infantry, and the 7th and 6th Dublin, in the centre of the line, came in for heavy shelling. They also report that, after their forward observing officer had been killed, shells from British batteries fell among them. These battalions fell back to the sunken road running through the centre of the village, and the 6/Munster on their left conformed to their retirement. Small bodies of Bulgarians followed up and entered the northern part of Yeniköi.

About 3.45 p.m. the action blazed up again. The bombardment, which had slackened a little, was renewed in its former violence, and large numbers of the enemy in close formation advanced on the village. A few minutes later men of the two Dublin battalions began to fall back from it. The spectators on the hills had a worse impression of what was happening than was actually warranted; for it was afterwards found that a considerable number of the men seen retiring from Yeniköi belonged to carrying parties returning after taking up wire and ammunition. The Munster battalions on the flanks maintained more or less their original position. The 6/R. Irish Rifles was then sent up, reaching the southern end of the village at 5.15 p.m., and there taking up a position in the sunken road. The stragglers were stopped by their own officers or carried back by the Irish Rifles, and the second position, through the middle of Yeniköi, was reoccupied. The British artillery had meanwhile put down a barrage to prevent the enemy from crossing the Seres road. In fact, however, the Bulgarians seem to have thrown in their hand at almost the same moment, and the god of war must have witnessed

CONFUSION AT YENIKÖI

a sight not unfamiliar to him but always fresh in its irony— that of both sides retiring simultaneously. **1916. 3 Oct.**
The excitements of the day were not yet over. At 7.40 p.m. Colonel Macpherson, evidently influenced by a report from Lieut.-Colonel Cox that had taken some time to reach him and represented the situation at the ugliest moment, ordered a withdrawal to the original line. News of the despatch of this order did not reach the headquarters of the 27th Division until 25 minutes later, and it was then at once cancelled. Unfortunately all lines to Yeniköi, except that to the 7/Munster on the east of the village, had been cut by artillery fire, and the message did not arrive in time to prevent the other troops of the 10th Division, with the exception, it would appear, of one company of the 7th and one of the 6th Dublin, from withdrawing. The situation was very confused, as the 2/D.C.L.I. was not in touch with the 7/Munster, but it appeared as the night wore on that there were few of the enemy in the village and those only in its northern part. It was, however, impossible to organize a counter-attack for several hours.

Meanwhile the two remaining battalions of the 82nd Brigade, the 1/Royal Irish and 1/Leinster, had arrived on the right bank of the Struma. The Royal Irish was sent across by Jungle Island bridge and held in divisional reserve. The Leinster battalion, which, after marching some 32 miles on the 2nd, had sent carrying parties across to Karajaköi Bala on the 3rd, was moved up to the bridge. The counter-attack on Yeniköi was ordered to take place at 3.30 a.m. on the 4th; but the two Dublin battalions, which were to move in first line, supported by the 6/R. Irish Rifles, were not ready until 4.45 a.m. When the advance did take place **4 Oct.** it met with no opposition; in fact one company of the 6/R. Dublin Fusiliers appears to have remained in the village all night. The Bulgarians had lost an excellent chance by giving up too soon.

The enemy's artillery was active at intervals throughout the day, but it appeared that his infantry had fallen back, possibly as far as the railway. General Briggs, when he rode out to Yeniköi, was assured by battalion commanders that with a fresh division he could have captured the Rupel Pass; and the reports by prisoners subsequently taken of hopeless confusion in their units for a full two days seemed to confirm this view. Though the British losses were heavy, those of the enemy, who was again and again caught by artillery and machine-gun fire in the open, must have been several times as great. Three officers and 339 rank and file were brought in as prisoners, and by the 10th October it was reported that 1,375 dead had been buried by the British. The casualties of the troops under Major-General Ravenshaw's command were 1,137, almost equally divided between the 10th and 27th Divisions.[1] The troops of the 28th Division, which were heavily shelled on the Seres road, had 111 casualties, bringing the total up to 1,248.

On the 5th two companies of the 2/Cheshire of the 84th Brigade entered Nevolyen unopposed, drove off a small party which attacked them after nightfall, and captured 16 prisoners. They then dug themselves in. Next day the 7th Mounted Brigade and the armoured cars crossed the Struma at Orlyak bridge and carried out a series of deep reconnaissances lasting several days, assisted by infantry patrols, to determine the exact front now held by the Bulgarians. It was proved that the enemy had, in fact, made a considerable retirement, approximately to the line of the railway, though he held several of the villages south and west of it with small detachments.

The Progress of the Monastir Offensive.

Map 2.
Sketch 7.

On the left flank of the Armée d'Orient the Bulgarian attack had been brought to a halt by the 1st September, but it had taken another ten days to mature General Sarrail's preparations for a counter-offensive. Perhaps, indeed, that phrase is inadequate to describe the hasty fashion in which the troops were pushed into action, short of supplies and ammunition, in this wild and almost roadless country.

General Sarrail made his principal effort to break the enemy's front with the Serbian Danube and Vardar Divisions, supported by the Morava Division, astride the road from Salonika, which runs north of Lake Ostrovo through Gornichevo and Banitsa, and then turns north-westward in the direction of Monastir. On their right the Šumadija Division and a brigade of the Timok were to advance up the track from Vodena to Prilep and attack the enemy on the frontier heights in the neighbourhood of the Vetrenik,

---

[1]

	Killed	Wounded	Missing
Officers	10	79	—
Other Ranks	179	818	51

The twin summits of the Kajmakčalan (right 7,769 ft., and left 8,284 ft.). (From the south-east.)

[*Photographic Boissonnes.*]

COUNTRY WEST OF THE VARDAR 185

and the Drina Division was to scale the Kajmakčalan, a vast, twin-peaked mountain mass rising to over 8,000 feet in height. On the left of the Serbians, General Cordonnier, with the French 156th Division, the Russian Brigade, the 57th Division when it should be in position, and later such troops of the 17th Colonial as had been relieved from the left bank of the Vardar, was to turn the enemy's right. Launching their offensive on the 12th September, the Serbians had a notable success on the 14th, capturing Gornichevo with 32 guns, and on their left flank reaching Ekshisu Station, though not before the Bulgarians had blown up the big viaduct at this point. The 156th Division had captured Rudnik on the 12th and was now moving on Florina; but the viaduct could not be quickly repaired and its destruction denied to the attackers the use of the line beyond Sorovich Station.

1916. Sept.

The country wherein the Armée d'Orient was now operating is strange in conformation, magnificent to the eye by reason of its extended perspectives, but most unfavourable to the manœuvring of modern armies. From north-east to south-west a great chain of hills, the Nidže Planina (rising to its greatest height in the Kajmakčalan, which may be likened to a tower flanking a vast building), the Stalkov Grob, the Malka Nidže, and the Mala Reka, sweep down to the valley of the upper Vistritsa. The north-westward slopes of the Nidže Planina and Stalkov Grob merge into a big *massif*, which stretches away for miles to the northward, still averaging about 4,500 feet, but on the westward side falls sharply to the bare, marshy plain of Monastir. Cutting right through this *massif* is a ravine through which the Crna runs to join the Vardar. The Crna presents a most curious spectacle, and reverses the normal behaviour of rivers. From north to south it runs past Monastir, a true river of the plains, slow, winding, and muddy. Then it apparently meets with a particularly hard rock formation and finds a natural rift in the *massif* overlooking its upper waters; for it turns northward in a great hairpin bend and enters a gloomy defile which bears it through the *massif*. Fed now by mountain streams, it becomes in wet weather a foaming torrent. Thence it emerges into the valley of the Vardar at its widest part, where we have already encountered it when considering the French expedition into Serbia.

General Sarrail's plan was dictated by this terrain, which was of more importance than any fortifications the Bulgarians had had time to create since their recent advance. The Serbians were to assault the positions on the Nidže Planina and the Stalkov Grob; the French and Russians, who had to scale the lower prolongation of the ridge at the Mala Reka, were to act as the marching wing, turning the position of the enemy on the heights, and then pressing northwards up the plain of Monastir. Monastir was the terminus of the railway; but a fairly good road ran northward from it to Prilep, half-way between the upper and lower courses of the Crna and a very important road centre.

Unfortunately the marching wing found great difficulty, owing to its weakness and the state of the communications, in fulfilling its rôle. It is not for us to deliver judgment regarding the bitter controversy between General Sarrail and his subordinate, General Cordonnier, especially as it does not affect British operations directly.[1] It may be said, however, that one of the British officers who saw most of the operations, Lieut.-Colonel C. C. M. Maynard, liaison officer between the War Office and Salonika,[2] considered that the chief responsibility for the slow progress of the French and Russians rested with the headquarters of the Armée d'Orient. The success of the operations hinged almost entirely upon rapidity of movement, yet the advance was hampered from the first by want of organization of the rearward services. It is in fact doubtful whether, but for the transport lent by the British, the French could have moved at all. None the less, a victory of considerable importance was gained. When we turn to the German official account we realize that by the middle of October the Bulgarian troops on this front had been thoroughly beaten and would have cracked but for the powerful German aid which was then sent to them.[3]

As a result of the Serbian success at Gornichevo, the enemy refused his right, pivoting on the Kajmakčalan and falling back to a line which ran thence through Florina.

---

[1] The course of this controversy may be followed in their respective books, General Sarrail's " Mon Commandement en Orient " and General Cordonnier's " Ai-je trahi Sarrail ? "

[2] Lieut.-Colonel Maynard was also British liaison officer between Chantilly and the Armée d'Orient, and reported direct to General Joffre each time he passed through France on his way to and from Salonika.

[3] " Herbstschlacht in Macedonien," pp. 32 *et seq.*

PASSAGE OF THE CRNA

Hindered by the fatigue of his troops after long marches, and by the difficulty of pushing on his artillery, the horses of which were debilitated and exhausted, General Cordonnier was not master of Florina until the 17th September. Even then he had great difficulties in freeing his left in the hills west and north-west of the town. This was not finally accomplished until the 2nd October, when the French captured the monastery of St. Marco, which dominated Florina.[1]

1916. Sept.

Meanwhile the Serbians had been fighting their way up the flank of the Kajmakčalan. By the 20th September they appear to have been in possession of the mountain, whence they looked down upon the bend of the Crna. They were driven off the summit by a counter-attack, but to the south-west pushed the enemy across the Brod and got a footing on the right bank. On the 30th they again stormed the Kajmakčalan. The loss of this magnificent buttress and observation post, combined with a Serbian advance to the crest of the Stalkov Grob and the French pressure north of Florina, caused another withdrawal. The Bulgarians fell back on the night of the 2nd October to a strongly fortified line along the bend of the Crna, through Kenali and Negochani, to German, near the spit of land between Lakes Prespa and Mala Prespa.

Oct.

The feel of their own soil beneath their feet seemed to give the Serbians new resolution. On the night of the 7th they forced their way across the Crna between Brod and Skočevir, though they gained only a very precarious hold on the left bank. In the plain of Monastir the Bulgarians held their ground. General Cordonnier, having on the 5th made a personal reconnaissance from an aeroplane of the Bulgarian position here, decided that, in view of its strength and the absence of cover under which to approach it, he could not attack it frontally with the means at his disposal. It appeared to him that an outflanking movement in the western hills, combined with Serbian pressure on the east, would gain it with small loss. He was, however, ordered by General Sarrail to attack at once in order to help the Serbians, and on the 6th was repulsed, his Russian troops suffering somewhat heavily. Another attack on the 14th, made against his own judgment, was still more

---

[1] Cordonnier, p. 296.

unfortunate. Coming up against uncut wire, the French lost 1,490 men and the Russians 600. Profoundly dissatisfied with General Cordonnier's conduct of the operations, and finding that his orders for the 20th contemplated no more than a reconnaissance in force of the enemy's position, General Sarrail on the 16th demanded his recall.[1] General Joffre then gave his permission for the Army commander to be replaced temporarily by General Leblois.

Map A.   This brief account will suffice to explain the calls which General Sarrail made upon General Milne not only to keep up his pressure upon the enemy but to set free more troops to take part in the offensive. On the 15th October the two generals had an interview at which the Commander-in-Chief asked General Milne to relieve the French detachment on the Struma at once. General Milne replied that he would give an answer as soon as possible, and took the opportunity to urge that the forces of the various nations at Salonika should be allotted definite zones of action, as he considered that the fashion in which they were at present intermixed was unfortunate. To the War Office he wired that he could relieve the Struma detachment, but that he would be glad to have for the purpose the 8th Mounted Brigade from Egypt, which he had previously been offered and which he had at first thought he would not require during the winter. This relief was not actually carried out until the 10th November. On the 23rd October, however, General Milne ordered the XII Corps to relieve the French 34th Colonial Brigade from Lake Dojran to north-east of Doljeli, which move would leave no French troops in line east of the Vardar except the small Struma detachment.

To meet General Sarrail's other demand, that of exerting continuous pressure upon the enemy, General Milne directed the commander of the XII Corps to keep up offensive action by means of wire-cutting, raids, and bombing attacks. Both divisions of the corps had already been active in this respect, having in general had strong patrols out each night and attempted a number of raids. The enemy, however, was alert and vigorous in defence, and it was a matter of great difficulty to enter his entrenchments. On the night of the 10th October the 12/Hampshire (79th

---

[1] Sarrail, p. 168.

Brigade, 26th Division) attacked Goldies Hill, a Bulgarian outpost 2,000 yards north-east of Dautli, and captured a prisoner at a cost of one casualty. On the following night, after a heavy artillery preparation, two companies of the 11/Worcestershire (78th Brigade) succeeded in fighting their way into the works on the Mamelon, 450 yards north-east of Doljeli, and found about 50 dead Bulgarians, the living having fled. The battalion's own casualties were, however, rather greater than this number.

1916. Oct.

On receiving General Milne's message, General Wilson arranged that the raiding should be intensified. The commander of the 22nd Division, Major-General Gordon, decided to carry out three raids the following week: the first on the night of the 18th against the vineyards on the bank of the Vardar between the enemy's trenches and Machukovo, by the 67th Brigade, under an artillery barrage; the second on the night of the 20th on the Nose, a little salient in the enemy's main line 2,500 yards north-east of Machukovo, by the 66th Brigade, without artillery support but after preliminary wire-cutting; and the third, a really strong one, on the night of the 21st against the Dorsale, where the attack of the 13th September had failed, by the 67th Brigade, after a thorough artillery preparation.

The first two raids were unsuccessful. The 7/S. Wales Borderers had no fortune in the vineyards; for pursuit of a platoon of the enemy which hastily retired when the raiding party advanced was checked by breast-high wire fastened from tree to tree. At the Nose a company of the 9/S. Lancashire found the enemy on the watch, sending up rocket lights and opening machine-gun fire. A "silent" raid can only hope to succeed by surprise; so there was nothing for it but to withdraw.

The weather was now worsening, and heavy rain on the 21st made wire-cutting and the bombardment of dugouts on the Dorsale impossible; so the third raid had to be postponed for twenty-four hours. This was the most important of the three, not only because of its size but because it was to establish whether or not the German *59th Regiment* was still upon this front. The British line opposite the Dorsale was still held by the 65th Brigade, but Major-General Gordon had decided that the raid should be carried out by troops of the 67th (Br.-General H. F. Cooke), which had not been engaged in any considerable operation. For

Sketch 6.

the bombardment the 132nd Siege Battery was placed under the orders of the C.R.A., Br.-General H. H. Bond, who also made arrangements for the co-operation of artillery of the French 122nd Division. The raiding party consisted of 300 officers and men of the 11/Welch, the 127th Field Company R.E., and the 67th Machine-Gun Company; but this included flank guards, the numbers destined to enter the enemy's trenches being eight officers and 166 rank and file of the 11/Welch and two officers and 20 rank and file of the Royal Engineers, under the command of Major R. Scott-Hopkins of the Welch.

The raiders came under very heavy artillery and machine-gun fire and had to lie down for 40 minutes, half their number on the position of deployment about 150 yards from the enemy's wire, the remainder 300 yards in rear and cut off from them by the enemy's barrage. At 1.10 a.m. on the 23rd the barrage became less violent, and the parties in rear managed to get forward and deploy. A quarter of an hour later Major Scott-Hopkins led the advance up the hill to within 30 yards of the wire, now almost destroyed by the British fire. Three telephone lines which had been reeled out during the advance had been cut; runners could not get through; and rocket signals could not be distinguished amidst the enemy's display of fireworks. The lifting of the artillery screen was done on surmise, but happily coincided with the firing of a rocket signal by Major Scott-Hopkins, who immediately afterwards assaulted the trenches. The enemy resisted stubbornly, throwing incendiary bombs and repeatedly counter-attacking, but was held off while 18 prisoners were sent back and the only machine-gun emplacement not destroyed by the bombardment was blown up by the sappers. Thirty-four dead were counted in the trenches, and it was thought that many more casualties were inflicted by the bombers on the flanks. The raiders were clear of the trenches by 2.30 a.m. and back behind their own wire two hours later. Their total casualties, including five in the 8/S. Wales Borderers, which battalion had lent some of its stretcher-bearers, were 34.

The 11/Welch had never before been in action, so that the resolution of its raiding party, after a long and difficult approach and after being caught and separated by the barrage in a manner so likely to be disturbing to young

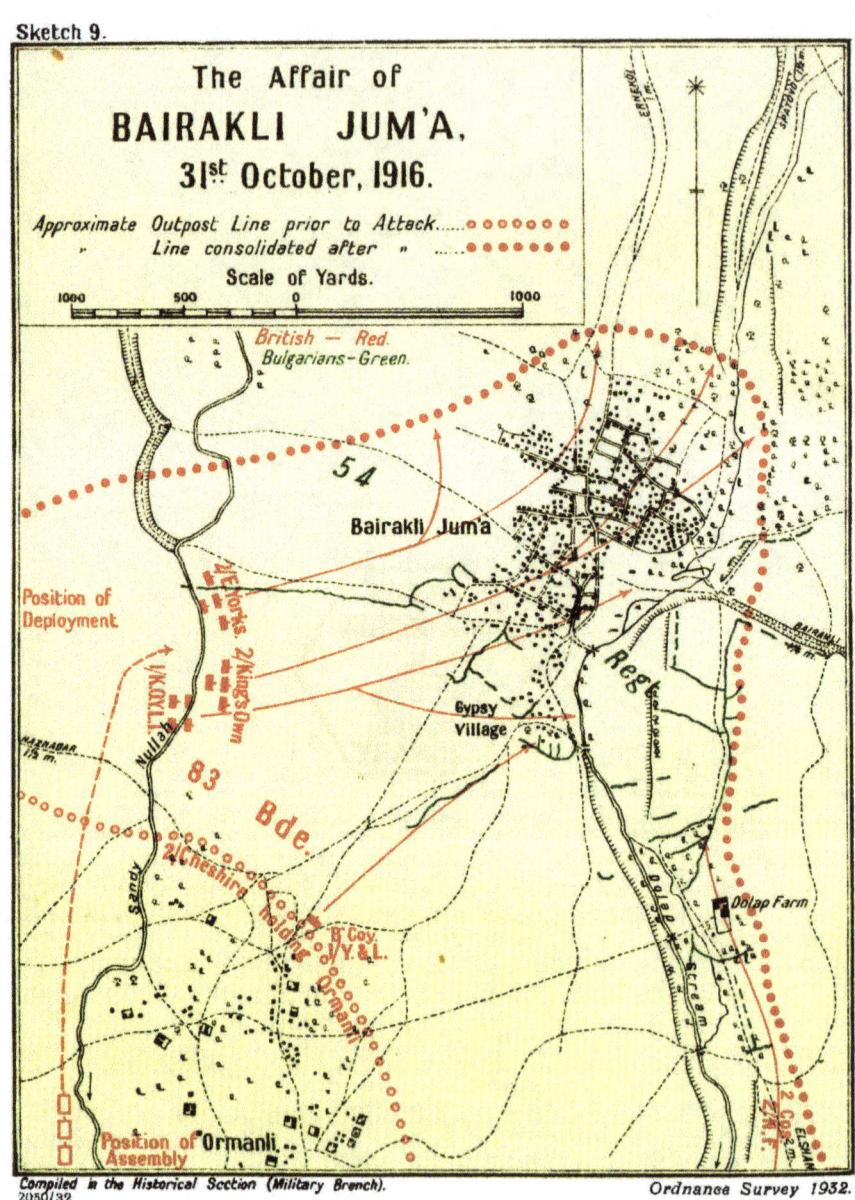

DIFFICULTIES OF XII CORPS

troops, was all the more creditable. One of the party, Private H. W. Lewis, who was thrice wounded, was awarded the Victoria Cross for conspicuous bravery and devotion. The prisoners were Germans of the *59th Regiment*.

1916. Oct.

Another raid on the Nose, on the night of the 28th, by the 12/Cheshire was unsuccessful, three parties entering the trenches, but being bombed out of them with a loss of 37. A second raid on the Mamelon in the early hours of the 1st October, by a party of the 7/R. Berkshire, was equally a failure, the enemy evacuating his front-line trench, retiring to another, newly dug and wired, in rear, and opening heavy fire. The raiders drew off, having suffered 22 casualties. On the other hand, two attempts by the Bulgarians, on the 1st and 17th, to enter the British trenches were easily repulsed.

This summary will show the difficulties which confronted the XII Corps. Raiding parties to points, like the vineyards of Machukovo, outside the enemy's main wire, could generally reach their objectives, but could not make certain of bringing him to action. A raid against the main line was, however, an operation demanding unlimited ammunition; and a concentration for the purpose of wire-cutting and demolition on only one point served to warn the defence. Though there was now only one German regiment on this part of the front, it had previously all been held by German troops, who had fortified it on the lines of the Western theatre of war. There were two or three strong belts of wire covering the whole front line from Dojran to the Vardar; the trenches were often ten feet deep; the dugouts were unaffected by field-howitzers, and it took a direct hit from a 6-inch howitzer to damage one of them.

The XVI Corps, faced as yet by no such defences, could accomplish something on a bigger scale. On the 14th October the Army commander directed General Briggs to work out plans for the capture of Bairakli Jum'a, a large village three miles beyond the Struma and nine miles north-west of Yeniköi the scene of the last action on this front.

The Affair of Bairakli Jum'a.

Map 8.
Sketch 9.
After the operations at Yeniköi and the Karajaköis the newly won bridgehead here was consolidated. The 81st Brigade, still with its right in touch with the French at Suhabanya Ferry, held this salient up to Karajaköi Zir; the 10th Division (29th and 30th Brigades) held Yeniköi and up to the right flank of the 84th Brigade at the 79th kilometre stone on the Seres road. Permanent patrols of the 7th Mounted Brigade and the divisional cavalry, supported when necessary by infantry, were out in front. An attempt by the 1/York and Lancaster of the 83rd Brigade to capture Bairakli Jum'a on the 11th October ended unfortunately. The battalion had been ordered to "drive the enemy out of the village" if possible, but not to become "so seriously engaged as to be unable to with-"draw." The divisional squadron of Surrey Yeomanry, an armoured car, and an 18-pdr. section of the XXXI Brigade R.F.A. had been put at the disposal of Lieut.-Colonel G. E. Bayley, and a section of the CXLVI Brigade R.F.A. was also to cross the river. The attack was held up by machine guns in the gypsy village on the southern outskirts of Bairakli Jum'a and by bodies of the enemy who advanced westward from Bairakli and southward from Erneköi. Their flanking movements were checked by the fire of the four 18-pdrs. on the left bank of the Struma and of the heavy artillery on the right bank. The battalion then withdrew slowly under heavy fire towards Ormanli, having suffered a loss of four officers and 92 other ranks, including three officers and 46 other ranks missing, out of a strength in action of about 320 all ranks.

This reverse was, however, the only check to General Briggs's otherwise entirely successful methods of patrolling. By means of reconnaissances, ambushes, and small raids the enemy's outposts were pushed gradually back from the river, a series of skirmishes taking place each day a little farther from the left bank. Finally, by the 12th October, these measures as well as reports and photographs from the air showed that the new Bulgarian main line of defence ran from the Struma south of Erneköi, Bairakli Jum'a, and Bairakli, then across the railway and along the foot-hills, round the southern skirts of Seres, and south-eastward to the shore of Lake Tahinos. This front was held by the

PREPARATION FOR ATTACK

1916.
Oct.

7th Division, consisting, apparently, of six regiments, with the *10th Division*, or part of it, on its left, north of Lake Tahinos. On the lower Struma, facing the British 80th Brigade, the Turkish *50th Division* had come into line, to some extent compensating for the withdrawal of Bulgarian troops from this front already recorded.

On the night of the 25th the 30th Brigade of the 10th Division relieved the 84th Brigade of the 28th Division. This relief involved, besides taking over the bridgehead defences at Mazirko, placing two companies each in Nevolyen and Cuculuk, which had been meanwhile occupied by the 84th. Nevolyen was taken over next night by the 31st Brigade, which was to co-operate in the attack on Bairakli Jum'a by occupying Prosenik. On the 26th also the villages of Elshan, Ormanli, and Haznadar were occupied without opposition by the 83rd Brigade. The occupation of these villages, together with that of Nevolyen and Cuculuk, extended the bridgehead of the Karajaköis and Yeniköi, and provided a good position of assembly for the attack. On the night of the 29th the 84th Brigade relieved the 83rd to set it free for the task it was about to carry out.

In accordance with Major-General Croker's orders the 83rd Brigade was to carry out the attack. The 84th Brigade was simultaneously to capture Dolap Farm, on the left bank of the stream of that name which runs southward to the Struma. The heavy artillery allotted to the attack, and which was placed under the orders of Br.-General H. E. T. Kelly, C.R.A. of the division, consisted of six 60-pdrs. and eight 6-inch howitzers,[1] which were to remain on the right bank of the Struma. All the divisional artillery, the 7th Mountain Battery (attached to the 83rd Brigade), and the Argyll Mountain Battery (attached to the 84th Brigade), were to cross the Struma, either by the existing road-bridge at Kopriva or by a new artillery bridge to be thrown a short distance upstream by the 2/1st Northumbrian Field Company R.E. Two bridges to take pack transport were also to be thrown by the 38th and 7/Hampshire Field Companies.

The bridging was a matter of some difficulty owing to heavy rains, which not only made the ground boggy but

---

[1] 143rd Heavy Battery and one section 153rd Heavy Battery, 127th and 134th Siege Batteries.

caused the Struma to rise two feet. All the field artillery was, however, got into position on the left bank between Elshan and Ormanli on the night of the 29th. During the 30th the battalions of the 83rd Brigade concentrated in Ormanli, where Br.-General F. S. Montague Bates established his headquarters. Rain fell steadily all that day and during most of the night.

1916.
31 Oct. Between 2 a.m. and 4.30 a.m. on the 31st the infantry moved into positions of deployment in a gulley about a thousand yards north-west of Ormanli. To increase the chances of surprise it had been decided that the artillery should not register until 7 a.m., and the night's fog fortunately cleared in time for this to be done. The advance began simultaneously with the opening of the bombardment at 7.15 a.m., was carried out by the 2/King's Own on the right and the 2/E. Yorkshire on the left, and was directed against the western side of Bairakli Jum'a. The 1/K.O.Y.L.I. moved in rear and clear of the right flank of the King's Own, with orders to detach sufficient troops, as it closed on the objective, to clear the gypsy village or encampment on the southern outskirts of Bairakli Jum'a. The 1/York and Lancaster sent one company to make a demonstration against this encampment from the south.

The attack was carried out with great speed. The enemy, whose patrols had probably kept under cover from the weather, was completely surprised, and, shaken by the bombardment (as prisoners afterwards stated), made but slight resistance. The York and Lancaster company, observing that he had little fight in him, entered the gypsy village from the south as soon as the 1/K.O.Y.L.I. was seen to enter it from the west, and drove a number of Bulgarians into the arms of that battalion. The enemy quickly brought artillery fire to bear on the village and showed some disposition to counter-attack; but the battalions which advanced from Spatovo and Bairakli were driven to ground by British artillery fire, and only a small party following a wooded gully from the north-east reached a point about 100 yards from Bairakli Jum'a. Carrying parties of the 85th Brigade began moving up as soon as the village had been occupied, and the wiring of the new position, begun in daylight, was completed during the night. Three officers and 317 rank and file, with two machine guns, were captured.

THE STRUMA

VALLEY, FROM KAJALI.

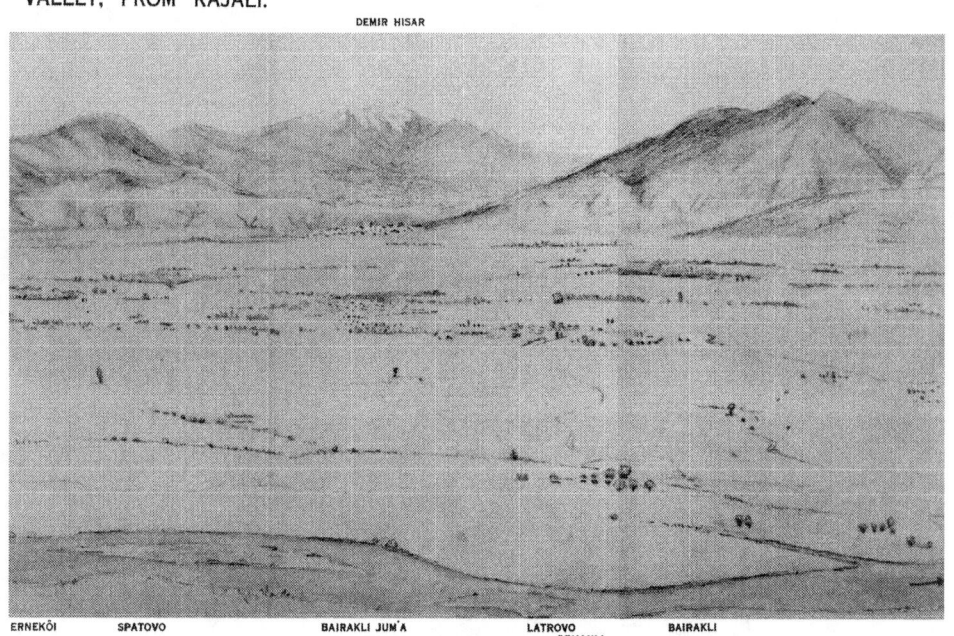

CAPTURE OF DOLAP FARM

1916.
31 Oct.

Meanwhile the 2/Northumberland Fusiliers of the 84th Brigade had advanced from a position of deployment on the left bank of the Dolap stream 2,000 yards south of Dolap Farm at 7.25 a.m., and by 8.45 a.m. had captured the farm. This battalion suffered more heavily than those of the 83rd Brigade, having 43 casualties, mainly from the fire of riflemen in the orchards, who had in some cases climbed the trees. A considerable number of the prisoners captured in Bairakli Jum'a were apparently men who had fled from Dolap Farm. A platoon of the 1/Suffolk advanced on Kumli and captured 13 prisoners, the rest of the small garrison withdrawing in haste. A section of " C " Battery LXVIII Brigade R.F.A. (10th Division) advanced to a position south of the village to shell Bairakli, but both it and the infantry patrol were forced to withdraw by a counter-attack. On the right the 31st Brigade, having occupied Topalova with the 5th and 6th R. Irish Fusiliers overnight, drove the enemy out of Prosenik on the railway and held that village until nightfall. The 29th Brigade (which had received sufficient drafts for it to be reorganized as four battalions) occupied Patrol Wood beyond the railway; but coming under heavy fire, was withdrawn to the line of the railway, where it was in touch with the 31st. Further east the 2/Gloucester of the 81st Brigade advanced from Hristian-Kamilla to the railway line, here embanked, before being checked by fire from trenches beyond it concealed in long grass and bushes. At this point there would probably have been but small opposition to an advance on Seres, to which parties of the enemy were observed retreating. On withdrawal, the brigade left a garrison in the village of Homondos, three miles east of Karajaköi Zir. The 7th Mounted Brigade, to which were attached the 1/Royal Irish and a small detachment of French troops, carried out demonstrations against Tumbitza Farm, Beglik, and Virhanli, between Seres and Lake Tahinos. At the mouth of the Struma the 80th Brigade after a heavy bombardment, mainly by naval artillery, carried out a big demonstration, advancing 2,000 yards from its trenches.

Thus, although the only point attacked in force was Bairakli Jum'a, the whole front of the corps was set in motion, and the Bulgarians were threatened by a general advance. The total casualties in the three divisions and

THE RUMANIAN CAMPAIGN

the 7th Mounted Brigade were 231.[1] Seeing that the enemy lost 338 in prisoners alone, almost entirely owing to the clever tactics of the 28th Division at Bairakli Jum'a, it may be said that the whole operation was a success won at not undue cost.

THE RUMANIAN CAMPAIGN AND ITS INFLUENCE ON BRITISH POLICY.

Map 1.   The operations of the Rumanians, to assist which was the object of the Allied offensive in Macedonia, after one brief moment of initial success, went steadily from bad to worse, to end in disaster. The German and Austrian commands had long anticipated the entry of Rumania into the war on the side of the Entente, and had been given further warning by the period of bargaining which preceded it. On the 29th July there was a conference at Pless between General von Falkenhayn, General von Conrad, and the Bulgarian Colonel Gančev, followed by another in Budapest on the 5th August between the two first-named and Enver Pasha, the Turkish Minister of War and Vice-Generalissimo. At these meetings the representatives of the four Powers came to agreement as to the common course of action to be followed in the event of a declaration of war by Rumania.[2]

Falkenhayn and Conrad knew very well that, from the Rumanian point of view, an advance in great strength through the Transylvanian Alps into Hungary, while comparatively small forces were left to hold the line of the Danube and the Dobruja, was unsound strategy. An attack with two-thirds of Rumania's available strength upon Bulgaria, tied down as she was by the Allied Army in Macedonia, might, on the contrary, have resulted in the complete defeat of that country and the severance of German communications with Turkey, the two mishaps together exercising an enormous but incalculable influence upon the future course of the war. The generals of the Central

---

[1]

	KILLED	WOUNDED	MISSING
Officers	2	17	1
Other Ranks	33	176	2

The losses of the French are unknown, but probably did not reach double figures.

[2] Falkenhayn, p. 279.

THE GERMAN PLAN

Powers were none the less convinced that Rumania would adopt the former plan. They knew that Transylvania was Rumania's " promised land," and recalled that for the Balkan peoples the oft deceptive proverb about the value of a bird in the hand had always governed military policy. They based their preparations upon this belief; and they were right. Directly hostilities began, Field-Marshal von Mackensen was to be placed in command of a new Army, made up of what Bulgarian, German, and Turkish troops could be collected,[1] on the Danube. His first operation was not to be so bold as an attempt to pass the Danube, but was to be the invasion of the Dobruja, into which he was to advance till he reached the shortest line between the Danube and the Black Sea, approximately the railway from Cernavoda on the Danube to Constantsa. The southern Dobruja once cleared, he was to force the passage of the Danube at Sistova in Bulgaria, 40 miles north-east of the historic fortress of Plevna, and actually the point where the Russians had crossed in 1877. The excellent Austrian bridging train, which had enabled him to cross from the left bank to the right into Serbia the previous autumn and was now to bear him from the right bank to the left into Rumania, was anchored near Sistova, behind the island of Bjelene. Meanwhile the Austrian *First Army* in Transylvania under General von Arz, consisting of three infantry divisions, one cavalry division, and smaller formations of various origin and doubtful value, was to delay the Rumanians as as long as possible until sufficient German and Austrian reinforcements could be brought up to permit of offensive action. For, though they knew that at best they would not be able to muster forces equal to those of the Rumanians, Falkenhayn and Conrad put the defensive out of their minds. Their plan was, in brief, a simultaneous invasion of Wallachia from north and south, and a swift march upon Bucharest.

When the moment came Falkenhayn was no longer in the saddle at Pless to direct the operations which he had planned. A gradually growing impatience with his methods

---

[1] Bulgarian *Third Army* of four divisions (whereof the *1st* and *4th* were already on the Danube, the *6th*, or the greater part of it, was to be sent at once from Macedonia, and the *12th* was apparently newly formed) and one cavalry division, the German *101st Division* from Macedonia, and two Turkish divisions from Adrianople.

had been long felt by the Government and had now affected his patron the Kaiser, having been fed by the failure of the offensive at Verdun, by the critical situation on the Somme, by the Italian success on the Isonzo in August, and by his opposition to the formation of the projected Polish State. The declaration of war by Rumania on Austria-Hungary and by Italy on Germany was the final blow; two days later, on the 29th August, he was superseded as Chief of the General Staff by Field-Marshal von Hindenburg. Within three weeks, however, he found himself in command of the newly formed German *Ninth Army*, with the task of playing the major part in a campaign which he had thought to direct from above.

The Rumanian campaign of 1916, one of the most interesting and on the victors' side the most brilliant in the annals of the war, must be here very shortly summarized.[1] Rumania had 22 big divisions, of which 16, in three Armies, were devoted to the invasion of Transylvania. This left six for the Dobruja and Danube fronts, and in the Dobruja she had been promised a corps of two Russian divisions, which was afterwards strongly reinforced. Even by mid-September, Falkenhayn, Arz, and Mackensen had not more than 17 German, Austrian, Turkish, and Bulgarian divisions, and of these all but the last-named were only about half as strong in numbers as the Rumanian. On the other hand, the Germans and their allies, including the Turks—whose troops in the Balkans were the flower of their Army—were in general better armed, equipped, and trained than their adversaries, and Mackensen's heavy artillery was exceptionally strong. Into the bargain, the two German generals were probably the ablest commanders of the world war.

The campaign began on the 28th August with the advance of the Rumanians through the Transylvanian Alps, from the Tolgyes Pass in the north to the Vulcan and Szurduk Passes in the south-west, a distance of 170

---

[1] There are numerous German accounts of this campaign, which has been chronicled by General von Falkenhayn himself as regards the *Ninth Army* and is described in full in General Schwarte's " Der Grosse Krieg " (Vol. II, Part II [German] and Vol. V [Austrian]). A good English account by Major-General W. M. St. G. Kirke will be found in *The Journal of the Royal United Service Institution*, November 1924, February 1925, and May 1925.

BATTLE OF HERMANNSTADT

miles.[1] They made fairly rapid progress, defeating and driving back the covering forces opposed to them. Yet they scarcely took full advantage of their wonderful opportunity, and General von Arz must be allowed credit for his delaying tactics. Meanwhile, moreover, Mackensen won an important success in the Dobruja, and on the 5th September captured the fortress of Turtucaia on the Danube, with 28,000 prisoners and a hundred guns.[2] The reverse had an unfortunate effect upon the spirits of the Rumanians. They abandoned the next Danubian fortress, Silistra, in hot haste, and denuded their Armies on the Transylvanian front of reserves, which they hurried southward by train. Mackensen pushed forward into the Dobruja till held up in mid-September south of the Constantsa railway by the Rumanians and Russians, who dug themselves in.

1916. Sept.

Such was the situation when Falkenhayn arrived on the 18th September in Karlsburg to take command of the *Ninth Army*, in part already engaged, in part moving up to the scene of action. He found the Austrian *First Army* giving way, but German and Austrian troops holding firm at Sibiu (Hermannstadt). The Rumanian columns were widely strung out. Leaving only a few battalions to hold that which had already been checked by German counter-attacks outside the Vulcan and Szurduk Passes, and one German and one Austrian cavalry division to cover the 30 miles between his left and the Austrian right on the Alt, Falkenhayn concentrated and struck at the Rumanian divisions of the Second Army in front of Hermannstadt. In four days' fighting between the 25th and 28th September he drove them back down the Red Tower (Rotherthurm) Pass, which his *Alpine Corps*, after a wonderful cross-country march, could not quite succeed in closing.

That was really the beginning of the end, though the end was not yet. Mackensen's troops, aided by floods, defeated an extraordinarily bold attempt by the Rumanians to take them in rear by crossing the Danube behind them at Rahovo on the 1st October. Between the 5th and 8th October Falkenhayn, having marched swiftly up the Alt,

Oct.

---

[1] If a division moving along the Danube to attack Orsova be included, the frontage becomes 230 miles.

[2] Schwarte, Vol. II, Part II, p. 593. Lon, p. 107, says 150 guns, but the Bulgarian sources from which he drew are never reliable as to numbers.

overthrew the Rumanians at Brasov (Kronstadt), and completely cleared Transylvania. The Rumanians still held the passes, and even inflicted a defeat upon Falkenhayn in the First Battle of Targu Jiu in the last week of October. But Mackensen had already routed the Russians and Rumanians in the Dobruja and captured Constantsa on the 23rd. Leaving a force strong enough to hold the narrow Dobruja front, at all events for so long as he judged would be necessary, he promptly marched back to Sistova, ready to pass the Danube when Falkenhayn had entered the Wallachian plain. In the Second Battle of Targu Jiu, between the 10th and 18th November, Falkenhayn won another victory over the Rumanians and contrived to debouch from the Szurduk Pass into the plain. On the 23rd, with the assistance of the Austrian flotilla and covered by the fire of massed heavy batteries, Mackensen crossed the Danube.

1916. Nov.

The battles in Wallachia, important as they are and interesting by reason of the strategical skill displayed—too late—by the Rumanian command, need not concern us. Completely defeated in the end, the Rumanians evacuated Bucharest on the 3rd December. Pivoting on the Russians, who held the northern crests of the Transylvanian Alps, their wretched remnants fell back into Moldavia. The front was in practice, if not nominally, placed under Russian command, and the Russians, who had no desire to see it extended in this quarter, withdrew it to a position south of the Siret. After more heavy fighting and a sharp check administered to Falkenhayn in the early days of January, the Russians fell back across the river. Simultaneously the Dobruja was evacuated. The Germans and Austrians, worn out with marching and fighting and faced by the worst part of the grim Moldavian winter, could do no more. They sat down upon the bank of the Siret. The Rumanians, in north-eastern Moldavia, were permitted to carry out such reorganization as was possible; but hunger and typhus were working for the enemy, if he himself was inactive. The Rumanian losses were enormous, the German *Ninth Army* alone having captured 148,000 prisoners and 312 guns.[1]

Dec.

In the whole course of the war no country, not Serbia

---

[1] Schwarte, Vol. II, Part II, p. 673.

even, suffered a more disastrous defeat or had to endure more terrible miseries than Rumania.

* * * * *

1916.
Oct.
Maps 1, 2.

By the end of October, then, if there was not yet cause for complete despair regarding Rumania, all the bright hopes had faded. On the Transylvanian front she might still be holding the passes, but who could say how long she would maintain them? On the Dobruja front she had lost Constantsa. In general the outlook was black. The offensive of the French and Serbians in the direction of Monastir, on the other hand, had not been brought to a halt but was progressing none too fast.

Three days before the fall of Constantsa, on the 20th October, an Anglo-French conference was held at Boulogne.[1] The first subject under discussion was the complicated situation in Greece, which will be outlined in the following chapter. With respect to the Rumanian situation, on which policy and operations in Macedonia hinged, there was a long debate, at the end of which it was decided that the General Staffs of Great Britain, France, Italy, and Russia should shortly meet in order to study the composition of the forces required at Salonika for three purposes: first, absolute security in case of a heavy attack by the enemy; secondly, a continuation of the offensive as far as Monastir and "the Vardar railway";[2] and thirdly, a strong offensive in combination with a Russo-Rumanian offensive against Bulgaria. The French representatives proposed that, without awaiting this meeting, the two Governments should make arrangements to bring the number of British divisions up to seven and that of the French to six. The British representatives agreed to give the proposal sympathetic consideration, and both Governments decided to

---

[1] Present: Mr. Asquith, Lord Grey, Mr. Lloyd George, Mr. Balfour, Generals Robertson and Haig; M. Briand (President of the Council and Foreign Affairs), General Roques (War), Admiral Lacaze (Marine), MM. Ribot (Finances), Bourgeois (without portfolio), and Thomas (Munitions), General Joffre; with certain staff officers and officials on each side.

[2] As the "Vardar railway" runs up the Vardar from a point 15 miles W.N.W. of Salonika to Skoplje, the phrase as it stands is meaningless. It must have referred to General Sarrail's project of advancing down the Crna and then crossing the plateau between its valley and that of the Vardar, striking the railway about Demir Kapiya station, and thus turning the Bulgarian defences which barred the Vardar valley further south.

request Italy to raise the number of her troops at Salonika to three divisions.

On the 25th General Milne was informed by the C.I.G.S. that, in view of very strong representations made to the British Government and the personal intervention of the Tsar and M. Poincaré, it had been decided to waive further discussion and to send another division from France. Britain reserved her freedom to withdraw it in the spring if necessary; and the move was conditional on the French force's being increased to six divisions—a condition which General Joffre had already stated he would fulfil. It did not modify the Government's view that a decision must be sought upon the Western Front. General Robertson himself had opposed in the War Committee the despatch of the division, in the belief that it would increase the chances of the British being drawn into major operations in the Balkans, which, now as ever, he considered would be a grave and perhaps fatal strategical error. Yet, while not believing that this reinforcement could serve any purpose but the sentimental one of showing a desire to help an ally in difficulty, he finally agreed that it was impossible to refuse it, seeing that the British General Staff was alone among those of the Allies in its attitude towards the Salonika Campaign.[1]

General Milne had already been promised, in addition to the 8th Mounted Brigade,[2] two battalions formed from dismounted Yeomanry in Egypt, garrison battalions and drafts amounting to 20,000 rifles, and a heavy artillery brigade headquarters with two 6-inch howitzer and two 60-pdr. batteries. Owing to the shortage of recruits from Ireland it was now impossible to find sufficient Irish reinforcements for the 10th Division, and he had therefore been instructed to transfer three Regular Irish battalions to it from the 27th, replacing them by the 10/Hampshire (the only English battalion in the 10th Division) and the two new arrivals.[3]

---

[1] " Soldiers and Statesmen," II, p. 130.

[2] The headquarters of this brigade reached Salonika on the 16th November.

[3] The changes in detail were : 1/Leinster from 82nd to 29th Brigade, 1/Royal Irish from 82nd to 30th Brigade, 2/R. Irish Fusiliers from 82nd to 31st Brigade, 10/Hampshire from 29th to 82nd Brigade, 2/Gloucester from 81st to 82nd Brigade. The dismounted Yeomanry on arrival were allotted to the 27th Division, the 10/(Lovat's Scouts) Cameron Highlanders forming part of the 82nd Brigade and the 13/(Scottish Horse) Black Watch of the 81st. The 5th and 6th R. Irish Fusiliers and also the 6th and 7th R. Munster Fusiliers were amalgamated.

General Milne's own opinions as to the requirements in the three situations discussed at the Boulogne Conference were given in a long and closely reasoned appreciation which he addressed to the War Office on the 30th October. This document is remarkable because it is the first from a British military hand which strikes a note of optimism regarding the campaign and, in particular, seizes upon the one serious weakness of the Bulgarian troops and suggests the measures to exploit it.

1916.
Oct.

The Army commander began with some remarks upon the Monastir offensive then in progress, which he thought had been embarked on without the plan of operations having been enough studied, the arrangements for supply having been inadequate and the troops having suffered unnecessary hardships. Turning to the future, he stated that, owing to the weakness of the Serbians, who could not hope to keep their formations up to establishment, and to the sickness in other contingents, he reckoned the Allied Armies to be the equivalent of only 14 divisions. Those divisions were now on a front more than double that of the Entrenched Camp. The Bulgarians had about 10 divisions of 24 battalions each,[1] and he took their strength to be, with the addition of Germans and Turks, that of 23 Allied divisions. The Allied rifle strength was low—about 34,500 British, 32,000 French, and 37,000 Serbians.

Then came the most important and most striking part of the document. The Armée d'Orient was, in General Milne's opinion, capable only of local offensives of a limited nature such as that then in progress against Monastir; but these local offensives might "*at any moment cause a "break-up in the Bulgarian Army*," which did not appreciate a long and trying campaign.

In order to achieve better results all administrative plans must be carefully worked out and all preparations made—possibly including the construction of roads and railways—prior to the concentration of the troops. For this purpose a "capable and genial" higher staff, able to appreciate the difficulties and to understand the idiosyncrasies of the various forces was necessary. When the arrangements were complete, the troops taking part in the

---

[1] Not all the Bulgarian divisions were of 24 battalions. On the other hand, the Bulgarians suffered very little from malaria and their battalions seem so far to have been kept up to a strength of nearly a thousand men.

operation must be moved rapidly against the objective so that local superiority of force and surprise might be obtained.

For the force's original rôle, the defence of Salonika, General Milne considered that if he had to undertake the task with British troops, 10 divisions would suffice, but owing to the cosmopolitan nature of the force he thought it would be well to have 12. That would be the garrison necessary for the Entrenched Camp. On the other hand, this line would have the disadvantage that it would permit the city and harbour to be shelled by long-range guns, and he therefore recommended holding the present line even in the event of a heavy attack. It could easily be held with 22 divisions.

For operations on a large scale with the object of co-operating with the Russians and Rumanians in defeating the Bulgarian Army and cutting off Turkey, he considered that with 24 good divisions and adequate artillery there was a reasonable prospect that the enemy might be forced back; with 29 divisions, the maximum numbers which could be served by the port and the railways, the odds were in our favour, so long as the enemy was not reinforced by German or Turkish divisions. This condition was attached because the enemy's positions were so strong by nature and so well fortified that determined troops adequately supplied with artillery and machine guns should be able to hold them for ever.

Next, General Milne gave his views, first, regarding the use of the present force with the reinforcements promised or likely to be received, and, secondly, as to the force needed for a decisive advance. In either case he would first clear Eastern Macedonia to the Mesta, which would permit the construction of a subsidiary base east of Salonika, probably at Stavros, which he preferred to Kavalla. This might be done in the early spring.

The strength of the Allies, when French and British divisions had been brought up to establishment, would be the equivalent of 15 divisions. Another French and another British division were expected, and it was hoped that three Greek Venizelist divisions would be ready to take the field by the spring; that made 20 divisions. With a force of this strength he would suggest leaving the Greek divisions with one British division to hold the Mesta, and attacking the Rupel Pass with the remaining five British, three carrying out the actual attack and the other two being held in reserve or employed to turn the flank *via* Brodi. Simultaneously the French should attack up the Vardar valley. With the help of the Italians in front of the Belašica Planina, he thought they might be able to force the enemy back far enough for the Allies to repair and take into use the railway from Dojran to Demir Hisar. Meanwhile the Serbians and Russians would attack in the Monastir area. Any subsequent advance would depend for success upon pressure on the enemy from the north, but even with the force mentioned it was possible that the Allies would be able to threaten Strumica seriously.

1916. Oct.

If the Armée d'Orient were increased to 29 divisions (say, eight British, eight French, four Russian, three Italian, three Serbian, and three Greek), the British would be able to operate on a much wider front. In addition to forcing the Rupel Pass (with three divisions)., one division would advance from Drama on Nevrokop, one from Seres in the same direction *via* Brodi and Lovča, and two divisions on Petrić by the passes which led across the Belašica Planina into the Strumica valley from Ramna and Poröi. Meanwhile nine divisions would advance astride the Vardar with a double object : first, to assist the forces operating from Eastern Macedonia to clear the Strumica valley, and, secondly, to break through the Demir Kapiya defile in the Vardar valley, and in conjunction with the force operating from Monastir to capture Veles and Skoplje. If this succeeded, there would then be an advance on Sofia, utilizing the Belgrade railway as far as Kumanova and thence the good road through Kyustendil, the Veles–Štip–Kočana road (together with the light railway from Veles to Štip), and the Struma valley, up which a railway would have to be laid during the advance.

We need not dwell upon the larger scheme because it was put out of court by the fact that the requisite troops could not be provided. Leaving Britain and France out of the question, Italy declared that she would send no troops beyond the extra brigade whereof mention has been made, and Russia would supply only another infantry brigade, from France. What is of chief importance is the principle, which we may put into the words of a slightly earlier telegram, that to secure a reasonable chance of success in Macedonia, " owing to lack of lateral communication "every zone of advance must be worked to its utmost "capacity in order that full advantage may be taken at "once of weakening on any front." General Milne emphasized these statements in a telegram on the 8th November. In this he urged that it was undesirable to give the British forces a purely defensive rôle and locality in 1917, as they would deteriorate in these circumstances; pointed out that troops could not remain next summer in the Struma valley owing to malaria, so that they must either come back—which meant a loss of prestige—or go forward— which involved a larger operation; and again insisted on the importance of the junction of the Struma and Strumica valleys near Petrić, from which point Sofia was threatened. In brief, while he agreed with the General Staff that no decisive action could be taken without large reinforcements, and left it, as was fitting, to the authorities at home to pronounce the last word on policy, he saw far greater possibilities even with the troops now in Macedonia than had ever appeared to Whitehall.

One aspect of the case with which General Milne was not concerned may also be mentioned. "British inter-"vention in the Balkans" is a term which applies equally to the proposals made in 1915 to send an Army to the succour of the Serbians and to those of a year later to carry out an offensive against the Bulgarians from Salonika. Yet the two proposals had little or nothing in common, and the complete change in the situation was in the main to the advantage of the Entente. In a campaign on the Sava and Danube the Central Powers would have been served by vastly superior communications. Both Germany and Austria could transfer troops with the greatest ease from several directions to this front and keep them supplied there, while a force operating against them from Salonika would have been dependent upon one railway which would have had to be held in strength from the Greek frontier to Belgrade. By going to the Danube Britain and France, so far from finding an easier method of approach by which to attack the Central Powers than the Western Front, would have been attacking them on a front which was peculiarly easy for them to defend. Now, not only was Germany much harder pressed elsewhere than she had been a year earlier, but the transport of large formations to the neighbourhood of the Greek frontier would have been for her a very slow and difficult matter, and their adequate supply still harder. There may be some exaggeration in Falkenhayn's statement that "the Entente could send a "division to Macedonia more easily than the Germans could "a battalion,"[1] but even if that phrase cannot be taken literally it represents the general situation well enough. In sum, a campaign on the Danube meant fighting Germany, Austria, and Bulgaria at their strongest, with a heavy disadvantage in communications; a campaign in Southern Macedonia meant fighting Bulgaria and such reinforcement as Germany, Austria, and Turkey could contrive to send her, with an advantage in communications against the two great Powers.

1916. Oct.

The British and French Governments had to discuss one other subject of a painful nature. The War Committee decided that the British Ambassador should represent to the French Government that several communications had been received, not only from British but also from Italian and Russian sources, as to the unsatisfactory conduct of the recent operations by General Sarrail. On the 3rd November Lord Bertie handed to M. Briand a memorandum on this subject. In reply M. Briand stated that the Minister of War had already been sent out to investigate affairs, doubtless in part because of the report made by General Cordonnier on arrival at Chantilly, in part because of unofficial representations already made by the Russian Ambassador.[2] The Minister, General Roques, actually arrived that day at Salonika and remained until the 12th November. His report was generally favourable to General Sarrail; it was, indeed, hardly to be expected that he would fail to support his compatriot in such circumstances. After the French Commander-in-Chief had, into the bargain, won a striking and important success by capturing Monastir on the 19th, the affair was allowed to lapse for the time being.

Nov.

---

[1] Falkenhayn, p. 183.
[2] Cordonnier, pp. 340–1. Mermeix, "Le Commandement Unique," II, p. 114.

CHAPTER X.

THE GREEK IMBROGLIO, AUGUST 1916 TO JANUARY 1917.

(Maps 1, 2.)

AFFAIRS IN OLD GREECE.

Map 1. THE political affairs of Greece at the end of the year 1916 were complicated and unhappy. They have not yet emerged into the clear light of history, because the dust stirred up by the strife which raged about them has not yet been allowed to settle. Perhaps, indeed, they never will emerge entirely. Even documentary evidence is not accepted by the partisans on either side. A riot with important results is, let us say, thus put on record. We have full evidence that it took place; but we are unable to draw inferences from it because of the suggestion that it was carried out or instigated by *agents provocateurs*. Fortunately, so far as the military situation in Macedonia is concerned, it is not necessary to weigh the motives of the two parties in Greece, still less to trace an alleged conflict of policy between the French Ministries of Foreign Affairs and of the Marine. Events and reports, not tendencies, have to be recorded. The sole point of view which needs to be taken into account is that of Great Britain; the sole evidence which needs to be considered is that given by the British diplomatic, naval, and military authorities on the spot.

After the formation of the Zaimis Ministry at the end of June 1916 there was a certain improvement in Greek relations with the Entente. There were still, however, minor matters of disagreement, and Sir Francis Elliot reported on the 5th July that General Sarrail in his dealings with the Greek authorities at Salonika made too little distinction between this Prime Minister and his very much less friendly predecessor. M. Zaimis looked upon himself as a stop-gap, and would, according to the British Minister's information, have been glad to bring about a reconciliation between the King and M. Venizelos before stepping aside to allow the latter's return to power.

Up to the 17th August, when the Bulgarians began their advance into Greek Eastern Macedonia, affairs were

going smoothly. It was to be long before that could again 1916.
be said. In the first place, the Bulgarian invasion and still Aug.
more the inhumanity of the invaders, who burnt and sacked
Greek villages, roused to action the Liberal party at Salonika,
which had for some time been eager that Greece should
intervene in the war. A meeting was held to protest against
the failure of the Government to defend Greek territory.
On the 30th a " Committee of Public Safety " was formed,
headed by Colonels Mazarakis and Zimbrakakis, and
supported by the artillery regiment in Salonika, the
gendarmerie, and the police. It proclaimed that Greek
Macedonia had ranged itself on the side of the Entente,
and appointed a commission to control the Greek administrative services. The Prefect took no action, while awaiting
instructions from Athens, and there was no disturbance
that day. In the early hours of the 31st, however, collisions
took place between the Royalist troops and those supporting
the new movement, from which six casualties resulted.[1]
After negotiations between the Committee and General
Sarrail, the Royalist garrison was disarmed. Some of
these troops decided to enrol themselves among the
supporters of the Entente; the rest were marched under
French escort to a temporary concentration camp. The
movement was not, according to Sir Francis Elliot's information, purely revolutionary; for, on the 31st August, he
reported his belief that the Committee had been about to
proclaim the autonomy of Macedonia but had not done so
owing to fear that the King might abdicate.

Meanwhile the Bulgarians were advancing in Eastern
Macedonia. Here and there the Greeks made some
resistance, but always against orders from Athens. Colonel
Christodoulos, acting commander of the 6th Division, was
apparently prepared to defend Seres, but found that
impossible. He then marched down towards the coast with
the field artillery of the IV Corps, which he picked up at
Drama. The 5th Division there refused to join him. He Sept.
exchanged some shots with the Bulgarians, but was not
opposed by them, and was allowed to enter Kavalla on the
4th September, though the Bulgarians, as previously
recorded, had possession of the forts.[2] Negotiations

---

[1] General Milne's telegram to the Director of Military Intelligence.
General Sarrail (p. 154) reports that there were three killed and five wounded.
[2] See p. 161.

followed between Colonel Hadzopoulos, the Greek corps commander, and the Allied naval authorities for the evacuation of the force; but when the former learnt that his troops would be taken to Salonika, where there was every chance that they would be induced to join the new movement, he refused the proffered aid. On the 10th a German officer demanded the surrender of Kavalla and the troops in it within 24 hours. A panic broke out in the town that night. Greek troops seized lighters in the harbour and put to sea in an endeavour to reach Thasos, but were washed back in the morning. Eventually Colonel Christodoulos got his troops, and a small proportion of the Kavalla (7th) Division, embarked, the total force being about 2,000 men and 10 batteries; the rest of the corps, about 8,000 men, surrendered with all the remaining artillery and the fortress guns on the evening of the 11th. The Greek troops were interned in Germany, but not treated as prisoners of war.

The Bulgarians finally occupied Kavalla on the 12th, leaving time for the Turkish population to break into the Greek magazines and arm themselves.

A second important effect of the invasion was that the Greek elections had to be indefinitely postponed. M. Venizelos had counted on winning many seats in Eastern Macedonia, and, though he appeared willing to take his chance without this strong factor in his favour, he eventually informed Sir Francis Elliot of his agreement with the Prime Minister, M. Zaimis, that it was impossible to hold the elections in these circumstances.

What was the part in the Bulgarian advance played by the Greek Government; how far did they connive in it? It seems that their rôle was no more friendly to the Allies, but possibly also no more hostile than in the case of the occupation of the Rupel Pass. It was afterwards discovered by the British intelligence service, and could not have been unknown at the time to the Greeks, that all preparations for the invasion had been made at the beginning of August. It was found also that arms had been brought in and handed over to the Bulgarian and Turkish population, while *comitaji* leaders had been actively organizing the villagers of those nationalities. Once again Germany had informed the Greek Government of her intention, and once again the Allies had been given no warning; nor had any attempt been authorized—or made, except by Colonel Christodoulos

—to prevent the artillery and warlike stores in Eastern Macedonia from falling into the hands of the Bulgarians. If there were suspicions that the Greeks went further than this towards collusion with the enemy, there was no proof.

1916.
Aug.

M. Venizelos, however, told the British Minister that he had information that the Bulgarian invasion was part of a plot to get possession of the whole of Greece, and that even an advance on Athens was possible. Sir Francis Elliot at first thought there might be something in the story, especially as he had noticed that recent events had caused unconcealed delight in Court circles. The suggestion was, of course, that this advance would take place not from Eastern but from Western Macedonia, where the Greek frontier was open for some forty miles owing to the left wing of the Allies having been driven in by the Bulgarians. There was actually a rumour that German cavalry had reached Larissa, 25 miles from the Ægean. This was false; but, on the other hand, M. Zaimis stated to Sir Francis Elliot on the 25th August that Bulgarians had penetrated as far as Kozana, 25 miles south of Lake Ostrovo, and 55 miles north-west of Larissa. The British military authorities thought the advance of any considerable force by this route to be out of the question, unless the Allies in Macedonia were first defeated. A raid was, however, clearly possible, though the chances were diminished in the next few days by the advance of the French and Serbians on this flank.

In the same interview M. Zaimis informed Sir Francis Elliot and his French and Russian colleagues that in no event would Greece undertake hostilities against Germany, but that it was open to the Allies to take what measures they chose. An occupation by them would be unpleasant, but, personally, he would much prefer it to an occupation by Germans or Bulgarians. Sir Francis and his colleagues recommended that preparations should be made to despatch troops if necessary, that an Allied squadron should be sent to Milos or Poros, one ship of each nationality coming to Piræus. No further action need be taken until a reply was received from Germany to a request made by Greece that a line should be fixed beyond which German or Bulgarian forces should not penetrate unless there were Allied troops on the other side. The Allied Governments could then decide whether or not they would, once and for all, make an end of the German organization in Athens. M. Briand informed the British Government that he was in agreement with their view as to the rumoured German invasion of Greece, and did not consider that any special military or naval counter-stroke was required.

The British Government were therefore astonished to receive on the 26th, first, a message through the French Naval Attaché that Admiral Dartige du Fournet had been ordered to proceed to Salamis Bay with his fleet and General Sarrail to prepare the transport of troops, and that British co-operation had been requested; secondly, a communication from the French Ambassador that a hostile advance on Larissa was possible, and that if it were attempted the Allies should be ready to take vigorous action. Lord Grey telegraphed to the British Ambassador in Paris that the Government deprecated any aggressive action, military or naval, and proposed to issue to their Vice-Admiral in the Mediterranean, who had been instructed to hold himself in readiness, no further orders. On the 30th, however, the War Committee had before it a memorandum from M. Cambon, to the effect that the French Government believed the enemy to be informed of every movement of the Armée d'Orient through Greek military channels. M. Briand did not think that the replacement of the Chief of the Staff, to which M. Zaimis had agreed, was sufficient.[1] While communication between Athens and the enemy by way of Florina was open, it would be possible for German agents to send not only news but supplies to the Bulgarians. The French Government thought it necessary to have their hands upon the posts and telegraphs, the railways, and the ports, and had prepared the embarkation at Salonika of a brigade to reinforce their demands. They would act only in agreement with the British, but considered it essential that the British should participate.

The War Committee gave way so far as to allow a squadron under Rear-Admiral A. Hayes-Sadler to be despatched to Salamis Bay to act under the French Admiral; but Lord Grey succeeded in persuading M. Briand to renounce his proposal to land troops. The object of the French Admiral was to seize Austrian ships interned at

---

[1] This was General Dousmanis, considered to be strongly Germanophil. He was succeeded by General Moschopoulos, formerly in command at Salonika, whose relations with the Allies had been fairly good.

SEIZURE OF GREEK FLEET 213

Piræus and to support the demands of the French Government regarding the posts and telegraphs and the expulsion of German agents. His powerful Allied fleet arrived off Salamis during the night of the 31st August; next morning the enemy ships were seized and towed to the fleet anchorage. The Greek fleet was paralysed, as it could not have put to sea without passing across the batteries of the Allied battle squadron in the bay.[1]

1916.
Aug.

A sudden and dramatic change, or hint of a change, in the Greek situation caused the British Government to reconsider their decision respecting the naval demonstration; but actually too late to stop it. In the course of the 30th August a series of overtures were made by King Constantine, M. Zaimis, and General Moschopoulos. They informed the Allied Ministers that, owing to the intervention of Rumania, the moment was approaching when Greece might alter her whole military policy and adopt one of active co-operation with the Entente. All three spoke as if an offer to do so were imminent, and M. Zaimis went so far as to sound the British Minister regarding the provision of arms, equipment, and money.

We see, then, how involved affairs had become by the time these messages were considered by the British Government. At Salamis the Allied fleet was approaching to seize the Austrian ships and immobilize the Greek fleet next morning; at Salonika the revolutionary movement had broken out, and General Sarrail was about to take it under his protection and march the Royalist troops ignominiously out of the city to a concentration camp; at Athens the head of the State, the head of the Government, and the head of the Army were suggesting that within a little while Greece would offer to range herself beside the Allies.

The Government, as we have said, could not stop the naval demonstration. Their problem was therefore now whether or not to associate themselves with the French demands. They decided to do so, unless, as Lord Grey telegraphed on the 1st September, there were " such a " change in the situation as to make them no longer " necessary." Sir Francis Elliot replied with some dryness that the demands were neither more nor less " necessary "

Sept.

---

[1] " Naval Operations," IV, p. 143.

—employing inverted commas for the word—now than they had been three days earlier, and, with M. Guillemin, addressed to the Greek Government on the 2nd a Note which embodied them. It ran as follows :—

"1. The two Allied Governments, knowing from sure "sources that their enemies obtain information in various "ways, and especially by the Greek telegraphs, demand "control of the posts and telegraphs with or without wires.

"2. The enemy agents of corruption and espionage "must leave Greece immediately and not return until the "end of the war.

"3. The necessary legal proceedings shall be taken "against Greek subjects who have been accomplices in the "above actions of corruption and espionage."

The Greek Government formally accepted the Note, but there was a great deal of discussion necessary to decide to what extent they should be allowed to communicate in cipher with their representatives in Allied countries, and also as to the measures to be taken against Greek subjects mentioned in the third paragraph. While negotiations were in progress Greece made a more direct approach to Great Britain and France. On the 5th September the Lord President of the Council, Lord Crewe (who was deputizing for Lord Grey at this moment), read to the War Committee a communication from the Greek Minister in London, M. Gennadius, to the effect that she was reconsidering her attitude. Owing to the state of her finances and equipment, it would be long before she could act in a military sense, and certainly for the moment, while her troops in territory occupied by the Bulgarians had not been disengaged, she must maintain reserve. The inquiry was therefore limited as to whether the Allies were disposed to assist with money and supplies her ultimate entry into the war.

There was some delay before this suggestion was crystallized into a formal offer. This was contained in a Note handed in to the Foreign Office by M. Gennadius, which was considered by the War Committee on the 20th, and was in the following terms :—

"The Government of Greece declare that they will "depart from their policy of neutrality, in favour of the "Entente Powers, as soon as she has, thanks to their "financial and military support, completed the refitting

" of her military forces, and proceeded, within a period
" fixed by common agreement, to a general mobilization
" of her Army.

" The Greek Government think, however, that, since
" common interest of course requires that the armed
" intervention of Greece should only take place as soon
" as it can do so with chances of success, Greece should
" not be held to the above engagement if at the time fixed
" there should be, in the opinion of the Allied General
" Staffs, a disparity of forces in the Balkan theatre of
" operations such as would not be balanced by the addition
" of the Greek military forces.

" In becoming an ally of the Entente Powers, Greece
" counts upon obtaining all the advantages which may flow
" from that alliance, as well during the course of the struggle
" as at the time of the settlement of peace.

" The Royal Government are also persuaded that during
" the war the Entente Powers will assist her in bearing the
" expenses of the war and of safeguarding the interests of
" commercial credit and of the country's shipping, and that
" at the peace, having in view the situation created in
" Northern Epirus, and the promises given at various times
" on the subject of an eventual territorial extension, notably
" in Thrace and on the coast of Asia Minor, they will be
" good enough to render all their help towards the possible
" realization of her national aspirations."

Vague as it was, this document might have met with a different reception had it been delivered a fortnight earlier. In that fortnight a great deal had happened, none of it calculated to improve the tempers of the Allies on one side or of the party of King Constantine on the other. A brawl in the courtyard of the French Legation on the 10th had caused the French Admiral to land a small party of sailors to guard it. The surrender of the Greek troops, guns, and war material at Kavalla next day had exasperated the Allies. The Salonika revolutionary movement was extending to the Greek islands, and had destroyed any slight hope there may have been that the King and M. Venizelos would be reconciled. Societies of army reservists, bitterly hostile to the Entente, were showing great activity. On the other hand, General Sarrail's treatment of the Royalist troops at Salonika had inflamed Greek opinion. The officers, who had been sent straight to Athens by ship, had been received on the 6th by the King, who had warmly congratulated them upon their loyalty to his person. What was still more serious, M. Zaimis had resigned, and had been succeeded by M. Kalogeropoulos, at the head of a political Cabinet, the constitution of which was considered to be a violation of the terms of the agreement that affairs should be in the hands of a " Business Ministry." Worst of all, King Constantine had by his words and general attitude caused Sir Francis Elliot to suspect that he had not been sincere in his overtures for co-operation, and that it was the discovery of this which had caused the resignation of M. Zaimis.

The short-lived Kalogeropoulos Cabinet (17th September to 9th October) was never recognized by the Allies, which was possibly a mistake on their part. After its fall, M. Polites, a strong Venizelist, who had been the chief official in the Ministry of Foreign Affairs, declared in the Athens Press that this Cabinet had been genuinely anxious to bring Greece into the war on the side of the Allies, and that it was the only recent one whereof that could be said.

In these circumstances, the Greek Note had lost some of its significance by the time it was delivered. Strangely enough, though French policy in Greece had been in the past and was to be in the future severe enough to cause Great Britain doubt and misgiving, on this occasion the French Ministry of Foreign Affairs was prepared to give a more favourable answer to the Note than it seemed to merit in the eyes either of the Foreign Office or of Sir Francis Elliot. To both it appeared that the proposals, coming from a Cabinet which had not the confidence of the Allies, were unsatisfactory. Lord Hardinge, the Permanent Under-Secretary of State for Foreign Affairs, in a memorandum drawn up for the War Committee, declared himself impressed by their " emptiness and duplicity." Nothing definite but mobilization was promised. Even then there need be no declaration of war if the situation should become menacing ; and if, through a leakage of their intentions, this should occur, the Greek Government would be released from all obligations, after having had their Army refitted by the Allies. It would be open to them to make such a leakage themselves and recover full liberty of action. In return they expected to be treated on equal terms, to reap commercial advantages, and to receive territorial concessions.

"It strikes me," continued Lord Hardinge, "as a very 1916. "brazen-faced proposal, and I do not think we should accept Sept. "M. Briand's views."

Both the Foreign Office and Sir Francis Elliot came independently to the view that guarantees must be given, and that the essential guarantee was the immediate recognition—the former suggested by the 1st October—of a state of war with Bulgaria. The unreadiness of Greece was no valid argument for delay, since the enemy could not now (that is, after the British had made secure the line of the Struma and the French and Serbians had captured Florina) advance further into Greek territory than he had already penetrated.

Before a reply had been agreed upon there was once again a long delay, and once again important events supervened. On the night of the 24th September M. Venizelos suddenly left Athens with his chief naval supporter, Admiral Condouriotis, for Crete, to head the revolt which had already broken out there,[1] and at the same time the Greek coast-defence ship *Hydra* and two torpedo-boats left their anchorage and joined the Allied fleet.

Probably in part as a result of this, the reservist Oct. societies instituted what Sir Francis Elliot described as "a reign of terror" against the Venizelists. The Government, moreover, had not kept its engagements, notably with regard to the removal of police officials hostile to the Entente. The French Admiral, who appeared to have instructions to take the conduct of affairs from diplomatic hands, informed Sir Francis Elliot that, in default of complete satisfaction of his demands, he contemplated landing three hundred sailors to reinforce the police of Athens and Piræus. The British Minister was not altogether averse to the plan, if due notice were given; and Lord Grey telegraphed on the 9th October that the British Government were prepared to agree to it. Before action had been taken there were fresh developments. On the 4th M. Venizelos sailed from Suda Bay in Crete, escorted by one Greek and one French torpedo-boat, visited Mitylene on the 7th, and reached Salonika on the 9th, to set himself at the head of the provisional government already formed by his adherents. On the 7th the

---

[1] An interesting account of affairs in Crete at this time is given by J. C. Lawson in " Tales of Ægean Intrigue," Chap. V.

Military Attaché reported a concentration of Greek troops in the neighbourhood of Larissa, and so in rear of the Allies.[1] On the 9th a new Ministry under Professor Lambros, of no marked political colour and apparently the mere mouthpiece of the King, was formed in Athens.

Suddenly the French Government ordered their naval commander at Salamis to take a step which was repugnant to the British Government, but not more so than to himself. On the evening of the 10th the Foreign Office learnt through the Admiralty that Admiral Dartige du Fournet had been instructed to demand the surrender of the Greek fleet next day, for the protection of the Allied fleet and in consequence of the assembly of troops and munitions near Larissa. Lord Grey at once protested strongly, telegraphing to Lord Bertie that the Government were much surprised at the setting on foot of " so startling a measure, in which British ships on " spot, being under command of French Commander-in- " Chief, will co-operate, without consultation with us or " explanation of reasons." Unless there were circumstances unknown to the British Government which called for immediate and drastic action, he begged that the admiral might be ordered to hold his hand.

It was too late. The operation was carried out next day without disturbance, the breech-blocks and munitions of the larger ships being removed and the crews reduced to care and maintenance parties.[2] Lord Bertie's telegram, reporting that the cause of the French action was the recent substitution, for the original crews, of hostile officers and men and the danger of a torpedo attack, did not reach Whitehall until that action was well in train. On the 16th, in view of public excitement, the admiral landed patrols at Piræus and sent 140 men to Athens.

The incident undoubtedly enraged a great number of Greeks as well as King Constantine, who compared M. Venizelos to Roger Casement, and declared to Sir Francis Elliot that, if he caught him, he would treat his former Prime Minister in the same fashion as Britain had treated the Irish rebel. The British Minister naturally declined

---

[1] General Milne reported on the 11th that his information tended to confirm that of the Military Attaché. Apparently, he telegraphed, the King wished to establish " a zone of independent action." This was a possible danger.

[2] " Naval Operations," IV, p. 152.

to continue that phase of the conversation, but pressed the King regarding the dissolution of the reservist societies.

1916. Oct.

It was in this atmosphere that the reply of the Allies to the Note of the 20th September was sent. The text was drawn up at the Boulogne Conference, and the British copy, handed to M. Gennadius on the 23rd October, was as follows :—

"In reply to the proposal of the King of Greece trans-
"mitted by the Greek Minister in London on the 20th
"September last, the Powers point out that they have never
"intervened with the King and his Government and have
"never desired to exercise pressure upon him to push Greece
"into the war on their side; they have asked for one thing
"only: the observation of that benevolent neutrality
"which was promised to them and which is indispensable
"to the security of the expeditionary corps of Salonika.

"The action of the Allies is inspired solely by these
"principles; they went to Salonika because they were called
"to the aid of the Serbians, Allies of Greece; every one of
"their interventions has had for basis their duties and their
"rights as Protecting Powers. If these interventions have
"been numerous, it is solely because Germanophil agents,
"with the complicity of Greek officials, have unceasingly
"by their machinations put our armies in peril, and because
"the Greek Government themselves, expected to defend
"their territory, have not scrupled to hand over to the enemy
"their fortresses, their troops, their guns, their munitions,
"and their stores.

"It has been quite spontaneously that the Royal
"Government has on several occasions since the beginning
"of the war offered to intervene on our side; but these
"proposals, and especially the last, were accompanied by
"conditions which made them unacceptable; in any case
"they bore with them no guarantee.

"The Powers will not welcome the adhesion of Greece
"without certain indispensable guarantees, unless the Royal
"Government, of its own initiative, considers that, in fact
"and as a result of the Bulgarian action at Kavalla and at
"Florina, a state of war exists between Greece and Bulgaria.
"That is the sole means of establishing unity in Greece and
"gaining the confidence and the support of the Allies."

The expression, "Protecting Powers" or "Guaranteeing Powers," refers to the Treaties of 1832 and 1863, guaranteeing the political existence and frontiers of the Kingdom of Greece. Under these Treaties Great Britain, France, and Russia assumed the position of Protecting Powers. This position imposed upon them the duty of assuring that the King and Government did not jeopardize the security of Greece. The argument was that the King and Government had gone so far in prejudicing the security of their country as to hand over to Bulgaria their fortresses, troops, guns, munitions, and stores; and that, in consequence, the Protecting Powers were compelled to intervene.

There was now little or no prospect that Greece would comply with the provisions of the Note. Some conversations which the King had at the end of October with a French deputy, M. Bénazet, seemed for a short time likely to improve the situation, but they were finally, as we shall see, so far from being useful that they led to a disaster. Swiftly the affair moved to its destined end. On the 31st October the German Legation issued a communiqué relative to an accident to the Greek steamer *Angheliki*. Sir Francis Elliot immediately pointed out that, whether the ship was injured by torpedo, mine, or infernal machine, this communiqué was an official avowal of the intention to sink Greek ships carrying " revolutionaries "—that is, troops from the islands on their way to support M. Venizelos at Salonika—and even of the possession of means of communicating information respecting such ships to submarines. He thought that here was a unique opportunity for insisting on the departure of all the enemy legations. The Ministers were finally ordered to leave, and sailed in a Greek steamer for Kavalla on the 22nd November.

1916. Nov. Here there was complete agreement between Britain and France. This was not the case regarding another measure taken by the French. Admiral Dartige du Fournet informed the Greek Government that he had received orders to employ for the protection of Greek waters Greek warships already sequestrated, and that he required the use of Salamis arsenal for repairs. The Greek Government would be indemnified. The demands were formally refused, whereupon, on the 7th November, the French flag was hoisted in the torpedo boats and the arsenal was taken over.

Royalist and Venizelist troops had come into conflict at Katerini in Thessaly, and the Allies were striving to form a neutral zone to keep them from each other's throats. The Greek Government showed so far no sign of fulfilling a promise made on the 17th October to withdraw all troops in Thessaly, except one division, into the Morea; and, though they were being maintained on the mainland to oppose the Venizelists, their presence so close in rear of the Allied forces was disquieting.

1916.
Nov.

Once again, though the French admiral had taken steps so drastic as to astonish the British Government, the French Foreign Office was more inclined than the British to make things easy for King Constantine with regard to M. Venizelos. Britain had not officially recognized the latter's Provisional Government at Salonika, but had, on the 24th October, authorized the British Minister to deal with him through the Consul-General in all questions relating to the districts and islands which accepted his administration. She would willingly have gone further, but M. Briand hesitated. Apparently he still hoped to conciliate the King, though how that was to be achieved now it was hard to see. He therefore persuaded the British Government to give M. Venizelos no formal recognition.

The next move was an intimation by Admiral Dartige du Fournet that he would demand warlike stores as a set-off against those handed over to the Bulgarians, and the immediate cession of ten mountain batteries to begin with. This was actually the King's own suggestion. It had been agreed between him and M. Bénazet that the Allies should make this demand in courteous terms and with a promise of payment, that the King should make a formal protest, and that he should then issue a proclamation that he agreed to the demands in order to maintain strict neutrality between the belligerents. He stipulated that the arms should not be handed over to the Venizelists, but apparently did not object to the Allies' enrolling volunteers in Thessaly and equipping them for their own resources.[1] The work of M. Bénazet was honest and ingenious, but it bore the marks of amateur craftsmanship. The withdrawal of negotiations from the hands of professional diplomacy was, in fact, the most noxious element in all this unhappy affair.

Now M. Bénazet was gone; General Roques, who had taken part in the preparation of the Note, was gone also;

---

[1] " Naval Operations," IV, p. 157.

and all the responsibility was left upon the shoulders of the admiral. The King, making one of those changes of resolution which rendered dealing with him so difficult, requested that the Note should not be delivered, though he gave orders to fulfil his promises by withdrawing the III and IV Corps to the Morea.[1]

The Note was presented by the admiral on the 16th November. The British Government had not been consulted with respect to its phraseology, but certainly could not have objected to it on the score of harshness; for it was mild and conciliatory in form. It expressed the French Government's appreciation of the orders given for the withdrawal of the troops, and then went on to remark that the surrender of Fort Rupel and the cession of the war material at Kavalla had upset the equilibrium to the advantage of the enemies of the Entente Powers. The French Government had therefore decided to demand the delivery of what war material was not now needed by Greece owing to the reduction of her army to a peace footing. They would ask for 16 field batteries, 16 mountain batteries, and 40,000 Mannlicher rifles, with ammunition, for which they offered reasonable payment. The Greek Government were requested to give proof of their good will by at once delivering 10 mountain batteries at the Thessaly railway station in Athens. There was in the Note no promise that these arms should not be given to the Venizelist troops. Such a promise, indeed, would have been unreasonable, and it was one of the worst weaknesses of the unofficial Bénazet negotiations that it should ever have been contemplated. The change of policy was none the less unfortunate.

The Greek reply, handed to the admiral on the 21st, was a complete refusal. Admiral Dartige du Fournet then stated that if the surrender of arms was not begun by the 1st December he would land 3,000 seamen to enforce his demands. The King replied that the situation had now got beyond his control, and that the public and the Army would not allow him to surrender the arms—" an unfortunate " confession from a monarch who had replaced the parlia- " mentary institutions of the country by a personal autocracy " of his own."[2] The admiral therefore informed him that the landings would take place, and asked whether the

---

[1] " Naval Operations," IV, p. 158.   [2] *Ibid.*, p. 164.

Government would keep order. He was given a reply by the hand of a Court official, Count Mercati, that the Venizelists should not be molested, if the Allies kept their hands off Greek subjects and the adherents of M. Venizelos refrained from acts of violence. Admiral Dartige also states that King Constantine informed him verbally that the Greek troops would have orders not to fire first.[1] The admiral seems to have been extraordinarily optimistic, since he must surely have had the information in the hands of the British Minister, that the doors of the Venizelists had been marked with paint, which could only have been done for identification by the Royalist mob, that reservists were pouring in and being collected in barracks, and that stores were being secretly removed from the military magazines.

The landing parties, consisting of three battalions of French sailors, three companies of the R.M.L.I. from the *Exmouth* and *Duncan*, acting under the orders of the French commander, and a small Italian detachment,[2] were put ashore early in the morning of the 1st December. The intention of the French admiral was to occupy the hills overlooking Athens from the south-west and the Zappeion theatre, and also to take possession of an arsenal and two munition factories outside the city. Most of the positions were occupied; but at 11 a.m. the Greek troops attacked each of the detachments simultaneously, evidently according to a pre-arranged plan. The French and British were surrounded, but beat off all attacks until at 11.45 a.m. the admiral sent a message to the French fleet to open fire on the Stadium, whence the Greeks were firing on the Zappeion. He now received a message from the King asking him to compromise and accept the surrender of six batteries. In view of the difficult situation of his own men, and of the risks run by the Legations and by Allied civilians in the city, Admiral Dartige agreed to negotiate. He was, however, forced by a renewal of the attacks to open fire again at 4.30 p.m. This time shells fell in the courtyard of the Diadoch's palace, where the King and his family were installed, and this speedily brought about the cessation of the Greek attack.

---

[1] Dartige du Fournet, " Souvenirs de Guerre d'un Amiral," p. 204.
[2] The Italians were opposed to the demonstrations owing to their hostility to M. Venizelos and withdrew at the first shot.

Eventually agreement was reached. The King promised to hand over the six batteries when the landing-parties had withdrawn. Admiral Dartige withdrew the landing-parties to the ships—except for a detachment at the Zappeion, which was also recalled next day—and the prisoners taken by both sides were exchanged. The casualties of the French were 191, and those of the British 21. The Greek Government behaved with decency towards the dead and with real consideration for the wounded who had fallen in the treacherous ambush prepared by their nationals.[1]

The parting words of Admiral Dartige were to the effect that this day's events would have grave consequences. He actually contemplated a bombardment of Athens, but was, Sir Francis Elliot reported, restrained by M. Guillemin from carrying this out. His warning did not prevent the Royalists from wreaking vengeance upon the Liberals. Throughout the two following days troops and reservists scoured the city, looting houses, inflicting barbarous cruelties upon men, mishandling their families, and filling the prisons to overflowing.

The political crisis which occurred in London just at the moment when it was necessary to deal with this miserable situation caused some delay. Mr. Asquith resigned on the 4th December, to be succeeded as Prime Minister by Mr. Lloyd George on the 7th. The War Committee did not meet after Mr. Asquith's resignation, and its successor, the War Cabinet, did not hold its first meeting until the 9th. Up till then the only step taken was an order to the British squadron in the Eastern Mediterranean to co-operate with the French in a blockade of the Greek coasts, which was begun on the 8th. The War Cabinet decided to maintain this blockade until reparation for the attack had been made and guarantees for the future had been given. On the 14th Sir Francis Elliot delivered an ultimatum—actually drawn up by Lord Grey before handing over to his successor, Mr. A. J. Balfour—demanding the withdrawal of all Greek troops to the Morea. The Minister then, in accordance with his instructions, left the Legation and went aboard a ship at Piræus. The ultimatum was accepted next day, but the

---

[1] " Naval Operations," IV, pp. 166–171. The account in the official naval history, of an affair which is important mainly from the naval point of view, is detailed.

Greek Government attempted to bargain, and the matter was not finally settled when the Allied Conference opened in Rome on the 5th January 1917.

1917.
Jan.

Admiral Dartige du Fournet was relieved of his command by the French Government, which also had a crisis to face. The Ministry was reorganized, with M. Briand still at its head, on the 12th. It was, however, in a precarious situation and depended for its retention of office largely upon the prestige of General Lyautey at the Ministry of War.

Affairs in Macedonia and Thessaly.

On the arrival of M. Venizelos at Salonika, General Milne asked for instructions as to the attitude to be assumed towards him, and was informed by the C.I.G.S. on the 10th October that the Provisional Government was not to be officially recognized. The Army commander had, however, been instructed on the 1st that he was to give his support to the National movement. After an interview with M. Venizelos, he telegraphed home that the new government hoped to raise four divisions, of about 10,000 infantry apiece. Their aim was to drive the Bulgarians out of Greek territory, and for this purpose they wished to operate in Eastern Macedonia. They declared that they had almost sufficient rifles, equipment, and clothing in their mobilization stores, but only three mountain batteries, though nine field batteries saved at Kavalla and lent to the Serbians might also be available. General Milne considered that, if the Struma front was to remain British and if the Greeks were to operate there, they should be placed under the British commander both tactically and administratively, though this would involve for Great Britain the provision of all their requirements. He deprecated dual control, and suggested that either British or French should take complete responsibility.

1916.
Oct.
Maps 1, 2.

The Government decided otherwise, however, arranging that while Britain and France should share the provision of the necessary equipment, the Greek troops should be " under the general control " of the French. At the same time the Greek battalions might be sent as they were ready to the Struma front to serve under General Milne's orders. By the 10th November three battalions, forming a regiment, had been taken over by General Milne, who was able to supply them temporarily.

1916. Dec. News of what had happened in Athens on the 1st December arrived at Salonika slowly, piecemeal, and at first in exaggerated form. Even the baldest truth had an ugly aspect. Greece was on the brink of a state of war with the Allies. Two days later, on the 3rd, the fall of Bucharest virtually brought the Rumanian campaign to an end. The exhaustion and heavy losses of the German troops were not known, and it was asked whether Germany would not now be in a position to direct a considerable force upon Monastir, in which quarter she had already reinforced the Bulgarians. Combined with a Greek attack from the rear, even if made in no great strength, this would be exceedingly dangerous. When the fate of the Venizelists in Athens was learnt, the civilian sympathizers with the Allies were thrown into the depths of despair, and it was hard even for the military authorities to avoid depression. Altogether this was a black moment.

General Sarrail immediately came to General Milne and informed him that he could not continue the Monastir offensive with a hostile Greek force threatening his rear. He proposed to drive the Royalist forces out of Thessaly, employing for the purpose the British 60th Division, which was in course of transport from France to Salonika, the Italian division, which had just been relieved by General Milne, and such French troops as he could spare. The British Army commander was convinced that an attack was neither necessary nor desirable, but he was no whit less anxious than General Sarrail to take such military action as would prevent the Royalist troops from endangering the communications of the Allies. There was no doubt that there had been a minor concentration about Larissa, that the battalions had been strengthened by reservists, and that food had been collected. General Milne considered that there were between 20,000 and 30,000 men, with at least 100 guns, within easy reach of Larissa. If mobilization were allowed to proceed, the strength of the concentration might reach 80,000, though food supplies were not yet sufficient to maintain more than half this force for any length of time. There were also 6,000 troops, with 50 guns, in Epirus. General Milne also noted that wireless communication between Athens and Sofia had been resumed, and, from the acknowledgments, partly in clear, he was of opinion that cipher messages intended for the Greek Minister in Berlin had been sent.[1]

1916. Dec.

General Milne decided to send the 179th Brigade (Br.-General F. M. Edwards) of the 60th (London) Division, with a detachment of artillery and engineers, to Katerini. The 60th, which was the reinforcement promised to meet the French demands, was a second-line Territorial Force division, not yet at its best, but containing excellent material, as it was later to prove in Palestine. It had been for six months in France, but had not been on the Somme front, and so had not been engaged in any action bigger than a trench raid. Its commander, Major-General E. S. Bulfin, arrived at Salonika on the 8th December.

Storms and floods having broken the Salonika–Athens railway at more than one point, the troops, guns, artillery wagons, and engineer stores had to be sent by sea, though one party of the Royal Engineers got as far as Tuzla by rail, repairing breaches in the line on its way. The transport, which was on the Salonika pack scale, mules and saddlery having been issued immediately on arrival, went by road, escorted by a squadron of the Lothians and Border Horse, and was delayed by the flooded condition of the country.

The brigade group[2] began embarkation at Salonika on the 11th. On arrival at Vromeris in the afternoon it was found that the jetty had been washed away; consequently the troops had to wade ashore. They began their expedition as miserably as those who first landed at Salonika, and for a similar reason. Their baggage was piled on the beach by naval ratings in heaps which it took two days to sort. Without attempting to do so then, the battalions collected driftwood to dry their clothes. After dark the 2/13th and 2/15th London marched to Katerini. Meanwhile another gale sprang up and the lighters had to be towed back to Salonika, some of the stores and baggage not yet landed being swept off their decks by heavy seas. Before sufficient

---

[1] We now know from the Greek "White Book" that several messages passed between the Kaiser and the Greek Royal family in December and January, including on the one hand demands that "Tino" should attack the left wing of the Allies, and on the other questions as to whether a German attack was in preparation, and, if so, when it would begin.

[2] 179th Brigade, headquarters and two 18-pdr. batteries CCCII Brigade R.F.A., 179th Machine-gun Company, 2/4th London Field Company R.E., 2/4th London Field Ambulance.

supplies arrived the troops had eaten their iron rations and begun requisitioning sheep. The two batteries arrived on the 14th and 17th, respectively. The 2/4th London Field Company R.E. set about repairing the jetty and throwing a trestle bridge across the Pelikas river.

The information given to Br.-General Edwards was that the attitude of the Royalist troops assembling in the Larissa district was threatening. The Venizelists were in possession of the country north of a line drawn approximately east and west three miles south of Katerini. Small detachments of French troops had already reached Katerini and Vlacholivadi, 25 miles to the south-west, and the Italian division, sent by railway from Salonika to Verria, was moving down towards Kozana and Servia. The brigadier was instructed to act with all military precautions and to place no trust in the inhabitants of the country, but not to provoke hostilities. On this subject there was again some conflict of opinion between Britain and France. The French view—or at least that of French naval and military opinion—was that the treacherous act of hostility committed in Athens merited severe punishment. General Sarrail was eager that the French admiral should destroy the bridges over the Corinth canal and that of Chalcis, thus cutting off the Morea and Eubœa from the rest of Greece and preventing any further concentration in Thessaly. He then intended to clear Thessaly by force of arms.[1] The British Government were as indignant as he, but they were also concerned for the safety of their nationals and the Venizelists. They thought it wiser to avoid risk and waste of energy by concentrating on one deadly weapon—the blockade—and at all events waiting to see whether King Constantine would carry out his promise to withdraw his troops to the Morea. There they would be deprived of all means of doing harm, confined in a " mouse-trap," as the King himself bitterly expressed it. For the time being the British view prevailed, though the whole matter was to be discussed between the Allies at the forthcoming conference in Rome.

Br.-General Edwards established an outpost line facing south, with one battalion from the sea to the railway (on which a company was established in a blockhouse just north

---

[1] Sarrail, pp. 193–211.

of the bridge over the Mavronero river); one battalion thence to Kundoriotista, three and a half miles south-west of Katerini; one battalion astride the Katerini–Elassona road, which follows the Mavronero through a deep defile; and the fourth battalion, with the remainder of the troops and brigade headquarters, in and round Katerini. The frontage was about nine miles.

1916. Dec.

Thus the British brigade barred the railway, the tracks which followed the coast, and the rather better route from Elassona to Katerini. French troops were astride the main road from Larissa, which forks north-west of Servia, one branch running through Verria to Salonika, and the other to Monastir. This proved sufficient protection until February, when irregular Greek bands began to work their way northward further to the west and General Sarrail was obliged to extend his outposts in that direction to bar their way.

The British detachment had no trouble with the Greek troops at Larissa, who remained quiet and did not enter the neutral zone. Nor were there any difficulties with the local inhabitants. The people of Katerini, sullen and hostile at first sight of the troops, became immediately most friendly. General Bulfin records that on the 13th, only two days after the landing, when he was engaged in inspecting the defences, a deputation, headed by the notables of the town, came to request that 200 young men of the district might be allowed to enlist in the London Scottish.[1] Here was, indeed, promising Venizelist material, but unfortunately the Allies had pledged themselves not to allow the Venizelist authority to extend into Thessaly.

Three months the detachment spent in this beautiful country, beneath the towering peak of Olympos. The troops on the slopes of the mountain suffered hardships from cold and wet, but the rest of the detachment was comfortable. Its life was very much that of a garrison in times of peace in a friendly country, and it had the happiest relations with the French troops in the neighbourhood. A number of officers procured sporting guns and enjoyed woodcock shooting such as Ireland at its best cannot match. Though the troops were withdrawn before the spring of 1917, when the land reached its best, they certainly had a peaceful and

---

[1] Dalbiac, "History of the 60th Division," p. 71.

pleasant interlude such as it was given to few of their comrades to enjoy in the course of the war. Being commanded by a brigadier with large experience of Indian mountain warfare, they also had training which was to prove valuable later that year in the Judean Hills.

One other result of the so-called "Athenian Vespers" was the recognition of the Provisional Government; for the Allies could hardly refuse any longer to their friends the formal respect which they continued to pay to those who had shot down their sailors. Recognition was accorded on the 19th December, and in January Lord Granville, formerly Counsellor of Embassy in Paris, was appointed British diplomatic agent. France and Britain, however, continued, as it were, to keep the ring, preventing, on the one hand, the forcible extension of Venizelism, and, on the other, any hostile action against it by the Royalists. The rôle was not an easy one. Several islands declared for M. Venizelos and accepted his administration, though in what degree spontaneous sentiment, the pressure of the blockade, or the instigation of Allied officers contributed to this decision it is not easy to determine. On the mainland, however, the neutral zone was preserved.

Salonika took on some of the importance and—so far as military conditions permitted—even some of the airs of a capital city. A number of upper-class Athenians had followed M. Venizelos and had brought with them an atmosphere of luxury and refinement, of which hitherto there had been no sign. This period was Salonika's short heyday.

The Rome Conference.

**1917.
Jan.** The conference of the leading political, military, and naval representatives of Great Britain, France, and Italy, which lasted from the 5th to the 7th January 1917, was held in Rome, in part for the convenience of the Italian representatives, in part to enable Generals Sarrail and Milne and the Allied Ministers at Athens to be present. The two main problems with which the conference had to deal were the increasing losses from submarine attacks in the Mediterranean and the differences of opinion as to the situation in Greece. To the former we shall presently return; for the moment the Greek imbroglio only concerns us.

In brief, General Sarrail stated that he feared an attack

THE ROME CONFERENCE

by the Central Powers and a simultaneous Greek attack upon his rear. He considered that this danger could be averted only by a swift march into Thessaly, so as to clear up the situation there before the enemy could move. In this he was supported by the Minister of War, General Lyautey. In a personal interview with Mr. Lloyd George, General Sarrail asked for a free hand in Greece. The British Prime Minister could not possibly grant this. The British point of view was that, while there undoubtedly was a danger to the Allies in Macedonia, and the Greek Government's replies to demands for the appointment of control officers to supervise the withdrawal of Greek troops to the Morea had been highly unsatisfactory, there was as yet no ground whatever for the extreme measures urged by General Sarrail. If the Greek Army could be got across the Isthmus of Corinth it would be innocuous. It would be madness, seeing that there was a good prospect that Greece would withdraw her forces to the Morea, gratuitously to become involved in a new campaign against a new enemy. Generally speaking, the Italians supported this thesis, though their nervousness about the ambitions of M. Venizelos and the probable effects upon Greek policy after the war of a victory gained by him over the King, made them not unbiased judges. The views of the three Powers as regards M. Venizelos have been excellently summed up by Field-Marshal Sir William Robertson : " France supported him ; Britain " admired him ; and Italy suspected him." [1]

It was decided eventually to present to the Greek Government a declaration, of which the following is a summary :—

The Allies were determined to protect their Armies against the menace created by the presence of the Greek forces in their rear. This could only be done if these forces were, as contemplated in the Note of the 14th December (and a second Note of the 31st December), transported to the Morea as soon as possible. It was also necessary that the Allies should have full liberty to control the movement. If within 48 hours of the receipt of this declaration it was not agreed to by the Greek Government, the Allies would assume full liberty to safeguard their Armies by other means.

This ultimatum—for it was nothing else—was presented

---

[1] " Soldiers and Statesmen," II, p. 134.

on the 8th January and agreed to on the following day. The French General Cauboue and the British Br.-General Phillips (formerly Military Attaché at Niš) were appointed chief control officers to supervise the withdrawal of the troops across the Isthmus of Corinth.

This movement had already been in progress for some time, under the supervision of the Military Attachés, having begun about the 18th December. In the first month, up to the 18th January 1917, Br.-General Phillips reported that, according to his calculations, there had been transferred to the Morea 8,948 men, 3,132 animals, 78 guns, 62 machine guns, 32,432 rifles, together with ammunition and a certain number of transport wagons. The great difficulty to be faced by the control officers was that, while it was not hard to check the numbers of troops and the quantities of munitions passing into the Morea, it was impossible to estimate what men and munitions were left behind. It was not known, within 50,000 or more—and 50,000 rifles in the hands of *comitajis* was a not insignificant number—how many rifles the Greek Army had possessed at the beginning of the war, still less what were its stocks of ammunition. Nor was it known exactly what stocks had been captured by the Bulgarians in Eastern Macedonia. Again, though the Greek Army was not on a war footing, that hardly accounted for the ludicrously small numbers of men representing its various formations : 350 being the highest figure for any infantry regiment. All the evidence showed that reservists called up in November, if not serving soldiers, were remaining behind and keeping their rifles. There were also reports, difficult to verify, that arms and ammunition were being buried.

By the end of January Br.-General Phillips reported that the transport of men and material would not be completed by the 4th February, the date fixed as a time-limit. He considered, however, that a sufficient proportion would have passed into the Morea to render the Greek Army innocuous for offensive purposes. His view was that the Greeks had tried to evade full compliance with the terms of the ultimatum, but that they were now honestly carrying out the transfer under the pressure of the blockade and the threat of further action by the Allies. This statement by the man on the spot represented, broadly speaking, the views of the British political and military authorities. They were far from being in accord with those of Generals Sarrail and Cauboue, who continued to demand stronger measures.

Meanwhile in Athens a solemn ceremony of reparation was carried out on the 29th January, in front of the Zappeion, detachments of Greek troops marching past and saluting the flags of Great Britain and France. The ceremony passed off quietly, the spectators, who were not allowed in close proximity to the scene, behaving with respect. On hearing this news and the fairly favourable reports from Thessaly, the British Government ordered on the 31st the release of sufficient ships with cargoes for Greece to supply immediate needs, though the blockade was not to be raised until all demands had been satisfied in full.

CHAPTER XI.

THE WINTER OF 1916–1917.

(Maps A, 1, 2, 8; Sketches A, 7, 10.)

THE END OF THE MONASTIR OFFENSIVE.

1916.
Oct.
Map 2.
Sketch 7.
In Chapter IX. the progress of the offensive towards Monastir was summarized up to the 16th October. On that date the French were held up by the enemy at Kenali and Negochani, while on their right the Serbians were fighting to secure the left bank of the Crna between Brod and Skočevir.

Having relieved General Cordonnier of his command, General Sarrail seems to have adopted the strategy which that officer had proposed, that is, to force the enemy out of his positions in the Plain of Monastir by operations in the hills.[1] For this purpose on the 23rd October he ordered the withdrawal of the 17th Colonial Division, the 2nd Zouaves, and a considerable force of artillery from the command of General Leblois, Cordonnier's temporary successor, and put them at the disposal of the Serbian headquarters, to be employed in part within the bend of the Crna, in part in the foot-hills between the Crna and Kenali. It has already been recorded that he arranged with General Milne for the relief of the last French brigade east of the Vardar. He also induced the Italian General Petitti to relieve the Cagliari Brigade by the Ivrea Brigade, newly arrived from Italy, and despatch the former to the extreme left flank.

Progress was slow still. Not only was the country very difficult—the hills inside the bend of the Crna being as craggy as the rest, if not so high as those to the east—but the weather, which had so far somewhat favoured the Allies, was worsening, and it was evident that winter with all its rigours was at hand. The Serbian were growing very weary, and the Germans had begun to reinforce the Monastir front.

At the beginning of the offensive they had been without means to do this, but had speedily taken over control of the

---

[1] Sarrail, p. 170.

menaced sector. The situation had appeared to them critical. Not only had the Bulgarian troops, after suffering heavy casualties and their first defeat in this war, lost confidence in themselves, but the Bulgarian command had become flurried and had begun to shower complaints and appeals upon Germany. On the 26th September the headquarters of the German *Eleventh Army* (Lieut.-General von Winckler, successor to General von Gallwitz) and of the Bulgarian *First Army* exchanged commands and sectors, the former taking over the front at Monastir and the latter that from about Huma to Lake Dojran, where it was in touch with the *Second Army* on the Struma. The commander of the *First Army*, General Bojadiev, was dismissed from his post and succeeded by General Gešov. At the beginning of October an Army Group headquarters under General Otto von Below was formed at Skoplje to control and co-ordinate the operations of the German *Eleventh* and Bulgarian *First Armies*.[1] There was still a Bulgarian Commander-in-Chief, General Gekov, but his control over the *First Army* appears to have been administrative only.

Until now the only German troops with the *Eleventh Army* had been a few heavy batteries and a mountain machine-gun detachment. As the fighting continued and the Bulgarian reinforcements from other parts of the line failed to hold up the attacks of the Allies, the Germans were forced, in order to avoid the complete rupture of the front, to bring in single units and detachments from wherever they could be spared. First came two more machine-gun companies from the valley of the Vardar; then, as previously recorded, two battalions of the *146th Regiment* from the same quarter, to be followed soon afterwards by the third. The *9th Jäger Battalion* was sent from the Vosges, the *11th Reserve* and *12th Saxon Jäger Battalions* from Champagne, the *42nd Regiment* from Volhynia. Batteries were collected, some of them also from the Western Front, and by mid-November a temporary division, with powerful artillery, had been formed on the Crna under the command of Major-General von Hippel.

Even this did not suffice to hold up the Serbians, who continued to make steady progress in the bend of the Crna. Within the next ten days, therefore, the equivalent of another

---
[1] The record from the German side is taken from the official monograph, "Herbstschlacht in Macedonien."

division was brought up : the *11th Grenadier Regiment*, the *Guard-Jäger Battalion*, the *Guard-Schützen Battalion*, and the *8th Reserve Jäger Battalion*, all from the Western Front ; the *45th Infantry Regiment*, which had already seen fighting in Macedonia and had taken part in the Rumanian campaign in the Dobruja ; and more artillery. Some Austrian batteries were also sent to the Crna front.

When the conduct of the campaign comes under criticism it must never be forgotten how considerable was the effort which General Sarrail forced Germany to make for the salvation of her Bulgarian ally ; nor that, in spite of it, he succeeded in capturing Monastir. Tribute is due to his indomitable will, and still more to the endurance and devotion of the troops under his command, above all to the Serbians. Even if it be admitted that the German official monograph quoted above makes the most of the German part in the battle, there is no reason to doubt that, but for German aid, the Bulgarians would have cracked and the situation foreseen by General Milne would have occurred.

On the 18th October the Serbian First and Third Armies renewed their attacks in the bend of the Crna, forced back the Bulgarians in its western half, and captured Veljeselo, a mile and a half north of Brod. On the following day the Bulgarians, blown out of their defences by an intense bombardment, fell back also in the eastern half to the heights south of Polog. The German troops were now being hurried to the front ; but counter-attacks carried out by them on the 20th and 22nd were repulsed, a single battalion (the *12th Saxon Jäger*) suffering 350 casualties.

1916.
Nov.

Then came a period of heavy fighting marked by little progress. The Germans had by now eight battalions in the western half of the bend, where they repulsed all attacks. But the Serbians were not to be denied. A series of fresh assaults beginning on the 10th November resulted in further success between Polog and the northern course of the Crna, the Serbian Danube and Morava Divisions with the French 2nd Zouaves taking 10 guns and a thousand prisoners.[1] So far the Germans had held fast, but on the 13th the Serbians broke into their front north of Veljeselo, capturing 660 prisoners ; and by the night of the 14th the enemy had withdrawn his whole line to Ribarci, Jarasok, and Hill

---

[1] Sarrail, p. 172.

HEAVY FIGHTING AT MONASTIR

1212, that is, to a chord drawn across the bend eight miles from the southernmost part of the arc. This position was a strong one; for it included the toe of the Selečka Planina, the long ridge running from north to south down the centre of the bend.

1916. Nov.

Meanwhile there had been a pause in the Plain of Monastir. On the 14th the French launched a new attack against the Kenali defences. After penetrating in places to the enemy's third line they were repulsed in bitter close fighting; but the Bulgarians promptly evacuated the defences they had held for the past six weeks, fell back that night to put the Bistrica stream between themselves and the attackers, and took up a position along its left bank, some three miles south of Monastir. On the western side of the plain the Italian Cagliari Brigade, which, owing to the congested state of the railway, had actually taken three weeks to come into action since leaving its old front south of the Krusa Ridge, was making its presence felt on the Baba Planina. Monastir, despite all the German efforts to save it, was doomed.

The conditions resembled those of the Austro-Serbian campaign on the Kolubara two years before. The battle was being fought out in winter at an altitude which exposed the combatants to winter's worst furies. Howling winds drove the snow horizontally before them. The snow buried the bridle-paths, so that troops often lost their way in the darkness, to wander in circles all night. In the plain men stood up to their knees in mud and water. Clothes were soaked through, and for weeks on end there was no chance of drying them. Small wonder that heavy losses from sickness were added to the enormous battle casualties, especially as both sides were wretchedly supplied. If the enemy had rather the better road communications, he had no normal-gauge railway nearer than Gradsko on the Vardar and not even a continuous light railway thence to Monastir, a gap between Drenovon and Prilep being covered by a cable-way.[1]

On the 17th November came new successes in the bend of the Crna. The 2nd Zouaves got a footing on Hill 1212, and though they lost it at night to a counter-attack, it was not for long. The very next day the Danube Division

---

[1] " Herbstschlacht in Macedonien," Map on p. 25.

took Hill 1378 to the north, the dominating height in all this region. The enemy then not only fell back a distance of some four miles on the western side and in the centre of the bend, he also, during the night of the 18th, abandoned Monastir. French and Serbian cavalry, closely followed by French and Russian infantry, entered the place on the morning of the 19th. It was the fourth anniversary of the capture of Monastir by the Serbians from the Turks.

After Salonika, Monastir is the principal town of Macedonia. At the outbreak of the war it had some 60,000 inhabitants, a true south-Balkan mixture of Turks, Slavs (both Mohammedan and Christian), Greeks, Albanians, and Jews. It was a considerable trading centre and had also some manufactures. Like so many towns of the Near East, it is fair at a distance, especially when the sun shines upon its slim white minarets, and less pleasing at close quarters; but, on the whole, it must be counted clean and well-built.

From Dobromir, just inside the bend of the Crna, the line of the Allies now ran through Kirklina, $2\frac{1}{2}$ miles north of Monastir, Bratindol, on the Koritza road, and along the slopes of the Peristeri Mountains to the shore of Lake Prespa. The defence was at its last gasp, and a swift attack launched by fresh troops up the main road might well have resulted in the capture of Prilep. But fresh troops there were none available, save the second Russian brigade, which was three or four marches from the front. The main road to Monastir was cut to pieces; the breach in the railway at Ekshisu had not been repaired—and was not to be until the 27th [1]; and the enemy had naturally blown up the bridges and destroyed the whole line between Kenali and Monastir. The weather added to the difficulties of supply and of pushing artillery forward. Troops and horses were exhausted by fatigue, exposure, and short rations. In short, had the enemy retired to the Babuna Pass, it would have been difficult enough to follow him; an attempt to break his new line as a preliminary to pursuit was found to be out of the question.

Very little change, indeed, was effected in the weeks which followed. On the 21st the Italian brigade made some progress at Bratindol, but other attacks failed. In

---

[1] Sarrail, p. 189.

END OF BATTLE OF MONASTIR 239

the last week of November the Serbians and the French 17th Colonial Division won more ground in the bend of the Crna, despite the fact that all the German reinforcements had now arrived. The assaulting troops were, however, driven by a counter-attack from Hill 1050, the most important height still in the enemy's hands on the Selečka Planina. East of the Crna the Drina Division captured Grunište on the 3rd December. Further attacks by the Serbians and the second Russian brigade against Hill 1050 on the 10th and 11th December were indecisive, though the highest peak remained in their hands.

1916. Dec.

The Serbian troops could do no more, and their difficulties of supply had become acute. With the Greek menace developing in his rear, with the knowledge that nothing more which he could do would avail to help Rumania, General Sarrail now decided to cease his attacks and regroup his forces. The Italian Division, relieved by General Milne and at first moved in the direction of Verria with a view to watching the Greek Royalist forces, was sent into the bend of the Crna. The two Russian brigades were attached to the Serbian First and Third Armies, which were thus enabled to withdraw a proportion of their troops for a rest. The 17th Colonial Division had moved into reserve in the Plain of Monastir, now held entirely by the Armée Française d'Orient with the 11th Colonial (newly-formed from troops in the country and others from France), 57th and 156th Divisions. Small French detachments were pushed out beyond Lake Prespa. The new French division from France, the 16th Colonial, was concentrated as it arrived in reserve south-east of Florina. In that town the headquarters of the Armée Française d'Orient was established after it had been found impossible to win space enough north of Monastir to prevent the enemy from shelling the town whenever he could spare the ammunition.

So ended the "Manœuvre of Monastir." It had resulted in an incontestable success, though without achieving nearly all that had been hoped for. The Bulgarians had lost not only the gains of their surprise march into Western Macedonia but some 400 square miles of Serbian territory. From a defeat infinitely greater—though exactly how far-reaching it is not possible to estimate—they had been saved only by the transfer of 18 German battalions, including some of the finest, and a large amount of artillery to this part of the front. Above all, they had been denied the opportunity of joining hands with the Greek Royalists.

The losses on both sides had been extremely high. Those of the Serbians, from August to December, were about 27,000 ;[1] those of the French 13,786.[2] The losses of the Russians and Italians are not known, but the former must have been considerable. If the 5,048 casualties sustained by the British in the subsidiary operations on the Vardar and Struma be added, the total must have been about 50,000.

Yet the losses of the enemy must have been higher still. Upwards of 8,000 prisoners had been taken on the Monastir front, and in the same period nearly a thousand by the British. When one comes to examine the casualties of the German troops they appear almost incredible. By the 21st November the *42nd Infantry Regiment* had, in four weeks' fighting, lost 50 officers and 2,615 rank and file.[3] It eventually came out of action at a strength of 146 all ranks.[4] The *45th Infantry Regiment*, which did not come into action until the 17th November, had 980 casualties (not including machine-gun personnel) up to the end of December.[5] The *146th Infantry Regiment* had at least 2,030 casualties in the same period.[6] The casualties of the *12th Saxon Jäger Battalion*, recorded from time to time but apparently not including every day's, amount to 628 ;[7] those of the *11th Reserve-Jäger Battalion* to 478.[8] That gives us 6,781 for 11 out of 18 battalions, and though those of the rest were doubtless not so heavy—the *Guard-Schützen Battalion*, for example, not being engaged before the December fighting round Hill 1050—the total, when the artillery is included, was probably at least 8,000. When it is remembered that not a single German battalion was in action until the latter half of October, that the Bulgarians had borne the full weight of the fighting till then, that they had about

---

[1] Various figures were supplied to the British from various sources, ranging between 25,000 to 29,000.
[2] Larcher, " La Grande Guerre dans les Balkans," p. 117.
[3] " Herbstschlacht in Macedonien," p. 98.
[4] " Geschichte des Infanterie-Regiments Prinz Moritz von Anhalt-Dessau (5. Pomm.) Nr. 42," p. 198.
[5] " Das Infanterie-Regiment (8. Ostpreussisches) Nr. 45," p. 175.
[6] " Das 1. Masurische Infanterie-Regiment Nr. 146," pp. 178 and 185.
[7] " Das Königlich Sächsische 1. Jäger-Bataillon Nr. 12."
[8] " Geschichte des Reserve-Jäger Bataillons Nr. 11," p. 182.

SITUATION IN STRUMA VALLEY

five times as many battalions as the Germans on the Monastir battle-front and lost five times as many prisoners, it may be estimated that their casualties here were over 45,000.[1] On the British front their losses were, as we have seen, very heavy also, certainly seven or eight thousand. Sixty thousand battle casualties would then represent the enemy's losses between August and December 1916.

THE BRITISH FRONT: NOVEMBER AND DECEMBER 1916.

On the 10th November, as previously recorded, the French Struma detachment commanded by Colonel Descoins was withdrawn for employment on the left of the Allied line.[2] The front hitherto held by it in the neighbourhood of Suhabanja Ferry was taken over by the 27th Division. The Greek battalion, which had been attached to the French, remained behind and came under the orders of Major-General Ravenshaw.

1916.
Nov.
Maps A, 8.

The struggle for Monastir was at this moment at its height. It therefore behoved the British to continue their minor operations on the Struma and to allow the lull following the capture of Bairakli Jum'a to last as short a time as possible. This lull had been occupied in improving the position and making semi-permanent bridges across the river. The heat was now over and the incidence of malaria was fast diminishing as the mosquito retired into winter quarters. The netting issued to the troops for protection against this pest was returned to Ordnance. The sun-helmets had been withdrawn in October. On the other hand, the rains had begun, and though the full force of the wet season was not to be felt for another month, the valley of the Struma was already becoming water-logged. Operations involving the movement of artillery were becoming more and more difficult, and on the scale of those previously carried out would presently be impossible.

On the 15th November General Briggs issued orders for a renewal of operations on the morrow. They were to be, except at one point, in the nature of a large-scale demonstration, there being little ground in front of the

---

[1] Prisoners of three different regiments on this front, the *23rd*, *39th*, and *44th* reported that their units had lost over three-fourths of their strength. In two cases three battalions had been formed into one.
[2] See p. 188.

positions now occupied which it was desired to hold permanently. The 10th Division was to seize the village of Prosenik on the railway, and the 28th Division the villages of Kumli and Bairakli, and in each case to hold their objectives for 48 hours. The other operation was to be carried out on the 17th some 15 miles to the south-east, where the 27th Division was to capture Tumbitza Farm, between the railway and the north-western end of Lake Tahinos, and in this case retain it.

The 16th was a dismal day, with sheets of rain from dawn to dusk, which made observation for the artillery impossible. Little assistance from the guns was, however, required on the front of the 10th Division. The 6/R. Dublin Fusiliers of the 30th Brigade moved out from Topalova at 3 a.m. and surrounded Prosenik without being observed. Then a company of the 7/R. Dublin Fusiliers entered the village on the southern side. The garrison, only about 40 strong, promptly ran. A handful escaped in the half light through a gap in the piquet-line, but 27 prisoners and a machine gun were captured.

On the 28th Division's front a short bombardment had been carried out against Bairakli on the 15th, continued at intervals during the night, and intensified before dawn. At 6.40 a.m. on the 16th it ceased and the 1/Suffolk of the 84th Brigade advanced on the village. Here the garrison was about 300 strong and made something of a fight before retiring hastily, leaving 12 dead and 3 wounded in the hands of the attackers. Simultaneously a company of the 2/Northumberland Fusiliers seized Kumli, almost without opposition. Strong bodies of the enemy subsequently advanced on Bairakli with the intention of carrying out a counter-attack, but made no attempt to press it in face of the British fire. The Bulgarian artillery shelled the villages fairly heavily throughout the day and the following night. At 5.30 a.m. on the 17th a company of the 2/Buffs, 85th Brigade, raided a trench west of Erneköi. The enemy fell back at once, leaving six dead behind him, and occupied another trench in rear, from which his fire became so hot that it was judged unwise to press the attack further.

In the fertile tobacco and grain country south-east of Seres large isolated farm-houses are commoner than elsewhere in Macedonia, where the rural population is for the most part concentrated in small villages. On the left

TUMBITZA FARM

bank of the Virhanli, a stream running in a south-easterly direction to enter Lake Tahinos, were two of these farms, Tumbitza and Virhanli, which were held by the enemy as permanent posts in front of his main line. The 82nd Brigade of the 27th Division was directed by Major-General Ravenshaw to carry out a surprise attack on Tumbitza Farm and to hold it when captured. The 7th Mounted Brigade received orders simultaneously to seize Virhanli Farm.

1916.
17 Nov.

Br.-General Brooke ordered the 2/D.C.L.I. to move out before midnight, take up a position in Pheasant Wood, a mile west of Tumbitza Farm, and attack the place at 6.30 a.m. on the 17th. The 10/Hampshire was to follow the D.C.L.I. and cover its left flank, and the 2/Gloucestershire was to continue the line thence through Salmah and Kispeki. The 1st Greek Battalion was to occupy the village of Kakaraska, 2½ miles south-west of the farm, and provide protection for two batteries of the C.XXIX Brigade R.F.A., which were to assist the operations of the D.C.L.I. and 7th Mounted Brigade. The brigadier established his battle headquarters south-west of Kakaraska half an hour before the attack was to be launched.

The night was dark and stormy, and though this was a hindrance to the troops, it seemed to favour the prospects of a surprise. Yet surprise there was none. A single rifle shot in Pheasant Wood, fired whether by friend or foe, by accident or design, is not known, probably sufficed to give the alarm.

The information given to Lieut.-Colonel J. W. C. Kirk, commanding the D.C.L.I., was that he would probably have to encounter a garrison of only 40 or 50. The one great difficulty was that the Virhanli stream appeared to be unfordable. In front of the gates of Tumbitza Farm a wooden footbridge spanned the stream, and success depended upon carrying this with a rush. When the leading company attempted to do so it was met by very hot fire and a great proportion of its men were hit. A second attack also failed. The situation of the battalion was now extremely difficult. The mule carrying the telephone cable had bolted, and by the time the signallers were ready to make their way forward with a line the dawn had come and the flat ground was so thoroughly combed by the enemy's fire that it was practically impossible to move across it.

There was no artillery officer present. Lieut.-Colonel Kirk had been told to expect a forward observing officer by 9 a.m., the earliest hour by which two 18-pdr. batteries could be in position at Kakaraska to support him; but he was not in communication with one until 3 p.m. On the right the Derbyshire Yeomanry of the 7th Mounted Brigade occupied Beglik, but was likewise unable to pass the Virhanli.

Telephonic communication with brigade headquarters was actually not established until after dusk, but at 10.15 a.m. Major E. N. Willyams, second-in-command of the D.C.L.I., arrived there—having taken three hours on his journey—and reported the failure of the first attack. Artillery fire was thereupon opened on the farm. Other messengers despatched by Lieut.-Colonel Kirk were all hit, until his adjutant, Lieutenant J. O'Brien, had the good fortune to get through and reach headquarters at 12.15 p.m. He reported that the D.C.L.I. was pinned to the ground, that a further attack was out of the question, and that casualties were apparently serious. A heavier bombardment was then directed upon the farm; but Lieut.-Colonel Kirk refused to withdraw under its cover, as it did not seem possible to get his wounded out in daylight. When the withdrawal did take place it was no easy matter. Parties had to move out and search in the darkness for the wounded, who had been lying out all day, and carry them back to Pheasant Wood. The bearer section of the field ambulance, sent up to the wood by Br.-General Brooke, there took them over and evacuated them. The battalion itself did not reach Kakaraska until 1 a.m. on the 18th. Its casualties proved less numerous than had been anticipated, but it had suffered 87, including 20 killed and 4 missing.

Meanwhile, at 2.40 p.m. on the 17th, General Briggs had visited the 82nd Brigade battle headquarters and, after consultation with the commander of the 7th Mounted Brigade, Br.-General F. F. Lance, instructed Br.-General Brooke to force the passage of the Virhanli stream a quarter of a mile south of the village of the same name, and capture Virhanli Farm. A column under the command of Lieut.-Colonel D. G. Baillie, 10/Cameron Highlanders, consisting of that battalion, the 2/Wessex Field Company R.E. with bridging material, one section of the 82nd Machine-Gun Company, and the 1st Greek Battalion, was ordered to move out from Beglik at 11.30 p.m. and on reaching the river to bridge it at once. After an artillery preparation the Cameron battalion was then to capture and consolidate the farm.

1916.
18 Nov.

This operation was a fiasco. The night was black as ink; there were no definite landmarks; and the sappers reached the stream at a point where it was between 50 and 60 feet in breadth. They had been told that it was about 30 feet, and had brought only sufficient material for a bridge of that span. After reconnaissance for some distance up and down stream, no point where the Virhanli could be bridged was found, and the column was withdrawn to Beglik, leaving two canvas boats hidden in the scrub 400 yards from the river. The Camerons and the Greek battalion were ordered to reoccupy their positions between Beglik and Salmah.

Br.-General Brooke was desirous of renewing his attempt to cross the Virhanli on the evening of the 18th; but he was ordered by Major-General Ravenshaw to devote the night to a thorough reconnaissance of the stream, making at the same time a demonstration in front of Tumbitza Farm. The reconnaissance showed that the enemy had strongly reinforced his position between Virhanli and Tumbitza Farms and was digging in upon it. General Briggs was just about to relieve one of the Italian brigades on his left, which would leave the rest of his own line somewhat thin; on the other hand, two more Greek battalions, making with that already on the spot the whole 1st Regiment of the National Army, had just arrived. On hearing that the enemy was on the alert, he judged it best not to renew the attack until he had moved some heavy artillery up to Kakaraska to support it and the Greek battalions were ready. He ordered the 10th and 28th Divisions to withdraw their battalions from Prosenik, Kumli, and Bairakli—where they had been kept longer than had first been intended owing to the check at Tumbitza Farm—on the night of the 21st. Before the withdrawal took place the 1/Royal Irish raided the village of Kyupri, capturing five prisoners.

The remainder of the month passed without active operations on the corps front, though artillery was lively on both sides and the British suffered a certain number of casualties daily. By the 29th the 83rd Brigade of the 28th Division had relieved the Sicilian Brigade in the valley of the Butkovo.

THE WINTER OF 1916–1917

1916. Dec. Between the 1st and 3rd December the headquarters of the XX Heavy Artillery Group, with the 153rd Heavy Battery and one section of the 130th Siege Battery, moved to the neighbourhood of Kakaraska. The 17th Kite Balloon Section was moved to Gudeli. The I Brigade R.F.A. of the 27th Division was relieved by an artillery brigade of the 10th Division in order to be available for the support of a renewed attack on Tumbitza Farm, which, in accordance with the verbal instructions of the corps commander, was to be carried out by the 82nd Brigade on the 6th.

Meanwhile the commanders both of the 27th Division and the 82nd Brigade had been superseded. Br.-General G. A. Weir, from the 84th Brigade, had taken over command of the division and Lieut.-Colonel J. H. Bailey, from the 2/K.S.L.I. of the 80th Brigade, that of the brigade, in each case temporarily.

After dusk on the 4th the 10/Cameron Highlanders, with two machine guns and four Stokes mortars of the 6th Light Trench-Mortar Battery, occupied Pheasant Wood, and a company of the 2/D.C.L.I., with two machine guns, Salmah. A dump of engineer stores, including canvas boats and trestles for a 75-foot bridge, was formed behind the wood by the 2/Wessex Field Company R.E. By midnight all the artillery was in position: the heavy guns and howitzers south-east of Kakaraska; two batteries of the I Brigade R.F.A. in the same neighbourhood, one at Osman, and one at Salmah; the CXXIX Brigade R.F.A. in the neighbourhood of Beglik.

A frontal attack against the bridge and the trenches dug to cover it on the left bank of the Virhanli being thought inadvisable in view of the recent failure, it had now been decided to bridge the stream from the cover of Rabbit Wood, which lay on the right bank upstream from the bridge and beyond a sharp bend, and to attack the position from this quarter. On the afternoon of the 5th, after a sharp bombardment, the 10/Cameron advanced quickly from Pheasant Wood and seized Rabbit Wood. The battalion then dug itself in and attempted to reconnoitre the bank of the Virhanli but was prevented from approaching it by heavy fire. Meanwhile the 10/Hampshire's patrols from Beglik had likewise been checked by fire and found themselves unable to reconnoitre the neighbourhood of Virhanli Farm closely. The enemy put down a barrage between

TUMBITZA FARM

Rabbit and Pheasant Woods, which stampeded a number of mules and delayed the carrying up of the bridging material and stores; but this work was completed by daylight on the 6th. The 2/Gloucestershire had reached Pheasant Wood the previous evening and moved up to Rabbit Wood before dawn. Its commanding officer, Lieut.-Colonel K. M. Davie, was placed in command of the two battalions to carry out the attack.

1916.
6 Dec.

The orders issued by Lieut.-Colonel J. H. Bailey, commanding the 82nd Brigade, were that at 11.30 a.m.[1] the two battalions in Rabbit Wood were to assault and capture Tumbitza Farm. Another group of two battalions, the 10/Hampshire and the 1st Greek Battalion, was to take up a position in front of Beglik and to be prepared to attack the Virhanli position on receipt of a signal that Tumbitza Farm had been captured. The 7th Mounted Brigade was ready to co-operate in this attack. The South Notts Hussars had taken up a position behind Pheasant Wood and was to move mounted round Tumbitza Farm after it was taken and attack Virhanli Farm from the north, while a squadron and a half of the Sherwood Rangers was to advance northward through Virhanli village.

The 2/Wessex Field Company had meanwhile ascertained that the stream opposite Rabbit Wood was only some 25 feet in breadth but that the current was swift. To take a sounding was impossible. High banks made bridging more difficult, though they would afford some protection to the bridge when thrown. An intense bombardment of the farm and the neighbouring trenches began at 11 a.m., and under its cover the sappers and a platoon of infantry went forward at the double with the bridging material. In less than ten minutes and despite heavy fire a bridge supported in the centre by one canvas boat was thrown. At 11.30 a.m. the attack was launched, the 10/Cameron advancing to the bridge, followed by the 2/Gloucestershire. So hot was the enemy's machine-gun and artillery fire that only three officers and about 50 men actually crossed. They were at once pinned to the ground, only partially in cover, and the bridge behind them was

---

[1] The hour was originally to have been 11.20. The attack was postponed ten minutes in order to allow half an hour's, instead of twenty minutes', bombardment, in view of the activity of the enemy's machine guns.

damaged by a shell. This party was eventually withdrawn, and orders were received to stand fast during the day.

At 4.35 p.m. Lieut.-Colonel Bailey ordered the 2/D.C.L.I. to move up to Rabbit Wood and relieve the 10/Cameron, with a view to the renewal of the attack, which was again to be carried out under the orders of Lieut.-Colonel Davie. The latter, from Pheasant Wood, issued orders at 8.50 p.m. for a night attack, headed by a party of bombers of the 2/Gloucestershire, who were to creep up and rush the Bulgarian trench on the other side of the bridge. When, however, the commanding officer of the D.C.L.I., Lieut.-Colonel Kirk, reached Rabbit Wood he protested against this plan. He found the crossing still commanded by half a dozen machine guns, against which the British artillery fire had had as yet no effect. The enemy was thoroughly on the alert and evidently strong in numbers. The ground and the trenches beyond the stream had never been properly reconnoitred. With the assent of the brigade commander it was decided to postpone the attack until dawn.

The two remaining battalions of the 1st Greek Regiment had now been put at the disposal of the 27th Division. One of them moved forward at night and took up a position from Pheasant Wood to Salmah, the 81st Brigade having previously extended its right to cover the latter place.

1916.
7 Dec.
After a quiet night the British artillery carried out two intense bombardments at 5 a.m. and 6 a.m., on each occasion five minutes' fire being followed by a two minutes' pause and then another five minutes' fire. In neither case did the enemy reply.

After a further bombardment, the attack was launched at 6.40 a.m. on the 7th. Again a small party—this time about one company and one platoon of the Gloucestershire—managed to cross under heavy machine-gun fire, and again no other troops could follow. The bridge was completely destroyed, but the sappers who had thrown it had found that the stream was now not much above waist-deep. The telephone line to brigade headquarters and to Lieut.-Colonel Davie in Pheasant Wood being cut, Lieut.-Colonel Kirk on his own responsibility ordered the party to wade back, under cover of a renewed bombardment.

Lieut.-Colonel Davie ordered another attack to be launched, but Lieut.-Colonel Kirk reported to brigade headquarters that it would be extremely costly and that its prospects of success were very small. Br.-General Weir came up to the brigade battle headquarters before noon and decided to postpone the attack. At dusk the 2/Gloucestershire was withdrawn to Kakaraska. The 8th was spent in consolidating Rabbit Wood, which was, however, abandoned next day, the new line running from Beglik to Pheasant Wood and thence to Salmah.

1916. Dec.

General Sarrail had in the meantime asked General Milne to hand over to him the Greek regiment on the 27th Division's front, and the Army commander had on the 8th given General Briggs instructions to send it to Salonika. The withdrawal of the Greek regiment (which had behaved well and showed good promise), following upon the extension of his front by the relief of the Italians, left General Briggs's line very thin. He had also learnt of the presence of fresh Turkish troops on the Struma front. On the early morning of the 6th the 2/Cameron Highlanders of the 81st Brigade had, in the course of a demonstration towards the railway, where the track from Homondos to Seres crossed it, rushed a post of the enemy, killing 20 men and taking two wounded prisoners. They proved to be Turks of the *146th Regiment, 46th Division*. They stated that they had arrived from Constantinople a fortnight before and had been in the line only 24 hours.[1] All things considered, General Briggs decided that it would be best to abandon the attack, and the ill-starred operations against Tumbitza Farm were therefore brought to an end. Without counting the abortive attack of the 17th November, they had cost, between the 3rd and the 9th December, 424 casualties.[2] The first surprise attack had had the best prospects of success. After it had failed, the shortage of ammunition, at a moment when the Seres road was at its worst, and the lack of observation posts for the artillery, had made the operation extremely difficult.

In consequence of this change in policy General Briggs decided that the line of resistance of the 27th Division should

---

[1] Information regarding the Turkish dispositions is given in Note at the end of Chapter.

[2]

	Killed	Wounded	Missing
British	57	293	15
Greeks	11	48	—

run from Fitoki Ford on the Struma through Yeni Mahale Osman Kamila, and Homondos (all taken over on the night of the 10th by the 82nd Brigade). By night Kakaraska, Salmah, Kispeki, and Ada were to be held by infantry outposts and by day by two squadrons of Yeomanry. Between that date and the end of the month several raids were carried out. At 2 a.m. on the 17th strong patrols of the 2/Buffs, 85th Brigade, entered the enemy's trenches south-east of Erneköi, and after a sharp bombing fight killed 38 Bulgarians and captured six prisoners, their own casualties being 13. On the night of the 20th the 1/Royal Irish, starting from Kumli, attacked Kyupri, sending two companies round to the east of the village to cut off the garrisons. The enemy got away before the circle was completed, only five prisoners falling into the hands of the Royal Irish, who had seven casualties. On the 31st a platoon of the 2/Gloucestershire entered Beglik, driving out a garrison of about 50 Turks. This village, which had been evacuated after the fighting at Tumbitza Farm, was then reoccupied and fortified.

The corps had serious troubles with its supplies in the middle of December. By the 13th the heavy rains had caused great damage to the Seres road. So deep were the ruts that the chains of certain small-wheeled lorries did not clear the mud and—the road-metal being churned up—carried grit up to break the teeth on the sprocket-wheels. As a consequence, lorry-head had to be moved back several miles and first-line transport substituted for it, while fresh quarries were opened and more labour, both civilian and military, put on the road.

During this period the XII Corps carried out a number of bombardments and raids. On the night of the 26th November the 66th Brigade of the 22nd Division raided the Nose, the scene of much previous activity. A party of nine officers and 275 other ranks of the 8/Shropshire Light Infantry under the command of Captain E. C. Day entered the enemy's trenches after an artillery preparation. The raiders killed all the enemy whom they encountered except for two prisoners, whom they brought in, and destroyed several dugouts. They remained in the enemy's position for an hour, during which they were under the continuous fire of artillery, trench mortars, and machine guns, which was made more accurate by the enemy's

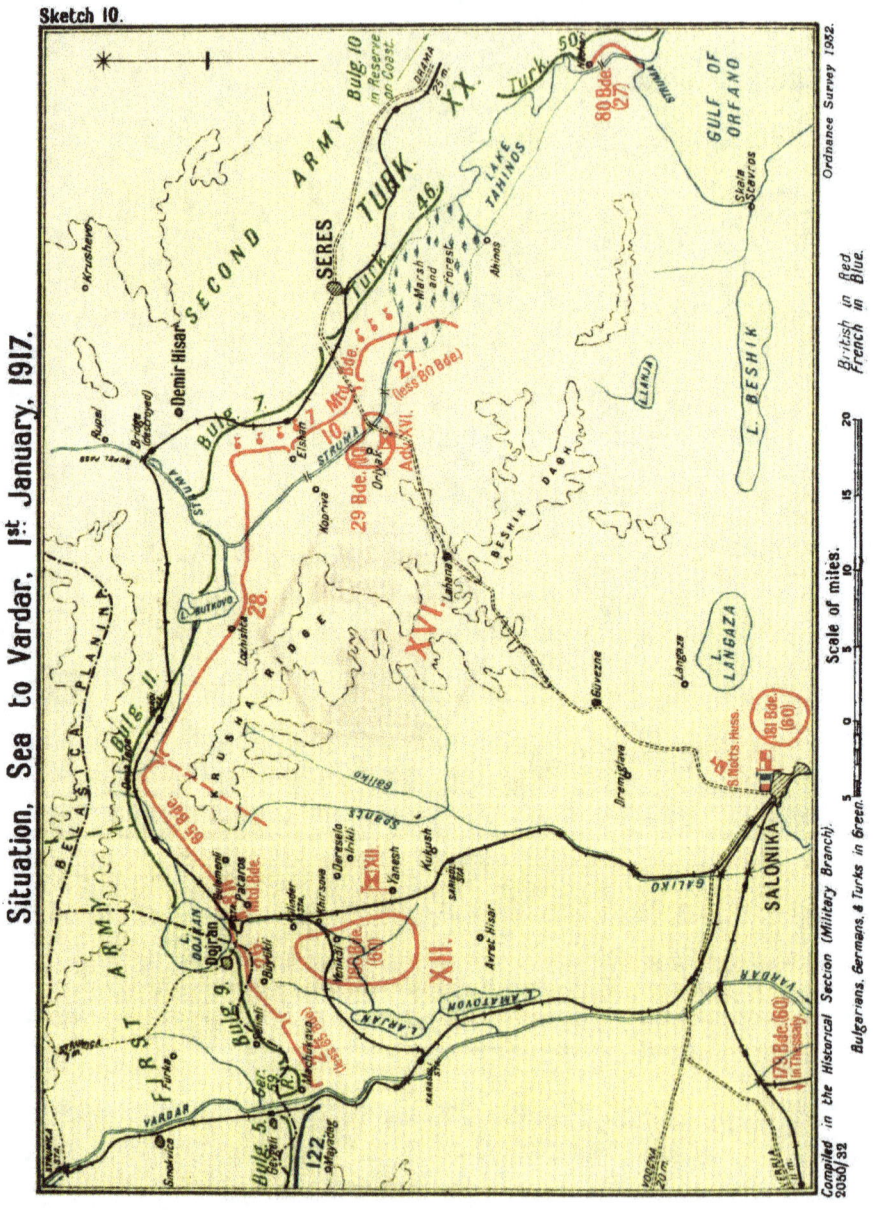

BRITISH RAIDS

use of searchlights and caused heavy loss. The casualties were 71.[1]

1916. Nov.

The 8th Mounted Brigade had reached Salonika from Egypt on the 16th November. It was put under General Wilson's orders for the purpose of constructing a new line of defensive works on the Gola–Kilinder ridge, its leading regiment reaching Irikli on the 26th. On the same day the 65th Brigade of the 22nd Division was withdrawn from the centre of the line in order to take over the front of the Italian Ivrea Brigade between Akbusalik, in the hills south of the Butkovo valley, and Dojran. This relief was completed on the 29th, by which date the XVI Corps had, as already stated, relieved the other Italian brigade in the line. The British now therefore held the whole front from the sea to the Vardar: 71 miles as the crow flies, but 90 miles owing to the curves of the front line, with the equivalent of six divisions, still much weakened by sickness. The arrival of reinforcements had left the front east of the Vardar no stronger than before. Three Italian brigades were gone and in their place had come the 8th Mounted Brigade and two brigades of the 60th Division, of which the 180th moved up behind the XII Corps as a reserve on the 24th December. The 181st remained in camp near Salonika, in case it should be required to join the 179th in Thessaly.

Sketch 10.

Raids carried out on the night of the 23rd December by the 7/Wiltshire of the 79th Brigade on a portion of the enemy's main line between Lake Dojran and the Petit Couronné, and by the 7/R. Berkshire of the 78th on an outpost on Hill 380, overlooking the Jumeaux Ravine, had ill fortune. In the former three Bulgarians were killed, but had no marks of identification upon them, and the attackers had eight men wounded. In the latter the enemy had evacuated his works, and the party, which appears to have charged in about two minutes too early, had serious losses, in part caused by the British barrage before it lifted. The total casualties, including engineer and trench-mortar personnel, were 34.

Dec. Sketch A.

On the night of the 26th a series of minor operations was carried out by the 65th Brigade from its new front,

---

[1]

	KILLED	WOUNDED	MISSING (believed killed)
Officers	—	4	—
Other Ranks	3	46	18

the chief of which was a raid on the village of Brest by a party of five officers and 200 other ranks of the 9/King's Own, with a small party from the 8th Mounted Brigade attached. The village was surrounded, but a number of the enemy managed to slip out and hide in the long rushes on the shore of the lake. Fourteen prisoners and a machine gun were captured, the total British casualties being three killed and 28 wounded.

POLICY AND ORGANIZATION.

Maps A, 2.

The new War Cabinet was averse to offensive operations in Macedonia, and would, indeed, have gladly seen the force there reduced to what was necessary for the defence of Salonika. Mr. Lloyd George was, however, anxious to obtain a victory or success somewhere. In Sinai Sir Archibald Murray was close to the frontier of Palestine and had been urged by the Prime Minister to " make the " maximum possible effort during the winter." For the purpose of advancing on Beersheba General Murray had asked for two more divisions,[1] which the Prime Minister considered should be found from Salonika and France.[2]

Prior to the 4th December, when General Sarrail came to the conclusion that he could no longer continue operations on a great scale against the Bulgarians in view of the Greek threat to his rear, he had been pressing General Milne to increase his activity on the Struma and suggesting that he should capture Demir Hisar. General Milne could have taken either Demir Hisar, which was under five miles from his front at Bairakli Jum'a, or Seres; but the capture of either would have meant an unwelcome extension of his long line. However, General Sarrail being for the moment more concerned with the Greek Royalists than with the Bulgarians, little was heard for some time of any considerable operations against the latter.

On the contrary, General Robertson had already renewed his criticisms. On the 2nd December he wrote to General Joffre, urging that the collapse of Rumania altered the whole situation and inviting him to consider the possibility of an attack by 35 Bulgarian, German, Turkish,

---

[1] " Egypt and Palestine," I, p. 260.
[2] From a note by Major-General J. H. Davidson of a message which he was asked by Sir W. Robertson to deliver to Sir Douglas Haig.

and Austrian divisions, combined with hostile action on the part of Greece, against the Armée d'Orient. He considered that preparations should be made to shorten the front, which would give General Sarrail a chance to create a reserve. General Milne, to whom the C.I.G.S. telegraphed in similar vein on the 4th, replied on the 6th that he had given the question serious consideration.[1] He had more than once pointed out to General Sarrail that a big attack down the Vardar valley would endanger the whole front at Monastir. He was already constructing a defensive line from Lahana through Kürküt and Irikli to Lake Arjan to permit of a gradual withdrawal if necessary. General Joffre, for his part, telegraphed on the 7th that if there was a probability of the enemy's diverting more troops to this theatre it was all the more necessary to bring the Allied force up to a strength of 23 divisions and to continue the offensive. He therefore urged that Britain should raise her contingent to nine divisions and Italy hers to five, and promised that France would send out two more divisions,[2] making a total of six.

1916. Dec.

General Joffre's directive to General Sarrail on the 11th—his last, as it proved—was in the nature of a compromise. The Armée d'Orient was to be established in a strong position to resist an attack and prepare for an ultimate resumption of the offensive; the territories held in pledge were not to be abandoned, except under military necessity; preparations were to be made to take rapid action in Greece if it was required. Every effort would be made by the Grand Quartier Général to accelerate the transport to Salonika of two more divisions.

The question of a withdrawal was, in fact, by no means a simple one. The Battle of Monastir had brought to the Allied arms a certain amount of prestige at a moment when it was badly needed. To abandon Monastir now would have been extremely humiliating. Upon the Serbians its effect would have been heart-breaking. General Milne went so far as to inform the C.I.G.S. on the 23rd December, after a conversation with their Chief of the Staff, General Bojović, that there was even a risk of the troops' not with-

---

[1] The slight shortening of the front on the Struma, which has been mentioned, was in part the result of General Robertson's telegram.

[2] They were the 11th and 16th Colonial, of which mention has already been made.

254 THE WINTER OF 1916–1917

drawing if they were ordered to ; some of them, at all events, might rather beg permission of the Bulgarians to return to their homes. It was, indeed, very fortunate that Monastir was not abandoned.

On the 26th December French Ministers came to London for a conference. That afternoon they discussed with the British Ministers, no military advisers being present, the question of withdrawal from Monastir, but without reaching any decision. On the 27th the main subject of discussion was the provision of reinforcements for Salonika. The British refused for the moment to send anything more than the drafts necessary to bring their force up to establishment ; but it was decided to reopen the whole question at a conference in which Italian Ministers and military authorities should take part. It was first of all proposed that this should be held in the south of France ; eventually, as we have seen, Rome was chosen as its seat.

1917. Jan. At Rome there was, in fact, a series of conferences, political, military, and economic. That of the military representatives ended in deadlock, the French and Russians urging that three more divisions for Macedonia should be found by Britain and Italy, the British and Italians declaring that they could send no more troops. Mr. Lloyd George advocated an offensive in Italy through the Julian Alps with the aid of British and French troops, above all of heavy artillery ; but the Italian Commander-in-Chief, General Cadorna, informed him that a tactical surprise was impossible and that the enemy would inevitably discover the arrival of the guns. Mr. Lloyd George based his arguments largely upon the parlous state of the maritime communications in the Mediterranean and the heavy loss of shipping. He pointed out that troops and guns moving to Italy would cause no fresh drain upon shipping, and added that there were 15,000 drafts in England unable to proceed to Salonika. In the last six months of 1916 the losses of the Allies in the Mediterranean had been 256 vessels of 662,131 tons, the British share being 32 per cent of the number of ships and 62 per cent of the tonnage. These losses were rapidly increasing, while the German submarines were operating almost with immunity.[1]

As so often happened, no final decisions were reached.

---

[1] " Naval Operations," IV, p. 175.

THE ROME CONFERENCE 255

The Conference paid tribute to Mr. Lloyd George's plan and decided that it merited further study ; it was, however, speedily pushed into the background by the project of General Nivelle for a series of great offensives on the Western Front. It was decided that Monastir should be held as long as this could be done without exposing the Armée d'Orient to defeat, and that meanwhile a shorter line should be prepared for occupation in case of need. The British were adamant in their resolution to send no more divisions, and the only immediate reinforcement despatched by them consisted of three 60-pdr. batteries.

The French, on the other hand, as advocates of a forward policy, were determined to make every effort to increase their force. The arrival of the 11th and 16th Colonial Divisions has already been recorded. Early in 1917 they sent two more divisions, the 30th and 76th. These divisions had only nine battalions apiece instead of 12, and formations already in the country were greatly under establishment—the total shortage being about 35,000, it was thought, by the end of February. There was some talk of cutting down other divisions to nine battalions, and, indeed, the necessity for this was only avoided eventually by attaching one Senegalese battalion to each Colonial regiment, that is, four Senegalese battalions to each of the three Colonial divisions. Moreover, these Senegalese troops had to be withdrawn from the line during the winter months. Though there were eight divisions, no corps headquarters were formed, but a group headquarters, with a staff for operations only, was formed under General Lebouc, who was to be entrusted with the command of any group of divisions assembled for attack. A new commander of the Armée Française d'Orient, General Grossetti—well known to the British as a fighting soldier and almost legendary hero of the Marne and the Yser—was sent out from France.

If the Rome Conference achieved nothing else, it opened a fertile field when, under the pressure of the threat to the maritime communications of the Armée d'Orient, it called for detailed reports upon the possibility of transporting troops to Salonika by way of Italy.

Regarding the question of command, it was decided that the relations of General Sarrail as Commander-in-Chief and the commanders of the various contingents should be similar to those of Sir Ian Hamilton and General

Gouraud during the Gallipoli campaign; that is, each commander should comply with the orders of the Commander-in-Chief with respect to military operations, " subject to the right of direct communication with, and " reference to his own Government." This formula represented a slight further delegation of powers to General Sarrail. The British Government, however, decided in January to raise the status of their force by giving its headquarters the style of " General Headquarters Salonika " Force." [1] Hitherto Major-General Travers Clarke had been head of both the Adjutant-General's and Quartermaster-General's branches, with the title of Deputy Adjutant and Quartermaster-General. On the 20th February the two branches were placed in separate hands, Major-General W. H. Rycroft being appointed Deputy Adjutant-General and Major-General Travers Clarke becoming Deputy Quartermaster-General. At the same time the office of Inspector-General of Communications was abolished.[2]

General Sarrail's position was altered by the removal from the French high command of General Joffre. The latter had been since December 1915 Commander-in-Chief of all the French Armies. On the 12th December 1916 the direct command of the Armies of the North-East—that is, on the Western Front—was handed over to General Nivelle, though until the 27th General Joffre remained nominally in command of all the French Armies. The Grand Quartier Général was transferred from Chantilly to Beauvais, and its section which dealt with Salonika was broken up. The Armée d'Orient, therefore, after having been almost exactly a year under Chantilly, was now again, and for the remainder of the war, directly under the Ministry of War. The change somewhat strengthened the position of General Sarrail, as a soldier of the political Left; but the favourable impression which he had made upon the Rome Conference was even more important in this respect.

---

[1] Yet they did not accord to their Army commander the temporary rank of general, as was usual. General Milne was promoted to the substantive rank of lieutenant-general in January 1917, but still held no higher temporary rank than his two corps commanders—to one of whom he was junior in that rank. Br.-Generals Gillman and Clarke had already been given the temporary rank of major-general. General Milne was given the temporary rank of general in June 1918.

[2] Major-General Koe returned to England, and the Base Commandant, Colonel D. K. E. Hall, was placed in command of an area known as Lines of Communication and Base Area.

THE VENIZELIST FORCES

Neither the organization nor the recruitment of the Greek National Army proceeded very fast, though it is only fair to add that in the islands recruiting was deliberately delayed because of the shortage of equipment. The islanders, and above all his own Cretans, were not only much warmer adherents of M. Venizelos but more reliable soldiers than the people of the mainland. For this reason the first design of the Provisional Government of raising two divisions on the mainland was abandoned, and even the first division was stiffened by troops from the islands, the last battalion formed being almost entirely composed of men from Samos. This battalion was ready for active service before the end of February; and by that time the whole of the first division, known as the Seres Division, was on the French front west of the Vardar. The Cretan and Archipelago Divisions—the latter recruited from the islands other than Crete—remained for the time being at home to carry out training. In the Seres Division there was a considerable amount of desertion among recruits from the peninsula of Khalkidike, upwards of a thousand men, almost all with their rifles, being missing during the month of January. Murders of police, interference with telegraph lines, and the general unrest resulting from this state of affairs forced General Milne to employ a regiment of Yeomanry, the South Notts Hussars, to assist the local authorities in rounding up the deserters.

The Serbians were compelled, for lack of reinforcements, to cut down their divisions from twelve to nine battalions, their force being then reduced to two "Armies." Even then the six divisions remained considerably under establishment, though the large numbers of lightly wounded men in the hospitals and the arrival of recruits by various channels gave prospect that this state of affairs would be to some extent remedied in the spring.

Only certain minor measures of reorganization have to be mentioned with regard to the British Army. On the 19th December General Milne issued orders, on instructions received from Whitehall, for the regrouping of the divisional artillery. Each division was now to have three brigades, each of two 6-gun 18-pdr. batteries and one 4-gun 4·5-inch howitzer battery. A fourth brigade was to consist of three 18-pdr. batteries, to be converted later to mountain artillery. This conversion had been discussed, advocated, and promised for over a year now, but still sufficient mountain batteries for the purpose had not been provided. Meanwhile, on the 24th November, the three batteries of the IV Highland Mountain Artillery Brigade had been temporarily divided up between the three divisions of the XVI Corps for instruction in work as divisional artillery.

In November the War Office decided that the garrison battalions [1] already at Salonika or in course of transport should be formed into a brigade and regarded as available for employment in front line. General Milne, though with some doubt regarding their marching powers, therefore constituted the 228th Brigade. It contained six battalions, and later in the year a machine-gun company, a trench-mortar battery, and a detachment of the 420th Field Company R.E. were added.

In December the cyclist companies and cavalry squadrons were withdrawn from their divisions, becoming respectively the XII and XVI Corps Cyclist Battalions and the XII and XVI Corps Cavalry Regiments. The cavalry regiments consisted of only two squadrons apiece, of Lothians and Border Horse and Surrey Yeomanry respectively, neither the 10th nor the 60th Division having divisional cavalry.

There already existed a Lewis-Gun School (formed in July 1916). An Army Training School for Infantry was established on the 10th December 1916, an Army Anti-Gas School on the 1st January 1917, and an Artillery Training School in March. A Greek Artillery Camp of Instruction, for the Greek National Army, was formed on the 17th February.

Hitherto leave had been given only in individual cases, small parties having been occasionally sent, by arrangement with the French, to Toulon. The first leave ship, with approximately 113 officers and 1,282 other ranks, sailed in November, and thereafter similar parties were sent home about once a month. This allowance of leave was, it will be seen, very small; but it was not possible to increase it until the opening of the Taranto route.

---

[1] These battalions were made up of elderly men, sometimes old regular soldiers, and younger men unfitted, by reason of wounds or other disabilities, for hard work or exposure. It had never been intended to use them in the line.

THE SANTI QUARANTA ROUTE

The Front during January and February 1917.

During January and February the whole Macedonian front was both stationary and quiet, with two important exceptions, neither of which concerned the British.

1917.
Feb.
Map 1.

Since his conversation with Mr. Lloyd George at Rome, General Sarrail had considered the possibility of extending his left far enough to make contact with the Italian force based on Valona, not so much because he was alarmed for his flank in the neighbourhood of Lakes Prespa and Ohrid as because he desired to establish communication with the Adriatic. The Italian right was now about Lyeskovik, some 40 miles from the sea and on the Yannina–Monastir road, which after passing through Koritza ran between the two lakes. Now, half-way between Lyeskovik and Yannina another road ran westward to the sea at Santi Quaranta. This was a poor little port without landing facilities, but it was only 80 miles from the Italian coast, only 100 miles from the port of Brindisi, and only 150 miles from what was to prove the much safer port of Taranto. Both roads were fair though neglected; but the section of the Yannina–Monastir road north of Lake Prespa was within the Bulgarian lines. There was, however, a road between Florina and Koritza, a very bad road indeed, which crossed a mountain pass at Pisoderi, but one not difficult to reconstruct for motor traffic if labour could be found. If this route could be opened and protected, there would be an alternative means of communication which would not require much shipping and would be little likely to be threatened by the enemy's submarines. Mr. Lloyd George had, according to General Sarrail's account, stated that he would even consider the despatch of British reinforcements by some route such as this. The Allied Commander-in-Chief also hoped that French aeroplanes and lorries, held up at Marseilles and Toulon for lack of shipping, might be sent to him across the narrow mouth of the Adriatic.[1]

At almost the same moment the importance to the Allies of the Santi Quaranta route occurred to the Austrians, who had one division, one brigade, and some irregular troops facing the Italian XVI Corps, based on Valona. On the 3rd February General Sarrail learnt that an Austrian brigade had moved down to Pogradec, on the south-western

---

[1] Sarrail, p. 225.

260 THE WINTER OF 1916–1917

shore of Lake Ohrid, and had pushed forward a detachment to within five miles of Koritza. At this place there was only a small French covering force of two battalions, two squadrons, and a couple of mountain guns—troops which had previously been on the Struma—under Lieut.-Colonel Descoins. General Sarrail decided to concentrate the newly-arrived 76th Division at Koritza, and did so by the 15th. By the 17th the road was clear, and a detachment from Koritza had joined hands with an Italian force at Herseg. There was now one Allied front from the Gulf of Orfano on the Ægean to Valona Bay on the Adriatic, a distance of 240 miles.

It must be added that the arrival of French troops at Herseg created some international feeling. The Italians did not, of course, suspect the French of direct political interests in Southern Albania, but they looked upon them as the chief patrons of the Venizelists, who, like the Royalist Greeks, desired to annex this country. Prior to her entry into the war, Italy had agreed, in the Pact of London, not to oppose Greek interests in Southern Albania, or Northern Epirus, as the Greeks preferred to call it, provided her own claims on the Adriatic coast were satisfied. She had, however, by now reconsidered the matter and was determined that the whole of Albania should be reconstituted after the war as a State under her influence. In these circumstances the Italian commander at Valona, General Ferrero, protested against French troops' remaining at Herseg, and General Sarrail ordered them to withdraw north of the Voditsa stream, which was henceforth to be the boundary of his command.[1]

Sketch 7.   The other operation in this period was much more limited in nature but led to much harder fighting. The highest point of the craggy mass known as Hill 1050, in the loop of the Crna, was in the hands of the Allies. On the evening of the 12th February German shock troops carried out a surprise attack with *flammenwerfer*, employed for the first time on the Macedonian front, and captured the position with 92 prisoners and five machine guns.[2] Bitter

---
[1] Sarrail, p. 226. With his account may be compared the Italian version given in " The Macedonian Campaign," by Luigi Villari, p. 121.
[2] The German troops were drawn from the *45th Regiment*, the *8th Reserve Jäger Battalion*, and the *11th Reserve Jäger Battalion*. In " Geschichte des Reserve-Jäger-Bataillons Nr. II," pp. 191–9, is an excellent account of the fighting.

and confused fighting followed, until on the 27th, after a heavy bombardment, the Italians obtained a lodgment in their lost trenches, capturing about 70 prisoners. A German counter-attack retook the highest point, 36 Italians falling into the hands of the enemy. The total Italian losses in these operations were about 400.[1]

During General Milne's absence at the Rome Conference, from the 3rd to the 10th January, General Sir H. F. M. Wilson was in command of the Army, Major-General Mackenzie-Kennedy officiating for him in command of the XII Corps for the same period.

1917.
Jan.
Maps A, 8.

On the long front held by the British from the Gulf of Orfano to the Vardar there was minor but unceasing activity. The weather was in general very bad, with constant rain and frequent snow. Macedonia had, every one was now beginning to realize, a very unsatisfactory climate for campaigning. The heat of the summer was oppressive, and autumn, which would otherwise have been pleasant, was spoiled by the mosquito. Winter stood for incessant wet and occasional intense cold. Yet, if the troops suffered great discomfort, especially on the Struma, where they lived and moved and had their being in water, their health was far better now than during the hot weather. The total evacuations for sickness in the XVI Corps were about 4,000 during January and February. This total included a few belated cases of malaria, but was for the most part made up of slight illnesses, rapidly cured. For a corps of three divisions and a cavalry brigade, with heavy artillery and auxiliary services, it could not be considered high.

The XVI Corps maintained active patrolling, despite the flooding of the Struma valley by the rains and snow. A number of civilians from Seres tried to enter the lines and were turned back. When it was found that some of them were in a starving condition it was decided from motives of humanity to let them pass through. The troops behaved with great generosity to these unfortunates and shared their rations with them. There was also a steady trickle of deserters, rather more Turks than Bulgarians.

---

[1] Villari, " The Macedonian Campaign," p. 124. It is here stated that the Italians retook all their lost positions except the crest, and that the enemy was not able to occupy this definitely. It is, however, certain that the command of the ground, from the point of view of observation, remained with the Germans.

Yet it was the Turks who carried out the only successful minor operation of the enemy during the two months. In the early hours of the 10th January they made a swift raid on Kalendra, which was held by a post of 30 men of the 6/R. Munster Fusiliers, and succeeded in carrying off a Lewis-gun section of eight men. The whole affair was over in ten minutes and the village was at once reoccupied. Two attempts by strong Turkish patrols, on the 14th and the 18th, to reach Kakaraska were beaten off by the posts of the 82nd Brigade and 7th Mounted Brigade, five prisoners being captured on the 14th.

If nothing serious was attempted on the Struma, it provided an excellent training ground. On the front of the 27th Division, while Kakaraska, Kispeki, and Ada were held at night by posts of the 82nd Brigade and during the day by those of the 7th Mounted Brigade, Salmah and Beglik were not held but were constantly visited by patrols, which had several brushes with the enemy. The Yeomanry also "lay up" for parties of the enemy who came out to cut maize, and killed a number of them.

Kyupri, on the front of the 28th Division, was raided on the morning of the 3rd. Two companies of the 1/Suffolk under Major D. R. A. Eley entered the village from the north-west, while a troop of the Derbyshire Yeomanry blocked the exits from the north and north-east and a company of the 2/Northumberland Fusiliers carried out a demonstration to the south-west. Three guns of the 100th Battery R.F.A. took up a position behind the village of Kumli to fire on the roads leading from Kyupri and cover the withdrawal if necessary. The raid was completely successful, 30 prisoners of the Bulgarian *7th Division* being captured, the British losses being only one man missing and one wounded.

On the front of the XII Corps an interesting operation was carried out by the 65th Brigade on the night of the 5th January. This brigade had, it will be recalled, taken over half the front formerly held by the Italian division. It was now independent of the 22nd Division, from which, in fact, it was separated by the 26th Division, and was directly under the orders of the XII Corps. The object of the raid was to surround the village of Akinjali from north, west, and south, prevent the escape of the garrison to the north-west by means of an artillery barrage, and close in upon the village. To accomplish this the village of Karali[1] and a work known as Hodza Redoubt, forming part of the enemy's advanced outpost-line, had first to be secured.

1917.
Jan.
Map A.

Lakes Dojran and Butkovo are connected by a deep valley, broken into two by the spur of Dova Tepe, which forms a watershed whence the Hoja (or Hodza) runs westward to Lake Dojran and the Butkovo eastward to Lake Butkovo. The main lines of the adversaries were naturally upon the hills north and south of this valley, that of the Bulgarians being, in fact, on the crest of the Belašica Planina. Yet, if the enemy's main line was five miles away from the British outposts, the villages in the valley were held by the Bulgarians in some strength.

The raid was carried out by parties from all four battalions of the brigade, with the support of $5\frac{1}{2}$ batteries of artillery, including one French 155-mm. battery, which had remained in this quarter in support of the Italians and had not yet been withdrawn. All the objectives were captured, but the garrison of Akinjali managed to escape and only four prisoners were taken, though some loss was inflicted upon bodies of the enemy who tried to approach from the north. The withdrawal was effected without incident, though a few men were wounded by the enemy's fire.

General Milne had now decided to relieve the 65th Brigade by the 181st Brigade of the 60th Division, which had hitherto been in reserve. The relief was carried out on the 19th. Major-General Bulfin then took command of this front, from Akbusalik to Lake Dojran, having under his orders the 181st Brigade, one battalion of the 180th, the Pioneer Battalion (12/Loyal North Lancashire), all the artillery except the brigade in Thessaly, and a proportion of the divisional engineers. The 1/County of London Yeomanry of the 8th Mounted Brigade was attached and was employed in the trenches. The 180th Brigade, less one battalion, remained in XII Corps reserve and was employed in road-making.

As often happened when a formation, especially a young formation, took over a new front under strange conditions, the 181st Brigade began with an unfortunate

---

[1] Akinjali and Karali lay quite close to one another and were at this time known to the British as "Akinjali West" and "Akinjali East" respectively.

experience. A patrol of one officer and 22 men visited Chakli in daylight on the 30th January and was ambushed on its way back by a party of the enemy about thrice its own strength. The patrol extricated itself, defeating two attempted bayonet charges, but had its commander and three men killed, two men missing, and three wounded.

1917. Feb. The brigade took vengeance in February by means of a small but successful raid by the 2/21st London on Palmis on the 6th, and a bigger one by the 2/24th on Brest. In the latter case parties from other battalions demonstrated in front of the neighbouring villages while the attack on Brest was in progress. Seven prisoners were brought in, the casualties of the brigade being only two men slightly wounded. A party remained in the village all night, beat off a small counter-attack at midnight, and returned to its lines at dawn.

Sketch A. A very much more serious operation was that of the 10/Devonshire of the 79th Brigade, against the Petit Couronné. This was the enemy's main line, and just about its strongest point, the lower slopes of the hill being very steep and the upper covered by broad belts of wire. There was an artillery preparation lasting two days, which resulted in the wire being considerably damaged. On the evening of the 10th February the battalion, under the orders of Lieut.-Colonel T. N. Howard, crossed the Jumeaux Ravine in two columns. At 9.16 p.m. a message was received from Lieut.-Colonel Howard calling for a ten minutes' bombardment to begin at 9.30 p.m. The sappers accompanying the battalion having completed the cutting of a gap through the wire by means of a Bangalore torpedo, the assault was launched and a lodgment effected in the trenches on the summit. The second objective was a concrete trench-mortar emplacement about 300 yards to the north-west, which it was particularly desired to destroy. One company fought its way with bomb and bayonet almost up to this emplacement, but was heavily counter-attacked and gradually forced back towards the original point of entry. Here also the enemy launched two strong and determined counter-attacks from the ravine on the far side of the hill. These were broken up mainly by the fire of a Lewis gun, the Bulgarians being lit up by the beam of one of their own searchlights. Eventually, however, Lieut.-Colonel Howard came to the conclusion that the enemy's numbers were

TWO BIG RAIDS

too great for him to complete his work and reluctantly gave the order to withdraw. The casualties were very heavy, about a quarter of the attacking force and a still higher proportion of officers. The losses of the battalion were 134, and those of all the troops engaged 158.[1] The commanding officer himself believed that the losses of the Bulgarians were greater still. Twenty-seven prisoners were brought in, but a number of Bulgarians captured in the trenches were too badly hurt to be taken across the rough Jumeaux Ravine. A considerable number were also killed with bomb and bayonet in the trenches and by rifle and Lewis-gun fire during the counter-attacks.

One other important raid was carried out by the 67th Brigade against the Piton des Mitrailleuses, on the left bank of the Vardar. There had been rumours of the departure of the old enemy, so often encountered in this quarter, the German *59th Regiment*. Orders were not issued for a raid until every effort had been made to bring one of the enemy's patrols to action and obtain an identification in this manner. A careful artillery preparation was carried out for two days, a gap being cut in the enemy's wire also at the Nose, 2,000 yards further east, in order to leave him in two minds as to the British objective. After two postponements, the first due to bad weather, the second because a thick belt of wire was found to be uncut, the raid was carried out in the early hours of the 21st February. There was no preliminary bombardment until a rocket signal was sent up to show that the attackers were in position; and the enemy was apparently surprised when a party, 86 strong, of the 11/R. Welch Fusiliers broke into his trenches, after a detachment of the 127th Field Company R.E. had cleared away the remaining wire by exploding torpedoes. The Germans, as usual, resisted stoutly, but six men were

---

[1]

	Killed	Wounded	Missing
Officers	—	9	4
Other Ranks	15	115	15

Two of the officers, including the medical officer attached to the battalion, Lieutenant J. M. Hammond, R.A.M.C., subsequently died of their wounds.

In view of the steepness of the hillside and the depth of the Jumeaux Ravine, a number of men had been trained to carry wounded on their backs, if necessary strapped on with putties. These men carried nothing but a long walking-stick and an extra pair of putties. The method of evacuation prove very successful, as the small figure of the missing in proportion to the total casualties shows.

bayoneted and five prisoners of the *59th Regiment* were brought back. The British losses were 21, including 16 slightly wounded.

Map A.   In the air it was the Germans who provided the surprise, and a very unwelcome one. They had established in secrecy at Hudova a squadron specially trained in formation bombing and equipped with fast and powerful modern machines, including one Gotha and a number of Rumplers. On the 26th February this squadron made its first appearance, 20 machines in V formation, flying swiftly down the Vardar, and surprised a French squadron at Gorgop on the right bank. Twelve French machines were damaged or destroyed, a very serious loss on a front where replacement was so difficult. In the afternoon the raiders visited the British aerodrome at Yanesh. No. 47 Squadron was expecting them, and most of its machines were in the air before the bombs began to fall. Little material damage was done on this occasion, but there were 28 casualties to personnel.

The next day the damage was even more disastrous. This time the bombers kept on straight down the Vardar and attacked Summerhill Camp, north of Salonika, causing nearly 300 casualties. They were attacked by seven machines of No. 17 Squadron, which succeeded in bringing down one Halberstadt Scout, and there was further fighting when No. 47 Squadron at Yanesh tried to intercept them on their way back.

The retaliation of the R.F.C. and R.N.A.S. will be mentioned in another chapter. Here it may be said that the British, with only two squadrons for 90 miles of front, and these containing few fast or quick-climbing machines, were at a serious disadvantage in dealing with the German bombing squadron. The latter, though it never equalled its exploits of the first two days, was to be a source of trouble for a long time to come.

Map 2.   General Milne was anxious, in view of the length of his front, that the 179th Brigade in Thessaly should be returned to him as soon as possible to act as a reserve. On the 10th February he was informed by General Sarrail that, far from withdrawing the brigade, he was desired to move it further from the fighting front, to Petra, in order to hold the defile south of that place. In accordance with his right to refer to his own Government decisions which in his opinion affected the safety of his force, he telegraphed home a message of protest. He had, he stated, great difficulties in relieving his troops in front line and would not find it easy to feed troops at Petra. In any case he considered that a move south, even within the neutral zone, required Government sanction. He added that since the Rome Conference General Sarrail had given him no indication of his plans, and that he was at a loss to understand the motive for this move, which the situation in Greece did not seem to justify. Not receiving a reply next day, he felt himself bound to order the 179th Brigade to move a battalion to Petra, where it was to send out patrols to watch the defiles. He was informed on the 13th that the War Cabinet had decided that the despatch of the brigade to Petra did not go outside the policy at present agreed to by the Government. General Robertson stated, however, that the French Government were being requested to instruct General Sarrail to keep General Milne sufficiently acquainted with his plans, and informed that it was desirable that the brigade should be returned as soon as possible.

1917. Feb.

At the same time another incident occurred, less easy to justify on the part of General Sarrail, but hardly important enough to mention here had it not been typical of General Milne's difficulties. The latter had obtained extended rights upon the quay at his disposal, without opposition from the Provisional Government, when General Sarrail put a veto upon the scheme in the interest of the Greek Customs. The affair had to be carried to the highest quarters in London and Paris before it was finally settled, and left upon the British Commander-in-Chief an impression of arbitrary and needless interference with his administration which was as painful as it was disquieting.

NOTE.

DISPOSITIONS OF THE ENEMY DURING THE BATTLE OF MONASTIR.

Owing to the dislocation of the big Bulgarian divisions, which took place in the course of the fighting, it is not easy to give the exact order of battle of the enemy during this period. The following represents the approximate distribution of his forces at the end of November 1916 :—

German *Eleventh Army* (Lake Ohrid to Huma), consisting of Bulgarian *2nd, 3rd,* and *8th Divisions,* with at least five regiments of the *6th* and *9th,* German " *Division von Hippel,*" *11th Grenadier Regiment, 45th Infantry Regiment,* and three rifle battalions.

Bulgarian *First Army* (Huma to a point on the Belašica Planina east of Lake Dojran), consisting of Bulgarian *5th* and *9th Divisions*, one brigade of the *11th Division*, and German *59th Regiment*.

Bulgarian *Second Army* (from left of *First Army* to about Dedeagach), consisting of Bulgarian *7th*, *10th*, and *11th* (less one brigade) *Divisions*, and Turkish *46th* and *50th Divisions* (*XX Corps*).

The infantry strength was approximately 190 Bulgarian, 24 Turkish, and 21 German battalions.

It has already been mentioned that the Turkish *50th Division* was identified in October. According to information supplied after the Armistice to the headquarters of the Army of the Black Sea, this division had moved to Drama on the 11th September, and its regiments had at first been interpolated between regiments of the Bulgarian *10th Division*. The *46th Division* followed on the 24th November, and headquarters of the *XX Corps* on the 4th December. Between the 1st and 10th December the *46th Division* took over a front of 20 miles south and south-east of Seres, between the Salonika–Seres road and Doksambos, on the shore of Lake Tahinos. The *50th* held the front from thence to the sea and along the shore to Leftera Bay, the Turkish *XX Corps* now having the Bulgarian *7th Division* on its right and the *10th* on its left. At the end of the year a single Turkish battalion with a mountain battery was sent to the Monastir front. It is not clear from the Turkish account whether their troops had already relieved the Bulgarians at Tumbitza Farm when the British attacks took place, but it is probable that the relief was actually in progress when that of the 6th December was launched, and that there was then a double garrison in the farm.

Both Turkish divisions consisted of three regiments of three battalions each. On arrival the regiments were increased to four battalions by the addition of battalions formed from the Mohammedan population of Kavalla, Drama, and Seres. The corps ration strength was then over 40,000. The divisions had only four artillery batteries apiece, but the Bulgarians put at their disposal a considerable amount of artillery, manned by Bulgarian gunners, but probably consisting of the guns taken from the Greeks in Eastern Macedonia.

CHAPTER XII.

THE WORKING OF THE MACHINE.

(Maps A, 1, 9.)

Exterior Communications and Supply.

In one respect Macedonia was unfortunate by comparison **Maps 1, 9.** with the other chief theatres of war. The British Expeditionary Force in France and Belgium depended directly for all but a small fraction of its requirements of every kind upon shipping from British ports; and throughout the war shipping in the Channel was relatively immune from submarine attack. It is true that a great proportion of those requirements, including food, ammunition, stores of every sort, and transport animals, had first to run the risks entailed in crossing the Atlantic; but purchases in the New World were made for all the theatres of war, which, therefore, shared these risks. The force in Mesopotamia and that in Sinai and Palestine could draw largely upon India and Australia by routes on which the submarine had not to be encountered. The Palestine campaign was, moreover, backed by the great resources of Egypt and the Sudan. The force at Salonika, on the other hand, was almost entirely dependent, wherever its supplies came from, upon shipping which had to make voyages of varying length in the Mediterranean. And from the spring of 1917 onwards it was upon the Mediterranean routes that the submarine attacks of the enemy were chiefly concentrated.

A statistical summary of the shipping required to maintain the British force at Salonika would be of interest; but it appears that its compilation would be a very lengthy and difficult task, if, indeed, sufficient data are now available. Most of the ships carried supplies for ports other than Salonika and theatres of war other than Macedonia. A ship would, for example, land a proportion of her cargo at Salonika and carry the rest on to Alexandria, Qantara, or even Aden. A note by the Quartermaster-General at the War Office, General Sir John Cowans, states that in November 1916 69 ships of 432,000 tons were employed in the maintenance of the British force at Salonika. The officials of the Board of Trade have been unable to give equivalent figures for any later period, and express doubt as to whether many of these ships were not also used for the purposes of the Egyptian Expeditionary Force. It may be presumed, however, for reasons which will be given, that the amount of shipping required in 1918 was less than in 1916.

Roughly speaking, each British division at Salonika required 1,400 tons of supplies, stores, and ammunition per week, with a considerable increase when operations on a large scale were in progress or in prospect. Fourteen hundred tons, dead weight, would require some 3,000 shipping tons for their transport. This, however, was only a proportion of the shipping tonnage required; for British vessels also carried to Salonika large quantities of supplies for the Serbians, for the French, and, in the latter part of the war, for the Greeks. Then there were the troop-carriers and horse-ships for reinforcements of men and animals, the hospital ships, and the leave ships.

As the shipping casualties in the Mediterranean increased, it was natural that the authorities at home should eagerly seek for a short sea route which would decrease both the risk from submarine attack and the total tonnage required; and that they should press for all possible measures to save shipping, from minor administrative economies up to a reduction of the force.

Regarding the short sea routes, that from Santi Quaranta to Taranto, of which mention was made in the last chapter, was of very little service to the British; the road to the coast was too hilly and the Monastir railway too overburdened already. It was, however, of considerable use to the Italians in their position near the Allied left flank. The route from Itea, on the Gulf of Corinth, to Taranto, proved invaluable, though mainly for personnel.

Regarding economy, General Milne issued urgent instructions for the prevention of waste. He also arranged, through Major-General Travers Clarke, his Deputy Quartermaster-General, for the fullest possible exploitation of the resources of the country. These were somewhat increased by Greece's entry into the war on the side of the Allies. They were, however, not very great, whereas Greece as an Ally in the field required large quantities of warlike stores. Greece was in times of peace an importer of grain, coal, textiles, and other manufactured products, her chief exports being fruit, tobacco, wine, olive oil, and certain minerals. Nevertheless, especially from 1917 onwards, something was accomplished, by means both of local purchase and of agricultural work carried out within the Zone of the Armies in Macedonia, to ease the strain upon shipping. Hay bought in Greece or cut by the troops in the occupied area made a large contribution; dried fruits, which were issued instead of jam, a smaller one. Large quantities of green vegetables were bought, and potatoes were grown on a big farm at Langaza. Divisions generally had their own vegetable gardens, and a quantity of fodder was obtained from the evacuated villages in the Struma valley. Charcoal burning was carried out on a fairly large scale, to take the place of coal. About 24,000 lbs. of locally made cigarettes were issued monthly, amounting to a quarter of the ration. It must be added that these cigarettes, made from the finest and most costly Turkish tobacco, were looked upon with no favour by the troops, who would have given a dozen of them for one American " fag." Beer was produced by two breweries in Salonika under military supervision, and soap and dubbin were manufactured from surplus fats, the machinery being improvised in the Ordnance workshops. All this was useful enough; but it did not compare with the great quantities of sheep and goats, grain, hay-stuffs, sugar, fresh vegetables, and oranges, which Egypt, the Sudan, and Palestine provided for the needs of the Egyptian Expeditionary Force. That force, moreover, was able to obtain a large proportion of its meat and flour, and all its atta, cheese, and tea, by way of the Red Sea, without risk of submarine attack.

Regarding reduction of the force, we shall see that the authorities responsible for the provision of shipping had their way, first in the reduction of the pack-transport scale, and secondly in an important reduction of the fighting troops. Yet we must beware of concluding that these reductions were wholly due to their arguments. There is a great difference in the attitude of a General Staff to such arguments according as they fit in or conflict with its own desires. The General Staff in this case was anxious, first, to supply Egypt with transport, and, secondly, to withdraw troops from Salonika.

It does not in any case appear that the total tonnage landed at Salonika was greatly decreased—though doubtless it was prevented from increasing largely, as was the inevitable tendency—by either economies or reductions. The equipment and maintenance of the Greek divisions tended to counterbalance any saving. In fact, the weekly tonnage landed, under 9,000 in the latter part of 1917, increased to nearly 11,000 in the first three months of 1918. But the fact that so many ships were now employed between Taranto and Itea or Taranto and Salonika, instead of between British ports or Marseilles and Salonika, makes it certain that a smaller total number of ships sufficed. Fortunate it was that this was so, for the number available was now considerably reduced.

The administrative services at Salonika were never without anxiety regarding supply. The working margin was always small, and when the enemy had an unusual measure of success in his attacks upon supply ships the shortage of reserves of food often became dangerous. On many occasions the British and French assisted one another by means of loans when necessities such as chilled meat or petrol were lacking to either.

These anxieties pressed more heavily upon the Army Service Corps than upon the other services concerned with supply. With engineer and ordnance stores and with ammunition the difficulties were naturally not so great. They could be husbanded more easily than food or even forage. The Macedonian campaign, where the British were concerned, represented trench warfare in an extreme form, and though this caused a big demand for stores, the demand was on the whole steady and regular. The front, moreover, though a wide one, was shallow. As a consequence, if the early period was one of breathless hand-to-mouth improvisation, there was afterwards well-controlled and smooth-working efficiency. At the outset depots were established on the nearest ground available. That of the Ordnance,[1] for example, was on a site where there was no room for expansion, so that new ones had to be found to accommodate the vastly increasing bulk of stores; and at one time there were three separate depots. The whole machinery was in chaos until the end of January 1916, by which time a railway had been laid between the docks and the depot, and even

---

[1] See "A History of the Army Ordnance Services," by Major-General A. Forbes, III, Chap. XVII.

ORDNANCE SERVICES

then months elapsed before all was running smoothly. But for a few store-tents, there was no accommodation for stores and clothing, and ammunition had for the most part to be stacked in the open, with unfortunate effects upon its reliability. Then the tents, the use of which was responsible for much loss through weather and theft, were gradually replaced by semi-permanent hangars; adequate workshops were at last installed; and a suitable ammunition depot was constructed.

The early confusion of the Ordnance services was in part inevitable, but in some degree due to there being, prior to the arrival of Br.-General C. M. Mathew on the 9th January, " no senior Ordnance officer present with sufficient " knowledge of what would be required and of sufficient " standing to be able to claim attention to the necessities " of his service."[1] It was due also in great measure, as has already been stated,[2] to the fact that the force was administered by a distant command not fully acquainted with local problems and preoccupied by its own.

Other difficulties of the Ordnance were also largely confined to the first few months, though some of them persisted throughout the greater part of the year 1916. At first the force had the leavings of the Gallipoli campaign. Large quantities of defective and unserviceable ammunition, which had been evacuated from the Peninsula and had then lain in the open at Mudros, had to be repaired and sorted. Dirty and even blood-stained clothing from the same source had to be repaired and cleaned. Repair work to vehicles of all sorts was unending. The effect of a hot climate and bad roads upon unseasoned wood was in itself enough to account for a proportion of this work, but the use of G.S. and G.S.-limbered wagons for carting road-metal caused far more damage still. The lack of a definite scale of transport allotted to Ordnance officers with formations, so that they had to depend upon the good will of officers of the A.S.C., was felt in the early stage of every campaign, but was felt here even more than usual owing to the general shortage of transport.

One technical problem deserves mention, as failure to solve it would have been disastrous. It was found in July 1916 that all amatol-filled shell in the command was

---

[1] *Ibid.*, p. 237

[2] See p. 100.

unserviceable, because the oozing of trotyl, as a result of the heat, had affected the fuzes. Practically all 60-pdr., 4·5-inch, and 6-inch howitzer ammunition was affected, as well as most of the bombs used by the R.F.C. Two Ordnance officers, Major W. M. Campbell and 2nd-Lieutenant G. J. Finch, devised a method of proofing this shell with paraffin wax. Despite the criticism of the Ordnance Committee at home—chiefly on the ground that the wax would melt at a temperature of 100 degrees—every shell and bomb was eventually repaired and proofed in this manner. The results were excellent, and the Ordnance Committee eventually gave its approval to the experiment.

Transport.

Maps A, 1, 9.

To turn now to transportation within the theatre of war, one of the most remarkable aspects of the Macedonian campaign is the development of the railways, a work in which the British contingent did something more than its share. There was no vast construction of standard-gauge track, such as was carried out on our side in Sinai and Palestine; nor did the construction of narrow-gauge track compare either as to its extent or as to the difficulties encountered with what was accomplished by the Germans and Turks in that theatre of war. New construction, however, especially that of narrow-gauge track, was fairly considerable. The greatest triumphs were those of organization and the achievement of an efficient service in face at first of political opposition and always with the handicaps of an indifferent permanent way required to carry five times its peace-time traffic, rolling stock deficient both in quality and quantity, and the barrier of language. This last had not to be surmounted by the French, for theirs was the official language of the railways, spoken and written by the officials.[1]

Of the four railways branching out from Salonika, all concerned the British, or at least their railway services, to some extent, but one in particular throughout the campaign. This was the easternmost, hitherto described in these pages

---

[1] In addition to the war diaries and a handbook prepared by the Admiralty War Staff Intelligence Division, a very interesting paper written in early 1918 by Lieut.-Colonel L. H. Kirkness, then Assistant Director of Railways, has been drawn upon for this summary.

as the "Dojran" or "Constantinople" railway, and officially known as the "J.S.C." (Jonction Salonique–Constantinople), which ran nearly due north to Dojran Station, and thence in an easterly direction to Seres, Drama, and Dedeagach, joining the main Constantinople railway some twenty miles south of Adrianople. It was entirely in Greek territory until it crossed the Bulgarian frontier at Okjilar, a distance of 195 miles from Salonika; but the furthest point to which the Allies ever ran trains was Dojran Station (44½ miles), and after early December 1915, Kilinder (39 miles).

The second railway, the "C.O." (from the name of the syndicate, Chemins de Fer Orientaux), ran up the valley of the Vardar to Skoplje and joined the main Constantinople line at Niš. Only 48 miles of this line, up to Gevgeli, was in Greek territory. These two lines were connected by a branch from Kilinder on the J.S.C. to Karasuli on the C O., which the Allies were fortunate in being able to use, though it was occasionally damaged by the enemy's fire.

The third was the "S.M." (Salonique–Monastir), a large portion of which was captured and damaged by the Bulgarians in their advance of August 1916, but which was employed by the Allies after the capture of Monastir to within a short distance of the town. As the French, Serbians, and Italians found to their cost, this railway had a very low capacity from the point where it entered the hills beyond Vertekop. Here trains had to be divided into two, each of which required one engine in front and one behind to take it up to the neighbourhood of Banitsa, where the line crossed the col between the Malka Nidže and the Mala Reka, over 2,500 feet above the sea.

At Plati, 21 miles from Salonika, was the junction with the Piræus–Athens–Larissa line. This railway originally extended no further north than Papapouli, on the old Turco–Greek frontier, 25 miles from Larissa; the section between Plati and Papapouli was officially opened by King Constantine as late as May 1916, but was not regularly used while he was on the throne. It was, however, of great significance, as it was a link between the hitherto unconnected Greek system and that of the Continent. As we have seen, it was employed for the maintenance of the 179th Brigade at Katerini. After Greece had entered the war as an ally it became much more important. In October

1917 the Allies opened a new route—already used by the French to a small extent in the summer—chiefly for personnel, including leave parties and hospital patients, along this line as far as Bralo, and thence by road to Itea on the Gulf of Corinth. From this point a sea-route was established to Taranto, and thence a direct rail service to Cherbourg, the worst dangers of submarine attack being thus avoided. The British and French would have been glad indeed to use the line to a far greater extent, but never found that possible owing to its long and steep gradients. To increase its capacity, stronger and consequently heavier engines would have been necessary, and neither the road nor the bridges were constructed for more than light loads.

Of the three lines in use when the Allies landed, the C.O. and S.M. were worked by an Austrian syndicate, and the J.S.C. by a Franco-Belgian company; but at that moment the Greek Government assumed control of them all, up to the frontiers, for the purposes of mobilization. A director arrived from Athens and installed himself in the office of the C.O. Though he was a brother of the well-known M. Nicolas Polites, whose enthusiasm for the cause of the Entente was undoubted, his sympathies appeared to the British officials who came in contact with him to be given to the other side. Perhaps it was that he found it impossible to assist the Allies owing to the pressure from above of the Greek General Staff and the obstruction from below of his own Austrian or Austrian-trained officials.[1] However that may be, every possible obstacle was put in the path of the Allies, and when the officials feared to risk a direct refusal they fell back upon passive resistance. To make matters worse, traffic was charged for at the rate of *grande vitesse*, three times that of goods (*petite vitesse*), whereas military traffic is normally carried at very low rates. The Greek Government was at the time actually paying for its military requirements one-third of the *petite vitesse* rate; that is, one-ninth of what the Allies were being charged. Meanwhile, to give the whole situation an air of farce, coal was consigned to Monastir after its occupation by the enemy; and, during the retreat, the mail train on the J.S.C. railway, which took precedence over the troop trains, bore a band

---

[1] See the debate in the Greek Chamber, 24th to 26th August 1917, as reported in "The Vindication of Greek National Policy," edited by J. Gennadius, p. 192.

of spies and agents to and fro between Salonika and the Bulgarian frontier.

The retreat from Serbia threw upon the two lines which ran northward from Salonika a strain which they were quite unfitted to bear; but on the British side no stores worth mentioning were lost. After the retreat was over, railways were little required for some time to come. When the advance from the Entrenched Camp had begun, the French, on the 5th May 1916, separated the J.S.C. railway from the other two and assumed partial control over it. Then, on the 3rd June, after the Bulgarians had occupied the Rupel Pass, General Sarrail proclaimed a state of siege and took over all three railways for such a distance as he was able to work them, establishing an international commission for their administrative control and installing a technical staff to supervise their operation. On the 25th September the working of the J.S.C. railway, which had always been mainly used by the British, was handed over to them; and in early October they took over also the Kilinder–Karasuli branch. The French continued to work the other two lines.

Among the difficulties encountered were the lack of accommodation for ships unloading and of room for stores in the neighbourhood of the port itself. These were overcome, first, by the construction of a special pier for lighters, into which the ships discharged their cargoes, and, secondly, by the construction outside the city of a sorting and marshalling station, known as Dudular, from a neighbouring village. Stores were landed in bulk and run into a group of sidings at Dudular, where the trains were broken up, the wagons being distributed to various depots. When trains were required for railheads, the wagons, after being loaded in the depots, were collected by shunting engines and marshalled into trains on a second group of sidings.

Another difficulty was the shortage of rolling-stock. This was to a certain extent remedied by taking over some hundreds of wagons, sent from the United States to the Serbian Government and diverted or reshipped to Alexandria and Malta after the disaster of 1915. Even then the shortage was so great that Colonel F. D. Hammond, the Director of Railway Services, was glad to accept some five hundred of the obsolete dead-buffered trucks which had been lying derelict for many years in British sidings, and to use them between the port and the depot, though they could not be put on to the main line. Sixteen mainline engines and six shunting engines were also taken over from the Serbians in the spring of 1917. The parts arrived without working plans, and a French engineer advised that they should be sent to France or England, erected, taken to pieces again, and reshipped with the parts labelled. The British locomotive engineers in the railway services could not bring themselves to lose so great a treasure, which would not return to them for six months at best, and might remain on the bottom of the Mediterranean. Therefore, although the design was American and utterly strange to them, they set to work on the erection of the engines, and had assembled several of them before the War Office sent to their aid a representative of the firm which had constructed them. These powerful engines were of the greatest service, especially on the S.M. line. They were the only ones not already old and out of date which ever arrived for use at Salonika.

Two extensions of the standard-gauge track were carried out. The first was a short one, from the Dudular yard to Lembet, a distance of five miles. It was projected when the troops were holding the Entrenched Camp, to serve the area wherein a considerable number were concentrated, known as Summerhill, but was not completed until July 1916. The second extension was constructed in the first half of 1917 and ran from Salamanli on the J.S.C. railway to Güvezne, 13 miles north-east of Salonika on the Seres road. It was built mainly to save traffic on that road and proved invaluable for the conveyance of stores to the XVI Corps, railhead for which was established at Güvezne. From Güvezne this line was subsequently extended southwards to Sarakli, near the shore of Lake Langaza, whence a narrow-gauge line was to run eastward.

Considerably more narrow-gauge track was laid. The first line was from Yanesh on the J.S.C. to Kalinova on the Kilinder–Karasuli branch, and was in the nature of a precaution, in case the enemy's fire should prevent the use of the junction at Kilinder. The line was constructed by the 26th Division, and afterwards maintained and worked by it, the personnel being for the most part railwaymen serving in the 8/Oxford and Bucks L.I. It was of great service in the winter of 1916–17, when the state of the roads made all four-wheeled traffic impracticable beyond Yanesh and the Kilinder–Karasuli branch was frequently under fire. A second important light line was that from Sarigöl on the J.S.C. railway to Snevche. This was constructed by the French when they held this part of the front, transferred to the Italians, and handed over by them to the British when the latter relieved them east of the Vardar at the end of November 1916. It was of value for the supply of troops holding the front between Lakes Dojran and Butkovo, an area served by no main road. The third light line was for some time unconnected. It ran from Stavros along the coast to a point three miles short of the mouth of the Struma, to supply, from the landing-place at Stavros, the brigade holding that part of the front, and was begun in March 1917. Though it was only 60-cm. gauge, the formation was broad enough to permit of its being converted to standard-gauge if the necessity arose and the material could be found; for General Milne did not lose sight of the possibility of linking it with the J.S.C. railway in the event of a general offensive. Alternatively, the 60-cm. track could be doubled. As the submarine pressure increased, it became necessary to provide an alternative means of communication with Stavros, hitherto almost entirely dependent on supply ships. A light railway, nearly fifty miles long, was therefore laid from Sarakli, on the standard-gauge branch already described, along the southern shores of Lakes Langaza and Beshik to Stavros, which was now linked by rail (though in somewhat roundabout fashion) to Salonika. Another light railway was laid along the right bank of the Struma, at right angles to the Seres road, for the supply of the troops on that front.

The railway material came from far afield. In addition to Egypt, which was able to spare a good deal of light-railway track from the old Canal Defences after the advance of the Egyptian Expeditionary Force across the Sinai desert, Great Britain, the United States, and India were drawn upon, the last-named especially for sleepers.

The French made one extension of the standard-gauge, from the J.S.C. station of Salonika, through the city, to Mikra, on the Gulf of Salonika, a distance of 13 miles. West of the Vardar they constructed two branch narrow-gauge lines, one from Bohemitsa on the C.O. railway, one from Vertekop on the S.M., towards the front line. Their most important new construction was a narrow-gauge line from Skočevir, on the left bank of the Crna, to Armensko, west of Florina. This crossed the S.M. railway north of Florina and then ran beside it for some distance, so that supplies could be transferred from the standard-gauge to the narrow to be carried either north-eastward to the Crna bend or westwards to Armensko.

On the enemy's side there was a good deal of fresh construction, but one line only need be described here,[1] as it alone promised to be of great service to the British in the event of their taking the offensive—all the more because it was of the same gauge as the British light railway through Stavros to the mouth of the Struma. It was a line from Radomir, south-west of Sofia, right down the Struma, to join the J.S.C. railway just south of the Rupel Pass. From its terminus a line was carried westward along the Strumica valley towards the town of that name, though, probably owing to shortage of rails, it never got so far. The existence of the Struma valley railway lightened the task of the Allies in case they desired to carry out an attack all along their front, since it provided direct communication with Sofia, the enemy's capital.

Possibly the XII Corps could have been maintained without mechanical road transport; the XVI Corps was, as has been explained, for a long time entirely and to the last largely dependent upon it. Of the three main roads capable of bearing heavy loaded lorries which radiated from Salonika on the British front the Seres road was therefore by far the most important. Unfortunately the ground over which it ran was in many places spongy, and a great proportion of the stone in its neighbourhood was a soft type of limestone. Work upon this road was consequently unceasing, but so was the traffic; and in wet weather the road-menders had to watch the fruit of their labours destroyed before it could ripen, as the passage of thousands of vehicles ground the stone to mud immediately it was laid down. The chief British mechanical-transport vehicle was the 3-ton lorry, of course with solid tyres. Despite its many merits, it proved, owing to its destructiveness to the roads, very inferior for work in this country to the Italian 30-cwt. light lorry. If the latter had to make two

---

[1] All fresh construction carried out by the enemy is shown on Map 9.

THE SERES ROAD

or even three journeys to transport the same weight, it did far less damage to metalled roads, and could also be driven on tracks where it was impossible to take a heavy lorry. The six-wheeled lorry of post-war days would have been a godsend in Macedonia.

After the breakdown of the road in December 1916,[1] greater and more methodical efforts had to be made to repair and maintain it. It was now realized that nothing short of a foundation of large stone as soleing, with at least six inches of rolled macadam on top, would carry the convoys. To lay this surface over a distance of 50 miles was an immense task, made possible only by a complete reorganization of the methods of work, by the diversion of any traffic which could possibly be diverted, and by the employment of thousands of Macedonian labourers, including women. The Engineer-in-Chief of the Army, Br.-General H. A. A. Livingstone, had the fortune to have at hand, in Lieut.-Colonel G. S. Pitcairn, one of the Deputy Directors of Works, a former contractor who had made roads and railways in the Balkans before the war, was a past-master in the organization and driving of Balkan labour, and had learnt from hard experience the quickest and cheapest method of carrying out any task set to him. His ingenuity and resource were invaluable, especially in repairing danger points before the complete reconstruction of the road. By the late summer of 1917 the Seres road was capable of standing any test, though it still required constant surface repair, especially after frost, and occasional complete "retopping."

The other two roads were, first, that which ran up the Galiko and forked at Kukush, one branch running to Snevche and the other to Chugunsi, and, secondly, that which left the Monastir road at Topji and ran up the Vardar, which it crossed at Karasuli. These two roads were practically new constructions. The second, though in the British area, was mainly required by the French for the supply of their troops on the right bank of the Vardar. In any case it branched off from the Monastir road, which always had to carry a vast amount of French, Serbian, and Italian traffic. A number of secondary roads, good enough for light motor transport and wheeled horse transport, were also constructed in the British area.

---

[1] See p. 250.

Work on the roads in winter, especially on the Seres road, was the hardest of hard tasks in Macedonia. In the course of each winter there were, in addition to ordinary bad weather, half a dozen terrific blizzards. Fine snow, driven by the bitterest of cold winds, would then fall for two or three days on end, freezing into a thick crust over the whole surface of the road. To drive a lorry along a road with constant bends and steep gradients was in such circumstances dangerous and difficult in the extreme. At the commencement of a blizzard, therefore, there was nothing for it but to turn out the Army Troops companies and the Macedonian labourers to work day and night in an endeavour to keep the surface clear by breaking up the ice and shovelling it off. Even when they had done so, their task was by no means finished; for now there were roadside drains blocked with ice and snow to be cleared. Then, amidst a sea of mud produced by the subsequent thaw, came the task of repairing the damaged surface.

The quantity of mechanical transport grew steadily. It has been mentioned that at the beginning of the campaign there were only some 350 lorries. Two years later there were, in round figures, 2,000 lorries and 1,400 light vans, including ten supply columns provided and driven by the British for the Serbians. Visiting the Serbian Second Army in late October 1916, during the Battle of Monastir, Br.-General A. Long, Director of Supply and Transport, found the British Ford vans working between the railway and Batachin, 2,000 feet up the lower slopes of the Stalkov Grob, over an almost incredibly bad road, with a maximum slope of one in four.

The adoption of pack transport has already been described in some detail. The Salonika establishment—"Salonika 4," as it was called—was doubtless the most perfect that has ever been devised for warfare in mountainous country from every point of view except that of cost and extravagance in forage. Unfortunately, it had hardly been completed when the War Office began to weaken it, and thenceforth to make inroads upon it until, but for General Milne's compromise of cutting down his divisional trains, it would have disappeared altogether.

The causes of this action on the part of the War Office were complex. One was undoubtedly the threat to maritime communications and the strong representations made to the War Office by the Ministry of Shipping as to the strain imposed by the number of forage-ships required by Salonika. (The Ministry's remedy was delightfully simple : it was, to sell the mules.) A second cause was the situation in Egypt. When the Egyptian Expeditionary Force was campaigning in Sinai it had little use for mules or draught horses. At the beginning of 1917 it reached the frontier of Palestine, with a country ahead of it on which wheels could play their part. Moreover, Egypt was, if one may put it so, coming into fashion, whilst Macedonia was going out. Mr. Lloyd George's Government were more or less in agreement with the General Staff in its hostility to the Macedonian venture, and the Prime Minister himself was becoming hopeful of winning a success against the Turks in Palestine. The First Battle of Gaza, in particular, caused the Government to entertain expectations of the capture of Jerusalem. It resulted that the shipment of mules, and to a lesser extent of horses, from Egypt to Salonika, which had taken place in the summer of 1916, was followed a few months later by a shipment in the opposite direction. Doubtless great numbers of the very animals which had come from Alexandria were now shipped back there. As some of them had done service on the Gallipoli Peninsula, they were becoming experienced travellers and campaigners ; and if, like the mule of Prince Eugene, they had not profited thereby, it must be owned that they had so far seen less that was profitable than that immortal beast.

The first demand upon General Milne was for a saving in British pack-transport drivers only. He was instructed to cut them down by 600 a division, or 3,600 in all. He pointed out that the malarial season imposed a heavy strain upon the drivers, who had at least their share of the total sickness. He had already abolished the divisional ammunition columns, forming instead two corps ammunition columns, each of about the same strength as a divisional column, and he was making arrangements to replace Army Service Corps personnel by Indian with his auxiliary horse-transport companies and reserve parks. The War Office replied that the 3,600 British drivers must be saved, but that it had no objection to the substitution for them of locally enlisted or other non-British personnel and was endeavouring to raise Indian personnel to replace British with ten auxiliary horse-transport companies.

The reductions were completed by the 25th March 1917. Shortly afterwards, on the 4th April—in the period between the First and Second Battles of Gaza, it is worth while to note—the War Office telegraphed that it had been decided, " owing to the necessity of meeting urgent requirements of " Egypt in transport animals and personnel, and having " regard to the military situation on the Salonika front, to " transfer 5,000 draught animals and 500 Army Service " Corps personnel . . . to Egypt." General Milne was informed two days later that the animals were all to be mules.

He replied on the 8th that he proposed to meet the demands partly by reduction in the divisional trains and field ambulances and partly by postponing the organization of two auxiliary horse-transport companies. Trains would in future consist of one pack and one wheeled echelon, in neither of which provision would be made for the carriage of hay; and in the field ambulances a proportion of the *cacolets* and *travois* would be withdrawn. He pointed out that there would now be great difficulty in supplying the troops in front line, and that all animals available to replace wastage would be absorbed. The War Office was, however, adamant, and, in reply to his request for the organization of the extra horse-transport companies, informed him that the reduction was permanent.

It was not, however, final. On the 5th May the War Office announced that it had been decided to go back to the old scale, and that, in addition to the 5,000 mules demanded, another 6,000 animals must shortly be sent to Egypt. This was, as it proved, a miscalculation, and the figure was finally settled at 4,500. General Milne made no attempt to disguise the fact that this reduction would make his difficulties greater than ever. He also stated that it was literally impossible to return to the " Salonika 3 " establishment for the fighting units. Their organization must be disturbed as little as possible; otherwise the troops would be able neither to make tactical movements nor to maintain their present positions. He considered that he could comply with the demands only by making fresh inroads upon his divisional trains, from the pack echelons of which he would withdraw another 750 mules apiece. This was the eventual solution. When added to the earlier reductions it resulted in the number of mules with the trains being halved, draught being cut down from 1,508 to 745 and pack from 1,040 to 521. This naturally resulted in the capacity of the trains being halved also, and they now carried only one day's rations in the two echelons combined. This was a serious loss in mobility, but at least the pack establishment, with very little reduction, had been preserved for the fighting troops.

WATER SUPPLY.

Macedonia being a primitive and sparsely populated country, there was no supply of water by pipe outside Salonika, though the towns and large villages were frequently equipped with aqueducts of masonry which carried water down to a fountain-head. Similarly, in the Dojran area water was obtained by the engineers by gravity fall from springs in the hillsides. Water was certainly not lacking anywhere; indeed one can call to mind few countries where there are so many very large lakes in an area of the same size, to say nothing of great rivers like the Struma, the Vardar, and the Crna. Unfortunately the surface water was frequently unfit for human consumption. The high ground behind Salonika, where so many of the troops and base services were quartered, had little surface water; and at Salonika itself the supply was barely sufficient for the city's own needs, and was speedily depleted to a dangerous extent by units and depots at the base.

A water-boring unit which had served on the Gallipoli Peninsula was transferred to Salonika early in 1916, and in the course of that year sunk 28 boreholes in the base area to serve the depots, the hospitals, the railway stations, as well as the camping-grounds on the foot-hills. The total capacity of these bores, some of which flowed naturally without pumping, was 500,000 gallons a day of pure, deep-seated water. The city's own supplies were augmented by extra wells, which were also artesian, sunk in the Vardar delta. A special bore was even sunk for the local brewery which supplied beer to the British forces.

In 1917 there were fresh demands for water, coming from much farther afield. As none of the other forces in Macedonia were equipped with plant for the development of subsoil waters, appeals for help were constantly made to the British, and during the year wells were sunk for the French, the Serbians, the Italians, and the Greeks. When the

Itea–Taranto route was opened fresh wells were drilled at Larissa and at Bralo, where troops left the railway for transport by motor-lorry to the Gulf of Gorinth.

The time taken to drill these wells, at an average depth of 180 feet, was about 13 days, and each could be relied upon to yield between 12,000 and 25,000 gallons a day. Where static water was estimated, after a geological examination, to be within 20 feet of the surface, and there were strata suitable for driving tubes, a much more expeditious method was employed. This was the Abyssinian tube well. In valleys, river beds, deltas, alluvial fans, lake shores, and sea beaches, a steam-driven percussion drill was used for the boring, and tubing, generally 1½-inch or 2-inch, was inserted, from which it was possible to pump by hand from 250 to 1,000 gallons per hour. On many occasions a tube well was driven, a hand-pump installed, and the well cleared of sediment within two hours of the arrival on the spot of the lorry with the driving outfit. Within a period of two years 211 tube wells were driven, with a remarkable proportion of success. Where large supplies were needed, wells were grouped and coupled to a power-pump, by which method several thousand gallons per hour could be raised. Thus the Army Service Corps potato farm, of which mention has been made, was provided with two groups of Abyssinian wells, coupled to Merryweather pumps, which yielded 18,000 gallons of water per hour during the dry weather.

Here, again, a great deal of assistance was given to the forces of other nationalities, numerous Abyssinian wells being sunk for them, especially in the Monastir district.

Mr. A. Beeby Thompson, an engineer without military rank [1] working directly under Br.-General Livingstone, records two remarkable cases in which the value of the Abyssinian wells was demonstrated to the profit of Allied Armies. On one occasion he visited an Italian formation near Brod. Though camped close to the Crna, the troops could not use its water and were found standing in long queues, water-bottles in hand, awaiting their turns at a few small springs. The lorry was unloaded; a tube well

---

[1] The writer is indebted to Mr. A. Beeby Thompson for most of the information upon which this summary is founded. He had previously served on the Gallipoli Peninsula in the same capacity, having been instructed not to apply for a commission, as it was thought that his status as a civil consultant engineer would give greater weight to his recommendations.

MALARIA

was sunk; a pump attached; and, to the joy and surprise of the Italian commander, a supply of 700 gallons per hour of pure water was at once provided for his men. The other case was that of a Franco-Serbian hospital at Arapli. Much money and energy had been expended by French engineers on infiltration chambers beside the Galiko river, but constant influxes of sand could not be stopped. Two tube wells were sunk within an hour by the British engineers, coupled to the existing pump by a flexible metallic suction-hose, and provided 2,000 gallons per hour of crystal-clear water.

Of equal value was the part played by these wells in the final advance, when, for example, wells sunk in the neighbourhood of Dojran Station provided 3,500 gallons an hour. At Dedeagach, where water was very scarce and there was some doubt as to what state the wells had been left in by the enemy, they were also employed with success for the supply of the troops landed in November 1918.

Incidentally, it was through British experience and example that the Greek Government obtained the knowledge necessary to supply with water at a later period the vast influx of Greek refugees—estimated at over a million—who immigrated from Turkish and Bulgarian territory.

Medical Services.

The British Salonika Army went through the whole campaign without a single battle with casualties heavy enough to strain seriously the resources of its medical services.[1] The greatest number of wounded evacuated was during the Battle of Dojran, 1917, but even then the total was less than 4,000, and was divided between two widely separated periods, the 24th and 25th April and from the 8th to the 12th May.

The most formidable, the almost unconquerable foe was malaria. Of the struggle against that something has already been said.[2] In the view of the medical authorities, it is very difficult to estimate the value of the measures taken

---

[1] The authority for the following summary is "Medical Services: "General History," Vol. IV, Chaps. II and III (Macedonian Front) and XIII (Ambulance Transport during the War). References to other volumes are indicated in footnotes.
[2] See p. 144.

to combat the mosquito. Those directed against its breeding were never satisfactory, owing to the vast amount of water and the changing courses of the streams, which constantly formed new pools. On the other hand, measures of protection, such as the provision of mosquito-proof huts and bivouacs, were always limited by the resources available. Had sufficient of these huts and a bivouac mosquito-net for each man been provided, there is no doubt that " a very " appreciable degree of protection would have resulted."[1] The difficulties of providing them would doubtless have been great, yet other stores, far heavier and bulkier, were provided because they were held to be essential. Had it from the first been possible to decide that in Macedonia protection from malaria was, after food and ammunition, the very first necessity, it is reasonable to suppose that the Salonika Army might have been kept at a higher standard of strength and efficiency, that a certain number of lives might have been saved, and that many thousands of men might have been spared ill health after the war.

Statistics seem to show that, even as it was, the battle with limited resources was not unavailing, and that it resulted in a decrease of the incidence of the disease. Thus, in September, the worst month of 1917, the admissions to hospital among British troops from this cause numbered 16,488 ; the worst month of 1918 was June, and in that month admissions numbered 7,655. As the ration strength had in the interval sunk only from about 180,000 to 145,000, this was a notable improvement, especially as a great proportion of the 1918 total was due to recrudescence of the disease among men previously affected.

Except for the universal epidemic of influenza in September 1918, there were few other serious diseases, though cholera, typhus, and plague, after famine the favourite handmaidens of Mars, were all hovering near at hand, eager to strike. The first was known to have appeared in the ranks of the Bulgarians and Turks ; the second had swept through those of the Serbians in 1915 and in a few cases had actually accompanied them to Salonika ; the third was prevalent on the coast of Asia Minor, whence Greek ships and Greek refugees continually arrived. All three were kept at bay. Another scourge that accompanies

---

[1] " Medical Services : Diseases of the War," Vol. I, p. 245.

warfare, venereal disease, was, as ever, a serious cause of inefficiency, but its incidence was lower than in the French, Palestinian, or Italian theatres.[1] Dysentery, though kept in check, stood second, *longo intervallo*, to malaria in the list of diseases.

One of the chief problems confronting Surg.-General W. G. Macpherson, the first Director of Medical Services, was the evacuation of wounded and sick from the forward areas to the roads, or at any rate to points at which horse ambulance wagons could be employed to carry them to roads suitable for motor transport. A number of methods were improvised by the field ambulances of divisions; some of them were abandoned or little used, but the varying nature of the ground over which the evacuations took place made uniformity impossible.

The "Salonika 4" pack-transport scale authorized 120 mules with *cacolets* to each field ambulance. The *cacolet* used in Sinai and Palestine with camel transport was of two types, a form of chair for sitting cases and a form of bed for lying cases, both carried in pairs, slung on either side of a camel. Only the type for sitting cases could, however, be carried by a mule. It was therefore decided to use only 60 of the mules with *cacolets* for sitting cases and the remainder with litters, wheeled stretchers, and *travois* for lying cases, and with saddles for very light cases. The litter had long shafts at either end, and required two mules, two drivers, and one attendant to each patient, but it was superior to the *travois* on ground covered with undergrowth. The stretcher and *travois* required only one mule, one driver, and one attendant. The *travois* was somewhat similar in appearance to the litter—in fact a combined *travois* and litter was invented, though found unsatisfactory—but the rear shafts were shorter, were shod with steel, and rested on the ground instead of being raised and slung astride a second mule. It was particularly serviceable on narrow hill tracks. Under the reduced establishment already described there were 30 *cacolets*, 14 *travois*, and 14 litters.

With regard to motor transport, the number of motor ambulance convoys steadily increased, and was not diminished with the reduction of the Army, though some cars were withdrawn to Egypt. By May 1917 there were

---

[1] "Medical Services: Casualties and Medical Statistics."

six convoys. Field ambulances were not supplied with motor ambulance cars, owing to the lack of suitable roads between the advanced and main dressing stations. Two ambulance train units arrived at an early stage, and the first train was assembled in June 1916. Ambulance trains were not, however, of very great utility in this theatre, except during the two battles in 1917 and 1918; and one constructed for Macedonia in 1917 was sent instead to France.

The final stage of the evacuation was from Salonika to Malta by hospital ship. The German submarine campaign had the effect of closing this route in the spring of 1917 and consequently greatly increasing the number of sick and wounded who had to be retained in the hospitals. The opening of the route to Itea, *via* Bralo, which has already been mentioned, enabled patients to be sent by the short sea route to Taranto, but until the end a large proportion of hospital patients were kept at Salonika.

The general and stationary hospitals were at first established on the Monastir road. The advantages of this site were its proximity to the railway and its good water supply; these were found to be more than counterbalanced by the neighbourhood of the malarial marshes and the risk of bombing, owing to the numerous depots of various sorts among which the hospitals were scattered. They were therefore for the most part transferred to the higher ground on the eastern slopes of the Gulf of Salonika, or to sites more distant from Salonika such as the Ortach plateau. Hitherto the hospitals had been under canvas, but in early 1916 the building of huts was begun. The spread of malaria and the maintenance of great numbers of patients in the theatre of war made necessary at Salonika no less than 17 general hospitals by the latter part of 1917, though by this time the 10th and 60th Divisions had been transferred to Palestine. In the summer of that year there were actually 29,000 beds in the general and stationary hospitals and the casualty clearing stations—an extraordinary number in proportion to the force's strength. It is all the more striking because it was not by any means the limit of the accommodation, which reached a figure of 50,000 beds, or more than one-third of the total strength of the force, when those in convalescent camps and depots were added. These conditions had no parallel in any other theatre of war.

In addition to their work for their own Army, the British medical services in Macedonia carried out a great deal for those of its Allies. A Scottish Women's Hospital, which came out with the French, was the first unit put at the disposal of the Serbians; subsequently four general hospitals and one stationary hospital were sent out for attachment to their Army. British motor and horse ambulance transport brought Greek sick and wounded to the Greek hospitals established in Salonika, and British hospitals were put at their disposal for the final operations. Medical and surgical stores were supplied from British depots to the Greeks, and the quinine supplied to the Greek refugees was all provided from England.

Veterinary Services.

The veterinary services of the Salonika Army had some problems peculiar to the theatre of war. The number of nationalities engaged in it, whose forces and transport frequently changed positions and used to a large extent the same roads, and the presence in the Zone of the Armies of a civilian population with no knowledge of animal hygiene, made the risk from infectious disease unusually great. Frequent shortage of forage due to the loss of supply ships had always to be faced. At the beginning of the campaign, too, shortage of grain crushers resulted in much of the barley issued being wasted. When conditions had become stabilized there remained the difficulty that the gun-horses were to a great extent idle, while the horse-transport companies were overworked. Both were widely scattered and difficult to supervise, and in the case of the former the high rate of sickness among the men made regular exercise and sufficient grooming almost impossible.

Lack of exercise was met by letting horses and mules run loose instead of keeping them constantly tied up in the lines. A striking passage in a report by Br.-General F. Eassie, Director of Veterinary Services throughout the campaign, describes the method and fruits of this innovation:—[1]

" The grazing was not always of great value, but the

---

[1] From the official history of the "Veterinary Services," edited by Major-General Sir L. J. Blenkinsop and Lieut.-Colonel J. W. Rainey, Chap. XII.

"freedom of movement, and the very considerable area of ground they covered in their wanderings, provided exercise. It was soon found that this of itself sufficed to enable the animals to digest the ration entirely. In a short time animals which were previously poor and unthrifty carried full flesh and healthy coats. It naturally took time before this practice became general. It spread largely by the force of example, the good results being obvious, but in the end it was insisted on by divisional commanders. Behind the whole of the front line the terrain was dotted with horses and mules. In cold and rain they turned tail to the wind and the weather. In the extreme heat of the summer they got together in groups, as sheep do, many with their heads in the shade of the flanks of others. They trailed out when let loose, knowing what to do and where to go, and they were punctual, almost to the minute, in filing back to their own lines at feed times, quite without direction and often at a slow jog-trot. Horses that were before unable, when called upon, to do half an occasional day's work without showing fatigue, now became capable of exhausting work. This was proved when, on more than one occasion, divisions were moved from one end of the long front to the other. It was proved more conclusively in the general advance. The whole force was then on half the grain and less than a quarter of the hay ration. With hardly a rise in the low sick rate, the 26th Division, starting from Dojran, marched 500 miles rapidly through the length of Bulgaria, under the worst weather conditions and over the worst roads. . . . (The animals) showed their fitness further, at the end of the advance, by their quick recovery of full muscle and strength."

The problem on the lines of communication was exactly the opposite. Here horses and wagons were on the roads, and had to be on them, almost without reference to the animals' fitness for the work. Something, however, could be and was effected by supervision and instruction in the arts of horse-mastership.

Disease was always kept under. Biliary fever caused considerable loss in the first summer, but was afterwards controlled and finally eliminated. Mange was fairly prevalent in the first eighteen months, when formations were in the course of arrival with their transport, but

Sketch II.

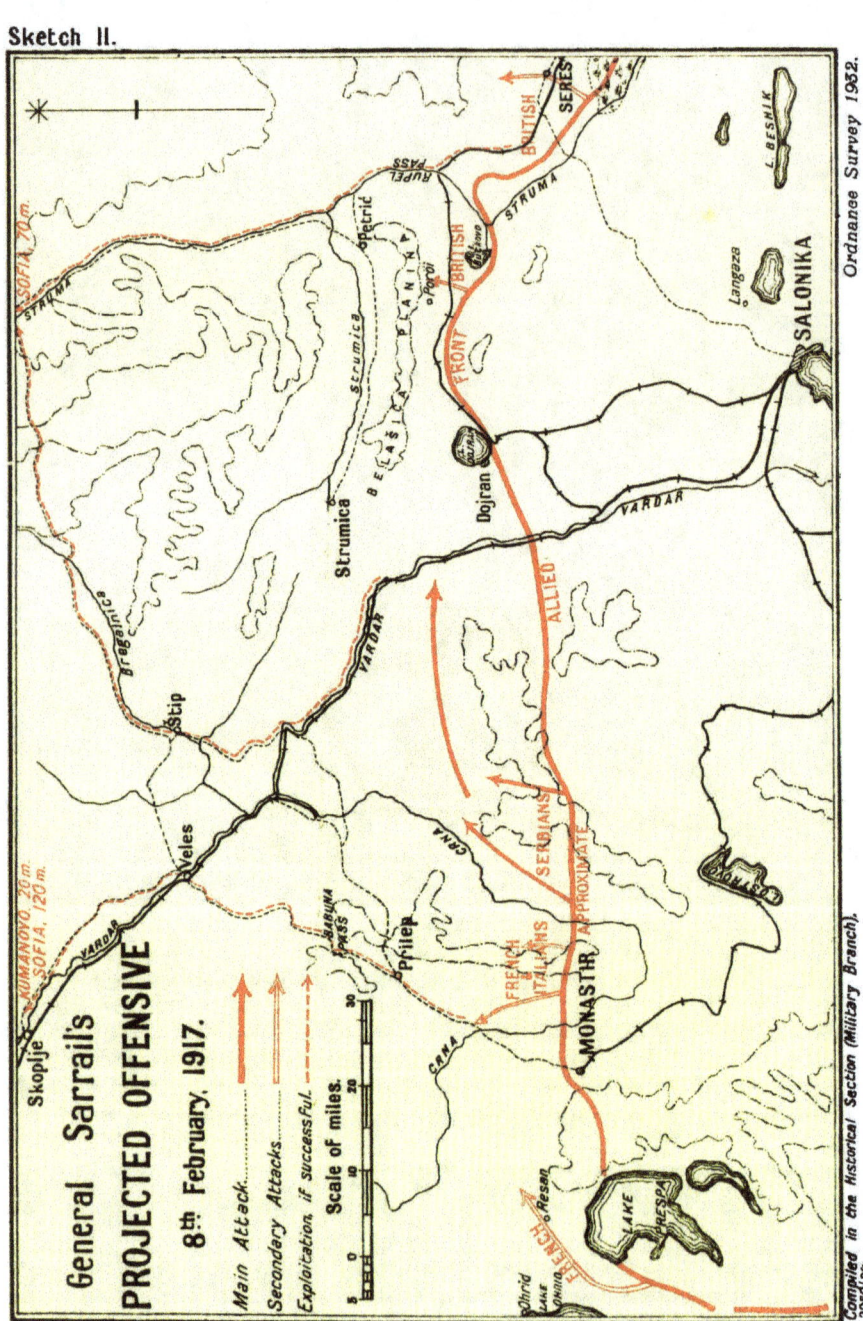

thereafter almost disappeared likewise. There were hardly any other diseases among the animals of the British Salonika Army, though those of other contingents were not so healthy.

The net wastage of animals, that is, the difference between the numbers killed or admitted to hospitals and the numbers recovered from the hospitals, was 24 per cent for the year 1916. For the year 1917 it fell to 12 per cent, including the remount depots, which had the highest proportion of the wastage. As was always obvious in France, if the French veterinary officers often took the lead in bacteriological research and blood-testing for disease, in preventive hygiene the British services were far ahead of allies or enemies.

CHAPTER XIII.

THE BATTLE OF DOJRAN, 1917.[1]

(Maps A, 2, 8, 10; Sketches A, 11, 12, 13.)

PRELIMINARIES OF THE OFFENSIVE.

1917.
Feb.
Sketch 11.
GENERAL SARRAIL had, in the latter part of 1916, just missed winning an important victory but had gained a fairly considerable success. He was eager to try his fortune again in the spring. He did not hope to begin operations on a big scale before March was out, partly because large bodies of troops could hardly be called upon to attack across inundated plains and snow-clad mountains, partly because he desired to await reinforcements in heavy artillery which he had urgently demanded, and partly because he did not care to move until the Greek problem was a step nearer to solution. He could, however, make a start by local operations, regardless of these conditions. The start suggested to him by his new Army commander, General Grossetti, was to win breathing-space around Monastir.

On the 8th February he outlined his plan to the Minister of War.[2] The Serbian right, which was still in Greek territory south of the frontier crest, was to assault and traverse that crest and, uniting with the left, which had scaled it, to advance eastward in the direction of the Vardar valley and take in rear the Bulgarian fortifications on the right bank of the river. Simultaneously, or earlier if possible, there was to be a secondary attack between Lakes Prespa and Ohrid upon Resan, to disengage Monastir and cover the left of the Army. Local offensives, especially in the Crna bend, would also be made at the same time. Lastly, he would demand of the British to hold down the enemy by an attack on Seres, by a threat against Poröi on the slopes of the Belašica Planina, and by bombardments and raids upon their whole front.

General Sarrail was then evidently questioned as to future plans; for he telegraphed next day that he had deliberately refrained from laying down any objective

---

[1] This is the British official title. The French official title for the whole series of operations is "The Battle of the Vardar."

[2] Sarrail, p. 399.

beyond the Vardar, but that if the development of the action was favourable the final objective would be Sofia. The British would advance up the Struma, and the other contingents by Štip and Kumanova. Again, on the 19th, when his hopes of receiving the heavy artillery seem to have been fading, he stated that he would attack in any case, but that if the guns did not arrive the results might well be smaller. His plan remained the same, except that on the British front the main attack would be in the neighbourhood of Lake Dojran, in accordance with the wishes of General Milne.

When this project reached Whitehall Sir William Robertson hastened to enquire of General Milne whether he had been consulted and whether he agreed. He had not been consulted in the drawing up of the plan, but he was not prepared to say that he disagreed. He did not desire to make two attacks on his 90-mile front, but he could make one if the brigade in Thessaly were returned to him. He preferred the Dojran front to the Struma, as he had told General Sarrail. The state of the Struma valley would render operations there impossible for some time to come, while by the middle of June malaria would make it dangerous to keep large numbers of troops in the valley. Seres could not be captured, certainly could not be held, unless the British also obtained possession of the heights dominating it and captured the enemy's strong position upon a broad front. Even that would have no great military effect, unless as part of a large scheme for the reoccupation of Eastern Macedonia, which would require many more troops. At Dojran the enemy was even more strongly entrenched, but the lines of approach were better covered, there were better opportunities for artillery co-operation, and success would have a greater effect in drawing in enemy troops.

Accordingly, General Milne directed General Wilson to prepare plans for an attack on the western shore of Lake Dojran. On the 28th he saw General Sarrail, who agreed to his proposals and promised to return the 179th Brigade. General Milne enquired of the C.I.G.S. whether he might expect any more heavy artillery, and learnt on the 3rd March that one 6-inch howitzer battery and two 60-pdr. batteries would be sent but might be delayed by shipping difficulties.

Meanwhile, on the 26th and 27th February, one of the

most important and fateful of all the Anglo-French Conferences had been held at Calais, where approval was given to the great series of offensives already planned for that spring. Regarding the Balkans, it was put on record that, "as the co-operation of the Russo-Rumanian forces against "Bulgaria is not yet possible, the Conference agrees to "confirm the decision of the Rome Conference and decides "that, for the present, the decisive defeat of the Bulgarian "Army is not a practical objective, and that the mission "of the Allied forces at Salonica is to keep on their front the "enemy forces now there, and to take advantage of striking "the enemy if opportunity offers."

Perhaps a certain vagueness in the formula was inevitable in such circumstances, but General Milne may well have felt some perplexity when told that it was the only answer that could be returned to his request for instructions. "It is for you and Sarrail to act in accordance "with the policy given." However, he learnt from the French Commander-in-Chief that the latter's Government had given their approval to the plan of attack, though it seemed to stretch the formula to its limit, if not beyond.

1917.
March.
Map 2.

The French began minor operations to win some room about Monastir in early March. The progress of the 76th Division on the western shore of Lake Prespa was, however, very slow, and on the 19th General Sarrail decided, as the ground was still deep in snow, to order this offensive to cease. North-west of Monastir affairs went better, and between the 16th and 18th the important Hill 1248, which overlooked the town, was captured by the 57th Division. The summit was afterwards lost, but useful gains were maintained. Directly north of Monastir only a very small advance was made in face of strong resistance, and here also the attack was brought to an end. Monastir was still very far indeed from being disengaged, but something had been done to improve the position there, and 2,000 prisoners had been captured. General Sarrail could do no more for the time being without exhausting troops required for the main attack or subsequent exploitation.

As General Milne, for his part, began his preparations he was plagued by the German bombing squadron at Hudova. The R.F.C. dropped bombs on its aerodrome at dawn on the 4th March, but that did not prevent the German bombers from carrying out an attack against the base

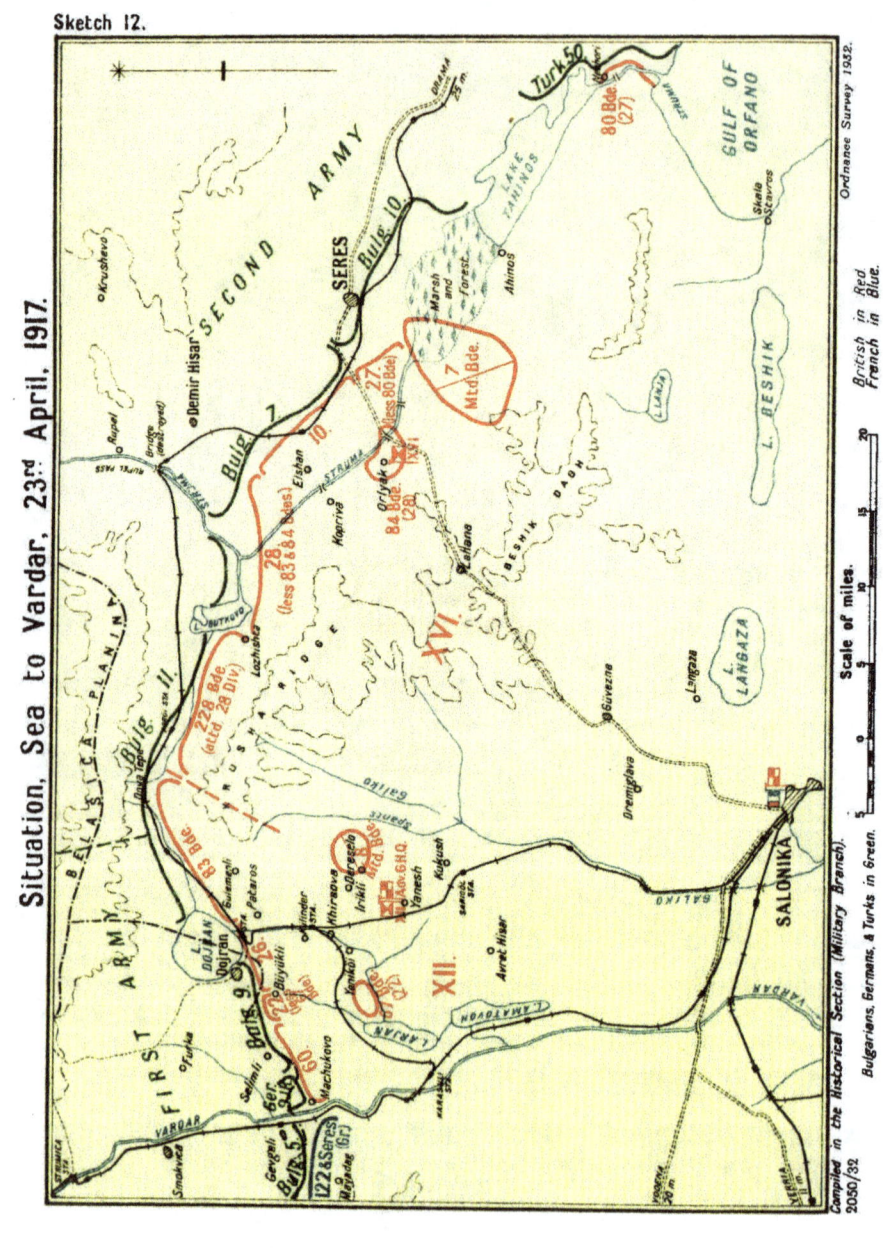

THE STRUGGLE IN THE AIR 297

area later in the day, causing 64 casualties, mostly in No. 29 General Hospital, which had now been twice bombed. On the very extended British front there were only eight anti-aircraft sections (16 guns), of which three had arrived in February. Two more arrived in April. General Milne therefore wrote direct to Vice-Admiral Sir Cecil Thursby, Commanding Eastern Mediterranean, with a request that machines of the R.N.A.S. should be put at his disposal, since his own resources were inadequate to cope with the hostile bombers. The vice-admiral had at this period under his command a squadron at Stavros and one on each of the islands of Imbros, Mitylene, and Thasos, with a base at Mudros. He proved a true friend in need, and at the end of March despatched four Sopwiths from Stavros. These were formed into a combined fighting squadron with five machines from the two R.F.C. squadrons. In April the vice-admiral formed another squadron, consisting of both bombing and escort machines, at Stavros, whence it flew to Amberköi, on the Dojran railway, arriving on the 29th.

1917. March.

The naval aid proved of very great value. The fighting squadron, known as " E " Squadron, constantly escorted R.F.C. bombers in attacks on the enemy's aerodrome and depots in rear of his lines; it also helped to break up his formations when he attacked, and shot down two of his aeroplanes in April. " F " Squadron, the bombing squadron, when it came into action, was equally effective. The enemy succeeded in carrying out only one more raid of any importance, on the 5th April, when his bombers set fire to and gutted some buildings, damaged the line, and destroyed a quantity of ammunition at Karasuli railhead. Finally, on the 11th May, it was discovered that the hangars at Hudova had been dismantled. The German bombers were gone and were not again seen on this front. After their departure, on the 27th, a disaster overtook " F " Squadron. Five machines, which had been taken out of the hangar and loaded with bombs, were wheeled back again owing to bad weather. A tremendous explosion followed; ten machines were destroyed, and four mechanics in the hangar were killed.

On the 4th March General Milne was able to send orders to the 179th Brigade in Thessaly to begin its long march up to Karasuli, where it would come under the orders of the XII Corps. On the 10th he informed the corps commanders that the newly-formed 228th Brigade was to be put at the disposal of General Briggs for the relief of the 83rd Brigade (28th Division), which was then to be handed over to General Wilson. The XVI Corps was also to detach the headquarters of a field artillery brigade and two batteries to the XII Corps. Headquarters of the XXXVII Heavy Artillery Group, with the 130th and 134th Siege Batteries, was also on its way from the Struma to the Dojran front. Two infantry brigades, two 6-inch howitzer batteries, and two field artillery batteries did not constitute a very strong reinforcement to the XII Corps, but it was all that General Milne could scrape together.

The 228th Brigade, to the command of which Br.-General W. C. Ross had been appointed, had hitherto been scattered for work. When four of its six garrison battalions, the 2/5th Durham Light Infantry,[1] the 2/Garrison Battalion R. Irish Fusiliers, the 22/Rifle Brigade, and the 1/Garrison Battalion Seaforth Highlanders concentrated about Sarigöl Station, they had no transport, no " specialists," and no Lewis guns. They were armed with the old long rifles, some of which were of the early pattern and not charger-loading. The march of the brigade to relieve the 83rd began unfortunately. The pack animals issued from the remount depot were scarcely broken and very difficult to load; on the march the new girths of the pack-saddlery stretched, causing the saddles to turn over and the wild mules to bolt, several of them being lost. However, the relief was completed by the 26th. The brigade received its supplies by means of Army Troops carts, from Snevche, the railhead on the light railway.

Maps A, 10.
Sketch 12.

During March and the early days of April the dispositions of the XII Corps were altered, in order to concentrate the more experienced troops of the 22nd and 26th Divisions for the attack and transfer the 60th Division to the left flank. When all the moves were over, the 26th Division held a front of about 8,000 yards (a large proportion of which was covered by Lake Dojran) from near Pataros to the Vladaya Ravine, west of La Tortue; the 22nd one of 2,000 yards from the Vladaya Ravine to the road running southward from Krastali; and the 60th one of eight miles

---

[1] The appearance of a 2nd-line Territorial battalion as a garrison battalion is due to the fact that its division, the (original) 63rd Division, had been broken up in the summer of 1916.

ACTIVITY ON BRITISH FRONT

thence to the Vardar. East of Lake Dojran the 83rd Brigade was holding the "independent brigade" area between Akbusalik, the left of the 228th Brigade, and the right of the 26th Division, a distance of eight miles.

On the front of the XVI Corps, which now had the 228th Brigade in line instead of the 83rd, the only other change in dispositions was that the 10th Division took over a small portion of the 28th Division's line, up to Bairakli Jum'a, thus enabling a brigade of the 28th to be withdrawn into reserve. General Briggs was instructed that his rôle during April would be to hold the enemy chiefly by demonstrations, but that large quantities of ammunition, especially of heavy natures, would not be available.

The whole British front was lively during the month of March, especially prior to the readjustments which have been described. Before leaving its sector east of Lake Dojran, the 181st Brigade of the 60th Division carried out a series of raids. The 2/22nd London searched Chakli Wood and encountered a body of about 60 Bulgarians, of whom they killed 12 and captured six. The 2/23rd found the Hodza Redoubt evacuated, and a party of the 522nd Field Company R.E. destroyed the wire and trenches. The 2/24th entered Brest, killing two and capturing two of the enemy. The casualties of the three battalions were only seven.

On the night of the 9th the 26th Division advanced its line south-west of Doljeli on a front of over 3,000 yards to a depth of 1,000 yards, occupying the mounds known as the Whale Back and Bowls Barrow, which were entrenched and wired. This new position was not within the enemy's line and was occupied without resistance. Prior to its relief by the 228th Brigade on the left of the XVI Corps front, the 83rd Brigade (Br.-General R. H. Hare) carried out a brilliant raid on Poröi Station on the morning of the 15th March. Detachments of the 1/K.O.Y.L.I. and 2/E. Yorkshire took the station by assault, killing four and capturing 24 of the enemy, and remained in occupation of it for nearly 20 hours. A raid that night by the 2/Cameron Highlanders of the 81st Brigade (27th Division) on the enemy's works west of Seres was unsuccessful. The battalion, which had a march of three miles to reach its objective, lost the track in the darkness, and the leading company came under heavy fire at close range. The enemy was driven back into Kavakli, but that village could not

1917. March.

Maps A, 8.

be carried and a withdrawal was ordered. The casualties were 36, including two missing.

During this period large columns of the enemy had been seen on the move towards Seres, and soldiers of the Bulgarian *10th Division*, captured on the front of the Turkish *46th Division* on the lower Struma, had stated that the Turks were being relieved. This information was confirmed later by a deserter, who stated that two regiments of the *46th* had already left for Constantinople. The *50th Division* remained on the coast between Doksambos and Leftera Bay until July, when it was also withdrawn for service in the East. The Bulgarians, now that the Rumanian campaign had been brought to an end, could spare troops for Macedonia. Their *1st Division*, which had taken part in that campaign, was known to be now in reserve behind the Macedonian front, though its exact situation was not certain. It would, indeed, have been sent earlier but for a serious rebellion in Serbia, of which the Allies were aware.[1]

Never yet had the Bulgarians used ammunition lavishly except to repulse an attack. On the 17th March, however, they began a bombardment of the British front between Lake Dojran and the Vardar and that of the French on the right bank of the river. At night their fire became very heavy indeed, especially on the front of the 22nd Division, and for the first time they used gas shell. Several thousand rounds fell upon the front of a single battalion. The troops were not equipped with box-respirators, for, though a consignment of these had recently arrived, indents for them had been received only the previous night. The older type, known as the " P.H. respirator," proved not completely impermeable. Casualties were, however, not high, except in the 67th Brigade, which had a loss of 164, whereof 103 were from gas-poisoning. They would doubtless have been more serious had not the enemy's gunners apparently failed to make the corrections to their fuzes necessary owing to the drop in the temperature at night. Box-respirators were rushed up by train and lorry and issued as speedily as possible.

---

[1] According to Lon (p. 241), the rebellion broke out in the first days of March in the mountainous district west of Niš, where some 8,000 men took the field. Their object was to cut the main railway in the valley of the Morava. The rising was put down by Austrian and Bulgarian troops, but not without sharp fighting.

Sketch 13

THE BATTLE OF DOJRAN
Night Attack of 24th April 1917.

Bulgarians .... Green.
British .... Red.

POSTPONEMENTS WEST OF VARDAR 301

The bombardment was continued at intervals on the 18th but then died down. It was at no time nearly so heavy on the front of the XVI Corps, but there also the Bulgarian artillery was more than usually active. *1917. March.*

At various points all along the front the Bulgarians pushed forward strong parties during the night of the 17th, presumably to ascertain what damage had been done. Only at Prosenik, on the 10th Division's front, did they show any determination. Here the British posts were withdrawn after dusk to the line of the Belitsa, and as soon as it was seen that the Bulgarians had entered the village heavy fire was opened upon it. A company of the 6/R. Munster Fusiliers afterwards reoccupied Prosenik without opposition.

On the 25th General Milne telegraphed home that he would be glad to have some gas shell, as the deep ravines between Lake Dojran and the Vardar were very suitable targets. He had little fortune in his demand. Out of 65,000 rounds asked for only 20,000 could be sent; these did not arrive till after the April attack, and 13,000 of them were defective.

General Milne had been warned that the Allied attack would take place about the 8th April, and he completed most of his own preparations by that date. The main attack was postponed until the 15th, and then again postponed until the 26th, the British operations being due to take place two days earlier. *April.*

Meanwhile another conference between British, French, and Italian political and military representatives had taken place on the 19th April, in a railway carriage at Saint-Jean de Maurienne, on the French side of the Mont Cenis tunnel. In view of the offensives in France, which had already begun at Arras, of the second attack on Gaza, which was actually launched that day, of the offensive in Mesopotamia, where Baghdad had been occupied, of the outbreak of the Russian Revolution, and perhaps especially of the fact that Turkish troops were moving eastward, the British Government were eager enough now for an offensive to be launched in Macedonia. They afterwards went so far as to despatch a message to the French Government, regretting that General Sarrail had postponed the attack, and urging that he should carry it out as soon as he could. Nevertheless, the British Prime Minister looked upon this operation as the last chance which could be given the Armée d'Orient. At

Saint-Jean de Maurienne he informed the new French President of the Council, M. Ribot, that if a considerable success were not achieved this time the British Government would be forced to consider a reduction of their troops in Macedonia, owing to the shipping difficulties. In this respect he was at one with the C.I.G.S., who in a memorandum to the War Cabinet urged that the Salonika expedition " had been a failure from the first," that it " had no " military justification," and that any troops which could be withdrawn and sent to Palestine were " likely to " contribute far more to winning the war " than if they were employed in the Balkans. In another respect, however, their views differed ; for, while the Prime Minister desired to reinforce the Palestine front, Sir William Robertson has put it on record that he consented to the despatch of troops there only as a *pis aller*.

On the 21st April the artillery of the XII Corps began cutting wire in preparation for the infantry attack.

THE NIGHT ATTACK OF THE 24TH APRIL—THE 26TH DIVISION.

Map 10.
Sketches A, 13.
The British Commander-in-Chief did not himself draw up the plan of attack of the XII Corps. Having first, as we have seen, directed the corps commander to submit his proposals, he then made his criticisms of the plan and limited it in accordance with his resources and his views on the possibilities of success.[1]

General Wilson's first draft plan was for an attack in three stages on the " P " Ridge and the enemy's works between it and Lake Dojran. In the first he proposed to capture the advanced works, including the Petit Couronné, Hill 380, and the crest known as P. 4½ on the " P " Ridge, consolidating a line approximately along the Dojran–Krastali track. The second stage would be the capture of the intermediate position, including the works of the Knot and the Tongue, from 800 to 1,000 yards beyond the first objective. The third stage would be the attack upon the

---

[1] In Sketch 13, of this attack, and also in Sketch 14, of the attack of the night of the 8th May, only the main fire trenches in the Bulgarian position are shown. The chief belts of wire are, however, shown on these sketches. In Sketch A the works (excepting those captured on the night of the 24th April) are shown in detail, but the wire is not marked.

enemy's third and main line of defence, including the Grand Couronné and P. 3 on the " P " Ridge.

General Milne replied that only the first objective need for the moment be considered. He pointed out that the enemy's position, though long, was not very strongly held, but that all lines of approach were covered by artillery fire which might cause heavy loss to troops advancing in large bodies. No more troops, therefore, should be employed than were considered necessary to capture and hold the position. Regarding the artillery plan, which was not yet drawn up, he remarked that, as two divisions were attacking in line, the artillery should be to a great extent controlled by the G.O.C. Royal Artillery of the corps; he issued a warning that a short period of intense bombardment immediately before the attack was inadvisable, as it would give away the exact time fixed for the assault; and emphasized the great importance of counter-battery work.

General Wilson's orders were issued on the 9th April.[1] In accordance with General Milne's instructions, they related only to the first stage of the attack which he had outlined, and even that was to be divided into two phases, the second of which—the consolidation of a position along the Dojran–Krastali road—was to take place at a subsequent date. All that he now contemplated was the capture of the enemy's first line: the works between the lake and the Petit Couronné, that hill, Hill 380, the Mamelon, and the most advanced work on the " P " Ridge. Simultaneously a raid was to be carried out against the enemy's salient opposite Machukovo.

The troops allotted to the main attack were the 26th and the 22nd (less the 67th Brigade Group in corps reserve) Divisions, supported by the XXXVII and LXXXII Heavy Groups, of two 6-inch guns, five batteries 6-inch howitzers, and five and a half batteries 60-pdrs. The 4·5-inch howitzers of the two divisions were to be divided into two bombardment groups, to which three 6-inch howitzer batteries were to be attached for the period of the bombardment only. From the Whale Back to the Vardar the front was to be held by the 60th Division, which was to carry out the raid on the Machukovo salient. The raid was to have the support of the LXXV Heavy Group, consisting of one 6-inch gun,

---

[1] XII Corps Order 24 is given in Appendix 7.

one battery 6-inch howitzers, and two batteries 60-pdrs., placed under the orders of Major-General Bulfin.

The attack was to be preceded by three days' bombardment, wire-cutting beginning a day earlier and being continued throughout the period. The 26th Division was to deliver the assault on the 3,000 yards' front between the lake and the Jumeaux Ravine, the 22nd on the 2,000 yards' front from thence to P. $4\frac{1}{2}$.

The attack was to be launched at dusk—the hour subsequently fixed being 9.45 p.m. on the 24th April. At this hour the infantry was to cross the enemy's parapet, with the exception of the 7/R. Berkshire, attacking the point known as O. $5\frac{1}{2}$ (in a re-entrant), which was to cross the parapet 20 minutes later. Except at this point, the 18-pdr. barrage was to lift, first on to points closely behind the front-line system, and a quarter of an hour later to a line 300 yards in rear of that selected for consolidation.

As there was no officer holding the appointment of commander of the heavy artillery of the corps, Br.-General H. D. White Thomson, the G.O.C. Royal Artillery, who considered that one was necessary for this operation, placed all the heavy artillery under the orders of one of his group commanders, Colonel O. C. Williamson Oswald. The allotment of ammunition was not great, considering the nature of the position, being approximately 200 rounds daily per 18-pdr., 175 per 4·5-inch howitzer, 150 per 6-inch howitzer, and 100 per 60-pdr. and 6-inch gun.

The ground immediately south-west of Lake Dojran is as tumbled and broken as any in Macedonia. Four to five thousand yards from the lake and following pretty closely its curves runs a steep-sided, knife-edged ridge, at its highest point well over 2,000 feet, and still over 1,800 at Horseshoe Hill—captured by the British in the previous August—where it begins to descend. To various points upon this ridge the French, at a time when their troops held the front between it and the lake, had given the name Piton (peak) 1, Piton 2, etc. On the maps these designations had been shortened to P. 1, P. 2, and therefrom had arisen the title of " P " Ridge—or, in the signallers' jargon, " Pip " Ridge—which will remain of grim significance so long as any memory of the Macedonian Campaign is in the mind of man.

Between the ridge and the lake is an extraordinary

jumble of hills of all shapes and sizes, broken up by deep gullies. The biggest, the Jumeaux Ravine, 400 feet deep, formed a fosse in front of 2,500 yards of the enemy's defences. Looking north-westward from the British lines above the lake shore the spectacle was presented of a rough and irregular terrace, rising to a peak about half-way between the lake and the " P " Ridge. This peak was the Grand Couronné, which will always share the notoriety of its neighbour, P. 2. Both dominated not only the British lines but all the country southward towards Salonika, as far as eye could see, overlooking trenches, battery positions, and communications so completely as to have a serious psychological effect upon the troops, who felt that all their existence was passed beneath the enemy's eye.

1917. April.

The enemy's third and main line ran across the " P " Ridge, along the forward slope of the Grand Couronné, to the shore of the lake, and was from one to two miles in rear of his front trenches. The whole position was, moreover, admirably fortified. The work had been begun by the two German divisions which had been on this front after the Allied retreat from Serbia; and their Bulgarian successors had profited by their example and continued their labours. The toil had been immense; for on the hills there was nowhere more than a few feet, and often not more than a few inches of soil above the rock. Trenches had been blasted from the rock itself, and were strongly protected by barbed wire. The British attack now about to be launched was directed, as has been explained, only against the first of the three Bulgarian lines of defence. If it were successful, it would still be faced by the formidable second position on the Hilt and the Tongue; behind that the Grand Couronné and its buttresses would still loom up unconquered.

To answer the question why the British should choose this immensely strong position for attack, we must turn from small-scale to large-scale maps. Between the Rupel Pass and the Crna, a distance of 100 miles, the valley of the Vardar was the only break in the frontier crest, and the key to the valley was this " P " Ridge—Grand Couronné system of defences. Strong as it was, it had no great depth, and if it fell the most promising of the three lines of advance would be open. The only question was whether strategy was demanding what was tactically possible.

The wire-cutting had been successful. On the front

of the 22nd Division there were by the evening of the 23rd April gaps of 100 yards in front of Hill 380, 45 yards at the Mamelon, and 60 yards at P. 4½. On the 26th Division's front the wire also appeared to have been sufficiently cut.

Early on the morning of the 24th a Bulgarian soldier gave himself up to the troops of the 22nd Division near the Horseshoe. On being interrogated, he declared that his battalion had been warned to expect an attack about 8 p.m. that evening. He also stated that the enemy had recently received reinforcements, which, it was subsequently discovered, amounted to four battalions. As the *9th Division* hitherto consisted of 18 battalions and the German *59th Regiment* was still presumed to be holding the position on the left bank of the Vardar, that made a total of 25 battalions between the river and Lake Dojran.[1]

The Bulgarian information regarding British intentions was all too nearly correct. When the news reached General Wilson at Yanesh that morning he went across to see the Commander-in-Chief, who had also established his advanced headquarters there. General Milne decided not to alter the programme. There had never been much doubt that the enemy had observed the British preparations, such as the laying of telephone wires and the digging of communication trenches to connect the gullies.

The 26th Division was now commanded by Major-General A. W. Gay, the former G.O.C. Royal Artillery of the XVI Corps, who had succeeded Major-General Mackenzie-Kennedy. It was attacking with two brigades in line: on the right the 79th Brigade (Br.-General A. J. Poole), with three battalions in line and one in reserve, up to and including the works on the Petit Couronné; on the left the 78th (Br.-General J. Duncan), with two battalions in line and one in reserve, on the remainder of the front up to the Jumeaux Ravine at Hill 380. The works which were the

---

[1] The reinforcements were the *39th Regiment* (*10th Division*) from the Crna front, which had arrived on the 8th, and a battalion of the *9th Division's* own *58th Regiment*, which had been separated from it throughout the campaign. The remainder of the *58th Regiment* did not arrive until after the first British attack. The four new battalions were held in Army reserve (Nédeff, p. 107). The British were also right in supposing that there was a German regiment on the *9th Division's* right, but not that it was the *59th*. This regiment had been relieved earlier in the month by the *9th Jäger Regiment*, made up of three Jäger battalions, all new arrivals and not among those mentioned in Chapter X as having been engaged on the Monastir front.

LOOKING ACROSS LAKE DOJRAN

DOJRAN STATION   LA TORTUE, & JUMEAUX RAVINE   PATTY RAVINE   CUSTOM HOUSE ON FRONTIER

Collotype by Waterlow & Sons Limited, London, Dunstable & Watford.

FROM SIGNAL GREC AVANCÉ (Map 10).

DOJRAN VOLOVEC TRACK

26th Division's objective had, by analogy with those on the "P" Ridge, been labelled "O. 1," "O. 2," etc. On the narrow front of the 22nd Division only one brigade, the 66th (Br.-General F. S. Montague Bates), was to carry out the attack, with two battalions in line, from Hill 380 to P. 4½. The 65th Brigade was in divisional reserve, with the exception of the 12/Lancashire Fusiliers, which held the Whale Back Ridge, in touch with the troops of the 60th Division. The 67th Brigade was in corps reserve about Galavansi, and the 8th Mounted Brigade in Army reserve.

The attack of the 79th Brigade was one of those complete and costly failures which recur so frequently in the grim annals of trench warfare, and which are as depressing to read about as they are to study and record. Forewarned as he was, the enemy put down a heavy barrage, chiefly of high explosive from heavy howitzers, before the troops had reached their assembly positions, causing great confusion and considerable loss. On the lake shore the right company of the 7/Wiltshire, climbing out of the steep Patty Ravine between its own trenches and O. 1, found the gaps in the wire covered by machine-gun and rifle fire and partly blocked by portable wire obstacles thrown out by the defenders. The Bulgarian supports were also seen hastening down the communication trench west of the work. Only a handful of the attackers entered the enemy's trenches, and they were not seen again. The centre company fought its way across the enemy's parapet and drove him out of the front-line trench, but owing to lack of support on either flank was forced to withdraw. The left company found the wire at O. 2 largely uncut, and was driven back by the enemy's fire and by showers of bombs to its own lines.

The left battalion, the 10/Devonshire, which was attacking O. 4 and O. 5 on the Petit Couronné, was cut in two by the enemy's barrage. Lieut.-Colonel T. N. Howard pushed on with the leading companies and captured O. 4 on the eastern slope of the Petit Couronné; but the two rear companies met the full weight of the barrage, which caused very heavy losses, and only a few men ever got through it. O. 5 was therefore never attacked.

The 12/Hampshire had the central objective of O. 3, but followed the Devon battalion up the Jumeaux Ravine. The enemy's shells of 150-mm. and over were bursting in this deep trough with terrific material and moral effect; the battalion was held up in the narrowest part by the losses and confusion among the troops in front of it, and only a proportion of the right company entered the enemy's trench. Lieut.-Colonel F. O. Koebel collected the remnants of the left company and what other men he could lay hands upon and led them forward in an attempt to prolong the line of the right company; but the men could not face the enemy's fire. With the troops already in the trenches, they were driven back into the ravine, the commanding officer himself being wounded.

On the front of the 78th Brigade the enemy's trenches were on the northern slope of the Jumeaux Ravine, here precipitous. The 7/R. Berkshire attacked with three companies, the first two to capture the enemy's front-line trench, the third to pass through to the assault on two isolated works in rear of the left section. The right company was stopped by the enemy's barrage; the other two carried their objectives and began to consolidate them. The 11/Worcestershire on the left had hardly begun its movement out of the Senelle Ravine when it came under heavy fire, which caused numerous casualties and temporary disorganization. The battalion pushed on, however, formed up, and launched its assault at the scheduled hour. The right company was beaten back by bombs and machine-gun fire from its objective, a circular redoubt, but the left company captured the trench west of it, and at 10.15 p.m. drove off a determined counter-attack. It also cleared a communication trench at right angles to the fire trench and blocked the latter 20 yards west of the redoubt. The supporting companies having now moved up, a fierce struggle followed, the fight swaying to and fro in the battered trenches, littered with dead and wounded.

The reports received by the commander of the 79th Brigade, Br.-General Poole, were at first vague and conflicting. His sole reserve was the 8/D.C.L.I., which had moved up before the attack was launched and at 10.40 p.m. had its two leading companies on Rockley and Silbury Hills, overlooking the Jumeaux Ravine. According to the brigade's war diary, it was not until 11.43 p.m. that the brigadier received a message from Lieut.-Colonel Howard of the 10/Devonshire that two companies were isolated in O. 4, that nothing was known of the other two, and that the situation was very serious if the enemy should counter-attack from O. 5. It is stated that Br.-General Poole at once ordered two companies of the D.C.L.I. to move to Lieut.-Colonel Howard's support.

There is a discrepancy of an hour between the diaries of the brigade and that of the Duke of Cornwall's battalion. In the latter it is stated that an identical message was received by the commanding officer, Lieut.-Colonel F. C. Nisbet, at 10.50 p.m. On the whole it seems probable that the battalion report is the correct one.[1]

The commander of the leading company, on approaching the enemy's trenches, halted and shouted: "Where are you, Devons?" and received the reply: "Here!" Directly the company moved forward it was met by a burst of fire, from which it recoiled. It was rallied and led forward again. This time the company commander got no answer to his calls, and, being again fired on, came to the conclusion that the Devon companies had evacuated the position. He therefore withdrew his men. It is probable that in the darkness he had approached the enemy's trenches to the right of O. 4. The second company, advancing in three waves, ran into the leading company retiring for the first time. The first two waves pushed on through it; the third, with which was the company commander, was cut off from it in the confusion; and the company commander, hearing the report that the Devon companies had withdrawn, also fell back to his own lines. Actually only about 40 men of the second company entered O. 4 to support the 10/Devonshire.

Meanwhile Lieut.-Colonel F. C. Nisbet, commanding the 8/D.C.L.I., had received orders to take the other two companies down to the "Sunken Road"—a track passing through the Jumeaux Ravine further down its course—for the purpose of supporting the 12/Hampshire in a renewed attack.[2] These companies could not follow their shortest route, which was blocked by an 18-pdr. battery firing across it. They therefore had to move down the Jumeaux Ravine, the second of them arriving at 1.30 a.m. on the 25th. In the Sunken Road Lieut.-Colonel Nisbet found two platoons

---

[1] It is to some extent confirmed by that of the commander of the second company, who moved off some little time after the first, and who states that his advance across the Jumeaux Ravine began "about 11.20 p.m."

[2] Exactly the same discrepancy as regards time is found here. The 79th Brigade reports that the order was sent at 12.1 a.m. on the 25th; the 8/D.C.L.I. that it was received at 11 p.m. on the 24th.

of the 8/Oxford and Bucks L.I. (Pioneers)—sent up with bombs and ammunition—and a handful of the Hampshire. He at once made preparations to attack O. 3, but was ordered to wait until the 12/Argyll and Sutherland Highlanders, from divisional reserve, should have arrived to co-operate by an attack on O. 2.

On the front of the 78th Brigade the 9/Gloucester in brigade support received orders at 12.10 a.m. to despatch one company to reinforce the Worcestershire in O. 6. This company passed through the barrage, still unabated, and reached its objective, though not without heavy loss. A second company was sent forward at 2.5 a.m., but does not appear to have entered the trenches.

If the information at the two brigade headquarters was vague, that at divisional headquarters was naturally no more precise. Major-General Gay believed (as did Br.-General Poole) that at 11.30 p.m. the right company of the Wiltshire was in O. 1. Actually, as we have seen, only a handful had ever entered the trenches at that point; it was the centre company which had made a lodgment west of O. 1, and it had apparently been driven out before this. He also believed that a party of the Hampshire was still in the enemy's trenches, though he knew that the main body of the battalion had been driven back. Reports as to the Petit Couronné (O. 4) were conflicting, but he was right in presuming that the two companies of the Devonshire were holding out there. He was aware that two companies of the Berkshire and three of the Worcestershire were upon their objectives. The most serious gap appeared to him to be at O. 2,[1] and this he decided to attack with a battalion of the 77th Brigade, in conjunction with Lieut.-Colonel Nisbet's attack on the Hampshire's front.

At 11.50 p.m. he sent orders to the 77th Brigade to put one battalion at the disposal of the 79th, his message being received at 12.8 a.m. on the 25th. At 12.30 a.m. the 12/Argyll and Sutherland Highlanders received orders to fall in on the Dojran–Kilinder road, and had done so by

---

[1] Looking back on the affair—which is naturally not the same thing as acting at the time—it seems possible that the most serious gap was really at O. 5, owing to the failure of the left of the Devonshire and the right of the Berkshire; and that, had the whole of the Petit Couronné been taken and firmly held, there was a chance, perhaps faint but still the best, of forcing the enemy out of O. 2 and O. 3 by enfilade fire.

THE ATTACK BROKEN OFF

1.30 a.m. The battalion was camped in the ravine through which the railway runs southward from Dojran Station, under orders to move at half an hour's notice. It had several hundred yards to move before reaching the road, and then a march of about two miles to the Jumeaux Ravine. It did not know this sector of the front, and as it moved up it found the trenches blocked with wounded and carrying-parties. Small wonder then that only the first two companies were ready to attack by 4 a.m.

1917.
25 April.

Br.-General Poole first decided to attack at 3.30 a.m., then, finding that the reinforcing battalion would not be ready so soon, at 4.10 a.m. But prior to this hour Major-General Gay received reports that the Wiltshire was not in O. 1 and that both the Berkshire and the Worcestershire had been driven out. He therefore cancelled the attack. One company of the Argylls, not receiving the message, moved out into "No Man's Land," but was withdrawn without loss.

It is difficult to ascertain at what hour precisely the two battalions of the 78th Brigade fell back, but apparently between 3.45 a.m. and 4 a.m., the Worcestershire having previously broken up two counter-attacks. That left only the two Devon companies on the Petit Couronné. Lieut.-Colonel Howard received orders to withdraw, apparently at 4 a.m., and at the very moment when parties of the 8/D.C.L.I. and 7/Oxford and Bucks arrived with bombs and ammunition. He did so as quickly as possible, realizing how urgent it was that the troops should be back in their trenches before dawn. The whole attack of the 26th Division had thus been a complete and, as it proved, a very costly failure.

The enemy's artillery fire did not slacken until after daylight. Then parties were sent out by the 78th and 79th Brigades into the Jumeaux Ravine, without arms, to collect wounded. In a few cases they were fired on by Bulgarian riflemen, and there were some casualties also from artillery fire; but generally speaking they were allowed to proceed with their work, and succeeded in bringing in a considerable number of wounded.

The Night Attack of the 24th April—The 22nd Division.

Map 10.
Sketches
A, 13.

The 66th Brigade (Br.-General F. S. Montague Bates) of the 22nd Division had two advantages over the troops on its right, in that its approach was easier and that the enemy's trenches which it had to attack were not continuous. They consisted of a short one on Hill 380, a longer one in the form of a horseshoe on the Mamelon, and a small wired-in redoubt on the " P " Ridge, known as P. $4\frac{1}{2}$. A continuous wire obstacle ran in front of the works, but, as has been mentioned, sufficient gaps had been cut in front of the three objectives. The wire-cutting seems, in fact, to have been more thorough on this brigade's front than on that of its neighbours of the 26th Division.

The attack was to be carried out by the 8/King's Shropshire Light Infantry on the right against Hill 380 and the Mamelon, and by the 13/Manchester on the left from thence to P. $4\frac{1}{2}$, each employing three companies in line and one in reserve. To each battalion was attached one company of the 9/Border Regiment (Pioneers) as a wiring party, and one section of the 66th Machine-Gun Company. Three sections of the 100th Field Company R.E. were detailed to construct three strong points after the two battalions had reached their final objective, which ran from Hill 380, keeping 100 yards north of a gully later known as Jackson Ravine and well behind the Mamelon, round P. $4\frac{1}{2}$, and thence back to the British lines. This plan of consolidation, not upon, but north of the enemy's former defences, deserves to be noted; for it had a great effect upon what followed. A special bombing party was also detailed to clear the sunken road running from the Mamelon trench to the Vladaya Ravine, at the foot of Hill 380. Just about where it crossed this road the ravine forked into three; and the bombing party, after clearing the road, was to block these three ravines. They represented covered approaches by which the enemy might counter-attack from his works on the Sugar Loaf, in his second line. The 66th Trench-Mortar Battery was also to detail two Stokes mortars to barrage these ravines in case of need.

The remaining battalions of the brigade, the 12/Cheshire and 9/S. Lancashire, were to occupy the British front-line trenches when the assaulting troops had left them. Two

ATTACK OF 66TH BRIGADE 313

companies of each were, however, to be held in brigade reserve, well closed up for employment if required.

1917. 24 April.

By 8.30 p.m. the 13/Manchester, and by 8.45 p.m. the 8/K.S.L.I. were in front of the British wire upon their line of deployment. At 8.50 p.m. a platoon of the Manchester occupied P. 5, a small outpost within the enemy's wire.

The enemy's barrage was again heavy, but it had been carefully located during the previous nights, and the troops, deploying beyond it, suffered few casualties. At 9.45 p.m. the six companies crossed the enemy's parapet, meeting with comparatively little resistance. By 10 p.m., after the British barrage had lifted off Jackson Ravine, the two battalions had established themselves on their objective. The wiring parties of the Border Regiment were then ordered forward.

The enemy's fire had now slackened, but soon broke out with the former intensity, this time largely directed upon his old works. A little counter-attack against P. $4\frac{1}{2}$ was driven off without difficulty by the Manchester company. At 4.15 a.m. on the 25th came a heavier counter-attack. The greater proportion of the enemy were stopped by the wire, which they were evidently surprised to find barring the way. Soon afterwards news arrived that the Worcestershire of the 78th Brigade had withdrawn from O. 6, and that the right flank was therefore in the air. Br.-General Bates at once ordered up a company of the 9/S. Lancashire to support this flank. Another small counter-attack was beaten off by the left company of the 8/K.S.L.I. in Jackson Ravine.

25 April.

After the sun was up the morning of the 25th was quiet, and though there were bursts of fire during the afternoon the Bulgarian artillery was not especially active considering the circumstances. At about 7.30 p.m., however, it began a heavy bombardment on P. $4\frac{1}{2}$, which quickly spread eastward along Jackson Ravine and was intense upon Hill 380. At P. $4\frac{1}{2}$, where the night garrison had not yet arrived, a Bulgarian attack got a footing in the trench; but the enemy was promptly driven back into the British barrage, which appeared to cause him considerable loss. At Hill 380 also he was repulsed without difficulty. The counter-attack had therefore been a complete failure.

When we come to compare the fates of the two divisions, it is clear that the success of the 22nd was due largely to its deployment beyond the line of the enemy's barrage. The attacking troops got through without serious loss and were able to repulse the enemy's counter-attacks without requiring reinforcements, so that the 66th Brigade was not tested in the handling of reserves as were those of the 26th Division. The second factor in the 66th Brigade's very fine feat was the consolidation of a line beyond Jackson Ravine, whereas the enemy expected to find it holding the crest at the Mamelon. The enemy's barrage was undoubtedly the decisive factor in the 26th's failure, since, as has been recorded, it brought a great proportion of the attacking troops to a halt. It opened in the fashion on which the artillery of the Bulgarian *First Army* prided itself, before the signal rockets calling for it had reached the ground,[1] and was dropped into the bottom of the Jumeaux Ravine with extraordinary accuracy. Here the heavy shells, especially those of a German 150-mm. naval battery, detonated with overwhelming effect. On one occasion a number of men were seen leaning against the wall of the ravine. An officer went up to them to urge them forward but found that they were all dead, though without an apparent wound.

It appeared to the British that the Bulgarians had considerably more artillery than they themselves, but there is no reason to suppose that this was the case.[2] The only possible conclusion was reached by the Commander-in-Chief when he wrote, after a study of the reports, that the Bulgarian artillery had not been sufficiently neutralized.

General Milne found also, however, that lack of speedy information and the slow handling of reserves, which were " dribbled into action " when they were used, had likewise contributed to the failure on the 26th Division's front. It is evident that there was great confusion in the Jumeaux Ravine, where battalions and companies collided in the darkness. This leads us to consider the balance of

---

[1] Nédeff, p. 97.

[2] According to Nédeff (p. 103) the front from the Vardar to Lake Dojran was covered by 147 German and Bulgarian pieces. The proportion of heavy artillery was high, there being 50 heavy pieces, ranging from 105-mm. guns (the equivalent of our 60-pdrs.) upwards. As the frontage was 10 miles, it is clear that not all these guns could fire upon the front of attack. The British had 44 guns and howitzers ranging from 60-pdrs. upwards on the front of the 26th and 22nd Divisions, and 57 from the Vardar to Lake Dojran.

BULGARIAN COUNTER-ATTACKS   315

advantages and disadvantages of a night attack. This **1917.** had been deliberately chosen because of the observation **24 April.** which the enemy's commanding position afforded him, but, though it may have saved loss in crossing " No Man's Land," it must have increased the difficulties of the troops attacking over very broken ground. Major-General Gay remarked in his report that it was a question " whether the attack " could not have been more profitably carried out at dawn." The effectiveness, now as always, of the enemy's searchlights also minimized the advantages of a night operation.[1]

The raid of the 60th Division was carried out by the 2/20th London against the Nose. Here it was discovered that the enemy had repaired the gaps in his wire and then retired to his second line. The raiders, with the aid of a Bangalore torpedo, penetrated the first line, but there came under heavy fire, the Bulgarian trench mortars causing serious losses and the searchlights again playing an effective part in the defence. Unable to reach the second line and finding not a living soul in the first, the attackers were compelled to withdraw.

On the night of the 25th Major-General Gay relieved **26 April.** the weary and depleted 79th Brigade by the 77th, from divisional reserve. Next morning he received orders to despatch the 79th to the relief of the 83rd Brigade in the " independent brigade " area. The 83rd was then to come into corps reserve, and the 67th was to be returned to the 22nd Division.

On the night of the 26th, at about 7.20 p.m., another determined counter-attack was launched against Hill 380. The company of the 8/K.S.L.I. fell back, but, being quickly reorganized, went forward again and drove the enemy to the northern slope of the hill. The Bulgarian artillery then subjected the works upon it to fire so heavy that the company could not endure it and fell back once more. As soon as the fire had died down somewhat, a company of the 9/S. Lancashire and the original garrison reoccupied the hill without opposition. On the evening of the 28th, after the **28 April.** 65th Brigade had relieved the 66th, there was another very heavy bombardment, and at 7.30 p.m. the fire lifted from Hill 380. It is not clear whether the enemy's infantry

---

[1] There were no less than 33 searchlights between Lake Dojran and the Vardar (Nédeff, p. 104).

attacked, but, if so, it was completely stopped by the British barrage.

Considering that only three brigades had been engaged in the attack, the casualties were very heavy. To estimate them exactly is difficult, because the various units give them for different periods. The figures given by the administrative branch of the XII Corps is for the week ending on the 29th April, and may be said to represent the casualties of the battle very fairly, as it covers the period from the opening of the bombardment until after the last counter-attack. The total losses of the XII Corps for this period were 3,163.[1] Of this number the 22nd Division's share was only 766, including casualties of the 65th Brigade during the bombardment on the night of the 28th. By far the greater proportion of those reported missing were undoubtedly killed, and nearly all the remainder had been wounded in the enemy's trenches.

Only 22 prisoners were captured by the two British divisions, and the losses of the defence must have been small by comparison with those of the attack.[2]

---

[1]

	KILLED	WOUNDED	MISSING
Officers	16	92	27
Other Ranks	180	2,271	577

[2] The losses of the Bulgarian *33rd* and *34th Regiments* on the front of the main attack, together with those of the *4th Regiment* at the Nose, are given by Lieut.-Colonel Nédeff (p. 116), but only for the 24th and 25th April. It is reasonable to suppose that the enemy had at least another couple of hundred casualties in the subsequent counter-attacks and bombardments. Lieut.-Colonel Nédeff's figures are as follows :—

	KILLED	WOUNDED	MISSING
Officers	8	11	1
Other Ranks	183	564	68

a total of 835. It is also mentioned that the Bulgarian and German artillery expended 17,492 rounds on those two days.

CHAPTER XIV.

THE BATTLE OF DOJRAN, 1917 (*continued*).
(Maps A, 8, 10, 11; Sketches A, 14, 15.)

THE NIGHT ATTACK OF THE 8TH MAY—THE 26TH DIVISION.

THE British attack, a subsidiary one according to General Sarrail's plan, had been made and had failed. Now the main attack, to which it was to have been the immediate preliminary, was again postponed. On the 26th April General Sarrail informed General Milne that the bombardment would begin on the 28th and the attack would follow as soon as the preparation seemed to be sufficient. The War Office was concerned upon hearing of the failure, the losses, and the fresh delay. Why had General Milne not referred the question to the War Cabinet if he had suspected that there was prospect of his attack being an isolated one?

1917. April.

To answer that question was not difficult. It was the British Government which had pressed for an early attack. He himself had urged General Sarrail that the two attacks should be synchronized. The French Commander-in-Chief had not agreed; but this difference of opinion hardly seemed to warrant a reference to the War Cabinet, seeing that the main attack was expected to follow so quickly, that the British troops had been ready since the first week of April, and that there was reason to believe that reinforcements were on their way to the enemy on the Dojran front. General Sarrail had stated in writing that the main attack would begin on the 26th, and it was not until after his own attack had been launched that General Milne had learnt of the postponement to the 28th. Now, he reported, bad weather and deep snow west of the Vardar had caused a further postponement.

The C.I.G.S. replied that he must leave the continuance of the offensive to General Milne's judgment. Another conference was about to assemble in Paris to discuss the Greek situation and the withdrawal of British forces from Salonika. This conference took place on the 4th and 5th May, when a number of resolutions were proposed by Mr. Lloyd George and accepted by the French representatives, *ad referendum* to their Cabinet. The bulk of these dealt with Greek affairs, and only the first four, which were of a strictly military character, need here be considered. They may be summarized as follows :—

(1) The British Government considered that the essential needs of the civil populations of the Allies could be met only by reducing the force at Salonika to what was necessary to hold an entrenched camp surrounding the harbour.

(2) The extent and methods of the reduction could be settled later on ; but the British Government insisted upon making arrangements forthwith to begin the withdrawal of one division and two cavalry brigades on the 1st June.

(3) If the offensive were remarkably successful, this action might be reconsidered.

(4) The French Government were requested (and to this their representatives agreed unconditionally) to direct General Sarrail to begin his offensive as soon as possible.

The General Staff had at last had its way. For the first time since the landing at Salonika there was about to be a reduction instead of an augmentation of the British force. Not only were the two latest-joined reinforcements the 60th Division and 8th Mounted Brigade, to go, but the 7th Mounted Brigade, which had been at Salonika almost from the first, was also to be withdrawn.

That, however, was not General Milne's immediate concern. He had first of all to face the question of continuing the offensive. His inclination was to comply with General Sarrail's desires. He had never, as we have seen, been a pessimist as to the possibility of beating the Bulgarians. They were a primitive people, unaccustomed to long wars. Brave as they were, it seemed certain that the moral discipline, the patience, the enduring resolution, and the intelligence of the troops of nations like Britain and France, whose high civilization had not weakened their native valour, would in the end prevail against them. As to his own part in the attack, that was difficult enough in all conscience, but it had a reasonable prospect of success if the mistakes of the last venture were avoided.

That the opportunity for which he looked had yet come was not certain, but there was some evidence that war-weariness was already at work in the Bulgarian ranks. Yet General Milne was not easy in his mind regarding the

Sketch 14

THE BATTLE OF DOJRAN
Night Attack of 8th May 1917.

Bulgarians....Green.
British........Red.

conduct of the offensive. A letter addressed on the 2nd May by Major-General Gillman, his chief General Staff officer, to the commander of the XVI Corps, with reference to a projected attack on Erneköi, reveals his misgiving lest the possible opportunity were about to be lost or had even been lost already. Had a synchronized attack by the Allies taken place and been pressed with vigour, General Milne thought it possible that the enemy might have been driven back upon the whole front between Lake Dojran and Monastir. At a recent interview General Sarrail had remarked that he did not intend to continue operations in the hot weather and that his primary object at present was to clear the enemy away from the immediate neighbourhood of Monastir. In these circumstances it was possible that the attack north of Monastir might have only a limited objective, in which case General Briggs's scheme would lose its chief *raison d'être* and would produce small benefit in return for its cost.[1]

On the same day the Commander-in-Chief ordered General Wilson to continue his operations as soon as possible, with the object of capturing the remainder of the Dojran–Krastali line as a preliminary to a further advance. He had now learnt from General Sarrail that the French artillery preparation would begin on the 5th and that the attack would take place a few days later. That of the XII Corps was fixed for 9.50 p.m. on the 8th, when there would be a good moon. An attack at dawn had, of course, been considered; but the project had been rejected. It was considered that the distance between the British and Bulgarian trenches on the shore of Lake Dojran would give the enemy too good an opportunity, in case of a dawn attack, of filling up gaps in his wire with fresh obstacles during the previous night. It was not possible now to advance closer by sapping forward and digging new trenches. The time for that would have been before the first attack, during the months of March and April.

The 26th Division's failure on the night of the 24th April and the simultaneous success of the 22nd Division had resulted in the salient hitherto existing in the British line between La Tortue and Horseshoe Hill becoming still more pronounced. It was hardly possible for the 22nd Division

---

[1] This letter is given in Note at end of Chapter.

to make further progress here until the 26th had gone forward to straighten out the right flank of the salient. General Wilson therefore proposed that the latter division should make a renewed attack upon the enemy's advanced line between Lake Dojran and the Petit Couronné. In order to induce the enemy to distribute the activity of his artillery, the 22nd Division was to simulate an attack against the line from the Petit Couronné to P. 4, a work on the " P " Ridge in the enemy's second line. West of the " P " Ridge and of the salient, the division was to advance its line at the Whale Back and simultaneously to raid the village of Krastali. The 60th Division was to co-operate by advancing its line to Tomato and Westbury Hills, east of Dautli, and by capturing Goldies Hill. All three had defences upon them, but only the last-named was regularly occupied by the enemy.

As previously stated, the 79th Brigade had, after its heavy losses in the first attack, relieved the 83rd Brigade east of Lake Dojran, and the latter had come into corps reserve. This left the 26th Division with only two brigades, but one battalion of the 83rd (the 2/King's Own) was put at Major-General Gay's disposal to be held in divisional reserve. The artillery arrangements were much the same as before, except that this operation was to be preceded by only two days' bombardment and that less wire-cutting would be necessary. Despite the importance attributed to the enemy's barrage-fire in the first attack, the counter-battery group was not strengthened. This could have been done only at the expense of the heavy artillery forming part of the bombardment groups, which was presumably considered undesirable. The right bombardment group, supporting the 26th Division, was now to have three 6-inch howitzer batteries attached; the left group, in support of the 22nd Division, one.[1]

In the interval between the two attacks the 22nd Division suffered a serious loss in the person of its experienced and successful commander, Major-General the Hon. F. Gordon, whose personality and gifts as a leader of men had given him a remarkable influence over his troops. Having strained his heart in the trenches, he was evacuated to

---

[1] The orders of the XII Corps, Letter G/4/919, are given in Appendix 8. This document was not formally described as an operation order because it was in continuation of that already issued.

ATTACK OF 77TH BRIGADE

hospital, and had finally to be sent home. Br.-General J. Duncan, the commander of the 78th Brigade, took his place temporarily and was soon afterwards confirmed in the appointment.

1917. May.

During the night of the 5th May the French 122nd Division west of the Vardar and the Greek troops attached to it advanced their line on a front of three miles and in places to a depth of over half a mile. In general, the enemy's positions captured were in the nature of posts.

The plan of attack of the 26th Division was based largely upon the desire to avoid as far as possible the deep Jumeaux Ravine, which had caused so much confusion on the night of the 24th April. For this purpose the 77th Brigade (Br.-General W. A. Blake) was first of all to capture and consolidate O. 1, O. 2, and part of O. 3, two of its battalions assembling beyond the ravine, in the trenches on Swindon Hill, and the third with its two leading companies beyond it, in the Sunken Road. The 9/Gloucester of the 78th Brigade and the 8/Oxford and Bucks Light Infantry (Pioneers) were attached to this brigade, the former battalion as a reserve. On the left of the 77th Brigade the 78th (Lieut.-Colonel T. N. Howard) was to hold a battalion in readiness to assault the Petit Couronné two and a half hours afterwards.

On the right the two leading companies of the 11/Scottish Rifles appear to have reached their objectives, but not without heavy loss, and to have been speedily driven out again by the enemy. The supporting company lost touch in the mist, thickened by a cloud of smoke and dust caused by the bombardment, and only a few men entered the enemy's trench, to be bombed out again. How long precisely any troops remained in the enemy's trenches is difficult to determine, for no news of any sort reached battalion headquarters until 2.15 a.m. on the 9th May, when one of the company commanders returned to report that the attack had been a complete failure.

8 May.

In the centre the 12/Argyll and Sutherland Highlanders entered the enemy's front line, in which a number of dugouts were bombed, and passed through to the final objective. Some consolidation was actually begun; but the battalion was isolated and enfiladed owing to those on either flank having failed; all the officers taking part in the attack were casualties; and after about half an hour's fighting it withdrew without the brigade headquarters' having any warning that it was hard pressed.

On the left the 10/Black Watch employed only two companies in the attack, the supporting company being directed to begin to move to the Sunken Road 15 minutes before the launch of the assault and there await orders. The right company was held up by uncut wire in Wylye Ravine, and only a handful reached the enemy's trenches. The left company was late and lost the barrage. It succeeded in entering the Bulgarian trenches, but was counter-attacked by the enemy with bombs and rifle grenades. It likewise was driven out, after its two Lewis guns had been destroyed. At 10.30 p.m. the supporting company was sent forward with the remnants of the right company to make a renewed attack, but ran into the same wire which had held up the first assault, and withdrew.

At 10.50 p.m. Br.-General Blake, who had as yet no suspicion that anything was seriously wrong, placed one company of the 8/R. Scots Fusiliers at the disposal of each of the commanders of the attacking battalions, to reinforce their troops which he imagined to be in the enemy's trenches, in case their fourth companies were required for carrying parties. We must for a moment leave these companies, which did not receive their orders till 11.45 p.m. in two cases and 12.10 a.m. in the third, painfully making their way forward over the open, up bombarded and congested communication trenches, or down the Winton Ravine, in the darkness, and turn to the attack on the Petit Couronné on the front of the 78th Brigade.

The 7/Oxford and Bucks L.I. was ordered to attack O. 4, the big work on the Petit Couronné, with three companies and their six Lewis guns, 150 minutes after the main assault, that is, at 12.20 a.m. on the 9th. Two platoons of the 8/Oxford and Bucks L.I. (Pioneers) had been put at the disposal of the battalion commander, and a company of the 7/R. Berkshire was to take over his trenches after his troops had gone forward. If the situation admitted of it, O. 5 was to be attacked from O. 4 at 3.30 a.m. after an intense bombardment of ten minutes. It was originally intended that this attack should be carried out by the 7/Oxford and Bucks, but at the last moment it was decided that it should be entrusted to two companies of the 7/R. Berkshire, which was to reach La Tortue at 11 p.m.

ATTACK ON PETIT COURONNÉ

1917.
8 May.

This order was not received by the latter battalion until about 5 p.m. on the evening of the attack.

The 7/Oxford and Bucks, including the reserve company, which was carrying ammunition, bombs, and water, and the two platoons of pioneers, left its trenches at 10.50 p.m., that is, 90 minutes before the scheduled hour of assault. The ample allowance of time is easily to be understood, but the result was very unfortunate. The Jumeaux Ravine was actually crossed very quickly and with few casualties; but the battalion, forming up in waves on the slopes of the Petit Couronné, now found itself with 45 minutes to wait, and began to suffer heavy loss, especially from trench-mortar fire. At 11.57 p.m. the brigade commander, Lieut.-Colonel Howard, received a message from the commander of the three assaulting companies, Major A. D. Homan: " Am going through in ten minutes." Lieut.-Colonel Howard, who did not think it would be possible to alter the artillery programme at such short notice, at once replied: " You must stick to programme and go in at ' B ' hours " (12.20 a.m.), not before."

9 May.

This message was certainly received on the Petit Couronné, but probably too late ; though, as Major Homan died of his wounds after the action, it is not known whether this was the case, or why he did not await zero hour. At all events, a report came from a forward observing officer of the field artillery at 12.13 a.m. that the attack had already been launched. Orders were issued for the guns to be switched off; but, according to the reports of survivors, shells from the British heavy batteries fell in O. 4, apparently even after 12.20 a.m., causing both loss and confusion.

During the advance up the hill Major Homan and almost all the company officers were wounded, and a subaltern, 2nd-Lieutenant C. P. Ker, took command of the three companies, until Major C. Wheeler came up to relieve him. The battalion, after being reinforced by its reserve company and the platoons of pioneers, made a lodgment in the south-eastern corner of O. 4 ; and four successive advances, pushed with great gallantry, were made from this point. In each case the troops were forced back by a trench-mortar barrage, under cover of which the Bulgarian infantry crept forward and counter-attacked.

Communication was now very difficult. All wires were cut ; dense smoke made lamp-signalling impossible ; and runners were frequently killed. Lieut.-Colonel Howard knew enough, however, to realize that the prospects of holding on to O. 4 were not bright. Reporting the situation to divisional headquarters, he was told at 2 a.m. to " make " good O. 4 and attempt nothing more." Major Wheeler, who now had two officers, both wounded, and about 150 men under his orders, decided he could do no more than cling to the south-eastern corner of the work until the Berkshire companies arrived. His weary and battered remnant had not lost their spirit. Pounded as they were by the trench mortars, they defeated all the enemy's efforts to push them down the hill.

The two Berkshire companies left the British trenches on La Tortue at 1.30 a.m., crossed the Jumeaux Ravine almost without loss, and formed up in two lines south of O. 4, in rear of a handful of the Oxford and Bucks, which had now been forced out of the work and was established about 50 yards south of it.

The general situation on the front of the 77th Brigade at 2.30 a.m., so far as it can be disentangled, was as follows :—

None of the three attacking battalions had a footing in the enemy's trenches. On the right the assaulting companies of the 11/Scottish Rifles had simply vanished; patrols sent out by the Scots Fusilier company which had moved to their support reported that they could find no trace of them and that the enemy had reoccupied his front line. The Argylls in the centre had likewise been driven out, but their survivors were more or less under the hand of their commanding officer, Lieut.-Colonel Falconar Stewart. A certain proportion of both these battalions had drifted back to their own trenches. On the left Lieut.-Colonel J. Harvey, commanding the 10/Black Watch, was attempting to organize a new attack with his own reserve company and the company of the 8/R. Scots Fusiliers which had been sent to his support. The 9/Gloucester, from brigade reserve, originally sent to the Wylye Ravine to enter O. 2 (still supposed to be held by the Argylls) and thence assist the Black Watch in an attack on O. 3, was now moving up in preparation for a new attack. The divisional reserve, the 11/Worcestershire, had been placed at Br.-General Blake's disposal, and he had sent his brigade major to guide the battalion to the Sunken Road.

PLAN OF NEW ATTACK

1917. 9 May.

At 2.46 a.m. the General Staff of the 26th Division reported by telephone to the XII Corps that Br.-General Blake would carry out a fresh attack with the aid of both the Gloucester and Worcestershire battalions; the British artillery was now firing shrapnel on O. 1, O. 2, and O. 3; it would later open with high-explosive, and, he hoped, lift for the assault at 3.30 or 3.45 a.m.; the Oxford and Bucks were still clinging to O. 4—actually there were probably no men in the work, though they still had a footing on the hill—and he had instructed them to hold on at all costs. Nine minutes later the G.S.O.1 of the division, Lieut.-Colonel P. L. Hanbury, informed Lieut.-Colonel Howard of the new attack, repeated Major-General Gay's instructions that O. 4 must be held, and bade him, if in any doubt, send up a third company of the Berkshire.

Between 2.50 and 3.15 a.m. Br.-General Blake issued instructions for the attack to be carried out in the following order from right to left: 11/Scottish Rifles, 9/Gloucester, 12/Argyll and Sutherland Highlanders, 11/Worcestershire, 10/Black Watch. During the same period Lieut.-Colonel Howard ordered the Berkshire to send up a third company to O. 4.

Then began a series of delays and misunderstandings, all the more unfortunate because the enemy's artillery fire had about this time to some extent diminished. It was quite evident that the troops would not be ready, and the final bombardment had to be postponed. Br.-General Blake called urgently for reports as to the progress being made in deployment for the attack. The 11/Worcestershire reported at 4.10 a.m. that it would be ready at 4.30. Its commanding officer apparently understood that this was to be the hour of assault and communicated the fact to the 10/Black Watch. At 4.22 a.m. the 12/A. and S. Highlanders reported that it could not attack for another hour. Br.-General Blake then directed that the company of the 8/R. Scots Fusiliers sent to its support should take its place in the attack. This unfortunate company had forced its way up a choked communication trench [1] and reached the front line at a point known as B. 6 at 3.10 a.m. Immediately on arrival it had received an order to go back again.

---

[1] It may be noted that this trench is marked on the brigade map as for "in" traffic, but that the company commander reports meeting a stream of wounded coming out.

The order had been given by Lieut.-Colonel Falconar Stewart, commanding the Argylls, who desired to clear the trenches on his right for the 9/Gloucester. He then intended to bring the Scots Fusilier company round in rear of his own battalion. The company went back down the communication trench, worse crowded than ever, and then got orders to move up the next to the left so as to reach the front line at B. 8. Up it struggled once more, two platoons being cut off by the congestion in the trench, and on reaching the front line received a message that it was to attack at 5.35 a.m. Just before this hour Captain J. G. Graham led his two platoons forward.

But meanwhile, at 5.15, Br.-General Blake had finally fixed 5.50 as the hour. Not only had that information not reached Captain Graham in time; it had also not reached Major M. W. Gloag, commanding the remnants of the 10/Black Watch (one company not yet employed and three others very much depleted) and one company 8/R. Scots Fusiliers, who had, as we have seen, arranged to attack at 4.30. And at that hour he had gone forward, the men, it was reported, moving as though on parade, and had reached the enemy's wire; but the gallant assault, unsupported and isolated as it was, was repulsed, and the Black Watch, falling back through the Worcestershire, now deployed in " No Man's Land," carried that battalion back also.

Then Lieut.-Colonel W. F. Barker, commanding the Worcestershire, received orders to attack at 5.50 a.m. He replied at 5.33 that he could see no other troops but his own battalion—Captain Graham's Scots Fusilier platoons being apparently hidden behind a low ridge—and that the wire was uncut at O. 3; and awaited instructions. It was now growing light. Before any message could reach Lieut.-Colonel Barker, he reported that his troops were so heavily shelled that they could not form up and that the troops on his right had withdrawn. He was thereupon ordered, about 5.55, to fall back to a position of security. Having been protected by a low bank, the battalion's casualties were only 10 wounded, of whom four remained at duty.

Actually Lieut.-Colonel Barker's second report was incorrect. Punctually to the moment the 9/Gloucestershire had attacked and crossed the parapet at O. 2. It found the

STRUGGLE ON PETIT COURONNÉ

1917.
9 May.

front-line trenches empty except for Bulgarian dead, but came under fire from O. 1, where the 11/Scottish Rifles had not attacked. Then an order was received to withdraw.

As often happens, while urgently important messages had lagged, the incorrect news from the Worcestershire had reached Major-General Gay with remarkable speed, and he had sent an order for the withdrawal of all troops. It was not received by Captain Graham's company of the Scots Fusiliers, which was close to the enemy's trench and engaging him with Lewis-gun fire; but, seeing the Gloucestershire withdraw, he likewise fell back.

To turn now to the situation of the two battalions of the 78th Brigade at the Petit Couronné, we left two companies of the 7/R. Berkshire and the remnant of 7/Oxford and Bucks L.I. lying on the slopes of the hill about 50 yards from O. 4. The commanding officer of the Berkshire, Lieut.-Colonel A. P. Dene, himself led the third company up in accordance with the orders he had received from the brigade commander, and reached this position without a casualty. He then made preparations to attack, placing the two original Berkshire companies in the first line, and the third company with what remained of the Oxford and Bucks in the second, and called for a half-hour's bombardment, after which he would attack at 5 a.m.

Weary as the troops were, they responded gallantly. The attack was successful; practically the whole of O. 4 was captured; and a bombing party actually forced it way along the communication trench leading to O. 5, half-way to that work. At this moment, however, the enemy turned his heavy artillery with terrible effect on to O. 4.[1] When his fire lifted again, the Bulgarian infantry came forward from O. 5 and forced the British back some distance. A line was now established, facing almost west, across the centre of the work.

It was by now 8 a.m. and the bombardment had died down, to be renewed again an hour and a half later. Soon afterwards Lieut.-Colonel Dene, who had been wounded some hours earlier, went back to have his wound dressed, his place being taken by Lieut.-Colonel A. T. Robinson of the Oxford and Bucks.

---

[1] The Bulgarian artillery had small consideration for their own garrison in O. 5, who were disputing the advance. Several of them were seen to be hit by their own shells.

There had been, as often in these circumstances, some confusion and misapprehension, such as orders to withdraw to the new line being mistaken by some of the troops for orders to retire from the position, and a number of men had fallen back down Tor Ravine. There remained only about 250 clinging to O. 4. It appeared hopeless to expect them to maintain their position, while the works on either side were in the enemy's hands. At 11.50 a.m. orders were received from Major-General Gay to withdraw them. Lieut.-Colonel Robinson having been mortally wounded just before mid-day, Captain S. A. Pike of the Berkshire took command. Organizing the men into parties of 12, Captain Pike sent these one by one down the Tor Ravine, and managed to bring away from the trenches all the bombs and much of the other material. All but four wounded [1] were brought back, even those on the very summit of the Petit Couronné being carried down by the medical officer, Captain M. S. Bryce, and one of his sergeants.

The heart-breaking action, marked by so many brave deeds and so many deplorable errors, so much good will and so much confusion, was at an end.

The Operations of the 22nd and 60th Divisions.

Map 10.
Sketch 14.

The rôle of the 22nd Division was in part to make demonstrations against the enemy on its front for the purpose of deceiving him as to the scope of the attack, and in part to occupy ground in front of his main line which he frequently held with night outposts or constantly patrolled. The division had made good progress in the consolidation of the positions captured in the previous attack, though the battalions in the new line could not move by day, the men lying for the most part in "slits" covered with brushwood. The new operations were to be carried out by the 65th Brigade (Br.-General G. E. Bayley), to which the 8/S. Wales Borderers of the 67th was attached, and the 67th Brigade (Br.-General H. F. Cooke), less two and a half battalions. The divisional reserve consisted of one and a half battalions of the 67th Brigade and the whole of the 66th, less one battalion which was held in corps reserve.

The tasks of the 65th Brigade were all in the nature of

---

[1] These were on the lower slopes of the hill and are all believed to have been brought in by stretcher-bearers after dusk.

SECONDARY OPERATIONS 329

demonstrations to attract the enemy's attention. They 1917. were to raid the work O. 6, captured and lost again by the 8 May. 26th Division on the night of the 24th April, and to make demonstrations against the Sugar Loaf, a fortified ridge facing the newly captured Hill 380, and trenches known as "Dol. L."[1] and P. 4, in the enemy's former second line (which now, owing to the capture of P. $4\frac{1}{2}$, had become at this point his first). All these tasks were to be carried out by quite small parties : the first by two officers and 59 rank and file of the 8/S. Wales Borderers, the second by one officer and 25 rank and file of the 9/King's Own R. Lancashire, the third by one officer and 25 rank and file of the 12/Lancashire Fusiliers, and the fourth by one officer and 24 rank and file of the last-named battalion. Gaps in the enemy's wire had been cut by the divisional artillery. A barrage was to be laid down from O. 6 to Krastali 16 minutes before the hour of the assault, 18-pdrs. sweeping and howitzers bombarding the enemy's front line. Prior to the hour the howitzers were to lift to "blocking points"; and at zero the 18-pdrs. were to lift to the support and communication trenches.

The brigade accomplished its general purpose without having much definite success. The raiding party of the 8/S.W.B. came into the ray of a searchlight from the Grand Couronné, and had to face a trench-mortar barrage. It succeeded in entering O. 6, which the enemy evacuated, and remained there ten minutes. After it had withdrawn, the Bulgarians were seen to re-enter their trenches and to fall back hastily when the British artillery was again turned on to them. The Sugar Loaf party could not get very far, but drew artillery fire which would doubtless otherwise have been directed against the 26th Division. It had only two casualties. The patrol against Dol. L. moved out at 9. 35 p.m. and passed through the battered copse known as the Corne du Bois. When within 350 yards of the enemy's trench it came into the beam of a searchlight and drew trench-mortar and rifle fire, to which it replied vigorously before withdrawing. The patrol to P. 4 moved up the west

---

[1] The enemy's trench system had been divided up into rectangles from the names of neighbouring villages, such as Doir. (Doiran), Dol. (Doljeli), Pal. (Paljorca), Sel. (Selimli), etc., inside which the principal points were lettered for quick reference. These titles are not used in this account where they are duplicated by the ordinary trench names.

side of the Corne du Bois and encountered a party of Bulgarians 150 strong in the open. It succeeded in driving in a bombing-party on the enemy's left; but the main body held its ground. The patrol withdrew at 10.20 p.m. without loss. The enemy's barrage signals were sent up, and a body at least 200 strong was seen to run forward to man the trenches, upon which the British artillery was then directed.

The 67th Brigade had a more definite rôle, though it had only the 7/S. Wales Borderers, one and a half companies of the 11/R. Welch Fusiliers, and one section of the 127th Field Company R.E. at its disposal, these troops being placed under the command of Lieut.-Colonel J. Grimwood of the 7/S. Wales Borderers. One company of this battalion and a detachment of the engineers, under Major P. Gottwaltz, was to carry out the raid on Krastali; the remainder of the battalion and half a company of the 11/R. Welch Fusiliers were to take up a new position on the Roach Back, a ridge beyond the line already held on the Whale Back.

The Krastali raiding party reached the outskirts of the village, but did not come into contact with the enemy, and was withdrawn at 10.50 p.m. It had come under heavy fire, but had suffered only eight casualties. The Roach Back was not occupied by the enemy, but its consolidation proved a difficult task, under heavy and continuous fire. The troops, however, worked with great pluck and energy, and before dawn had constructed a series of dummy trenches on the forward slope—to draw the enemy's fire by day but also for night outposts—and the real fire trenches on the reverse slope. The total casualties for the night were 37, including one officer and six other ranks killed.

The hills to be occupied by the right of the 60th Division, known as Tomato, Single Tree, Turtle Back, and Westbury Hills, were none of them held by the enemy, though he sometimes had a night outpost on Tomato Hill. Northwest of this chain of hills and at right angles to them was the long, narrow ridge known as Goldies Hill, on the further end of which the enemy had a small work. This work was to be raided and outpost trenches were to be dug towards the British end of the ridge. All these operations were to be carried out by the 179th Brigade (Br.-General F. M. Edwards). There was to be no preliminary artillery fire, but special barrages had been registered and were to be called for if required.

The whole affair was carried out with complete success, and without opposition from the enemy, who was found to have abandoned his outpost on Goldies Hill. A continuous belt of wire was put up in front of the new position, excluding Goldies Hill. At dawn the enemy's artillery opened fire, hindering the work of consolidation, which, however, made good progress during the night of the 9th. Before dawn on the 10th small parties of the enemy attacked the little posts on Goldies Hill but were beaten off. The post in the enemy's old work, half a platoon in strength, was more than once during the day forced to withdraw slightly, owing to the very heavy fire directed upon it, but always reoccupied the position.

1917.
9 May.

On the 9th General Milne ordered the bombardment on the front of the XII Corps to be continued. To assist the operations west of the Vardar, it was his intention to capture a large redoubt on Flat Iron Hill, beyond the new line occupied by the 60th Division. For this purpose the corps further advanced its line on the night of the 14th, occupying a ridge known as Fish Back and digging a chain of posts, protected by wire, from thence to Tomato Hill. On hearing, however, that the 60th Division was at once to be withdrawn, in accordance with the decisions of the Conferences of Saint-Jean de Maurienne and Paris, and on being informed by General Sarrail that the Franco-Serbian attacks had ceased for the time being, he cancelled this minor operation.

14 May.

* * * * *

The losses incurred were, in proportion to the numbers engaged, as heavy as those of the April attack, and for the night of the 8th May alone amounted to 1,861—1,743 in the 26th Division, 108 in the 22nd, and 10 in the 60th.[1] The 26th Division had had 3,888 casualties in the two attacks, with no success in either to compensate for them. But the figure of 1,861 does not represent the total loss resulting from the operations of the 8th May. In the ensuing days the new positions were heavily bombarded and a considerable number of men were killed and wounded. The 60th Division had 65 casualties in the next four days and each of the others about half that number.

---

[1]
	Killed	Wounded	Missing
Officers	7	43	17
Other Ranks	68	1,435	291

So far as the British were concerned, the causes of failure were very much the same as in the April attack. On this occasion, it is true, the assaulting troops of the 77th Brigade crossed "No Man's Land" with little loss from the enemy's barrage; but in General Milne's view lack of information and delay in using reserves were as apparent as before. In the foregoing account some indication has been given, without going into all the details, of the delays and confusion which occurred owing in part to mistakes and errors of judgment, but much more to the lack of sufficient trenches for assembly and communication. As the Commander-in-Chief pointed out, he had ordered preparations for the attack to be carried out at the end of February. The fact appears to be that new trenches were less necessary for the attack on a broad front of the 24th April than for the operations of the 8th May, and that there was little time to dig them between the two attacks. It is, indeed, probable that the digging in this rocky ground of even a couple of extra communication trenches and of slits for a "jumping-off" line would have been impossible in a fortnight. Existing trenches had, however, been widened and deepened by Br.-General Blake's orders.

Signal communication forward of the British lines failed everywhere, with one exception, and adequate measures to ascertain the fate of the companies in the attack were either not taken or taken too late. The one exception was at the Petit Couronné. Here the forward observing officer of the artillery, Lieutenant J. B. White, "A" Battery CXV Brigade R.F.A., was in constant communication with the British lines and sent through a steady stream of messages—interrupted only when the smoke from the enemy's barrage was exceptionally thick—reporting the situation of the infantry and directing fire on the enemy's trench mortars and upon a counter-attack at dawn, which was broken up. He had gone forward with the assaulting companies of the Oxford and Bucks, without a telephone; and though he had a signalling lamp he did not use it, all his messages being flashed with a torch.

It will have been noted that the two attacks had been carried out at night and at almost the same hour. The enemy's complete command of the ground had been the chief reason for this. Yet the time chosen was without certain advantages which dawn or dusk would have had.

CONDUCT OF THE DEFENCE

An early morning attack, at an hour when the troops could just see their way but could not be seen from the enemy's observation posts, might have enabled objectives to be reached with less loss and have avoided some of the confusion in " No Man's Land " ; then, as the light improved, the British artillery observers would have had a better chance of breaking up the enemy's counter-attacks. (This was clearly proved by the attack of the 7/R. Berkshire on the Petit Couronné in daylight on the morning of the 9th, when the British artillery held the Bulgarians off by observed fire.) An attack at dusk would have had similar advantages in the crossing of " No Man's Land," but assembly would have been very difficult. On the other hand, the attackers would have been given, say, twenty minutes of half light in which to consolidate themselves, and would then have been shrouded in darkness.

It may be added that, according to a letter from G.H.Q. written before the first attack—and there is no evidence that this state of affairs was remedied before the second—all the pamphlets on the employment of artillery in possession of the Army were written before the Battle of the Somme. Possibly some system of searching and sweeping in rear of the objective might have checked the enemy's counter-attacks, which had, according to his own story, no great difficulty in passing through the barrage.[1] But probably no such system would have fully availed. The essence of the affair, so far as artillery was concerned, was that the British had insufficient guns and ammunition for their task, and no 8-inch howitzers to deal with concrete emplacements.

As regards the defence, it made full use of its many advantages. The enemy's trench mortars, generally firing from deep ravines in which it was exceedingly hard to knock them out of action, had great moral and material effect. The Bulgarian gunners fired without hesitation upon their own trenches as soon as they knew that the British were in them ; and a skilful system of coloured rocket-signals enabled them to increase the range when their infantry moved forward to counter-attack. Their excellent observation posts, especially that on the Grand Couronné, were, of course, of the greatest possible service to them in this

---

[1] Nédeff, p. 135.

respect. The infantry dugouts, in some cases mined, in others covered with nearly five feet of concrete,[1] kept the garrison safe until it was time to issue from them to repel the attack; and altogether the losses appear to have been very slight.[2]

The Bulgarian soldier gave proof not only of the tenacity expected of him, but also of a quickness and a standard of training which were only now beginning to be fully appreciated by the Allies. He had fine physique, good eyesight, and the mountaineer's sense of direction; he was a good bomber, and had also a liking for the bayonet which made him an ugly opponent at close quarters. Writing afterwards to Sir William Robertson, General Milne stated frankly that, however great was the superiority of British troops on the flat, in hill fighting the superiority was with the enemy.

Finally, for what they are worth, the enemy's comments on British tactics may be given. Neither the rifle nor the bayonet was used to any extent : " il paraît que les soldats "anglais ne tiraient presque pas."[3] The attack relied chiefly on the Lewis gun and the bomb, and it was the latter which caused the heaviest loss to the Bulgarians.

The Operations of the XVI Corps.

Maps A, 8. General Briggs had been instructed to draw up a plan of operations to be carried out in the Struma valley; he was, in brief, to avoid heavy losses, but as far as possible to prevent the transfer of Bulgarian troops to other parts of the Macedonian front. He had on the 25th April issued orders for steady pressure to be begun upon a fairly wide front, culminating in an attack on the enemy's main line upon a narrow one, which was all that his resources would permit. The first phase, lasting about four days, was to consist of increased artillery activity between Tumbitza Farm, five miles south-east of Seres, and Mirsla, on the right bank of the Struma, four miles north-west of Bairakli Jum'a, a front of over 22 miles as the crow flies. During

---

[1] " Un mètre et demi " (Nédeff, p. 126).
[2] They are given by Colonel Nédeff (p. 123) as 489, almost all in the *34th Regiment*. He also mentions that 28,874 projectiles were expended, more than half as many again as in the first attack.
[3] Nédeff, p. 137.

the second phase, lasting about three days, the front of the 10th and 28th Divisions was to be pushed forward towards the enemy's main line. By the end of this phase the two divisions were to be in possession of Prosenik, Kyupri, Bairakli, and an important series of outpost trenches between Bairakli Jum'a and the Struma. The third phase, lasting four days, was to consist of final preparations for the attack upon the very strong defences of the main line from Spatovo to the river, and was to include bombardment and the necessary wire-cutting. During the last day there were to be artillery demonstrations on the whole front. In the fourth phase, to be carried out in one day, the 28th Division was to capture the villages of Spatovo and Erneköi, and to hold the ground gained. Beyond taking part in the artillery demonstration, the 27th Division, now commanded by Major-General G. T. Forestier-Walker, had no part to play.

It was in the last phase only that considerable loss might be anticipated, and here the Commander-in-Chief hesitated to give his approval when it began to appear possible that General Sarrail's operations might be less extensive and prolonged than had at first been anticipated. As we have seen, he wrote to Lieut.-General Briggs on the 2nd May that this last stage of his operation might have to be abandoned.

The corps had now at its disposal a very small amount of heavy artillery for an operation such as this—one 6-inch gun of the 43rd Siege Battery, the 143rd and 153rd Heavy Batteries (60-pdrs.), and the 127th Siege Battery (6-inch howitzers). The 6-inch gun was to be kept at the disposal of the corps to engage batteries beyond the range of the 60-pdrs. and bombard distant targets such as camps and bridges. The 153rd Heavy Battery was put at the disposal of the 10th Division, and the two remaining batteries, under the XX Heavy Group, at that of the 28th Division. The field artillery of the 28th Division was to be reinforced by the LXVIII Brigade R.F.A. of the 10th. The ammunition allotment was fairly liberal, especially to the 28th Division.

The first phase began on the 12th May, by which time the field artillery of the 10th and 28th Divisions had been moved forward and most of the heavy guns and howitzers had crossed the Struma. The main operation of the second phase, the occupation of the line Kalendra–Prosenik–

1917.
15 May. Kyupri–Bairakli by the 10th Division, and the capture of the outpost works, known as the "Ferdie" and "Essex" trenches, by the 85th Brigade of the 28th Division, took place on the night of the 15th.

At 6.45 p.m. the 6/R. Irish Rifles of the 29th Brigade moved forward to the attack on Kyupri. All three brigades of the division—the 31st on the right, the 30th in the centre, and the 29th on the left—took part in the operation, but the only serious part of it was the capture of the village, and this was supported by 16 field guns and howitzers, in addition to the 153rd Heavy Battery. The 6/Leinster had instructions to cover the left of the Irish Rifles and link its new position with that held by the 1/Leinster on the outskirts of Bairakli.

At 7.30 p.m. a barrage was laid upon the south edge of the village, and began to move quickly through it two minutes later. The attack met with little resistance, except on the left, where the 6/Leinster was slightly delayed by a small Bulgarian post. Here three prisoners were captured. The intention was to hold Kyupri as an outpost with one company in four posts to east, north, and north-west, and to establish a new main line, held by two companies, 200 yards south of the village.

These dispositions were taken up, and by 10.45 p.m. touch had been obtained with the 30th Brigade on the right and the 6/Leinster on the left. Work was at once begun on the four posts and carried on as quickly as possible, so as to have some cover and protection by daylight. At 3.30 a.m. on the 16th the covering parties were withdrawn.

16 May. The enemy had been shelling Kyupri all night. Now, as it began to grow light, his fire increased. At 5.15 a.m. he launched his first counter-attack, a line of some 150 men creeping through the corn towards No. 4 post, north-west of the village. Caught by the barrage and by Lewis-gun and rifle fire, the Bulgarians withdrew, but quickly re-formed and at 6 a.m. returned to the attack, now trying to work round the left of the post. Again they were beaten off. Then came a short artillery preparation, which inflicted several casualties in No. 4 post. At 6.45 a.m. a stronger force attacked upon a frontage covering No. 3 as well as No. 4 posts, many of the Bulgarians having tied sheaves of corn round their bodies and stuck small tufts of it into their caps. This time the British barrage did not come down directly

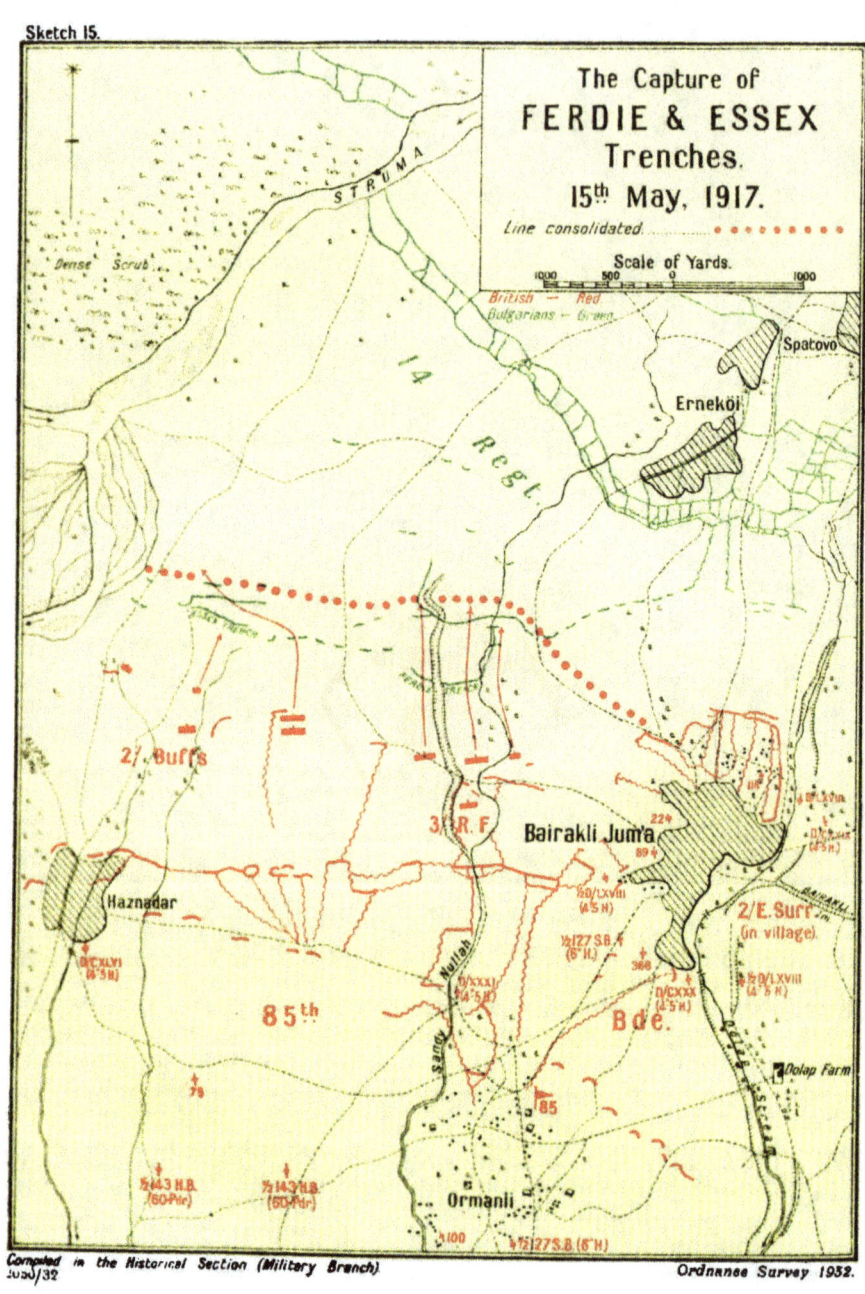

it was called for, but the result could not have been more fortunate. When fire was opened, the barrage fell right on the Bulgarian line, now 150 yards from the British works, and just as the enemy sprang up to rush forward with his traditional hurrah. The attack was completely broken up. Shouts could be heard from the officers urging their men on, but the reply was " frenzied cries of discord from the rank " and file." The Bulgarians fled in disorder, only the cover from view afforded by the high crops saving them from very heavy losses.

1917.
16 May.

That was the last of the counter-attacks. The enemy now turned his artillery on again, and until noon shelled the four works, but especially Nos. 3 and 4. Both were hit several times, and it was impossible to communicate with them or remove the wounded owing to the enemy's shrapnel. When Br.-General R. S. Vandeleur came out to visit the posts he found that in No. 4, out of a platoon about 28 strong, five men had been killed, the officer and 11 men wounded, and the Lewis gun knocked out. In No. 3 there were two killed and six wounded. He had these posts withdrawn somewhat closer to the village. The courage and endurance of the platoon under 2nd-Lieutenant F. Burkett in No. 4 post had been extraordinary, and the possibility of having to abandon the position had not even been mentioned.

The enemy's main line ran round the outskirts of Erneköi, and then turned sharply north-west to the Struma. There was, however, a system of outpost trenches, covered by a continuous belt of wire, running south of the village due westward to the marshy bed of the river. These trenches were to be captured by the 85th Brigade (Br.-General B. C. M. Carter) as a preliminary to an attack on the main line at Erneköi and Spatovo. The artillery preparation had begun on the 13th, and gaps in the wire had been cut. The main British line ran from the southern outskirts of Bairakli Jum'a to Haznadar, but there was an advanced line of small works, connected with the main line by long, recently dug communication trenches, and about 500 yards from the objective. It was upon this advanced line that the leading companies of the 3/Royal Fusiliers and the 2/Buffs formed up.

15 May.
Sketch 15.

Then, at 6.30 p.m., under cover of a bombardment of the enemy's front-line works, two companies of each battalion deployed and advanced to within 100 yards of the wire, moving swiftly through the gaps when the barrage lifted. The Bulgarians were grouped in parties of about a dozen men in various short trenches, and did not put up a very strong resistance. A good many were killed and 89 prisoners were taken, which showed that there had been a garrison unusually strong for a position of this sort. Carrying parties held in readiness at once moved up, and work was begun with vigour to put the captured position in a state of defence. Two small counter-attacks were beaten off before midnight by the Royal Fusiliers. A more determined one, supported by the fire of artillery and a trench mortar, was launched about 2 a.m. on the 16th against the extreme right. By this time a belt of wire had been put up, and the enemy was driven off, leaving nine dead.

During the 16th the Bulgarian artillery was active in registering the new British position, and at 10 p.m. a fourth counter-attack was launched, this time against the Buffs in the Essex trenches. Like its predecessors, it was repulsed. The operation had been completely successful, at a cost of 64 casualties. The enemy must have suffered much more severely as, apart from the 89 prisoners captured, he undoubtedly had numerous casualties in his abortive counter-attacks.

The third phase—that of preparation for the capture of Spatovo and Erneköi—began on the 20th May. On the 22nd, however, General Milne cancelled the attack, which had no longer any useful object. The Franco-Serbian offensive, to which all the British operations had been subsidiary, had, in fact, resulted in total failure.

There was to be, however, a more far-reaching result of this failure. The British Commander-in-Chief had come to the decision some time ago that he would not leave his troops during another hot weather in the malarial and enervating valley of the Struma. If they could not go forward they must draw back. The movement would affect the whole front of the XVI Corps—which was to come right out of the valley and take up a new position on the hills—and the right of the XII Corps. On the 26th General Milne gave orders for preparations to fall back to a " summer " line " to be begun.

DISPOSITIONS WEST OF THE VARDAR

THE OFFENSIVE WEST OF THE VARDAR.

West of the Vardar, where the main attack was to take place, there had been, since the preliminary affairs about Monastir described in the last chapter, no operations of importance prior to the 9th May, except the attack of the French 122nd Division on the 5th. The Allied dispositions were now as follows :—

1917.
May.
Map 11.

From the right bank of the Vardar to Nonte, on the southern slopes of the Duditsa Mountain, there were the French 122nd Division, a regiment of the 30th Division, and the Greek Seres Division, all under the command of General Gérôme. Thence, to the northward course of the Crna, were the Serbian Second and First Armies, with one of the Russian brigades attached. Each of these Armies had one of its three divisions in reserve. In the bend of the Crna was the "Groupement Lebouc," [1] consisting of, from right to left, the 17th Colonial Division, the 2nd Russian Brigade, the 16th Colonial Division, and the Italian 35th Division, with the 11th Colonial Division (less one brigade) and a brigade of the 76th Division in reserve. From the Crna to Lake Prespa was the "Groupement Regnault"—one brigade 11th Colonial Division, 57th and 156th Divisions. Between the lakes was the 76th Division. The "Groupement Lebouc," the "Groupement Regnault," and the 76th Division were under the orders of General Grossetti, commanding the Armée Française d'Orient. The detachment between the Vardar and Nonte, the 30th Division in reserve at Banitsa, and the cavalry, concentrated about Kozana and Lapsista, were directly under General Sarrail's command.

The enemy forces, including those upon the British front, consisted of the Bulgarian *Second Army* (Bulgarian *7th, 10th,* and *11th Divisions* and Turkish *50th Division*) ; Bulgarian *First Army* (Bulgarian *5th* and *9th Divisions,* and German *9th Jäger Regiment*) ; and German *Eleventh Army* (Bulgarian *1st, 2nd, 3rd, 6th Divisions* and part of the *8th Division,* German *302nd Division* and other German troops, as well as some Austrian and Albanian battalions). There were estimated to be about 255 Bulgarian, German, Turkish, and Austrian battalions, to 274 of the Allies ; but the Bulgarian, which numbered about 220 of the enemy's total,

---

[1] See p. 255.

were much the strongest.¹ In field and mountain artillery the Allies were estimated to have a superiority of over five to four, and in heavy artillery of 16 to 15. The command of the Army Group in which were the German *Eleventh* and Bulgarian *First Armies* had been taken over at the end of April from General von Below by General von Scholtz.

The weather, which had favoured the Allies during the Battle of Monastir, had amply restored the balance. In return for a prolonged autumn in 1916 there had now been a prolonged winter. The month of April had been terrible in the hill country. Blinding snowstorms, landslides, and avalanches had hindered the preparations and had left General Grossetti with no alternative but the postponement of the offensive. Even now there had been hasty improvisation. No one was satisfied that he was thoroughly ready, and the Serbians seem to have been even less advanced in their preliminary measures than the troops in the bend of the Crna under the orders of General Lebouc.

The main attack here was to be carried out by the 16th Colonial Division, considered one of the best in the French force, and the Russian brigade on its right. The right of the Russians was to be covered by the 17th Colonial Division. On the left the Italian 35th Division was to recover the summit of Hill 1050 and capture another peak called the Piton Brûlé. The 16th Division was attacking on a front of nearly three miles, the main enemy works which were its objectives being known as the Mamelon des Tranchées Rouges, the Piton Jaune, and the Piton Rocheux. The artillery preparation began on the 5th, and the attack was launched at dawn on the 9th.

1917.
9 May.
The Franco-Russian attack, carried out with confidence and dash, ended in a complete failure, after a good beginning. On the right the Russians captured their objective, and one battalion appears to have broken clean through the enemy's second line and captured the village of Orle in rear of it. By nightfall, however, the troops had been forced back to their own lines. The 16th Division took the Mamelon, but was first driven to its lower slopes by German bombing attacks and finally had to withdraw also. On the left the

---

¹ This total does not include the Austrians and Albanians west of Lake Ohrid on the one hand, or the Italian XVI Corps on that flank on the other. In Note II at end of Chapter some further details of the enemy's dispositions are given.

Italians captured the first line on the Piton Brûlé, but likewise fell back at night. The losses were heavy, even if not quite on the scale of those of the British 26th Division at Dojran, the 16th Division having 1,053 and the 17th 526 casualties.[1] {1917. 9 May.}

Next day the attack was to have been renewed solely on the left, against the Piton Jaune, the Piton Rocheux, and the Piton Brûlé, two battalions of the 11th Colonial Division being put at the disposal of the 16th for the purpose. At the last moment General Dessort, commanding the 16th, declared that it was impossible for his troops to be in position by 8 a.m., and at 7.30 the attack was cancelled. One French and one Italian battalion, not receiving the order in time, went forward and suffered appreciable losses.[2] On the 11th the attack took place as ordered, but again failed. {10 May. 11 May.}

Meanwhile, on the 9th, the Serbian Second Army east of the Crna bend, had captured Hill 1824 on the Moglena heights. One of its divisions had made a slight further advance on the 11th, but since then there had been no move. The Serbian command now suggested to General Sarrail that their Armies should be held in reserve, to exploit any success won in the bend of the Crna. General Sarrail could not possibly agree at this stage.[3]

The French Government were becoming alarmed. On the 15th the Minister of War telegraphed to General Sarrail that, in view of the general situation and that of Greece in particular, offensive operations in the Balkans should not be pursued at the price of sacrifices out of proportion to the goal to be reached. " It is, in consequence, for you to " judge at what moment these operations should be " stopped."[4] General Sarrail replied on the same day that his attacks in the bend of the Crna had been made mainly with the object of containing the enemy forces concentrated there. He was now going to attempt " to take by bits what " could not be taken simultaneously." In any case he had confidence that no hostile troops would be withdrawn from the bend. He had also prepared an attack west of the bend to hold down the enemy in that quarter, while the activity of the troops on the right bank of the Vardar had caused

---

[1] " Historique des Troupes Coloniales," p. 100.
[2] *Ibid.*, p. 101 ; Villari, p. 132.
[3] Sarrail, p. 250.   [4] *Ibid.*, p. 405.

342 DOJRAN—THE MAY ATTACK

anxiety to the Bulgarians. He hoped that all this pressure would yet permit the Serbians and the Russian brigade at their disposal to obtain a decision east of the bend. If a break-through did not occur, he would call a halt on the whole front.[1]

1917.
17 May.
The last attack in the bend of the Crna was launched on the 17th, after four days' artillery preparation. Their repeated failures had not daunted the French troops, and it was with great dash and determination that the 42nd Regiment of the 11th Division, under the orders of the 16th, advanced to the attack on the Piton Rocheux. The leading companies reached their objective, the German second line. But the barrage prevented supports from coming up to their aid ; they had run short of bombs ; and they were subjected to fierce counter-attacks by the Germans. Completely isolated, they were fortunate in being able to fight their way out, with a loss of 413.[2] The simultaneous attack north of Monastir had no better success, and this time the losses amounted to over 700.

There remained the Serbians. They made another small attack, and then demanded that the offensive should be brought to an end. On the 21st General Sarrail issued orders to that effect. The Serbian First Army, immediately east of the Crna bend, had not been in action.

Thus the whole offensive had failed. At a cost of some 14,000 casualties the enemy's front line had been captured on a narrow front west of Dojran by the 22nd Division, and near the Sokol by the Serbians. That and a few unimportant advanced works were all there was to show for great efforts and heavy sacrifices. Only a handful of prisoners had been taken, and it was certain that, in contrast to the Monastir battle of 1916, the enemy's casualties had been far smaller than those of the Allies.[3]

The failure, General Milne reported, was in his opinion due to an increase of the enemy's artillery and to the difficulty experienced by the French in obtaining superiority of fire. For this the bad weather was in part responsible.

There is more than this to be said on the subject,

---

[1] Sarrail, p. 250.
[2] " Historique des Troupes Coloniales," p. 103.
[3] They must have been fairly heavy, however, in the bend of the Crna. Here the *11th Reserve-Jäger*, opposed to the Italians, reports 131 casualties (" Geschichte des Reserve-Jäger-Bataillon Nr. 11," p. 217).

however. General Milne stated that there appeared to have been friction between the Allies, and—telegraphing before the Serbians had refused to continue the action—that the Serbians were determined not to bear the brunt of the fighting again, as they had last year. Mistrust had caused each ally " to look over his shoulder at the other."

1917. May.

Why did the Serbians, for the first time in the campaign, refuse to continue an attack for which all the others had been but a preparation? It is probable that Prince Alexander and General Bojović realized that the troops had not recovered, physically or morally, from their tremendous efforts of the previous year. Anticipating another failure, such as had occurred in the bend of the Crna, the command feared that it would break the instrument in their hands irreparably. There had been a great deal of Austrian propaganda in the Serbian ranks, and though so far it seemed to have had no effect to speak of, it was dangerous. It could not be expected that these men, many of them five years under arms, would not at the least brood upon the Austrian offer that they should return to their families and their farms. Then there was the bad influence of their fellow-Slavs, the Russians. The brigade under General Dietrichs in the bend of the Crna had done all that men could, but that under General Leontiev, which was attached to the Serbians east of the bend, was already under the disintegrating and contagious influence of Bolshevism. The Serbians had also, by General Sarrail's account, gone through a serious internal crisis, and partisans of the society known as the " Black Hand," including many senior officers, had been relieved of their commands and sent to Bizerta.[1]

Yet all these stumbling-blocks seem to have been of secondary importance. The chief had been lack of confidence in the plan, and this had been shared by French generals. In its broad lines the plan was good, but it had been carried out piecemeal, without co-ordination or sufficient concentration. In fact, except in the bend of the Crna, where the Italian front had been closed up and fresh troops had come in, there had been little concentration. The lack of preparation has also been mentioned; but here the British Government cannot be wholly acquitted

---

[1] Sarrail, p. 218. The " Black Hand " was responsible for the Sarajevo murder.

of responsibility, since they had pressed General Sarrail to attack as soon as possible when they heard that Turkish troops were being relieved and moving to the East.

It is not easy to say definitely that an opportunity had ever existed. Lieut.-Colonel E. A. Plunkett, liaison officer with the War Office,[1] reported to Whitehall that in his view it had, and we have seen that General Milne himself had held the same belief. General Lebouc informed Lieut.-Colonel Plunkett that he had submitted to General Sarrail a detailed plan for the Crna attack. It involved the concentration under one command of four French divisions, the big Italian division, the two Russian brigades, the Serbian First Army of three weak divisions, and, if possible, one or two British divisions. The general idea was to break through in the bend of the Crna with the main force, and to hold back the Serbian First Army, whose marching power and endurance were unequalled, to advance into the gap and exploit the break-through. "Judging," wrote Lieut.-Colonel Plunkett, "from the fact that part of a " Russian regiment, without the help of reserves, actually " broke through and reached the village of Orle, which is " some distance in rear of the hostile defensive lines, " Lebouc's plan should at least have gained some " considerable success."

At all events, the contrary had not been proved; for the Bulgarians had not been fully tested. As in the previous year, it was the Germans who had saved them in the bend of the Crna. Dojran was a special case. Here their excellent *9th Division*, called also the *Division of Plevna*, working under the eye of the commander of their *First Army* at Dedeli, had not only made its already strong position into a fortress, not only organized with intelligence and foresight all its defensive measures, but also preserved a moral power to resist which was unequalled elsewhere. This was apparent even now on the British front, when the quality of the opposition met with from these troops was compared with that encountered in the valley of the Struma. It was to be proved conclusively in 1918, when, with all melting about it, this division did not flinch. It is not without cause that the name of Dojran is to-day considered

---

[1] Lieut.-Colonel Plunkett had succeeded in this post Lieut.-Colonel C. C. M. Maynard, who had been appointed to the command of the 82nd Brigade, 27th Division.

GENERAL SARRAIL'S DIFFICULTIES

1917.
May.

in Bulgaria to be as honourable as any in the military annals of the country.

Any plan such as that of General Lebouc would, of course, have involved a risky thinning-out of the rest of the front; but victories are seldom won either without concentration or without risk. There was another risk: the Greek situation, which induced General Sarrail to keep throughout the battle the equivalent of two divisions in reserve. According to British views, this risk was not immediate. If the British were wrong, then all that can be said is that the offensive should not have been launched, at any rate on this scale.

It must be admitted that General Sarrail's difficulties, apart from weather and terrain, were great. He had an ill-matched team of six to drive, and with far more tact, affability, and personal activity than his it would have been hard to keep the coach on the road and all the horses pulling equally. The British had been hitherto, and would be again, tied down by restrictions from home; the Italians were unfriendly and in a certain sense a force sent for a political object, the assurance of Italy's future on the Adriatic coast; the Russians were beginning to weaken; the Venizelist Greeks were not yet ready; the Serbians were tired and for the moment discouraged; his own French subordinates were doubtful of his plan. One and all lacked confidence in him and in his Chief of the Staff, General Michaud.

That was perhaps the most fatal defect of all in the Armée d'Orient: its command no longer inspired it with confidence. General Lebouc might argue that there had been an opportunity to break through and that it would recur in the autumn. How was it to be taken? The British Government had given up Macedonia as a bad job and were intent upon removing as many troops thence as possible. The authorities of the other Allies, depressed by that decision in itself, were not much more sanguine. The tragedy of the Army was that there was no hope of its achieving under its present Commander-in-Chief, experienced, resourceful, and in some ways remarkably gifted as he was, any decisive success.

NOTE I.

LETTER TO LIEUT.-GENERAL C. J. BRIGGS.

XVI Corps.

The Commander-in-Chief directs me to explain to you the present situation on the Allied fronts here, and how they affect our operations in general, more particularly with reference to your proposed scheme for an offensive in the direction of Erneköi.

After repeated changes of date, the attack near Dojran by the XII Corps was fixed eventually for the 24th April, and took place on that date. Its main object was to draw as many of the enemy's reserve troops as possible from the Monastir area to the country east of the Vardar. This it has to a certain extent already succeeded in doing. The Allied attack near Monastir was to have been commenced on the 26th, but, chiefly on account of the recent unprecedented snowfall, it was postponed, and the latest instructions from General Sarrail are that it will commence about the 8th of this month. In an interview with the Commander-in-Chief, General Sarrail also stated that he did not intend to continue operations into the hot weather and that his primary object at present was to clear the enemy from the immediate vicinity of Monastir.

These factors may make a material difference in the general policy here. Had a synchronized attack by the Allies taken place and been pushed forward with vigour, it was possible that the Bulgarian forces would have been driven back all along the line from the Dojran Lake to Monastir, and while they were thus hard pressed your proposal for an attack on Erneköi might easily have been productive of great results. Now, however, the attack north of Monastir may have a limited objective, and, in consequence, the object of your scheme may cease to exist unless something unforeseen occurs, as it would appear to involve an unnecessary loss of life without a sufficiently corresponding advantage. It would at best take your troops further into the Struma valley at the commencement of the hot weather. Under these circumstances and in case it may become necessary to abandon your proposed attack, the Commander-in-Chief directs you to consider plans for one or possibly for more than one minor operation accompanied by a limited bombardment, with a view to causing serious loss to the enemy and at the same time preventing the transfer of troops elsewhere.

It may also be necessary to transfer one of your divisions to the XII Corps front in exchange for a division of that corps which may suffer serious casualties in the forthcoming operations.

W. GILLMAN,
Major-General, General Staff,
British Salonika Force.

G.H.Q.,
Salonika.
2nd May 1917.

NOTE II.

THE ENEMY'S DISPOSITIONS IN MAY 1917.

His disposition by divisions affords no full indication of the enemy's strength or even of the composition of his formations. It is the inevitable fate of divisions as big as those of the Bulgarian Army to be split up in a long war, and this had now occurred. The *9th Division* on the Dojran front now consisted of seven or eight regiments, and the *3rd Division* between Nonte and the Vetrenik of eight. The German troops were now practically all in line in the bend of the Crna or in reserve to that sector, the battalions which had been moved to the Monastir front to oppose the initial French attacks having returned to meet the threat of the main offensive. West of the Crna the *1st Division*, of which mention has been made in the last chapter, had apparently come into line, and two regiments of the *4th Division* had appeared from Rumania. The *8th Division*, formerly shown on British intelligence maps west of Monastir, now appears on the coast east of the mouth of the Struma, but this does not imply that regiments had been moved from one end to the other of the 150-mile front. The headquarters may have been, and certainly ended up, in Eastern Macedonia.

CHAPTER XV.

THE END OF THE GREEK IMBROGLIO.

(Map 1.)

Reaching a Decision.

1917.
Feb.-April.
BEHIND the Armée d'Orient still remained a Greece split into two opposing camps, whose hatred now smouldered but was ready to burst into flame at any moment. So menacing was the attitude of the reservists that Sir Francis Elliot felt himself obliged to go back upon the advice which he had given in January 1917, that the blockade should be completely raised, and to telegraph on the 5th February that he now advocated the admission of wheat and coal only. A month later, on the 7th March, he was directed by the Foreign Office to address a strong protest to the Greek Government on the subject of the terrorization of the Venizelists which was reported from Epirus. On the 3rd April he stated that he had received information that new attacks on the Venizelists in Athens and even upon the diplomatic representatives of the Entente were possible and suggested that a solemn warning might be salutary.

Meanwhile in France M. Briand had resigned, and a Ministry with M. Ribot as President of the Council, M. Léon Bourgeois as Minister of Foreign Affairs, and M. Painlevé as Minister of War, had assumed office on the 20th March. The change had a considerable effect upon French policy. The new Prime Minister had neither his predecessor's tenderness for the established order in Greece nor his indifference to public opinion in France, which had become extremely hostile to King Constantine. M. Ribot was, in short, disposed to take stronger action than M. Briand.

The attitude of M. Venizelos at Salonika was stiffening also, as anti-dynastic and even Republican sentiment developed among his adherents. Twice in the course of April he spoke to the British diplomatic agent, Lord Granville, of the impossibility of reconciliation and of the need for the King's abdication, which appeared to him the only means of saving the dynasty. If the King would abdicate now, his eldest son, the Diadoch, might be accepted; after the war it would be too late. Sir Francis Elliot's

THE THESSALIAN HARVEST 349

comment, addressed on the 22nd April to Lord Robert Cecil (acting Secretary of State during Mr. Balfour's absence in the United States), was that, except as regards the dissolution of the reservist leagues, the Greek Government had carried out their engagements, though only after delay and opposition. All things considered, it did not appear that the conduct of the Lambros Ministry was such as to justify the withdrawal of guarantees given by the Allies against the forcible extension of Venizelism. He added, however, that there would be advantage in the removal of King Constantine if it could be effected by a stroke of the pen. An invasion by the Allies and the Venizelists would, he felt sure, be resisted.

1917. April.

Another question causing anxiety was that of the ripening harvest in Thessaly. Thessaly was the only important granary of Greece, and its harvest would feed Old Greece—which meant Royalist Greece—for six or seven months. Moreover, were that harvest in the possession of the Royalists, the German submarine commanders would be given a free hand to torpedo all grain-ships, knowing that their cargoes could be destined only for the hostile Venizelists. M. Venizelos informed Lord Granville that he had learnt of the formation of a committee of officers who had determined to seize the harvest with the aid of the reservists or to burn it if that proved impossible. He protested that the people of Thessaly were strongly in his favour and that, if the Allies would give him a free hand, he could secure possession of the crops himself. Lord Granville notified the Foreign Office on the 1st May of reports that General Sarrail intended to seize them for the benefit of the Armée d'Orient. Politically, this would be more desirable than that the Royalists should have them, but morally the action would be indefensible.

Map 1.

May.

On the 4th May M. Zaimis once more took office at Athens. His Ministry was colourless, and depended entirely upon the skill and prudence of the veteran at its head. M. Zaimis, a strong and faithful Royalist, who had yet always been anxious to come to an understanding with M. Venizelos and always well disposed to the Allies, with many of whose leading men he was on terms of personal friendship, was King Constantine's last card. But the card was played too late, if it would ever have availed. On the same day Sir Francis Elliot reported the discovery near

Athens of a *cache* of 480 new Mannlicher rifles and a quantity of ammunition. This was the first discovery of hidden arms, and, as the British Minister remarked, confirmed the French belief that arms had been hidden.

The next event of importance was a mass meeting at Salonika of 30,000 men, which proclaimed the deposition of King Constantine and his dynasty. In a telegram of the 7th May Lord Granville reported that the object of this meeting was to force the hand of M. Venizelos. The latter knew it and was angered. He declared that his first desire was the reunion of Greece, and that to attain this end he would accept the Diadoch as King. The more extreme of his followers were evidently determined to make compromise impossible.

We have spoken already of the military problems discussed at the Paris Conference of the 4th and 5th May. The decisions on Greek affairs were not final, but were significant of the direction in which political opinion was moving. The French representatives desired, in order to guarantee the safety of the Armée d'Orient, to instruct General Sarrail to send a contingent of troops into Thessaly to secure the crops. The British agreed to this and promised to send, for their part, a detachment 500 strong, stipulating that they should not be called on for reinforcements if complications arose. It was decided that the Allies should announce their intention of raising the blockade if permitted to purchase the harvest, which would be divided between Royalist and Venizelist Greece. Posts would be established at Larissa, Volos, and other points to secure control, and grain would be sent to Royalist Greece only under permits signed by an International Commission in Athens. Venizelist forces were not to be employed, but if there was a spontaneous rising in Thessaly in favour of the Provisional Government, the latter would be allowed to send in troops for the maintenance of order after the establishment of a Venizelist régime. It was agreed that General Sarrail should be directed to carry out the work in a pacific and friendly manner; and Mr. Lloyd George asked that the Commander-in-Chief should be thanked for his adherence to the spirit and letter of his pledge to take no military action against Greece without the consent of the Allied Governments.

Then came by far the most important decision. In

view of the failure hitherto of Allied policy in Greece, it was agreed that one Power should in future speak for the Allies, and that that Power should be France. The French Government undertook to recall M. Guillemin and to replace him by a man of " exceptional position," acceptable to the British Government. The British would recall Sir Francis Elliot and leave their representation at Athens in the hands of a Chargé d'Affaires.

1917. May.

Another factor in the approaching crisis in Greece was the departure of British troops from Salonika. It will be recalled that at the Paris Conference the British Government had announced that they would at once make arrangements to withdraw one infantry division and two cavalry brigades.[1] This decision had been accepted with regret by the French, who had good reason to believe that further withdrawals would follow. The weakening of the Allied forces made it the more necessary to clear up the uncertainty in Greece, and clear it up if possible before the troops were gone. " Against our judgment," said the French Government in effect, " you are taking away your troops. Allow " us, then, at least to carry out the measures which we " consider necessary to the safety of ours." The argument was reasonable. It was reinforced by the prospect that a Venizelist Greece would dispose of forces ample not merely to fill the gap caused by the British withdrawal and any further gaps that might be made, but to give the Allies in Macedonia predominance over the Bulgarians.

These were the skeins; let us knot them by briefly resuming the facts which have been set out. There was the failure of King Constantine to carry out his pledges strictly; there was a new French Government determined upon strong measures; there was the stiffer attitude of the Venizelists, the spread of Republican sentiment among them, and the impossibility of a reconciliation of the opposing factions; there was the question of the Thessalian harvest; there was the coming weakening of the Allied front in Macedonia; and there was the decision of the British Government virtually to resign the solution of the Greek problem to France. Such were the main causes of the drastic action about to be taken in Greece. That which was to be announced to the world was a justification rather than a

---

[1] See p. 317.

cause. It was the old argument that King Constantine had violated the constitution and jeopardized the security of Greece, for which the Protecting Powers had a responsibility. Finally, we may add that Russian Tsardom, by instinct always a patron and supporter of monarchy, was no longer in a position to plead for King Constantine.

Yet if the British Government were to be borne forward to action on the stream of French opinion and that of the British public, it was not without hesitation or misgiving that they committed themselves to the current. On the 23rd May the Secretary of State for War, Lord Derby, outlined to the War Cabinet new French proposals, which he had had from the mouth of M. Painlevé. They were nothing less than to march into Thessaly, depose the King, and establish a Venizelist Government. The French authorities had no hostility to the King and no particular brief for M. Venizelos; but the former was hostile to them and the latter was the only statesman in Greece upon whom they could rely. The British Government's naval and military advisers were strongly against compliance with the French policy, Sir John Jellicoe, the First Sea Lord, arguing that the danger of German submarines using Greek ports had been exaggerated. At any rate he thought this danger considerably less than that of bringing about war with Greece. After a long and earnest discussion, in which vital differences of opinion were revealed, the War Cabinet put off a decision until they had heard from M. Ribot himself the reasons for his change of policy; and authorized Lord Robert Cecil to invite the President of the Council and his colleagues, civil and military, to London for that purpose.

This meeting, known as the London Conference, took place on the 28th and 29th May, and resulted in the almost complete acceptance of the French view. It was decided that, having obtained control of the Thessalian harvest, the representatives of France and Britain should inform King Constantine that, as Guaranteeing Powers for the Treaty of 1863, the Allies would tolerate neither his continued violation of the Greek Constitution in governing the country as an absolute monarch, nor the prolonged division of Greece into two factions. They must therefore insist upon his abdication in favour of one of his sons, who would have to bind himself to rule as a constitutional monarch, with M. Venizelos or his nominee as Prime Minister. After the abdication of the King, the harvest would be equitably distributed between the different parts of Greece and the Allied Armies.

1917. May.

The French representatives stated that, in order to forestall organized resistance, it would be necessary from the outset of the Thessalian operation to carry out a military occupation of the Isthmus of Corinth. At the simultaneous conference of naval and military advisers of the two Governments, General Foch, the French Chief of the General Staff, remarked, in response to British objections to this, that a landing on the isthmus was no more an act of war than was an advance into Thessaly. The formal conclusion was, however, that General Sarrail should hold troops in readiness to proceed to the isthmus "in case of necessity." If the necessity arose, the British Government assented to the inclusion of a small British contingent—additional to what they had already promised to send into Thessaly—for either the isthmus or Piræus, on the understanding that they should not be called upon for any further assistance, naval or military, or for transport, with the exception of four vessels already lent to the French. As a fact, it was difficult to decide from Downing Street or the Quai d'Orsay whether it would be necessary to land troops; this was really a question for the man on the spot, who had to carry out the work and bear the responsibility for the maintenance of order and the safety of Allied troops and nationals.

With regard to the "man on the spot" it was decided that M. Charles Jonnart was to be "High Commissioner for "Allied purposes in Greece, representing France and Great "Britain, and, if they will agree, Russia and Italy as "well,"[1] and that in all political matters General Sarrail was to act under his orders.

The French Government had certainly fulfilled their promise to find a man of "exceptional position." In the formation of the modern French colonial empire it has been as a rule soldiers who have played the greatest parts as administrators and proconsuls. On that distinguished roll, which contains the names of Bugeaud, Galliéni, and Lyautey, M. Jonnart, as Governor-General of Algeria, was one of the few civilians who had fairly won a place. Where

---

[1] Neither did eventually agree, but the point was not of great importance, since Italy was not a Guaranteeing Power, and Russia, which was, was already in a state of turmoil and dissolution.

354 THE END OF THE GREEK IMBROGLIO

a combination of firmness, prudence, and political experience was required, no better choice could have been made. His personal knowledge of Greece was not profound, though he had been to Athens on a mission before the war; but he set out with a civil and military staff qualified to fill that deficiency.

Yet if—or because—M. Jonnart was the best choice for the work in hand, he was not a man who, once he understood what he had to do, would be easily controlled over telegraph wires, and certainly not from Whitehall. He would carry out the affair in the manner he thought best and give his explanations afterwards. Having put their interests, about which even now they were not any too decided, into the hands of such a man, the British Government would have henceforward little power to influence him and little right to complain of his methods.

The Abdication of King Constantine.

1917.
June.
Map 1.

M. Jonnart reached Brindisi, where two French destroyers awaited him, on the 4th June. At Corfu he had an interview with Admiral Gauchet, the Naval Commander-in-Chief in the Mediterranean, and then passed on through the Corinth Canal to Salamis Roads. Here he had interviews aboard the cruiser *Vérité* with the French and British Ministers. He had at once decided that the only way in which he could avoid disorder and bloodshed was to persuade M. Zaimis to remain in office and to act through his Ministry. If M. Zaimis resigned, a military Cabinet, vowed to resistance, was inevitable. Having received a private pledge from M. Zaimis to remain in power until he returned,[1] M. Jonnart sailed for Salonika, to arrange with General Sarrail and Rear-Admiral Salaün questions of naval and military dispositions and of transport.

The High Commissioner and his advisers were determined to have troops on the spot, without regard to the clause "in case of necessity." When M. Jonnart re-embarked at Salonika on the morning of the 9th he was accompanied by General Regnault, destined to command the force which was to be sent to Piræus and the Isthmus of Corinth; and his destroyer caught up the first transports

---

[1] R. David: "Le Drame ignoré de l'Armée d'Orient" (from which the record of M. Jonnart's movements is taken), p. 214.

in the Skopelos Channel. That night, in Salamis Roads, 1917. there arrived a telegram from the Quai d'Orsay, which June. stated that the British Government had expressed their astonishment on learning that, contrary to the decisions of the London Conference, there was to be a disembarkation of troops prior to the delivery of the ultimatum to King Constantine. The Ministry of Foreign Affairs desired that every consideration should be given to British sentiment. General Regnault, consulted on the matter, urged that it was necessary, owing to the excessive heat, that men and horses should be disembarked immediately on arrival, and that the decision reached at Salonika to deliver the Note and disembark the force simultaneously should be adhered to. Very unwillingly he agreed to keep the troops for Piræus in their transports for 24 hours after their arrival the following evening.[1]

M. Zaimis had kept his word and remained in office, though there had been rumours that he was about to resign. On the evening of the 10th he was requested to meet the High Commissioner aboard the *Bruix* at Piræus. On this occasion only two demands, for the purchase and control of the harvest and the reinforcement of the posts already stationed on the Isthmus of Corinth, were made. They were accepted without difficulty. M. Jonnart was here acting strictly in accordance with his instructions, to wipe the affair of the harvest off the slate before he approached the more serious matter of the abdication.

That was reached next morning, again aboard the *Bruix*, when M. Jonnart demanded the abdication of King Constantine in favour of one of his heirs; his eldest son, the Diadoch, being declared unacceptable to the Powers. The troops would not disembark until the Greek Government's reply, demanded within 24 hours, had been received. The landing on the Isthmus of Corinth had taken place without incident the previous evening. In Thessaly the advance of a mixed division, formed largely of cavalry, had also begun under the orders of General Venel.[2] The two British detachments had not yet been sent.

M. Zaimis, deeply moved and stricken with grief, promised the High Commissioner to do all in his power to

---

[1] R. David: "Le Drame ignoré de l'Armée d'Orient," p. 221.
[2] Sarrail, p. 243.

persuade the King to abdicate. At the Crown Council, summoned immediately on the Prime Minister's return to Athens, he encountered stiff opposition and prevailed only because the King agreed with him that resistance would be useless. That evening he sent an official down to Piræus, where the French squadron lay stripped for action, with a draft reply of acceptance, to the terms of which M. Jonnart agreed. The King, " mindful as ever only of the " interests of Greece, was decided to leave the country with " the Crown Prince, and nominated as his successor Prince " Alexander "—his second son.[1]

All was not over yet, however; indeed, the most anxious moments were to come. In Athens there was great excitement, and as the news leaked out a crowd surrounded the Palace to stop the King's departure. On the afternoon of the 12th, the King and the Royal Family left the Palace secretly and motored to Tatoi, the summer palace, some 25 miles north of Athens, intending to embark at the little neighbouring port of Oropos in order to avoid a demonstration. Meanwhile the new King's proclamation that he intended to " walk in the glorious footsteps of his " father " was not precisely what the Allies had hoped for, though it cast a ray of humour upon a sombre episode.[2] That afternoon French troops began their disembarkation at Piræus, and moved forward to occupy a strong position between the port and the city of Athens. On Thursday the 14th the Royal Family embarked at Oropos for Italy, whence the King had decided to go to Switzerland.

At Athens there was calm, to which the immediate announcement by M. Jonnart that the blockade had been lifted contributed. In Thessaly, however, there was bloodshed. The French cavalry moving on Larissa was fired on, and had two officers and four men killed. The French speedily routed the assailants with heavy loss, capturing over three hundred of them. That was the only resistance or disturbance; indeed, whatever was the sentiment of Athens, the people of Thessaly showed themselves markedly Venizelist in sympathy. The two British

---

[1] Translations of M. Jonnart's Note and of the reply of M. Zaimis are given in Note at end of Chapter.

[2] The proclamation was signed by M. Zaimis, and it is said that King Alexander himself did not see it for two days. The allusion was, of course, to King Constantine's victories in the Balkan Wars, and was designed to soothe the feelings of the Royalists.

detachments now arrived upon the scene. The first, drawn from the 4/Rifle Brigade and commanded by Major H. G. Moore-Gwyn, landed at Piræus on the afternoon of the 14th, and was employed partly in guarding the Custom House and partly in holding a hill which commanded the town. The second, formed from the 2/E. Yorkshire under Lieut.-Colonel R. Scott-Hopkins, reached Larissa on the 16th and was moved forward by General Venel to support his cavalry 25 miles further south. The two detachments were, as has been explained, provided merely to show the solidarity of the Allies and could have little effect on the military situation in Greece. At Piræus the other contingents consisted of two French regiments and one Russian, with a proportion of artillery; in Thessaly there were four French cavalry regiments, one infantry regiment, and two Territorial battalions; on the Isthmus of Corinth a French infantry regiment, two companies of Senegalese, and artillery.

1917. June.

A complication was caused by the sudden march, without warning to Great Britain or France, of Italian forces into Epirus, where they occupied Yannina on the 8th June, and moving swiftly south, the port of Preveza on the 10th. Whereas the French advance had been welcomed by the Venizelists, the Italian move was as little appreciated by them as by the Royalists. It was, indeed, obviously directed against the pretensions believed to be entertained by M. Venizelos regarding southern Albania. The situation was somewhat strained until Italy agreed to remove her troops as soon as those of the Entente had been withdrawn from Athens and Thessaly; and even then it was only after long negotiations that the question was finally settled.

Little more remains to be said. By the desire of M. Venizelos himself it was decided that there should be, before his return to Athens, a brief period of transition which would allow passions to cool. Once more M. Zaimis consented to remain in office, to carry out this work of reconciliation. A number of Germanophil soldiers and politicians were banished from the mainland of Greece for the duration of the war. When the reassembly of the Chamber of Deputies came in question, however, and it was decided not to hold fresh elections—which would not in any case have been complete owing to the Bulgarian occupation of Eastern Macedonia and the situation in Epirus—but to convoke the Chamber of May 1915, which had been illegally dissolved, M. Zaimis refused to take that responsibility. The return of the *Sphacteria*, the yacht which had carried King Constantine to Messina, and news of the imminent arrival of M. Venizelos, resulted in a fresh outbreak of Royalist unrest in Athens, and caused General Regnault to move forward artillery to points of vantage such as the Stadium and the Acropolis, and detachments of infantry into the suburbs. On the morning of the 27th they occupied the principal squares and gardens of the city. At 11 a.m. M. Venizelos drove in, going straight to the Palace to take the oath. Next day his Ministry took office, its first act being to instruct the Greek Ministers in Berlin, Vienna, Constantinople, and Sofia to ask for their passports.[1]

The abnormal representation of both Britain and France by a French High Commissioner did not survive the crisis, M. Jonnart withdrawing early in July. For some time longer the two Governments left their legations in the hands of Chargés d'Affaires, Mr. Dayrell Crackanthorpe and M. Clausse, and then appointed as Ministers to Athens Lord Granville and M. de Billy, their former representatives with the Provisional Government at Salonika.

So, unable to untie the knot, the Allies had cut it. The affair will always be the subject of debate, which is never likely to end in an unanimous judgment. The problem before Britain and France had been one of great difficulty. Here was a State, on the soil of which their Armies were fighting and where a comparatively small hostile force in rear of those Armies might have brought about a disaster. In this State were two parties, so far as could be ascertained about equal in strength. One was hostile and dangerous, the other friendly and helpful. The Allies had attempted to disarm the former and restrain the latter from spreading its influence, and had thus made themselves responsible for the division of the country into two. That had been an experiment, made in the hope that reconciliation would result. It had failed. Then they had decided to remove the head of the hostile party—not necessarily so hostile as his followers, but still their head— and give their complete support to his opponent.

Had these parties been in all respects equal, there

---

[1] Officially, the declaration of war by the Provisional Government, which had been made on the 23rd November 1916, was considered binding upon the whole of Greece from the 27th June 1917.

could have been no question as to the justice of the action, which in this case would, indeed, have been carried out much earlier. It was because the leader who was to be removed was the King that there was doubt and delay. It was Great Britain's respect for constitutional forms, abroad as at home, which had caused her to hesitate and to follow France's lead without enthusiasm. Wellington's maxim has never been forgotten by British statesmen : " I always " had a horror of revolutionizing any country for a political " object. I always said, if they rise themselves, well " and good, but do not stir them up; it is a fearful " responsibility."

At all events, the experiment was this time successful. Its success was partly due to the fact that, unlike earlier experiments, it was timely. If we analyse the quarrel between the opposing parties in Greece, it resolves itself finally to this : the Royalists believed that victory would rest with the Central Powers ; the Liberals believed that the Entente would prevail in the end. These views were, of course, complicated by other factors. For example, the King of Greece was the Kaiser's brother-in-law, and on the Royalist side there were many important personages sympathetic to Germany, apart from their belief in German invincibility; whereas the Venizelists had their share of the disinterested affection for Britain and France, and of the belief in the righteousness of their cause, which were shown by the most generous and enlightened in nearly all neutral countries. There were many other influences too ; but, in its simplest terms, the conflict was between men whose views differed as to the result of the World War.

It must be noted that the scales were not even. Defeat for Greece as an ally of the Entente would have been a terrible disaster. She would have lost her territories in Macedonia, and probably also in Thessaly and Epirus, to Bulgaria ; she would have lost many of her islands to Turkey. Defeat on the side of the Central Powers would have been unhappy for her, but it may well have been felt that Britain would prevent her being ruthlessly dismembered. On the other hand, she had more to gain at the expense of Turkey and Bulgaria defeated than as the ally of those countries in victory. M. Venizelos, who always played high—though with extraordinary judgment—played for the greater prize, taking the greater risk. King

Constantine, disinclined to play for the smaller and from the beginning of 1916 largely in the power of the Entente, fell back upon neutrality. Yet when, in August 1916, the Bulgarians made their advance on the flanks of the Armée d'Orient and it seemed to an outside observer like himself that that Army was facing the risk of a rout, he showed by his attitude that his neutrality was not to be trusted.

When M. Venizelos had set up his Provisional Government at Salonika, caused it to declare war on Germany and Bulgaria, and obtained for it the recognition of Great Britain and France, the King and his adherents found the situation in some respects actually improved. Greece was now " on velvet." If the Central Powers won the war, the King could claim that he had resisted, to the best of his power and at risk to himself, the demands of Britain and France. If the latter were victorious, then they would owe gratitude to the Provisional Government, which had supported them, and to its levies, which had fought on their side. In either case Greek territory appeared to be safe. The presence of M. Venizelos at Salonika was an insurance policy. Collusion between King and Minister must not be alleged, since kings with a leaning to absolutism do not incite to rebellion democratic ministers who overshadow them in intellect and personality. Yet the King and his party could now see their advantage in an action which had surprised and angered them.

Then had come another development. The Russian Revolution had for a moment given the advantage to the Central Powers; but hard upon its heels, on the 6th April 1917, had followed the declaration of war against Germany by the United States of America. That was the turning-point. Greece, with a wider international view than other Balkan countries, realized that the odds on the victory of the Entente were now heavy. In consequence, the enforced abdication of the King in June 1917 provoked less opposition than would have been the case three months earlier, and there was no armed resistance, as there would then almost certainly have been. There was, inevitably, deep indignation at the King's removal; but already it was recognized, clearly by the instructed, vaguely by the rest, that Greece had no further need to keep a foot in Germany's camp. In fact, all but the extremists accepted the new régime without bitterness. The division of Greece into two was ended.

The Greek Army began, slowly but steadily, to take its place beside the Allies in Macedonia; and its coming gradually transformed the military situation there.

British hesitations were therefore in some sort justified, because they had delayed action until the best moment for action was come. That the British Government had not followed this line of reasoning is true; nevertheless, their scruples had had the same effect. Instinct, we say, luck, say our critics, has often served this country well in like cases. And yet, perhaps, it may be allowed that scruples are not cause for shame, and that those under their influence, who are the scrupulous, are not undeserving of some reward, if reward should come.

NOTE.

NOTE DEMANDING THE ABDICATION OF KING CONSTANTINE AND THE REPLY.[1]

Aboard the *Bruix*,
10th June 1917.

M. Jonnart, High Commissioner of the Protecting Powers of Greece,
To H.E. M. Zaimis, President of the Council of Ministers, Athens.

Monsieur le Président,

The Protecting Powers of Greece have decided to reconstitute the unity of the Kingdom without prejudice to the monarchical Constitution which they have guaranteed to Greece.

H.M. King Constantine, having manifestly violated, on his own initiative, the Constitution of which France, Great Britain, and Russia are the guarantors, I have the honour to declare to Your Excellency that the King has forfeited the confidence of the Protecting Powers, and that they consider themselves liberated, where he is concerned, from the obligations resulting from their rights of protection.

My mission is therefore, in order to re-establish constitutional verity, to demand the abdication of H.M. King Constantine, who will himself nominate, in accord with the Protecting Powers, a successor from among his heirs.

I am under the obligation of requesting a reply within a period of twenty-four hours.

Please accept, Monsieur le Président, the assurance of my high consideration.

JONNART.

The High Commissioner of the Protecting Powers has the honour to inform H.E. the President of the Council of Ministers that, since the Diadoch does not represent the guarantees which France, Great Britain, and Russia are now constrained to demand on the part of the constitutional sovereign of the Hellenes, they can assent only to the nomination of another of the heirs.

---

[1] Translated from the French original, quoted by R. David.

Athens,
10th June 1917.

The President of the Council and Minister of Foreign Affairs,
To H.E. the High Commissioner of the Protecting Powers of Greece.

Monsieur le Haut Commissaire,

France, Great Britain, and Russia, having by your Note of to-day demanded the abdication of H.M. King Constantine and the nomination of his successor, the undersigned, President of the Council of Ministers and Minister of Foreign Affairs, has the honour to inform Your Excellency that H.M. the King, mindful as ever only of the interests of Greece, has decided to leave the country with the Crown Prince, and nominates as his successor Prince Alexander.

Please accept, Monsieur le Haut Commissaire, the assurance of my high consideration.

ZAIMIS.

APPENDIX 1.

ORDER OF BATTLE
OF THE
ALLIED ARMIES IN MACEDONIA, DECEMBER 1916.

COMMANDEMENT DES ARMÉES ALLIÉES EN ORIENT.
Commander-in-Chief .. .. .. General Sarrail.
Chief of the Staff .. .. .. General Michaud.

ARMÉE FRANÇAISE D'ORIENT.
G.O.C. .. .. General Leblois.[1]
    57th, 122nd, 156th, 11th Colonial,[2] 16th Colonial,[3] 17th Colonial Divisions, 1st, 4th, and 8th Regiments of Chasseurs d'Afrique

BRITISH SALONIKA ARMY.[4]
G.O.C. .. .. Lieut.-General G. F. Milne.

XII CORPS.
G.O.C. .. .. Lieut.-General Sir H. F. M. Wilson.
    22nd, 26th, and 60th Divisions.

XVI CORPS.
G.O.C. .. .. Lieut.-General C. J. Briggs.
    10th, 27th, and 28th Divisions.

    6th and 8th Mounted Brigades.

SERBIAN ARMIES.
Commander-in-Chief .. .. .. The Prince Regent Alexander.
Chief of the Staff .. .. .. General Bojović.

FIRST ARMY.
G.O.C. .. .. General Mišić.
    Morava and Vardar Divisions.

---

[1] Temporarily holding the appointment; succeeded in January 1917 by General Grossetti.
[2] Formed December 1916.
[3] Completed disembarkation at Salonika in the first week of January 1917. The 30th and 76th Divisions arrived shortly afterwards.
[4] A detailed Order of Battle is given in Appendix 2.

APPENDIX 1

Second Army.
G.O.C. .. .. General Stepanović.
Šumadija and Timok Divisions.

Third Army.
G.O.C. .. .. General Vasić.
Drina and Danube Divisions.

Cavalry Division.

Italian Detachment.
35th Division.[1]

Russian Detachment.
2nd and 4th Brigades.[2]

Note.—The Greek National (Venizelist) Force consisted at this time of two regiments fit for service.

---

[1] Three brigades, each of 6 battalions, etc.
[2] Each of 6 battalions, but without artillery.

APPENDIX 2.

ORDER OF BATTLE

OF THE

BRITISH SALONIKA ARMY,[1]

DECEMBER 1916.

GENERAL HEADQUARTERS.[2]

Commander-in-Chief [2]	Lieut.-General G. F. Milne, C.B., D.S.O.
Major-General, General Staff	Major-General W. Gillman, C.B., C.M.G., D.S.O.
Deputy Adjutant and Quartermaster-General [3]	Major-General T. E. Clarke, C.B.

Attached—

Br.-General, Royal Artillery	Br.-General W. H. Onslow, C.B.
Chief Engineer	Br.-General H. A. A. Livingstone, C.M.G.
Inspector-General of Communications	Major-General F. W. B. Koe, C.B., C.M.G.

XII CORPS.

G.O.C.	Lieut.-General Sir H. F. M. Wilson, K.C.B.
Br.-General, General Staff	Br.-General F. G. Fuller, C.M.G.
Deputy Adjutant and Quartermaster-General	Br.-General H. L. N. Beynon, C.M.G.
G.O.C. Royal Artillery	Br.-General H. D. White-Thomson, C.B., D.S.O.
Chief Engineer	Br.-General G. Walker.

---

[1] The force is variously described in official documents as "British "Forces at Salonika," "British Forces in Salonika," "British Salonika "Force," and "British Salonika Army."

[2] The headquarters of the force was actually known as "Army "Headquarters," and the commander as "General Officer Commanding," until January 1917.

[3] That is to say, the Adjutant-General's and Quartermaster-General's branches were combined under Major-General Clarke. On the 20th February 1917 they were separated, Major-General W. H. Rycroft, C.B., C.M.G., being appointed D.A.G. and Major-General Clarke becoming D.Q.M.G.

APPENDIX 2

22nd Division.

G.O.C.	Major-General the Hon. F. Gordon, C.B., D.S.O.[1]
65th Brigade	Br.-General G. E. Bayley, D.S.O
9/King's Own.	14/King's.
9/East Lancashire.	12/Lancashire Fusiliers.
66th Brigade	Br.-General F. S. Montague Bates.
12/Cheshire.	9/South Lancashire.
13/Manchester.	8/Shropshire L.I.
67th Brigade	Br.-General H. F. Cooke.
11/R. Welch Fus.	8/South Wales Borderers.
7/South Wales Borderers.	11/Welch.
Artillery	XCVIII, XCIX, C, and CI Brigades R.F.A.
Engineers	99th, 100th, and 127th Field Companies R.E.
Pioneers	9/Border Regiment.

26th Division.

G.O.C.	Major-General E. C. W. Mackenzie-Kennedy, C.B.[2]
77th Brigade	Br.-General G. L. Hibbert, D.S.O.[3]
10/Black Watch.	11/Cameronians (Scot. Rif.).
12/Arg. and Suth. Highrs.	8/R. Scots Fus.
78th Brigade	Br.-General J. Duncan, C.M.G., D.S.O.[4]
9/Gloucestershire.	7/Ox. and Bucks L.I.
11/Worcestershire.	7/R. Berkshire.
79th Brigade	Br.-General A. J. Poole.
8/D.C.L.I.	7/Wiltshire.
10/Devons.	12/Hampshire.
Artillery	CXIV, CXV, CXVI, and CXVII Brigades R.F.A.
Engineers	107th, 108th, and 131st Field Companies, R.E.
Pioneers	8/Ox. and Bucks L.I.

---

[1] Succeeded on the 7th May 1917 by Br.-General J. Duncan, C.M.G., D.S.O.

[2] Succeeded on the 14th January 1917 by Major-General A. W. Gay, C.B., D.S.O.

[3] Succeeded on the 6th February 1917 by Br.-General W. A. Blake, D.S.O.

[4] Succeeded on the 6th May 1917 by Lieut.-Colonel T. N. S. M. Howard, D.S.O.

APPENDIX 2

60th (London) Division.

G.O.C.	Major-General E. S. Bulfin, C.V.O., C.B.
179th Brigade	Br.-General FitzJ. M. Edwards, D.S.O.
2/13th London.	2/15th London.
2/14th London.	2/16th London.
180th Brigade	Br.-General F. M. Carleton, D.S.O.
2/17th London.	2/19th London.
2/18th London.	2/20th London.
181st Brigade	Br.-General E. C. Da Costa.
2/21st London.	2/23rd London.
2/22nd London.	2/24th London.
Artillery	CCCI, CCCII, and CCCIII Brigades R.F.A.
Engineers	3/3rd, 2/4th, and 1/6th London Field Companies R.E.

Corps Troops.

1/1st Lothians and Border Horse (less one squadron).

XVI CORPS.

G.O.C.	Lieut.-General C. J. Briggs, C.B.
Br.-General, General Staff	Br.-General G. N. Cory, D.S.O.
Deputy Adjutant and Quartermaster-General	Br.-General H. J. Everett, C.B.
G.O.C. Royal Artillery	Br.-General A. W. Gay, C.B., D.S.O.[1]
Chief Engineer	Br.-General H. L. Pritchard, D.S.O.

10th (Irish) Division.

G.O.C.	Major-General J. R. Longley.
29th Brigade	Br.-General R. S. Vandeleur, C.M.G.
6/R. Irish Rifles.	1/Leinster.
5/Conn. Rangers.	6/Leinster.
30th Brigade	Br.-General A. D. Macpherson, D.S.O.
1/Royal Irish.	6/R. Dublin Fusiliers.
6/R. Munster Fusiliers.	7/R. Dublin Fusiliers.
31st Brigade	Br.-General E. M. Morris.
5/R. Innis. Fusiliers.	2/R. Irish Fusiliers.
6/R. Innis. Fusiliers.	5/R. Irish Fusiliers.

---

[1] Succeeded, on promotion to the command of the 26th Division, by Br.-General H. E. T. Kelly, C.M.G.

APPENDIX 2

Artillery	LIV, LVII, LXVII, and LXVIII Brigades R.F.A.
Engineers	65th, 66th, and 85th Field Companies R.E.
Pioneers	5/Royal Irish.

27th Division.

G.O.C.	Major-General G. T. Forestier-Walker, C.B.
80th Brigade	Br.-General A. C. Roberts, D.S.O.
2/Shropshire L.I.	4/K.R.R.C.
3/K.R.R.C.	4/Rifle Brigade.
81st Brigade	Br.-General B. F. Widdrington, D.S.O.
1/Royal Scots.	2/Cameron Highrs.
13/(Scottish Horse) Black Watch.	1/Arg. and Suth. Highrs.
82nd Brigade	Br.-General C. C. M. Maynard, D.S.O.[1]
2/Gloucestershire.	10/Hampshire.
2/D.C.L.I.	10/(Lovat's Scouts) Cameron Highrs.
Artillery	I, XIX, XX, and CXXIX Brigades R.F.A.
Engineers	17th, 1/1st Wessex, 1/2nd Wessex Field Companies R.E.
Pioneers	26/Middlesex.

28th Division.

G.O.C.	Major-General H. L. Croker, C.B.
83rd Brigade	Br.-General R. H. Hare, C.M.G., M.V.O., D.S.O.
2/King's Own.	1/K.O.Y.L.I.
2/East Yorkshire.	1/York and Lancs.
84th Brigade	Br.-General G. A. Weir, D.S.O.
2/Northumberland Fusiliers.	2/Cheshire.
1/Suffolk.	1/Welch.
85th Brigade	Br.-General B. C. M. Carter, C.B., C.M.G.
2/The Buffs.	2/East Surrey.
3/Royal Fusiliers.	3/Middlesex.
Artillery	III, XXXI, CXXX, and CXLVI Brigades R.F.A.
Engineers	30th, 2/1st Northumbrian, 1/7th Hampshire Field Companies R.E.
Pioneers	23/Welch.

---

[1] Actually assumed command on 12th January 1917.

APPENDIX 2

Corps Troops.

1/1st Surrey Yeomanry (less one squadron).

GENERAL HEADQUARTERS TROOPS.[1]

Mounted Troops .. .. .. *7th Mounted Brigade.*
G.O.C. .. .. Br.-General F. Fitz H. Lance.
   1/1st Sherwood Rangers.
   1/1st Derbyshire Yeomanry.
   1/1st South Notts Hussars.

                         8th Mounted Brigade.
G.O.C. .. .. Br.-General A. H. M. Taylor, D.S.O.
   1/1st City of London Yeomanry.
   1/1st County of London (Middlesex) Yeomanry.
   1/3rd County of London Yeomanry.

Royal Flying Corps .. .. .. Headquarters " A " Wing.
   No. 17 Squadron ⎫
   No. 47 Squadron ⎬ 16th Wing.
   No. 17 Kite Balloon Section (Naval).

Artillery .. .. XX, XXXVII, LXI, and LXXV Heavy Artillery Groups.[2]
                                III Mountain and IV Highland Mountain Artillery Brigades, R.G.A.
                                Nos. 24, 32, 73, 74, and 91 Anti-Aircraft Sections, R.G.A.

Royal Engineers .. .. .. 37th, 137th, 139th, 140th, 143rd, 286th, and 287th Army Troops Companies R.E.

NOTES.—There were six Garrison battalions as G.H.Q. Troops or on the Lines of Communication, formed into the 228th Brigade (Br.-General W. C. Ross), but at this time for administrative purposes only, one British Labour Battalion, and one Maltese Labour Battalion.

The transport included under G.H.Q. Troops consisted of 13 Mechanical Transport Companies A.S.C. (of which one was attached to each Army Corps as a Corps Troops Supply Column and three as Divisional Supply Columns), five Reserve Parks (wheeled horse transport), and four Indian Mule Cart Corps units. There were four further Mechanical Transport Companies on the Lines of Communication, and six Special Supply Columns (four heavy and two light) attached to the Serbian Army.

In addition to the troops given above, each Division had a Signal Company R.E., a Cyclist Company (except the 60th Division), a Divisional Train, a Divisional Ammunition Column, a Sanitary Section, and a Mobile Veterinary Section.

---

[1] With the exception of the R.F.C., practically all the G.H.Q. Troops were attached to one or other of the two corps.

[2] Comprising seven 60-pdr. batteries, seven 6-inch howitzer batteries, one (3-gun) 6-inch gun battery, and one battery composed of two 4·7 naval guns and four 6-inch guns.

Each Brigade had a Machine-gun Company, a Light Trench-Mortar Battery (eight 3-inch Stokes guns, in process of organization), and a Field Ambulance. Battalions at this date were equipped with eight Lewis guns apiece, and the cavalry was in process of being equipped with one Hotchkiss gun per troop.

There were three 2-inch Medium Trench-Mortar Batteries (not officially numbered by the War Office) attached to the XII Corps.

The Garrison of Lemnos, Imbros, Tenedos, and Thasos, which was under G.H.Q., consisted of the 1/2nd W. Lancs. Field Company R.E., detachment of 28th Fortress Company R.E., Mudros Signal Section, 3rd Battalion Royal Marines, and detachments of auxiliary troops.

APPENDIX 3.

ORDER OF BATTLE

OF THE

BULGARIAN AND GERMAN FORCES IN MACEDONIA, DECEMBER 1916.

BULGARIAN GENERAL HEADQUARTERS.

Commander-in-Chief	Prince Boris.
Assistant Commander-in-Chief	General Gekov.
Chief of the Staff	Colonel Lukov.

MACEDONIAN ARMY GROUP.

G.O.C. .. .. General Otto v. Below.[1]

BULGARIAN FIRST ARMY.

G.O.C. .. .. General Gešov.

Bulgarian 5th and 9th Divisions, 1st Brigade of the 11th Division. German 59th Regiment.

GERMAN ELEVENTH ARMY.

G.O.C. .. .. Lieut.-General v. Winckler.

Bulgarian 2nd, 3rd, and 8th Divisions, 6th Division (less one brigade), 58th Regiment of the 9th Division, 39th Regiment of the 10th Division.
German " Division v. Hippel," 22nd Brigade.

BULGARIAN SECOND ARMY.[2]

G.O.C. .. .. General Todorov.

Bulgarian 7th Division, 10th Division (less one brigade), and 11th Division (less one brigade).
Turkish XX Corps (G.O.C. Major-General Abdulkerim Pasha), 46th and 50th Divisions.

NOTE.—The Bulgarian division commonly consisted of 24, and the brigade of eight battalions.

Each Turkish division consisted of nine regular battalions and three battalions of militia formed in Eastern Macedonia.

The German " Division v. Hippel " consisted of 12 battalions, and the 22nd Brigade (comprising the reinforcements sent at the end of November) of nine battalions, etc.

The Bulgarian Third Army on the Rumanian front consisted of the 1st, 4th, and 12th Divisions, with certain regiments of the 6th and 7th.

---

[1] Succeeded at the end of April 1917 by General v. Scholtz.
[2] Directly under Bulgarian G.H.Q., whereas the Bulgarian First Army and the German Eleventh Army were under the Army Group v. Below.

APPENDIX 4.

SALONIKA TRANSPORT

(Known as

S.A. SECTION AMM

Detail	Existing	
	Vehicles	Drivers
1st Line		
Water	—	—
Wagons, limb., G.S., S.A.A.	43	86
Cooking pots	—	—
Grenades [2]	—	—
Farrier's tools, forge, and anvil	—	—
Saddler's material, vet. chest and office	—	—
Officers' mess and baggage	—	—
Spare	—	27
Total	43	113
Train		
Baggage	1	2
Supplies	3	6
Total	4	8

[1] To save space only units of the greatest importance and most affected that the field artillery of a division was very little altered in the new establish it with pack guns.
No precise date is given for this establishment, as it was adopted
[2] Each ammunition mule carries one box Mills Grenades or proportion

NOTE.—Under the series of revisions begun in the spring of 1917, pack echelon, consisting of 15 limbered wagons for S.A.A., 30 drivers, and 60 supplies, was put once more on a wheeled basis.

ESTABLISHMENTS.[1]

" Salonika 4.")

UNITION COLUMN.

Scale		Pack Scale			
Mules		Vehicles	Drivers	Mules	
Draught	Pack			Draught	Pack
—	—	—	2	—	2
172	—	—	180	—	240
—	—	—	1	—	2
—	—	—	—	—	—
—	—	—	1	—	1
—	—	—	1	—	1
—	—	—	—	—	1
34	—	—	13	—	25
206	—	—	198	—	272
4 12	—	} —	12	—	24
16	—	—	12	—	24

by the change in establishments are given below. It must be recalled ments, as to convert it to a pack scale was impossible, short of rearming

gradually during the latter part of 1916.
of " Very " Lights.

mules were reduced to 142. To compensate for the deficiency, a wheeled draught mules, was formed. The Train detachment, for baggage and

FIELD COM

Detail	Existing	
	Vehicles	Drivers
1st Line Headquarters		
Water	—	4
Searchlights [1]	1	2
Wagons, pontoon [1]	2	6
Wagons, trestle [1]	1	3
Wagons, limb., G.S., technical stores and baggage	2 [2]	4
Officers' mess and baggage	—	—
Spare drivers, animals	—	12
4 Sections		
Cooks gear	1	2
Water	—	—
Carts, tool, R.E. (two per section)	8	8
Wagons, limb., R.E., technical stores and baggage	4	8
Drivers, pack animals	—	8
Total	19	57
Train		
Supplies	2	4

[1] To be parked under Corps arrangements and sent forward when re
[2] To Divisional Reserve.

NOTE.—Under the series of revisions begun in the spring of 1917, the virtually unaltered, except that the Train now again provided two limbered

PANY, R.E.

Scale		Vehicles	Drivers	Pack Scale	
Mules				Mules	
Draught	Pack			Draught	Pack
—	4	—	1	—	1
4	—	—	—	—	—
12	—	—	—	—	—
6	—	—	—	—	—
8	—	—	5	—	10
—	—	—	1	—	2
14	—	—	12	—	7
4	—	—	2	—	4
—	—	—	4	—	4
16	—	—	12	—	24
16	—	—	20	—	32
—	8	—	—	—	—
80	12	—	57	—	84
8	—	—	6	—	12

quired.

transport establishment of this unit remained on a pack basis and was wagons for supplies instead of 12 pack mules.

INFANTRY

Detail	Existing	
	Vehicles	Drivers
1st Line Headquarters		
Medical equipment	—	2
Water	—	8
Officers' mess	1	2
S.A.A.	5	10
Tools	2	4
Signalling equipment	—	—
Cooks	4	8
Q.M. Stores	—	—
Spare animals	—	14
Battalion Machine-Gun Section		
4 machine guns and ammunition	4	8
4 Companies		
Officers' mess	—	—
Water	—	—
Tools	—	—
Ammunition	—	8
Cooks	—	—
Scouts	—	—
Total	16	64
Company Detail		
Officers' mess	—	—
Water	—	—
Tools	—	—
Ammunition	—	2
Cooks	—	—
Scouts	—	—
Company Machine-Gun Section		
2 machine guns and ammunition	—	—
Total	—	2
Train		
Baggage, H.Q.		
„ M.G.	12	24
„ 4 Companies		
Supplies		
Total	12	24

[1] When number of machine guns is increased to 2 Lewis guns per com be absorbed in companies. (Editorial Note: This indicates a state of establishment for which is given below.)

[2] When 2 Lewis guns per company are issued in place of battalion

[3] One additional driver and 2 mules required when 2 Lewis guns per

Note.—Under the series of revisions begun in the spring of 1917, the machine guns had been transferred to machine-gun companies, and 40 mules wagons and 8 pack mules for supplies and baggage instead of 37 pack

APPENDIX 4

BATTALION.

Scale				Pack Scale		
Mules		Vehicles	Drivers	Mules		
Draught	Pack			Draught	Pack	
—	2	—	2	—	3
—	8	—	1	—	1
4	—	—	—	—	1
20	—	—	20	—	40
8	—	—	1	—	2
—	—	—	2	—	3
16	—	—	—	—	1
—	—	—	2	—	4
12	8	—	4	—	8
16	—	—	20 [1]	—	28 [1]
—	—	—	2	—	4
—	—	—	4	—	8
—	—	—	4	—	8
—	8	—	8	—	8
—	—	—	2	—	4
—	—	—	4	—	4
76	26	—	76	—	127
—	—	—	1	—	1
—	—	—	1	—	2
—	—	—	1	—	2
—	2	—	2	—	2
—	—	—	1	—	1
—	—	—	1	—	1
—	—	—	10 [2]	—	14 [2]
—	2	—	17	—	23
48	—	{ — — —	1 — 2 16	— — —	2 — 4 [3] 31
48	—	—	19	—	37

pany, drivers will be 40, mules 56, and battalion machine-gun section will transition. Some divisions had already machine-gun companies, the

machine-gun sections.
company are issued.
transport establishment of this unit was virtually unaltered, except that were now provided for Lewis guns. The Train now provided 4½ limbered mules.

MACHINE-GUN

Detail	Existing Scale			
	Vehicles	Drivers	Horses	
			Draught	Heavy Draught
1ST LINE HEADQUARTERS				
Bicycles	4	—	—	—
Carts { cooks'	1	1	1	—
{ water	1	1	2	—
EACH SECTION				
Wagons, limbered, G.S. :—				
For 4 machine guns, tripods, ammunition and 4 ammunition pack saddles	2	4	8	—
For ammunition	1	1	2	—
Total Company	18	22	43	—
TRAIN				
Wagons, G.S., for baggage and supplies	1	1	—	2
Total	1	1	—	2

NOTE.—Under the series of revisions begun in the spring of 1917, the virtually that given under " existing scale."

APPENDIX 4

COMPANY.

Detail	Pack Scale		
	Vehicles	Drivers	Mules Pack
1st Line Headquarters			
Cooks' and officers' mess	—	1	2
Water	—	2	2
Stores { artificer, shoeing smith, signallers' }	—	1	1
Spare animals	—	5	9
Each Section			
For 4 machine guns, tripods, and spare parts	—	4	4
For 1st supply ammunition (3,500 rounds per gun in belts)	—	4	8
For 2nd supply ammunition (18,000 per section in boxes), sandbags, and sig. equipment	—	5	10
Total Company	—	61	102
Train			
Baggage	—	1	2
Supplies	—	6	12
Total	—	7	14

establishment of this unit was brought back to a wheeled basis and became

DIVISIONAL TRAIN.

Detail	Vehicles	Drivers	Mules Draught	Mules Pack
H.Q. Divisional A.S.C. Wagons, limb., G.S., for baggage and supplies	2	4	8	—
Total H.Q. Divisional A.S.C.	2	4	8	—
Pack Echelon Headquarters Pack mules for water and baggage	—	1	—	2
Carts, Maltese, for medical equipment	1	1	2	—
Carts, Maltese, for postal equipment	1	1	2	—
Total H.Q. Pack Echelon	2	3	4	2
Headquarters Company				
Headquarters of Company				
Pack mules for water	—	1	—	2
Wagons, limb., G.S., for :—				
Baggage, stores, etc.	2	4	8	—
Cooks' and men's rations	2	4	8	—
Forage	4	8	16	—
Spare mules	—	23	22	24
Spare drivers	—	14	—	—
Baggage Section				
Wagons, limb., G.S., for H.Q. Division	2	4	8	—
Carts, Maltese, for 4 F.A. Brigades (15 Batteries)[1]	23	23	46	—
Pack mules for :—				
H.Q. Divisional R.E.	—	1	—	2
3 Field Ambulances	—	21	—	39
1 Pioneer Battalion	—	3	—	6
1 Cavalry Squadron	—	1	—	1
Divisional M.G.	—	1	—	2
Supply Section				
Wagons, limb., G.S., for :—				
H.Q. Division	1	2	4	—
H.Q. Divisional R.A.	1	2	4	—
4 F.A. Brigades (15 Batteries)[2]	23	46	92	—
Divisional Ammunition Column	7	14	28	—
Sanitary Section	1	2	4	—
Mobile Veterinary Section	2	4	8	—

[1] If a division has 4 F.A. brigades of 16 batteries, add 1 Maltese cart, 1 driver, 2 mules.

[2] If a division has 4 F.A. brigades of 16 batteries, add 1 G.S. limb. wagon, 2 drivers, 4 mules.

APPENDIX 4

Detail	Vehicles	Drivers	Mules	
			Draught	Pack
HEADQUARTERS COMPANY—*contd.*				
Supply Section—contd.				
Pack mules for :—				
H.Q. Divisional R.E.	—	2	—	3
3 Field Ambulances	—	36	—	69
3 (Field) Coys. R.E.	—	18	—	36
1 Cavalry Squadron	—	7	—	14
Divisional Signal Coy.	—	8	—	15
Divisional M.G. Coy.	—	6	—	12
1 Pioneer Battalion	—	19	—	36
Divisional Cyclist Coy.	—	3	—	5
Total H.Q. Company	68	277	248	266
EACH BRIGADE COMPANY				
Headquarters of Company				
Pack mules for :—				
Water	—	1	—	2
Baggage, stores, etc.	—	5	—	9
Cooks	—	2	—	3
Supplies	—	11	—	22
Spare mules	—	12	—	24
Spare drivers	—	7	—	—
Baggage Section				
Pack mules for :—				
H.Q. Infantry Brigade	—	2	—	4
Infantry Battalions	—	12	—	24
Brigade M.G. Company	—	1	—	2
Supply Section				
Pack Mules for :—				
H.Q. Infantry Brigade	—	2	—	4
4 Infantry Battalions	—	64	—	124
Brigade M.G. Company	—	6	—	12
S.A. Sec. Ammunition Column	—	12	—	24
Total each Brigade Company	—	137	—	254
Total Pack Echelon	70	691	252	1030
WHEELED ECHELON HEADQUARTERS				
Carts, Maltese, for :—				
Baggage and supplies	1	1	2	—
Medical equipment	1	1	2	—
Postal equipment	1	1	2	—
Limb. G.S. wagon for supply officer	1	2	4	—
Total H.Q. Wheeled Echelon	4	5	10	—

382 APPENDIX 4

	Vehicles		Drivers	Mules	
Detail				Draught	Pack
HEADQUARTERS COMPANY [1]	Per Sec.	Per Coy.			
Headquarters of Company					
Water, pack mules..	—	—	2	—	4
Waggons, limb., G.S., for :—					
Baggage, stores, etc.	2	4	8	16	—
Cooks	1	2	4	8	—
Supplies	5	10	20	40	—
Spare mules	—	—	31	62	—
Spare drivers	—	—	17	—	—
Vehicles for Supplies					
Wagons, limb., G.S., for :—					
H.Q. Division	1	2	4	8	—
H.Q. Divisional R.E.	1	2	4	8	—
3 Field Companies, R.E.	4	8	16	32	—
3 Field Ambulances	7	14	28	56	—
1 Pioneer Battalion	4	8	16	32	—
Divisional M.G. Company	1	2	4	8	—
4 F.A. Brigades (15 Batteries) [2]	23	46	92	184	—
Divisional Ammunition Column	6	12	24	48	—
1 Cavalry Squadron	2	4	8	16	—
Divisional Cyclist Company	1	2	4	8	—
Divisional Signal Company	2	4	8	16	—
Mobile Veterinary Section	1	2	4	8	—
H.Q. Coy. 1st Echelon	4	8	16	32	—
Carts, Maltese, for :—					
H.Q. Divisional R.A.	1	2	2	4	—
Sanitary Section	1	2	2	4	—
Total H.Q. Company Wheeled Echelon	67	134	314	590	4
EACH BRIGADE COMPANY [3]					
Headquarters of Company					
For water	—	—	2	—	2
Wagons, limb., G.S., for :—					
Baggage, stores, etc.	1	2	4	8	—
Cooks and supplies	2	4	8	16	—
For supply officer	—	1	2	4	—
Spare mules	—	—	10	20	—
Spare drivers	—	—	6	—	—

    [1] Consists of 2 sections, each carrying 1 day's supplies for Divisional Troops.
    [2] If a division has 4 F.A. brigades of 16 batteries, add 1 G.S. limbered wagon, 2 drivers, 4 mules per section.
    [3] Consists of 2 sections, each carrying 1 day's supplies for 1 Infantry Brigade.

APPENDIX 4

Detail	Vehicles		Drivers	Mules	
				Draught	Pack
EACH BRIGADE COMPANY—*contd.* *Supply Vehicles* Wagon, limb., G.S., for :—	Per Sec.	Per Coy.			
4 Battalions Infantry	16	32	64	128	—
S.A.A. Column	2	4	8	16	—
Brigade M.G. Company ..	1	2	4	8	—
Brigade Company, 1st Echelon	2	4	8	16	—
Total each Brigade Company Wheeled Echelon	24	49	116	216	2
Total Wheeled Echelon ..	—	285	667	1248	10
Total H.Q. Divisional A.S.C. ...	—	2	4	8	—
,, Pack Echelon	—	70	691	252	1030
,, Wheeled Echelon ..	—	285	667	1248	10
Grand Total Divisional Train ..	—	357	1362	1508	1040

NOTE.—Under the series of revisions begun in the spring of 1917, the transport establishment of this unit was the most seriously curtailed of all. Under the later scale the division of the Train into two separate echelons was abolished. The headquarters company and the three brigade companies were placed entirely on a wheeled basis, but one pack company was retained. The strength of the Train was approximately halved, vehicles being reduced from 357 to 183, drivers from 1,362 to 617, draught mules from 1,508 to 745, and pack mules from 1,040 to 521. The Train now carried one instead of two days' supplies.

APPENDIX 5.

Secret.

ARMY OPERATION ORDER NO. 22.

Salonika,
8th June 1916.

Map A. 1. As the result of an agreement arrived at with the French Commander-in-Chief, it has been decided to allot to the British Army the zone approximately south and east of the line Butkovo Lake–Bahisli Dere–Sariköi to junction with the French about the Matterhorn.

The boundary between areas for which Corps will be tactically and administratively responsible will be the Salonika–Seres road (inclusive to XVI Corps).

2. The French cavalry and their 17th Colonial Division are under orders to move as soon as possible in a north-west direction. The defence of the line of the Struma will devolve on British from the evening of the 9th June.

3. The XVI Corps will arrange to send at once the 29th Brigade Group, of which the infantry is now near Likovan, towards Orlyak.

This Corps will take over from the French the defence of the line from Butkovo Lake to the Gulf of Orfano. For this purpose a divisional squadron of the XII Corps is placed at disposal of G.O.C. XVI Corps until relieved above Orlyak by the XII Corps. Care is to be taken to keep touch with the French.

4. The XII Corps will detail one division to take over at the earliest possible date the defence of the line from Orlyak exclusive to the French right flank. The divisional squadron mentioned in Paragraph 3 will be moved rapidly forward to Orlyak and placed temporarily under the orders of the XVI Corps until the arrival of the division.

The 7th Mounted Brigade (less one regiment) and the 22nd Division will remain in their present positions until relieved by the French in about eight days' time. When relieved, the 7th Mounted Brigade (less one regiment) will remain under the orders of the XII Corps and is to be employed in guarding any interval between the French right and our left flanks.

The 26th Division will remain for the present in Army reserve.

5. The XVI Corps will continue to be responsible for the reconstruction and maintenance of the Salonika–Orlyak road.

6. Army Operation Order No. 21, Paragraph 8, is cancelled.[1]

W. GILLMAN,
Br.-General, General Staff, Salonika Army.

Issued at 6.30 p.m.

---

[1] This paragraph referred to a projected move to XII Corps headquarters.

APPENDIX 6.

27TH DIVISION OPERATION ORDER NO. 40.

28th September 1916.

Reference: Part of Struma Valley 1/100,000 No. 122.

1. In order to hold the enemy to his ground, operations will take **Maps A, 8.** place against enemy positions on the left bank of the Struma on Saturday **Sketch 8.** 30th September.

2. The 81st Brigade Group, consisting of 81st Infantry Brigade with its Machine-Gun Company and 1st Wessex Field Company R.E., will on Saturday 30th September attack and occupy the village of Karajaköi (Bala and Zir) on the left bank of Struma, and will hold the ground gained.

The 82nd Brigade Group, consisting of 2/D.C.L.I. and 2/R. Irish Fusiliers with Brigade Machine-Gun Company and two sections 2nd Wessex Field Company R.E., will act as a reserve under the orders of Br.-General B. F. Widdrington, Commanding 81st Infantry Brigade.

3. The 29th Infantry Brigade (10th Division, attached 27th Division) will guard both flanks of the 81st Infantry Brigade. The force detailed to guard the left flank should be slightly stronger than that destined for guarding the right flank of the attack.

After the capture of Karajaköi (Bala and Zir) the battalions guarding right and left flanks of 81st Infantry Brigade will respectively establish themselves in continuation of 81st Brigade line on its right and left flanks, up to the River Struma.

4. The Struma will be crossed by means of two bridges and rafts which have been constructed by the 10th Division at points about 1,000 yards magnetic north of Karajaköi on the right bank of the Struma and which will be ready for use at 11 p.m. on 29th September.

The 81st Infantry Brigade, followed by the 29th Infantry Brigade, will cross by the above-mentioned bridges and rafts in sufficient time to enable the 81st Brigade attack to issue from the woods on the left bank of the Struma at 5.30 a.m. on 30th September. (Our artillery will open fire at 5.45 a.m.)

The troops of the 82nd Brigade Group will cross the Struma as ordered by G.O.C. 81st Infantry Brigade.

G.O.C. 81st Infantry Brigade will arrange for the control of the traffic across the river.

5. The I Brigade R.F.A. and two field artillery brigades of 10th Division will come under the orders of C.R.A. 27th Division at 6 a.m. on 29th September.

The artillery of the 28th Division will assist in the protection of the left flank of the attacking force.

The Argyll Mountain Battery will come under the orders of G.O.C. 81st Infantry Brigade at 12 noon 28th September; camp west of Mahmudli Road, ¼ mile south-east of 10th Divisional Headquarters.

The 81st Small Arms Section, Ammunition Column, will forthwith come under the orders of G.O.C. 81st Infantry Brigade.

Separate instructions have been issued to C.R.A. as to the rôle of the artillery.

Infantry liaison officers will be detailed by 81st and 29th Infantry Brigades to accompany the artillery forward observation officers.

The signals for the artillery to lengthen their range will be two white Very Lights instead of two green lights. The signal for barrage remains one red and one green light in quick succession.

6. Further instructions concerning supply arrangements will be issued later. Two days' rations will be carried.

7. Dressing Stations will be established at Sakavcha and near Karajaköi (right bank of Struma) under arrangements made by A.D.M.S. 10th Division. A dressing station will be established at a later stage of the operations on left bank of Struma.

8. Prisoners of war to be sent to kilometre 61 on Salonika–Seres Road.

9. The troops at Neohori under the G.O.C. 80th Infantry Brigade will engage the enemy on their front with artillery and patrol activity on Saturday 30th September.

Special instructions have been issued.

10. Watches will be synchronized at 9 p.m. on 29th September.

11. Reports to Advanced 27th Division at kilometre $67\frac{1}{2}$ on Salonika–Seres Road.

E. GROGAN,
Lieut.-Colonel, G.S., 27th Division.

Issued at 10.15 p.m.

NOTE.—No Operation Order or extracts therefrom or marked maps must on any account be taken across the river.

APPENDIX 7.

Secret.
XII CORPS OPERATION ORDER NO. 24.

Yanesh,
9th April 1917.

Reference 1/50,000 and 1/20,000 Dojran Edition 2 A.

1. *Information regarding the Enemy.*—The information available **Maps A, 10.** from all sources regarding the enemy on the XII Corps front between **Sketch 13.** Lake Dojran and the Vardar is summarized in Memorandum No. 1/4/231, dated 24th March 1917.

2. *Intention.*—As a commencement to further offensive action the XII Corps will, on a date to be notified later, attack the enemy's advanced position between Lake Dojran and P. 4½, and will subsequently advance and consolidate a position roughly along the line of the Dojran–Krastali road.

3. *General Plan.*—The attack will be carried out in two stages. The *first stage* will include the assault and consolidation of the enemy's advanced line system running Lake Dojran–Petit Couronné–Hill 380–Mamelon–P. 4½. A raid will be made simultaneously against the enemy's salient opposite Machukovo.

In the *second stage*, which will take place on a subsequent date, our right will be pushed forward and a position will eventually be consolidated on the line Dojran Hill–Teton Hill–Hill 340, to Hill 380.

4. *Allotment of Troops.*—(a) The troops allotted to *the attack* will be the 26th Division and the 22nd Division (less one infantry brigade group), supported by the bulk of the Corps Artillery, namely, by the

XXXVII and LXXXII Heavy Groups,

consisting of
    Two 6-inch Mk. VII Guns.
    Five batteries 6-inch Howitzers.
    Five and a half batteries 60-pdrs.

The 4·5 Howitzers of the two divisions will be formed into two "bombardment groups" and three 6-inch Howitzer batteries will be attached to these groups for the bombardment period only, returning to their Heavy Artillery Groups on completion of this period.

(b) The remainder of the Corps front from the Whaleback (exclusive) to the Vardar will be held by the 60th Division, which will also carry out the raid against the Machukovo salient.

The raid will be supported by the LXXV Heavy Group, which has been placed under the direct orders of the G.O.C. 60th Division, and consists of
    One 6-inch Mk. VII Gun.
    One battery 6-inch Howitzers.
    Two batteries 60-pdrs.

(c) The *Corps Reserve* will consist of the 67th Infantry Brigade Group (Br.-General H. F. Cooke, D.S.O.), consisting of
    67th Infantry Brigade.
    67th Trench-Mortar Battery.
    67th Machine-Gun Company.
    67th Field Ambulance.
    67th S.A. Section Ammunition Column.

APPENDIX 7

It will be located in the area Malovsi–Galavansi with headquarters at Galavansi.

(d) The 8th Mounted Brigade will be in Army Reserve.

5. *Method of Attack.*—The main attack and the raid will be carried out simultaneously, and the method of attack in each case will be as far as possible identical. Each will be preceded by three days' bombardment in accordance with the Corps Artillery Plan (copies of which are attached as per distribution) and with the 60th Division Artillery Plan. Wire cutting will be carried out during this period, but will commence the day before the beginning of the bombardment.

6. *The Main Attack.*—The main attack will be carried out as follows:—

The 26th Division on the right will attack and occupy the enemy's advanced line works from the Lake to the Jumeaux Ravine inclusive.

The 22nd Division on the left will attack and occupy the enemy's advanced works from the Jumeaux Ravine (exclusive) to P. $4\frac{1}{4}$ (inclusive).

The infantry, with the exception of one battalion, will deliver the assault after dusk simultaneously along the front at " X " hours, at which time they will cross the *enemy's* parapet. (The time " X " hours will be notified later.) The above-mentioned battalion, namely, that attacking O. $5\frac{1}{4}$, will cross the enemy's parapet at X + 20 minutes.

The bombardment of the front line system will meanwhile have continued at the normal intensity of the previous days until ten minutes to X hours (X − 10 minutes) at which time it will change to an 18-pdr. H.E. barrage, except on O. 5 and the portion of O. $5\frac{1}{4}$ eastward of co-ordinate 12465, upon both of which the bombardment will continue (see last sentence of this paragraph). The 18-pdr. H.E. barrage will continue for five minutes (X − 5 minutes) and then again change to 18-pdr. shrapnel barrage till X hours. It will then lift from the front trenches on to points closely behind the enemy's front line system, where applicable. Fifteen minutes later (X + 15 minutes) the barrage will again lift on to selected barrage lines and blocking points about 300 yards beyond the line selected for consolidation.

On sections of the front where the enemy's defence consists of a single line of trenches this second lift in the barrage will be unnecessary and the first lift will be direct on to the selected barrage lines and blocking points, where it will remain.

On O. 5 and the portion of O. $5\frac{1}{4}$ eastward of co-ordinate 12465 the bombardment will continue until ten minutes after X hours (X + 10 minutes), at which time the 18-pdr. H.E. barrage will commence, changing to 18-pdr. shrapnel barrage at X + 15 minutes and lifting at X + 20 minutes on to the selected barrage line.

7. *Consolidation.*—The enemy's advanced line system will be cleared of the enemy and consolidated under the protection of covering parties pushed forward under cover of the barrage by troops detailed for the purpose. The 22nd Division will pay special attention to the protection of their left flank, particularly from the direction of Krastali.

8. *Patrol Boundary.*—The boundary between the two divisions for purposes of patrols will be Ravin de Senelle where it crosses " D " Sector (inclusive to 26th Division) to the Jumeaux Ravine where the enemy wire crosses it between O. 6 and Hill 380, thence along the Jumeaux Ravine (inclusive to the 26th Division).

9. *Completion of First Stage.*—During the day subsequent to the assault the bombardment will be continued on selected works and ravines by the Divisional Artillery.

The Corps Artillery will be employed on counter-battery work.

Meanwhile, the 26th Division will carry out reconnaissances along

APPENDIX 7

their front in order to decide the final details of the plan for the second stage of the operation.

10. *The Raid on the Machukovo Salient.*—The raid will be carried out against a point on the front of the Machukovo salient to be selected by the G.O.C. 60th Division, the troops actually entering the enemy's trenches being limited to a strength of approximately one company.

The time during which this party may remain in the enemy's trenches will be limited to three-quarters of an hour.

The time at which the assault will be delivered and the timing and duration of the barrage will follow closely those given for the main attack (see paragraph 6).

11. *Synchronization of Watches.*—The synchronization of watches will be done daily, from the date of the commencement of the bombardment, at 7 a.m. and 7 p.m., by the General Staff of the Corps with the General Staffs of Divisions and by the B.G.R.A. of the Corps with the counter-batteries. Bombardment groups will obtain their time from the Divisions to which they are affiliated.

12. *Medical Arrangements.*—Details of arrangements as to regimental aid posts and advanced dressing stations and evacuation from these to main dressing stations have been issued to all concerned.

Main Dressing Stations will be as follows :—

For " B " Sector	The 78th Field Ambulance : $1\frac{1}{4}$ miles north-west of Kilinder.
For " C " Sector	The 80th Field Ambulance : just south of Col de Rates.
For " D " and " E " Sectors	The 68th Field Ambulance : at Chugunsi Church.

Evacuations from main dressing stations will be by motor ambulance to 31st Casualty Clearing Station at Yanesh or 28th Casualty Clearing Station at Karasuli and, if necessary, owing to the number of casualties, to 35th Casualty Clearing Station at Sarigöl.

Ambulances will be demanded as required from detachments of the M.A.C. at Malovsi.

In addition, empty supply trains fitted up for carrying both lying down and walking cases will leave Kilinder at 2.30 a.m. for Yanesh, and will leave Chugunsi at 1 a.m. for Karasuli.

A decauville ambulance train will run from Chugunsi at 3 p.m. and from Malovsi at 6.30 p.m. to Yanesh—extra trains will be arranged for if required.

13. *Prisoners of War.*—Prisoners of War taken by the 22nd and 26th Divisions will be sent under escort from Divisional control posts to a Corps control post which will be established at Yeniköi, whence they will be despatched by batches to Yanesh.

Prisoners taken by the 60th Division will be sent to Karasuli, and after XII Corps has been informed will go from there by rail to Dudular under arrangements to be made by the 60th Division direct with P.M., General Headquarters.

The 26th Division will furnish a guard of one platoon for the Corps control post at Yeniköi from the date decided on for the commencement of the operations, to act under instructions which will be issued by the A.P.M., XII Corps.

14. *Clearing the Battlefield and collection of effects from enemy dead.*—Arrangements will be made divisionally for collecting the effects of enemy dead, which will be forwarded to Yenköi, where they will be taken over by the A.P.M., XII Corps, or his representative.

15. *Supplies.*—Four days' full rations and fuel for the advanced Brigades of the 22nd and 26th Divisions will be dumped in advanced Brigade areas for consumption on first four days after the attack commences. Other troops will draw rations daily from advanced railheads.

Two days' rations included in the above will accompany the attacking troops either on the man or taken up by carriers.

16. *Ammunition.*—Gun ammunition for six days is dumped on divisional charge, in the case of the 22nd and 26th Divisions, and four days in the case of the 60th Division. In addition, two days' firing is held for all Divisions in Corps charge. Throughout all stages of the operation ammunition dumped in gun positions will not be allowed to fall below two days' firing, exclusive of rounds carried in the echelons.

17. *Corps Report Centre.*—The Corps Report Centre will remain at Yanesh.

A Corps advanced report centre will be established at Piton Rocheux, but reports will only be sent there on receipt of special orders from the Corps.

F. G. FULLER,
Br.-General, General Staff.

XII Corps.

Issued at 7 p.m. on 9th April 1917.

APPENDIX 8.

Headquarters XII Corps,
General Staff,
G/4/919.

Secret.
Reference Map 1/20,000.

With reference to XII Corps Operation Order No. 24, dated 9th April 1917.   **Maps A, 10. Sketch 14**

1. The XII Corps will continue the operation described in paragraph 2 of Operation Order No. 24 at an early date to be specified later.
The intention is to advance our right and consolidate a position in prolongation of the line newly occupied by the 22nd Division, roughly along the Dojran–Krastali road.

2. As a first step towards the attainment of this object, the 26th Division (less one infantry brigade, M.G. company and T.M. battery) will attack and consolidate the enemy's front line system on the front O. 1–O. 2–O. 3. It will at the same time be prepared to occupy O. 4 if opportunity offers.

3. In order to attract the enemy's attention from the 26th Division front of attack and to reduce the sharp salient at P. 4½ on the new portion of the 22nd Division front, the 22nd Division will, simultaneously with the attack of the 26th Division, advance its line between P. 4½ and the south-western end of the Whaleback and will at the same time raid Krastali village.
In addition, the 22nd Division will carry out an artillery and musketry action against O. 6 to synchronize with the attack of the 26th Division.
The 60th Division will also at the same time advance the right sub-section of its line to include Tomato Hill and Westbury Hill, and will attack and occupy Goldies Hill as an advanced post.

4. During these operations the tactical boundary between the 26th and 22nd Divisions will be :—Boris Ravine (inclusive to the 26th Division) –Jumeaux Ravine from its junction with Boris Ravine to its junction with Mortar Ravine (inclusive to 26th Division)–Mortar Ravine (inclusive to 22nd Division).
The tactical boundary between the 22nd and 60th Divisions will remain as at present, namely, a line from where the Castle Hill–Krastali track crosses our wire to the Spotted Dog.

5. The operations described above will be preceded by two days' bombardment and such further wire-cutting as may be necessary.
The allotment of Heavy Artillery to Bombardment Groups will be as follows :—

   To Elliot's Group under the orders of the G.O.C., 26th Division :
      12 6-inch Howitzers.
   To Arbuthnot's Group under the orders of the G.O.C. 22nd Division :
      4 6-inch Howitzers.

6. *Ammunition.*—The 22nd Division and 26th Division will arrange that six days' firing, including echelons, is held in divisional areas.
The 60th Division will hold four days' firing, including echelons.

7. Watches will be synchronized daily at 7 a.m. and at 5 p.m., commencing on the first day of bombardment.

F. G. FULLER,
Br.-General, General Staff.

XII Corps.
2nd May 1917.
Issued at 7.18 p.m.

GENERAL INDEX.[1]

Administrative services, Chap. XII.
Admiralty, its objection to landing in Gulf of Iskanderun, 46; 94; 107 (f.n.); its dislike of French policy in Greece, 352
Agamemnon (British battleship), 114
Air raids, 104, 114, 266, 296, 297
Albania, state of in late 1915, 35
Alexander, King of Greece, 356, 362
Alexander, Prince-Regent of Serbia, 9, 12, 120, 343
Alexander the Great, 3
Alexiev, Gen., 138
Allies in Macedonia, their strength in May 1916, 121; rôle of in July 1916, 138; policy of in February 1917, 296
Amery, Captain L. S., 28
Angheliki (Greek S.S.), 220
Angista bridges, destruction of, 159
Armée d'Orient, under orders of General Joffre, 92; reinforced, 108; begins advance from Entrenched Camp, 111; takes up new front, 114; formation of Armée Française d'Orient, 146. (Henceforward A.O. stands for Allied Armies and A.F.O. for French Army.) Length of front in August 1916, 149; possibilities open to in General Milne's view, 203; prospects of its being attacked, 253; strength of in battalions, May 1917, 339; its attack, May 1917, 340; its situation with regard to Greece, 348
Armée Française d'Orient, formation of, 146; in Dojran operations, August 1916, 153; attacked on Struma front, 158; in Battle of Monastir, 184, 234; regrouped, 239; reinforced from France, 239, 255; operations of in March 1917, 296

Artillery, in Action of Kosturino, 66; lack of heavy artillery after landing, 88; suitability of mountain artillery, 112; shortage of heavy and mountain artillery in early 1916, 121, 123; reorganization of field artillery, July 1916, 142; mountain artillery sent, 142; reinforcements in heavy artillery, 142, 162; reinforcements in anti-aircraft artillery, 142; (heavy) artillery in Dojran operations, Aug. 1916, 152; in Action of Machukovo, 166, 168; in Action of the Karajaköis and capture of Yeniköi, 173, 175; in Affair of Bairakli Jum'a, 193; in attacks on Tumbitza Farm, 246; second reorganization of field artillery, Dec. 1916, 257; defective ammunition, 274, 301; in Battle of Dojran, April 1917, 303; and in May 1917, 320, 328, 333; in Struma valley, May 1917, 335

Arz, General von, 197, 199
Asquith, Rt. Hon. H. H., 48, 49, 63, 201 (f.n.), 224
Augagneur, M., 42
Austro-Hungarian Army, situation of (against Serbia) in 1914, 10; first invasion of Serbia by, 11; second invasion, 12; third invasion, 15; on the Kolubara, 16; rout of by Serbians, 20; in campaign of 1915, 30, 32 *et seq.*; in campaign against Montenegro, 36; offensive of in Trentino, 121; defeated by Brusilov, 134; occupies Pogradec, 279
Austro-Serbian campaign of 1914, 8 *et seq.*
Ayas Bay. *See* Iskanderun, Gulf of

---

[1] Names in orders of battle and operation orders in the appendices are not indexed.

393

Bailey, Lieut.-Col. J. H., 246
Baillie, Lieut.-Col. D. G., 244
Bailloud, Gen., 40, 41, 53, 71, 72, 73, 74, 98
Bairakli Jum'a, attempted capture of, 192; capture of, 193
Balfour, Rt. Hon. A. J., 42, 44 (*f.n.*), 48, 201 (*f.n.*), 224, 349
Balkan Wars, The, 7
Barclay, Sir George, 137
Barker, Lieut.-Col. W. F., 326
Basil II (the Bulgar-Slayer), 3, 4
Bates, Br.-Gen. F. S. Montague, 194, 307, 312, 313
Bax-Ironside, Sir H., 25, 27
Bayley, Br.-Gen. G. E., 192, 328
Beckett, Lieut.-Col. J. D. M., 166
Beeby Thomson, Mr. A., 286
Below, Gen. Otto von, 235, 340
Bénazet, M. Paul, 220, 221
Berlin, Congress of, 5
Bertie of Thame, Lord, 207, 218
Billy, M. de, 358
" Birdcage," The. *See* Entrenched Camp of Salonika
Birdwood, Lieut.-Gen. Sir W. R., 56, 95
Blake, Br.-Gen. W. A., 321, 322, 324, 325, 326, 332
Bogdanov, Col., 60, 61
Bojadiev, Gen., 31, 235
Bojanović, Gen., 14
Bojović, Voivode (Marshal), 120, 158, 253, 343
Bond, Br.-Gen. H. H., 190
Borradaile, Major B., 57 (*f.n.*)
Bourgeois, M. Léon, 201, 348, 355
Bratianu, M., 135, 139
Briand, M., 48, 49, 136, 201 (*f.n.*), 207, 212, 217, 221, 225, 348
Briggs, Major-Gen. (later Lieut.-Gen.) C. J., 86; appointed to command XVI Corps, 125; 144, 147; reinforces Struma front, 158; ordered to carry out demonstrations, 162; his orders, 163; 165; decides to capture the Karajaköis, 172, 174; orders capture of Yeniköi, 180; 181, 183; ordered to capture Bairakli Jum'a, 191; 192; orders renewal of operations, 15th Nov. 1916, 241; 244; gives up attacks on Tumbitza Farm, 249; 298; his rôle in April 1917, 299, 319; and in May 1917, 334; Gen. Milne's letter to, regarding attack on Erneköi, 346

British Adriatic Mission, 36
British Government. *See* Great Britain
British Salonika Army, landing of first troops of, 33, 42, 51; reinforcements sent to, 52, 65, 85, 107, 202, 251; headquarters of formed, 56; relieves French troops near Kosturino, 56; its sufferings in Serbia, 64; attacked at Kosturino, 69; its retreat on Salonika, 71; its deficiencies, 88; two Corps H.Q. formed, 95; placed under orders of Gen. Sarrail, 97; false conception of its existence, 104; begins advance from Entrenched Camp, 112; dispositions of, June 1916, 125; new boundary of, 126; new importance of owing to Rumanian intervention, 135; prepares for active operations, 140; occupies lower Struma, 147; dispositions of, 3rd August 1916, 147; rôle of in offensive to aid Rumania, 150; dispositions of, September 1916, 162–163; rôle of during Battle of Monastir, 162, 241; removed from control by Egypt, 172; holds whole front from Ægean to Vardar, 251; its development of local resources, 271; in Battle of Dojran, Chaps. XIII. and XIV.
Brooke, Br.-Gen. C. R. I., 174, 243, 244, 245
Bruix (French cruiser), 355
Brulard, Gen., 97 (*f.n.*), 98
"Brusilov Offensive," 134, 136, 139
Bryce, Captain M. S., 328
Bucharest, Treaty of, 7
Bugeaud, Marshal, 353
Bulfin, Major-Gen. E. S., 227, 229, 263, 304
Bulgaria, Allies seek aid from or neutrality of, 26; mobilizes, 29; attacks Serbia, 33; not enthusiastic about an attack on Salonika, 105; her anxiety regarding Rumania, 121
Bulgarian Army, its dispositions for attack on Serbia, 31; advance of, 33 *et seq.*; comes into contact with French, 53; engaged with French in Vardar-Crna loop, 57 *et seq.*; its pursuit of French, 68; attacks

GENERAL INDEX 395

Bulgarian Army (*continued*)—
British at Kosturino, 69; its boldness in pursuit, 74, 75; halts on Greek frontier, 79, 81, 93; not available on other fronts, 117; strength of in May 1916, 121; good positions of, 122; occupies Fort Rupel, 124; dispositions of, 3rd August 1916, 149; crosses Greek frontier south of Monastir, 153; advances on Allied flanks, 157; digs in on Struma front, 161; occupies Kavalla, 161, 209; checked by Serbians, 161; its successes against Rumania, 163; in Struma fighting, Sept. 1916, 165; its fighting qualities, 165; transfers troops to Monastir front, 173; counter-attacks in Action of Karajaköis, 179, 181; its retirement after that action, 192; Gen. Milne's view of its weak point, 203; its loss of heart in Battle of Monastir, 235; its dispositions in that battle, 267; reinforced after Rumanian campaign, 300; its work on Dojran defences, 305, 334; its artillery in defence of Dojran position, 314, 333; strength of, in battalions, May 1917, 339
Burkett, 2/Lieut. F., 337

Cadorna, Gen., 254
Cambon, M. Paul, 137, 212
Campbell, Major W. M., 274
Captures by British, in Action of Karajaköis, 178, 184; in Affair of Bairakli Jum'a, 194, 196; in capture of "Ferdie" and Essex trenches, 338
Carter, Br.-Gen. B. C. M., 337
Castelnau, Gen. de, 92, 93
Casualties—
Austrian, in campaign of 1914, 13, 16 (*f.n.*), 20
British, in expedition into Serbia, 82; at Horseshoe Hill, 156; on Struma, 23rd September 1916, 166; in Action of Machukovo, 168; in Action of Karajaköis, 178, 184; in Affair of Bairakli Jum'a, 194; Aug.-Dec. 1916, 240; at Tumbitza Farm, 244, 249; in raid on Petit Couronné, 265; from German

Casualties (*continued*)—
British (*continued*)—
air raid, 27th Feb. 1917, 266; from gas bombardment, 17th March 1917, 300; in Dojran attack, April 1917, 316; and in May 1917, 331; in capture of "Ferdie" and Essex trenches, 338
Bulgarian, against Franco-British expedition into Serbia, 82; in Battle of Monastir, 241; in Battle of Dojran, April 1917, 316; and in May 1917, 334
French, in expedition into Serbia, 81; in Dojran operations, Aug. 1916, 154; in Battle of Monastir, 240; in attack of 9th May 1917, 341; total casualties (of Allies) in attacks of May 1917, 342
German, in Battle of Monastir, 240
Serbian, in campaign of 1914, 12, 13, 21; in campaign of 1915, 35; in Battle of Monastir, 240
Cauboue, Gen., 232, 233
Cecil, Lord Robert, 349, 352
Charles, King of Rumania, 25, 134
Charles, Lieut.-Col. E. M. S., 174
Christodoulos, Col., 209, 210.
Clarke, Br.-Gen. (later Major-Gen.) T. E., 56, 256, 270
Clausse, M. Roger, 358
Clermont-Tonnerre, Gen. de, 75, 76, 80
Command, formulas regarding, 97, 137, 150, 255
Condouriotis, Adm., 217
Conferences of Allies (Political and Military), Chantilly (7th July 1915), 22; Calais (5th Oct. 1915), 42; London (29th Oct. 1915), 44, 62; Calais (4th Dec. 1915), 48, 63; Chantilly (6th Dec. 1915), 49; Chantilly (12th March 1916), 110; London (9th June 1916), 136; Boulogne (20th Oct. 1916), 201, 219; Rome (5th Jan. 1917), 230, 254; London (26th Dec. 1916), 254; Calais (26th Feb. 1917), 296; St. Jean de Maurienne (19th April 1917), 301, 331; Paris (4th May 1917), 317, 331, 350; London (28th May 1917), 352, 355

GENERAL INDEX

Conferences of Central Powers, Pless (29th July 1916), 196; Budapest (5th Aug. 1916), 196
Conrad von Hoetzendorff, Gen., 10, 15, 23, 29, 31, 196, 197
Constantine, King of Greece, 27; orders mobilization of Army, 38; dissolves Greek Parliament, 38; asks for Allied landing to be postponed, 39; refuses to fulfil treaty obligations, 46; his interview with Lord Kitchener, 47; refuses to hand over Fort Kara Burun, 89, 100; receives Gen. Sarrail, 109; again dissolves Greek Parliament, 129; 131, 208; his overtures to Allies, 213; 215, 216; his indignation against M. Venizelos, 218; his suggestion to M. Bénazet, 221; attitude to landing of French sailors, 222; his correspondence with Kaiser, 227 (*f.n.*); 275, 348; mass meeting at Salonika demands his abdication, 350; 351, 352; Allies decide to demand his abdication, 352; his abdication demanded, 355; leaves Greece, 357, 358; 359; note demanding his abdication, 361
Consulates, Affair of the enemy, 99
Cooke, Br.-Gen. H. F., 189, 328
Cordonnier, Gen., 146, 150, 156, 158; in Battle of Monastir, 185; removed from command, 188, 234; 207
Cory, Br.-Gen. G. N., 96
Cowans, Gen. Sir. J., 269
Cox, Lieut.-Col. P. G. A., 66, 70, 71, 181, 183
Crackanthorpe, Mr. D., 358
Crewe, Marquess of, 214
Croker, Major-Gen. H. L., 127, 180, 193
Cyprus, offered to Greece, 46

D'Amade, Gen., 98
Dardanelles. *See* Gallipoli Campaign
Dartige du Fournet, Admiral, 130, 132; ordered to Salamis Bay, 212; lands sailors to guard French Legation, 215; takes conduct of Greek affairs from hands of diplomacy, 217; forces surrender of Greek fleet,

Dartige du Fournet, Admiral (*continued*)—
218; takes Greek ships into use, 220; demands warlike stores from Greece, 221, 222; lands force from fleet, 223; withdraws, 224; relieved of command, 225
Dauvé, Gen., 152
Davidson, Major-Gen. J. H., 252 (*f.n.*)
Davie, Lieut.-Col. K. M., 247, 248
Day, Captain E. C., 250
Debenham, Major F., 155
Delcassé, M. Théophile, 26
Demidov, Prince, 132
Dene, Lieut.-Col. A. P., 327
Derby, Earl of, 352
de Robeck, Vice-Admiral J. M., 41, 45, 88
Descoins, Col., 158, 160, 163, 174, 241, 260
Dessort, Gen., 341
Diadoch (Crown Prince) of Greece, 348, 350, 355, 356, 361
Dietrichs, Gen., 343
Dojran, operations of Aug. 1916, 152 *et seq.*; Battle of, April 1917, 302 *et seq.*; May 1917, 317 *et seq.*
Dousmanis, Gen., 212 (*f.n.*)
Drage, Lieut.-Col. G., 70
Drina, Battles of the, 11
Duncan (British battleship), 223
Duncan, Br.-Gen. J., 154, 155, 306, 321

Eassie, Br.-Gen. F., 291
Edwards, Br.-Gen. FitzJ. M., 227, 330
Egypt, administration of British Salonika Army from, 97, 100, 141, 172
Eley, Major D. R. A., 262
Elliot, Sir F., 26, 39, 47, 88, 122, 208, 210; his recommendations in Aug. 1916, 211, 213; his opinion of M. Zaimis's resignation, 216; describes "reign of terror" against Venizelists, 217; presses King Constantine to dissolve reservist societies, 218; suggests expulsion of enemy Ministers, 220; his knowledge of Royalist plot, 223; leaves Legation, 224; his protests against treatment of Venizelists, 348; 349; recalled, 351

GENERAL INDEX 397

Emery, Br.-Gen. W. E., 174
Engineers, Royal, Army Troops Coys. sent, 142 ; bridging of Struma, Sept. 1916, 175 ; wiring in action of Karajaköis, 178 ; bridging of Struma for attack on Bairakli Jum'a, 193 ; at Tumbitza Farm, 246, 247 ; and water supply, 285. *See also* Road work, Seres road
Entrenched Camp of Salonika, formation of the, 85 *et seq.* ; advance from, 104 *et seq.* ; strength of, 105
Enver Pasha, 196
Essad Pasha, 35
Essex Trench. *See* " Ferdie " Trench
Eugene, Archduke, 20
Everett, Br.-Gen. H. J., 96
Exmouth (British battleship), 223

Fair, Lieut.-Col. F. K., 73
Falconar Stewart, Lieut.-Col. R., 324, 326
Falkenhayn, Gen. von, launches offensive of Gorlice, 23 ; his plans regarding Serbia, 29 ; 30, 31, 37 ; decides against attack on Entrenched Camp, 106 ; turns to Western Front, 107 ; 117 (*f.n.*), 133 ; his plans regarding Rumania, 196, 197 ; in command against Rumania, 198 ; his comment on difficulty of German communications with Macedonia, 207
" Ferdie " and Essex Trenches, capture of, 336
Ferdinand, Tsar of Bulgaria, 28 ; orders mobilization, 29
Ferrero, Gen., 260
Finch, 2/Lieut. G. J., 274
Fleuriau, M. de, 137
Flying Corps, Royal, aircraft sent, 143 ; 152, 266, 296. *See also* Index of Arms, Formations and Units
Foch, Gen., 353
Forestier-Walker, Major-Gen. G. T., 335
France, promises troops to aid Serbia, 39 ; differences of opinion with Britain as to campaign, Nov. 1915, 49 ; alarmed for safety of her force, Nov. 1915, 62 ; result of clash of her policy with British, 84 ;

France (*continued*)—
her arguments in favour of offensive, April 1916, 116, 121 ; urges reinforcement in Macedonia, 201 ; her action against Greece, Aug.–Sept. 1916, 212 *et seq.* ; her attitude to Greek Note of Sept. 1916, 216 ; her attitude to M. Venizelos, 221, 352 ; demands warlike stores from Greece, 221 ; her attitude at Rome Conference, 230, 254 ; brings offensive of May 1917 to an end, 341 ; effect of M. Briand's resignation on her Greek policy, 348 ; empowered to speak for Great Britain in Greece, 351 ; determined to depose King Constantine, 352 ; consideration of her action in Greece, 358
Franchet d'Espèrey, Gen., 98
Frank, Gen., 19, 20
Franz Ferdinand, Archduke, 8
French Army, first troops to land at Salonika, 33, 42 ; reinforcements sent to, 52 ; moves up into Serbia, 52 *et seq.* ; its operations in Varda–Crna loop, 56 *et seq.* ; and north of Lake Dojran, 58 ; its retreat from Serbia, 62, 66, 74 ; its rôle in offensive to aid Rumania, 146. *See also* Armée d'Orient, *and* Armée Française d'Orient
French Government. *See* France
French, Field-Marshal Sir J. D. P., 38, 44
Frotiée, Gen., 111, 148, 156, 157, 158
Fuller, Br.-Gen. F. G., 95 (*f.n.*)

Gabbett, Lieut.-Col. A. C., 76
Galliéni, Gen., 48 (*f.n.*), 353
Gallipoli Campaign, 27, 37, 39, 43 ; Gen. Monro recommends evacuation, 45 ; orders for evacuation of Suvla and Anzac, 50 ; 64, 84, 86, 95 ; evacuation of Suvla and Anzac, 96 ; and of Helles, 97, 118
Gallwitz, Gen. von, 23, 29, 33, 106, 235
Gančev, Col., 28, 196
Garsia, Major W. C., 37, 166
Gauchet, Adm., 354
Gay, Major-Gen. A. W., 306, 310, 311, 315, 320, 325, 327, 328
Gekov, Gen., 235

Gennadius, M., 214, 219
German Army, takes part in campaign against Serbia, 30 *et seq.*; troops advance to Greek frontier, 111; divisions withdrawn from, 121; reinforces Monastir front, 173, 235; in action at Hill 1050, 260; saves Bulgarians in Crna bend, May 1917, 344
Gérôme, Gen., 79 (*f.n.*), 154, 339
Gešov, Gen., 235
Gill, Lieut. J. E., 57 (*f.n.*)
Gillman, Major-Gen. W., 124, 256, 319, 346
Gloag, Major M. W., 326
Gordon, Major-Gen. Hon. F., 73, 74, 75, 76, 78, 80, 85, 113, 114, 167, 189, 320
Gorlice, The Break-through of, 23
Gottwaltz, Major P., 330
Gouraud, Gen., 37, 98, 256
Graham, Captain J. G., 326, 327
Grand Couronné, 152; described, 305
Granville, Earl of, 230, 348, 349, 350, 358
Graz, Sir C. des, 26, 28
Great Britain, attitude of to campaign in Macedonia, 43, 48, 49, 50, 82; declares war on Bulgaria, 43; agrees to co-operate with France in Macedonia, 44; her reply to Greek threat, 46; her demands, 47; refuses to consider offensive, 108, 116; growing divergence of her policy from French, 118, 121; proposes an offensive after Battle of Somme, 136; agrees to offensive when Rumania enters war, 137, 138; her attitude on Greek affairs, Aug. 1916, 212; Note to Greece by, 2nd Sept. 1916, 214; protests against seizure of Greek fleet, 218; ultimatum to Greece, 14th Dec. 1916, 224; and of 8th Jan. 1917, 231; demands that Gen. Sarrail shall launch attack, 301, 317, 318, 343; hands over control of policy in Greece to France, 351; against a disembarkation at Piræus, 355; justification of her policy, 358
Greece, negotiations with in 1915, 26; refuses to aid Serbia, 32; mobilizes, 38; terms of her treaty with Serbia, 38; threat of her Government to intern

Greece (*continued*)—
Allied troops, 46; comes to an agreement, 48; her attitude regarding railways, 54, 89, 276; attitude of her troops during reteat of Allies, 78; protests against expulsion of enemy consuls, 99; her promise of neutrality to Germany, 107; refuses to allow Serbians to go overland to Salonika, 119; attitude regarding Fort Rupel, 124, 130, 132; obtains loan from Germany, 130; Note addressed to, 21st June 1916, 132; agrees to comply with demands of Allies, 133; demobilizes, 145; Allies' relations with after Bulgarian advance, Aug. 1916, 208 *et seq.*; her rôle in this advance, 210; her offer to Allies, 214, 216; concentrates troops at Larissa, 218, 226; seizure of her fleet, 218, 220; British reply to her offer, 219; Ministers of hostile Powers ordered to leave, 220; refuses to hand over warlike stores, 223; affair of the landing parties, 1st Dec. 1916, 223; accepts Allied ultimatum, 232; transports her Army to Morea, 232; her ceremony of reparation for events of 1st Dec. 1916, 233; split into two camps, 348; crisis in May 1917, 351 *et seq.*; deposition of King Constantine, 356; consideration of Allied action in, 358
Greek National (Venizelist) Forces, 174, 220, 225, 241, 245, 257
Grey, Sir Edward (later Viscount), his offer to Greece in 1915, 26, 27; his offer to Serbia, 28; dissuades Serbia from attacking Bulgaria, 31; discusses landing at Salonika, 39; his speech alarms M. Venizelos, 40; his urgent appeal to Greece, 46; 48, 49; his action after Rupel incident, 132; 137, 138; his attitude to Greece in Sept. 1916, 213, 217; protests against seizure of Greek fleet, 218; draws up ultimatum to Greece, 224
Grimwood, Lieut.-Col. J., 330
Groener, Gen., 106
Grossetti, Gen., 255, 294, 339, 340
Guillaumat, Gen., 98
Guillemin, M., 47, 88, 130, 132, 214, 224, 351

GENERAL INDEX

Hadzapoulos, Col., 161, 210
Haig, Gen. Sir D., 96, 137, 201, 252
Hall, Captain G. F., 159
Hall, Col. W. K. E., 256 (*f.n.*)
Hamilton, Br.-Gen. A. B., 40
Hamilton, Gen. Sir Ian, 37, 40, 42 (*f.n.*), 43, 98, 255
Hammond, Col. F. D., 277
Hammond, Lieut. J. M., 265 (*f.n.*)
Hanbury, Lieut.-Col. P. L., 325
Hardinge of Penhurst, Lord, 137, 216
Hardman-Jones, Lieut.-Col. A. C. L. 164
Hare, Br.-Gen. R. H., 299
Hare, Br.-Gen. S. W., 90
Harrison, Lieut.-Col. A. P. B., 22, 24, 28
Harvey, Lieut.-Col. J., 324
Hayes-Sadler, Rear-Adm. A., 212
Hentsch, Lieut.-Col., 30
Herbert, Br.-Gen. L. N., 73, 166, 167
Hermannstadt, Battle of, 199
Hickman, Br.-Gen. H. O. D., 113
Hindenburg, Field-Marshal von, 198
Hippel, Major-Gen. von, 235
Hoffmann, Major-Gen. Max, 106
Homan, Major A. D., 323
Horseshoe Hill, capture of, 154
Howard, Lieut.-Col. T. N. S. M., 264, 307, 308, 311, 321, 323, 324, 325
Howell, Br.-Gen. P., 51, 124
Hudson, Lieut.-Col. A. R., 173 (*f.n.*)
Hunter, Lieut.-Col. C. G. W., 91
Hydra (Greek coast-defence ship), 217

Inspector-General of Communications, appointed, 143; office abolished, 256
Iskanderun, suggested landing in Gulf of, 45, 56 (*f.n.*), 84, 86
Italy, enters the war, 22, 29; her attitude to Salonika campaign, 108; her occupation of Albanian coast, 110; declares war on Germany, 139; sends a division to Salonika, 146; refuses to send further troops, 205; is suspicious of M. Venizelos, 231; and of French in Albania, 260; her contingent in attack of May 1917, 340; her attitude to Gen. Sarrail, 345; sends troops into Epirus, 357

Jackson, Adm. Sir H. B., 44
Jellicoe, Adm. Sir J., 352
Joffre, Gen., 38, 44, 58, 62; C.-in-C. of all French Armies, 92; his estimate of force required for offensive, 108, 110, 123; definitely favours offensive, 116, 136; 137; calls for Gen. Sarrail's plan, 145, 151; differs from Gen. Robertson regarding Rumanian convention, 156; 188; decides to increase strength of French contingent, 202; his last directive to Gen. Sarrail, 253; removed from command, 256
Johnson, D. W. (*quoted*), 29 (*f.n.*)
Jonnart, M. Charles, High Commissioner of Powers in Greece, 353; decides to bring troops to Piræus, 354; demands abdication of King Constantine, 355; raises blockade of Greece, 356; withdraws, 358; his Note demanding King's abdication, 361
Jourdain, Lieut.-Col. H. F. N., 70
Jurišić-Sturm, Gen., 158

Kalogeropoulos, M., 216
Kara Burun, Fort, 88, 100
Karajaköis, Action of the, 173
Kelly, Br.-Gen. H. E. T., 152, 193
Ker, 2/Lieut. C. P., 323
Keyes, Commodore Roger, 45, 48, 50
King-King, Br.-Gen. J. G., 66, 69, 72, 87
Kirk, Lieut.-Col. J. W. C., 243, 244, 248
Kirkness, Lieut.-Col. L. H., 274 (*f.n.*)
Kitchener, Field-Marshal Lord, 24; dissuades Serbia from attacking Bulgaria, 31; discusses Mediterranean question with French authorities, 38; suggests despatch of troops to Salonika, 39; promises further troops, 42; cancels moves, 42; orders moves to proceed, 43; refuses to order evacuation of Gallipoli, 45; visits Mediterranean, 45; suggests landing in Gulf of Iskanderun, 45; visits Salonika, 46; visits Athens, 47; 48; visits Paris to discuss Macedonian campaign, 49; permits Gen. Mahon to enter Serbia, 54; 55, 63, 92, 95
Koe, Major-Gen. F. W. B., 143, 256 (*f.n.*)

Koebel, Lieut.-Col. F. O., 308
Kolubara, Battle of the, 16
Kosturino, Action of, 64 *et seq.*
Kövess, Gen. von, 29
Kronstadt, Battle of, 200
Kut, retreat on, 48; siege of, 50; surrender of, 118

Lacaze, Adm., 48, 201
Lambert, Lieut.-Col. W. J., 167
Lambros, Professor, 218, 349
Lance, Br.-Gen. F. FitzH., 244
Lardemelle, Gen. de, 59, 60, 61, 79 (*f.n.*)
Lawrence, Major C. T., 168
Leave, to Salonika, 105; to United Kingdom, 258
Leblois, Gen., 57, 59, 62, 67, 79, 80, 188, 234
Lebouc, Gen., 255, 339, 340, 344, 345
Leontiev, Gen., 343
Levant Base, and British Salonika Army, 96, 101
Lewis, Pte. H. W., V.C., 191
Livingstone, Br.-Gen. H. A. A., 281, 286
Lloyd George, Rt. Hon. D., proposes despatch of troops to Salonika in Jan. 1915, 26; 49; refuses " free hand " to Gen. Sarrail, 231; his attitude to Macedonian campaign, 252, 283; advocates despatch of British troops to Italy, 254; decides to withdraw British troops, 301; 317, 350
London, Treaty of, 27
Long, Br.-Gen. A., 282
Long, Lieut.-Col. W. J., 159
Longley, Br.-Gen. (later Major-Gen.) J. R., 87, 90, 128
Lyautey, Gen., 225, 231, 353

Macdonald, Lieut.-Col. A. C., 36
Macedonia—
  Boundaries of, 1
  Climate of, 127, 261, 294, 340
  Communications in, 52, 82, 274, 280
  History of, 3
  Nature of country, north of Lake Dojran, 64; in general, 122; west of Vardar, 185; west of Lake Dojran, 304
  Races of, 3
  See also Malaria, Salonika
Machukovo, Action of, 166

Mackensen, Gen. (afterwards Field-Marshal) von, 23; in command against Serbia, 29, 31, 33; in command of southern forces against Rumania, 197, 199, 200
Mackenzie-Kennedy, Major-Gen. E. C. W., 85, 261, 306
Maclachlan, Major A. F. C., 159
Macpherson, Col. (later Br.-Gen.) A. D., 180, 183
Macpherson, Surg.-Gen. W. G., 289
Mahon, Lieut.-Gen. Sir B., 42, 43; gets permission to advance into Serbia, 46, 54; 51; asks for new transport establishment, 55; 58, 65; urges retirement from Serbia, 68; his anxiety for 10th Division, 69; reinforces 10th Division, 71; places Major-Gen. Gordon in command of troops in Serbia, 73; 87; reconnoitres line of Entrenched Camp, 89; orders work on defences to begin, 90; extends defences to Ægean, 92; 93, 94, 95, 97; protests regarding affair of enemy consulates, 99; and against occupation of Fort Kara Burun, 100; his view of strength of Entrenched Camp, 106, 107; 108; his view of possibility of offensive, 109, 123; 111, 114; to Egypt, 115; his good work in Macedonia, 115; 118, 123, 140, 157
Malaria in Macedonia, 3, 102; in Struma valley in 1916, 128, 143, 241; precautions against, 128, 287; incidence of, 288
Marquette (Troopship), 82 (*f.n.*)
Marshall, Major-Gen. W. R., 96, 163, 173
Mathew, Br.-Gen. C. M., 101, 273
Martial Law (state of siege) at Salonika, 130
Maxwell, Lieut.-Gen. Sir J., 43, 45, 96
Maynard, Lieut.-Col. (later Br.-Gen.) C. C. M., 186, 344 (*f.n.*)
Mazarakis, Col., 209
Medical Services, 143, 287; medical pack transport, 289. *See also* Malaria
Mercati, Count, 223
Michaud, Gen., 345
Millerand, M. Alexandre, 23, 37, 38, 42

GENERAL INDEX 401

Milne, Major-Gen. (later Lieut.-Gen.) G. F., 85; appointed to command XVI Corps, 95; 98; succeeds Gen. Mahon in command of Army, 115; 123, 124; is warned not to be drawn into an offensive, 125; demands definite zone, 125; dislikes proclamation of martial law, 131; 132; his position as regards Gen. Sarrail, 137, 146, 150; 140; concerned by incidence of malaria, 144; 145; relieves French troops east of Vardar, 147; his embarrassing position, Aug. 1916, 154, 156; 158, 159, 160; relieves further French troops, 161, 162; 165, 169; orders Gen. Briggs to take the offensive, 172; 175; relieves further French troops, 188; orders capture of Bairakli Jum'a, 191; informed of arrival of 60th Div., 202; his appreciation, Oct. 1916, 203; his opinion of Greek concentration in Thessaly, 218 (f.n.); 226; instructed to support Venizelist movement, 225; sends a brigade to Thessaly, 227; attends Rome Conference, 230; 236, 239, 249, 252; on possibility of Bulgarian attack down Vardar, 253; 257, 258, 261, 263; demands return of brigade from Thessaly, 266; his dispute with Gen. Sarrail about landing facilities, 267; his instructions regarding economy, 270; 279, 283; his methods of cutting down transport, 284; prefers to attack at Dojran rather than on Struma, 295; his indefinite instructions from home, 296; obtains aircraft from Navy, 297; learns of postponement of main attack, 301; his instructions regarding attack, 302, 306; his comments on attack of 24th April 1917, 314; explains his action to Gen. Robertson, 317; decides to continue offensive, 318; brings offensive to an end, 331; 332; his opinion of Bulgarian troops, 334; 335; cancels attack on Erneköi, 338; decides to withdraw from Struma valley, 338; his view of failure of main attack, 342

Mišić, Gen. (later Voivode), 15, 17, 19

Monastir, Battle of, 184 *et seq.*, 234 *et seq.*; capture of, 238
Mondésir, Gen. de, 36, 37, 120
Monro, Gen. Sir C., 43, 45; proposed for command at Salonika, 55; in command of Mediterranean forces, 56, 87, 95; at Salonika, 88; returns to France, 96; 115
Montenegro, ally of Serbia, 8, 9; in campaign of 1914, 13; in that of 1915, 32; overrun by Austrians, 36
Moore-Gwyn, Major H. G., 357
Moreau, Vice-Adm., 133
Morris, Lieut.-Col. (later Br.-Gen.) E. M., 87, 164
Moschopoulos, Gen., 212 (f.n.), 213
Murray, Lieut.-Gen. (later Gen.) Sir A. J., 44, 49; appointed to command in Egypt, 96; in control of administration at Salonika, 97; 115, 141, 252

Navy, the, at Salonika, 47 (f.n.); institutes partial blockade of Greece, 131; carries out demonstration off Piræus, 133; its part in landing of Dec. 1916, 223; aids Salonika Army with aeroplanes, 297
Nicholas, Grand Duke, 22
Nicholas II., Tsar of Russia, 202
Nicol, Br.-Gen. L. L., 54, 56, 65, 66, 69, 71, 72, 75, 76, 78, 80, 87, 180
Nisbet, Lieut.-Col. F. C., 309, 310
Nivelle, Gen., 255, 256
Norseman (Troopship), torpedoed, 85, 100 (f.n.)

O'Beirne, Mr. H. J., 28, 31
O'Brien, Lieut. J., 244
Ordnance services, 101, 272

"P" (or Pip) Ridge, 152; described, 304; 312
Pack transport. *See* Transport
Painlevé, M. Paul, 348, 352
Pallis, Lieut.-Col., 48, 88, 90
Pavlović, Lieut.-Col., 31
Perceval, Br.-Gen. C. J., 95
Peter, King of Serbia, 19
Petit Couronné, 154, 156, 264; attack on, 24th April 1917, 307; and on 8th May 1917, 322
Petitti, Gen., 234
Philip of Macedon, 3
Phillips, Col. (later Br.-Gen.) G. F., 31, 232
Pike, Captain S. A., 328

Pitcairn, Lieut.-Col. G. S., 281
Plunkett, Lieut.-Col. E. A., 344
Poincaré, M. Raymond, 202
Polites, M. Nicolas, 216, 276
Pont, Col., 44 (*f.n.*)
Poole, Br.-Gen. A. J., 306, 308, 310, 311
Porro, Gen., 110
Potiorek, Feldzeugmeister, 10, 12, 13, 14, 16, 18, 19, 20, 30
Protecting Powers (with reference to Greece), 132, 219, 352, 361
Provisional Government at Salonika, 225; recognized by Allies, 230; islands declare for, 230, 257; 360
Putnik, Voivode (Marshal), 9, 11, 13, 14, 15, 17, 19, 24, 31, 34, 58, 120

Radoslavov, M., 27
Railways, attitude of officials on, 53; Greek Government takes control of, 54; carrying-power of, 83; 89; French guard bridges on Monastir line, 113; 129; general system of, 274; Allies take over, 277; new construction on, 278, 279; light railways, 278
Ravenshaw, Major-Gen. H. S. L., 173, 177, 180, 184, 241, 243, 245
Regnault, Gen., 111, 339, 354, 358
Retreat from Serbia. *See* Serbia
Ribot, M. Alexandre, 201, 302, 348, 352
Richardson, Br.-Gen. G. S., 95
Road work in Macedonia, 90, 128, 129, 280
Roberts, Br.-Gen. A. C., 159
Robertson, Gen. Sir W. R., appointed C.I.G.S., 96; against an offensive, 109, 110, 124; promises to make Salonika Army more mobile, 111; considers limited offensive, 112; 116; his grave view of Gen. Sarrail's plans, 125; 131; his instructions to Gen. Milne, Aug. 1916, 154; differs from Gen. Joffre as to Rumanian convention, 156; gives away about despatch of 60th Div., 202; his *mot* regarding M. Venizelos, 231; desires Macedonian front to be shortened, 252; 267, 295; considers campaign has "no military justification," 302; leaves continuance of Dojran attack to Gen. Milne's judgment, 317; 334

Robinson, Lieut.-Col. A. T., 155, 327, 329
Roques, Gen., 201 (*f.n.*), 207, 221
Ross, Br.-Gen. W. C., 298
Ruef, Col., 75
Rumania, prospects of intervention of, 116, 121, 133; signs military convention, 138, 153, 170; declares war on Austria-Hungary, 139; will not attack south of Danube, 154; her campaign against Central Powers, 196
Rupel, Fort, occupation of by Bulgarians, 124; effects of surrender of, 130, 132, 222
Russian Brigades, arrival of 1st, 145, 146; in Battle of Monastir, 185, 186; second brigade promised, 205; arrives, 238; brigades attached to Serbian Armies, 239; in attack of May 1917, 340; appearance of Bolshevism in, 343; detachment from at Piræus, 357
Russo-Turkish War of 1877, 5
Rycroft, Major-Gen. W. H., 256

Salaün, Rear-Adm., 354
Salonika, importance of, 2; first proposal to land troops at, 26; landing of Franco-British force at, 33, 37 *et seq.*; pessimistic British estimate of port, 44, 62; situation at in Oct. 1915, 51; its advantages from Allies' point of view, 83, 89; natural defences of, 89; air raids on, 94, 104, 114; life at, 104; water-supply of, 128; force required for defence of, 204; Venizelist revolt at, 209; arrival of M. Venizelos at, 217; Venizelist mass meeting at, 350. *See also* Macedonia
San Stefano, Treaty of, 5
Sarrail, Gen., 37, 38; despatches troops into Serbia, 43, 52; 48, 53; asks for British assistance, 54; his plan to aid Serbians, 58; orders preparations for retreat from Vardar–Crna loop, 62; 65, 67, 68; his coolness during retreat, 74, 79, 98; 80; gives orders to take up new line of defence, 81, 88; 93; blows up Demir-Hisar bridge, 94; appointed C.-in-C. of Allies, 92, 103; characteristics of, 97; expels enemy consuls, 99; occupies Fort Kara Burun, 100; considers

GENERAL INDEX 403

Sarrail, Gen. (*continued*)—
possibility of offensive, 103;
visits King Constantine, 109;
said to have misunderstood
instructions, 109; orders advance
from Entrenched Camp, 111, 113,
114; his plan in May 1916, 123;
126; proclaims state of siege
at Salonika, 130, 277; new
definition of his relationship with
Gen. Milne, 137, 150; his plan
to aid Rumania, 145, 146, 147;
requests Gen. Milne to relieve
French troops, 147; postpones
attack, Aug. 1916, 153; 154, 156;
his first action after Bulgarian
advance, 157, 169; his later
plan, 158, 184, 186; 160, 166;
his dissatisfaction with Gen.
Cordonnier, 186; asks for British
assistance in Battle of Monastir,
188; British memorandum on
his conduct of the campaign,
207; 208; his aid for Venizelist
revolt, 209, 213, 215; his proposals for dealing with Royalists
in Thessaly, 226; at Rome
Conference, 230; 233; his conduct
of Battle of Monastir, 234, 236;
decides to break off battle, 239;
249, 252, 253, 254; his position
affected by resignation of Gen.
Joffre, 256; extends left to cover
Santi Quaranta route, 259; refuses to return British brigade
in Thessaly, 266; vetoes British
port arrangements, 267; his
projects for 1917, 294; meets
Gen. Milne's wishes regarding
Dojran attack, 295; breaks off
minor operations at Monastir,
296; postpones main attack, 301,
317; decides not to continue
operations in hot weather, 319;
brings offensive to an end, 331;
335, 341, 343; lack of confidence
in, 345; 346, 349, 350; to act
under orders of M. Jonnart, 353;
sends troops to Piræus, 354

Sazonov, M., 26
Schenk, Baron, 132 (*f.n.*).
Scholtz, Gen. von, 340
Scott-Hopkins, Major R., 190, 357
Seeckt, Gen. von, 29
Senussi, the Grand, 50
Serbia, attempts to conciliate Bulgaria, 28; demands Allied aid,
31; prepares to meet Bulgarian
offensive, 32; terms of her treaty

Serbia (*continued*)—
with Greece, 38; Allied advance
into, 50 *et seq.*; Allied retreat
from, 67 *et seq.*; consideration
of expedition into, 81; revolt in,
March 1917, 300
Serbian Army, situation of in 1914,
8; its advance into Syrmia, 12;
and into Bosnia, 13; is defeated
on the Drina, 15; in Battle of
the Kolubara, 16; victory of, 20;
state of in early 1915, 22;
dispositions of in Oct. 1915, 32;
defeat of, 33; its retreat to
Adriatic, 34; losses of, 35;
transported to Corfu, 36; transported to Salonika, 119; deaths
in at Corfu, 119; strength of on
arrival at Salonika, 120; its rôle
in offensive to aid Rumania, 145;
attacked by Bulgarians, 157;
succeeds in checking Bulgarian
advance, 161; its part in Battle
of Monastir, 184, 235; reduction
of battalions in, 257; in attacks
of May 1917, 341; refuses to
continue offensive, 343
Seres road, 128, 250, 280
Shipping. *See* Transport by Sea
Signal communications, 129, 152,
332
Sir Thomas Picton (British Monitor),
161
Skouloudis, M., 46, 47, 130, 133
Somme, Battle of the, 135
Sphacteria (Greek yacht), 358
Struma valley, British troops enter,
126; withdrawal from to higher
ground, July 1916, 144; occupation of Neohori position in, 147,;
minor operations in, Sept. 1916,
164; Action of the Karajaköis,
173; Affair of Bairakli Jum'a,
193; minor operations in, Nov.-
Dec. 1916, 241; large operations
impossible in winter, 295; capture of "Ferdie" and Essex
Trenches, May 1917, 334;
decision to withdraw from, May
1917, 338. *See also* Malaria

Taranto route, 258, 270, 290
Targu Jiu, Battles of, 200
Taylor, Br.-Gen. F. P. S., 36
Tersztyánsky, Gen. von, 29 (*f.n.*).
Thessalian harvest, problem of, 349,
353, 355
Thomas, M. Albert, 49, 201 (*f.n.*).
Thomson, Lieut.-Col. C. B., 139

GENERAL INDEX

Thursby, Vice-Adm. Sir C., 297
Tisza, Count, 29 (f.n.)
Todorov, Gen. 31, 60, 61
Townshend, Major-Gen. Sir C. V. F., 48, 50
Transport, first changes in British establishment, 55; lack of motor lorries in early stages, 88; transfer to pack establishment, 112, 121, 128; completed, 140; deficiencies in June 1916, 128; effect of lorries on roads, 280; growth of mechanical transport, 282; cutting-down of pack transport, early 1917, 282; medical pack transport, 289
Transport by rail. *See* Railways
Transport by sea, 86; losses of ships in Mediterranean, 254, 268, 270; general conditions of, 269 *et seq.*, 302
Tumbitza Farm, operations at, 242
Turkish Revolution, the, 6
Turkish troops in Macedonia, 193, 249, 268, 300

United States, declaration of war by, 360

Vandeleur, Br.-Gen. R. S., 66, 73, 78, 80, 174, 337
Vardar corridor, the, 2, 3, 5, 29, 53
Vardar–Crna loop, French operations in, 33, 53, 56 *et seq.*; French retreat from, 67
Venel, Gen., 355, 357
Venizelos, M. Eleutheros, seeks support of Rumania, 26; first resignation of, 26; returns to office, 38; mobilizes Greek Army, 38; asks for Allied aid, 39; is alarmed by speech of Sir E. Grey, 40; again resigns, 41, 42; boycotts elections, 129, 132; comment of on Rupel incident, 133; 174, 208, 210, 211, 215; at Salonika, 217, 225; 218; 220; islands declare for, 230; 257; considers King should abdicate, 348; on Thessalian harvest, 349; 352; delays return to Athens, 357; takes office as Prime Minister, 358; 359
Verdun, Battle of, 109, 121
Verité (French Cruiser), 354

Veterinary services, 291
Via Egnatia, 2
Voelckers, Lieut.-Col., 106 (f.n.)

War Cabinet, first meeting of, 224; its policy in Macedonia, 252, 302; 317; its decision regarding deposition of King Constantine, 352
War Committee, first meeting of, 45; memorandum by, 116, 124; considers action on Rumanian intervention, 137; considers Greek Note, 214, 216; dissolution of, 224
Water supply, 285
Weir, Br.-Gen. G. A., 164, 246, 249
Wemyss, Rear-Adm. R. E., 50
Wheeler, Major C., 323
White, Lieut. J. B., 332
White Thomson, Br.-Gen. H. D., 303, 304
Widdrington, Br.-Gen. B. F., 174, 176
William II., German Emperor, 198, 227 (f.n.)
William of Wied, Prince, 35
Williamson Oswald, Col. O. C., 304
Willyams, Major E. N., 244
Wilson, Lieut.-Gen. Sir H. F. M., 55; appointed to command XII Corps, 95; 96, 147, 152; asked by French to attack Petit Couronné, Aug. 1916, 154; orders capture of Horseshoe Hill, 155; orders continued pressure on enemy, Oct. 1916, 188; in command while Gen. Milne is at Rome Conference, 261; prepares to attack at Dojran, 295; his orders, 302, 306; prepares for second attack, 319
Winckler, Lieut.-Gen. von, 235

Yarde-Buller, Br.-Gen. Hon. H., 109
Yeniköi, capture of, 180

Zaimis, M., 46, 129, 133, 208, 210, 212, 216; in office, May 1917, 349, 354; receives demand for King's abdication, 355; persuades King to abdicate, 356; 357, 361
Zimbrakakis, Col., 209

INDEX TO
ARMS, FORMATIONS, AND UNITS.

Artillery—
  Anti-Aircraft Sections, Garrison.
    No. 24—127; No. 32—127;
    No. 73—142; No. 74—142
  Batteries, Field—
    99th—159; 100th—262
  Batteries, Garrison, Heavy—
    13th—88, 127, 162; 18th—88,
    127, 162; 20th—88, 127, 162;
    143rd—142, 160, 162, 173,
    193, 335; 153rd—142, 160,
    162, 173, 193, 246, 335, 336
  Batteries, Garrison, Mountain—
    2nd—88, 142; 5th—88, 142;
    7th—88, 142, 193; Argyll—
    142, 173, 176, 193; Bute—
    142; Ross and Cromarty—142
  Batteries, Garrison, Siege—
    43rd—88, 127, 152, 162, 335;
    84th—88, 127; 127th—142,
    162, 173, 193, 335; 130th—
    142, 162, 246, 298; 132nd—
    142, 162, 190; 134th—142,
    162, 193, 298; 138th—142,
    162, 298
  Brigades, Field—
    I—160, 173, 246; XXXI—
    192; LIV—50, 66, 75, 173;
    LVII—50, 54, 66, 70, 173;
    LXVII—173; LXVIII—50,
    66, 78, 79, 80, 81, 173, 195,
    335; XCVIII—154; XCIX
    —153, 168; CI—85, 154;
    CXV—155, 332; CXXIX—
    243, 246; CXLVI—192;
    CCCII—227
  Brigade, Garrison, Mountain—
    IV Highland—142, 258
  Groups, Heavy Artillery—
    XX—127, 162, 246, 335;
    XXXVII—127, 152, 162,
    172, 175, 298, 303; LXI—
    162, 167; LXXV—303;
    LXXXII—303
Cavalry—
  Brigades (Yeomanry)—
    7th Mounted, 107, 111, 113, 126,
    127, 147, 148, 157, 158, 160,
    163, 164, 166, 184, 192, 195,
    196, 219, 243, 244, 247, 262,
    318

Cavalry (*continued*)—
  Brigades (Yeomanry) (*continued*)—
    8th Mounted, 188, 202, 251,
    252, 263, 307, 318
  Regiments (Yeomanry)—
    1/1st Derbyshire, 144, 166, 244,
    262
    Composite Regt., 51, 78, 107
    1/1st County of London
    (Middlesex), 263
    1/1st Lothians and Border
    Horse, 144, 166
    Nottinghamshire—
      1/1st Sherwood Rangers, 126,
      127, 158, 247
      1/1st South Notts Hussars,
      126, 144, 247, 257
    1/1st Surrey, 147, 159, 192
Corps—
  XII, formation, 95; 112, 125,
    126; its dispositions on 3rd
    Aug. 1916, 148; rôle of, Aug.
    1916, 152; extends left to
    Vardar, 161; its dispositions
    at end of Aug. 1916, 161;
    extends right, 162; minor
    operations in Oct. 1916, 188;
    minor operations, Nov.-Dec.
    1916, 250; minor operations,
    Jan.-Feb. 1917, 262; prepares
    for Dojran attack, 298; its
    attack, April 1917, 302 *et seq.*;
    and in May 1917, 317 *et seq.*
  XVI, formation, 95; 125, 126;
    its dispositions on 3rd Aug.
    1916, 147; its dispositions in
    Sept. 1916, 161; demonstrations on Struma by, 162; in
    Action of the Karajakôis, 173
    et seq.; in capture of Bairakli
    Jum'a, 192; minor operations,
    Nov.-Dec. 1916, 241 *et seq.*;
    and in Jan.-Feb. 1917, 261;
    its dependence on Seres road,
    280; detaches troops to XII
    Corps, 298; its rôle in April
    1917, 299, 319; its operations
    in May 1917, 334
Divisions—
  10th (Irish), arrival, 40, 42, 50;
    begins move into Serbia, 55;

Divisions (*continued*)—
10th (Irish) (*continued*)—
relieves French troops, 59; sickness in, 64; in Action of Kosturino, 65; rear-guard actions of, 70; its retreat into Greece, 71; condition in Nov. 1915, 87; 91; takes over defence of Rendina and Eiri Dere valleys, 92, 94; withdrawn to reserve, 107; in Struma valley, 125; malaria in, 127, 144; 147, 148, 158, 160; in minor operations on Struma, 163; 166; in Action of the Karajaköis, 173 *et seq.*; 192, 193; minor operations, 31st Oct. 1916, 195; change in composition of infantry, 202; minor operations, Nov. 1916, 242, 245; 258, 299, 301, 335; capture of Kyupri and other minor operations, May 1917, 335

11th (Northern), 40

13th (Western), 40

22nd, arrival, 52, 55, 65, 85; a detachment in Serbia, 71, 73, 75, 76; in retreat on Salonika, 80, 87; in Entrenched Camp, 90, 95; begins advance from Entrenched Camp, 113; 125, 126, 127, 142, 148; in Dojran operations, Aug. 1916, 152; in Action of Machukovo, 166; raids, Oct. 1916, 189; raids, Nov. 1916, 250; raid, Feb. 1917, 265; 298, 300, 303; dispositions before Battle of Dojran, April 1917, 307, 312; in attack of 24th April 1917, 312, 319; rôle in May attack, 320; operations May 1917, 328

26th, arrival, 55, 56 (*f.n.*), 65, 85; in Entrenched Camp, 90; 95; in Army reserve, 125; 127, 142; on Dojran front, 148, 152, 162 (*f.n.*); raids, Dec. 1916, 251; raid on Petit Couronné, 10th Feb. 1917, 264; constructs Yanesh-Kalinova light railway, 278; 298; in Battle of Dojran, attack of 24th April 1917, 303 *et seq.*; and attack of 8th May 1917, 319 *et seq.*, 331

27th, 45, 56 (*f.n.*); arrival, 65, 85; in reserve at Lembet, 90; 95; relieves 10th Div. in

Divisions (*continued*)—
27th (*continued*)—
Rendina and Eiri Dere valleys, 107, 126; dispositions 3rd Aug. 1916, 147; 80th Brigade's raids on Angista bridges, 159; 160, 163, 164; in Action of the Karajaköis, 173 *et seq.*; in minor operations on Struma, 195; change in composition of infantry, 202 (*f.n.*); 241; in Tumbitza Farm operations, 242, 246; 262, 299, 335

28th, 45, 56 (*f.n.*); arrival, 65, 86; in Entrenched Camp, 90; 95; in reserve east of L. Arjan, 125; dispositions 27th June, 1916, 127; malaria in, 127, 144 (*f.n.*); transferred to XVI Corps and enters Struma valley, 147; 160; in minor operations on Struma, 164, 166; occupies Mazirko during attack on Yeniköi, 180, 184; occupies Nevolyen, 5th Oct. 1916, 184; attempted capture of Bairakli Jum'a, 192; capture of Bairakli Jum'a, 193; capture of Bairakli and Kumli, 242; raid near Erneköi, 17th Dec. 1916, 250; raid on Kyupri, 3rd Jan. 1917, 262; 83rd Brigade transferred to XII Corps, March 1917, 299; 335, 336; capture of "Ferdie" and Essex trenches, 337

31st, 86

46th (North Midland), 86

53rd (Welsh), 40

60th (London), arrival, 226; 179th Brigade Group in Thessaly, 227, 266; 251; division in line east of L. Dojran, 263; raids in February 1917, 264; on left of British front, 298; raids in March 1917, 299; rôle in Battle of Dojran, April 1917, 303; raid on the Nose, 24th April 1917, 315; to be withdrawn from Macedonia, 318, 331, 351; rôle in Battle of Dojran, May 1917, 320; operations of May 1917, 330

Royal Naval, 94, 107

Engineers—
Field Companies—
17th—159; 38th—193; 65th—178; 66th—54, 73, 175, 178; 100th—312; 127th—

Index to Arms, Formations, and Units 407

Engineers (*continued*)—
  Field Companies (*continued*)—
    265; 131st—155; 420th—258; 522nd—299; 1/7th Hampshire—164, 181, 193; 2/4th London—227, 228; 2/1st Northumbrian—193; 1/1st Wessex—178; 1/2nd Wessex—244, 246, 247
Flying Corps (R.F.C.)—
  Middle East Brigade—143
  Kite Balloon Section, 17th (Naval)—143, 246
  Squadrons, No. 17—143, 152, 266, 296, 297; No. 47—143, 266, 296, 297
  Wing, Sixteenth—143
Infantry—
  Brigades—
    29th—42, 51, 54, 59, 65, 66, 72, 75, 78, 80, 93, 94, 126, 127, 148, 160, 166, 173, 174, 175, 179, 182, 195, 202, 245, 336
    30th—54, 55, 59, 64, 65, 66, 67, 69, 72, 73, 75, 79, 87, 93, 127, 147, 148, 160, 164, 166, 180, 181, 192, 193, 202, 336
    31st—59, 64, 66, 70, 72, 73, 75, 80, 81, 87, 127, 148, 160, 193, 195, 202, 336
    65th—71, 73, 75, 76, 80, 82, 113, 148, 161, 166, 189, 251, 262, 263, 307, 315, 316, 328, 329
    66th—90, 113, 148, 153, 161, 189, 250, 307, 312, 313, 314, 315, 328
    67th—148, 161, 189, 265, 300, 307, 315, 328, 330
    77th—148, 310, 315, 321, 324, 332
    78th—148, 154, 251, 306, 308, 310, 311, 313, 321, 323, 327
    79th—148, 251, 264, 306, 307, 308, 310, 311, 315, 320
    80th—86, 90, 91, 92, 94, 147, 159, 160, 163, 174, 195, 246
    81st—86, 90, 166, 173, 174, 175, 178, 180, 192, 195, 202, 248, 249, 299
    82nd—86, 87, 90, 127, 160, 164, 166, 174, 176, 183, 202, 243, 244, 245, 246, 247, 250, 262
    83rd—127, 160, 173, 192, 194, 195, 245, 298, 299, 320

Infantry (*continued*)—
  Brigades (*continued*)—
    84th—127, 128, 160, 164, 166, 180, 192, 193, 195, 246
    85th—127, 160, 194, 242, 250, 336, 337
    179th—227, 266, 267, 275, 295, 297, 330
    180th—251, 263
    181st—251, 263, 299
    228th—258, 298, 299
  Regiments—
    Infantry of the Line and Territorial—
      Argyll and Sutherland Highlanders, 1st Bn., 175, 176, 177, 178
      ——, 12th Bn., 310, 311, 321, 324, 325, 326
      Berkshire, Royal, 7th Bn., 154, 191, 251, 304, 308, 311, 322, 324, 325, 327, 333
      Black Watch (Royal Highlanders), 10th Bn., 322, 324, 325, 326
      ——, 13th Bn. (Scottish Horse), 202
      Border, 9th Bn. (Pioneers), 65, 66, 69, 73, 75, 80, 114, 312, 313
      Buffs (East Kent), 2nd Bn., 242, 250, 337, 338
      Cameron Highlanders, 2nd Bn., 175, 176, 177, 178, 179, 249, 299
      ——, 10th Bn. (Lovat's Scouts), 202, 244, 245, 246, 247, 248
      Cheshire, 2nd Bn., 164, 184
      ——, 12th Bn., 191, 312
      Connaught Rangers, 5th Bn., 51, 65, 66, 68, 69, 70, 73, 81, 82
      Devonshire, 10th Bn., 264, 307, 308, 309, 310, 311
      Dublin Fusiliers, Royal, 6th Bn., 66, 69, 70, 71, 72, 181, 182, 183, 242
      ——, 7th Bn., 65, 66, 70, 72, 181, 182, 183, 242
      Duke of Cornwall's L.I., 2nd Bn., 178, 179, 181, 183, 243, 244, 246, 248
      ——, 8th Bn., 308, 309, 311
      Durham L.I., 2/5th Bn., 298
      East Lancashire, 9th Bn., 76, 167

Infantry (*continued*)—
  Regiments (*continued*)—
    Infantry of the Line and Territorial (*continued*)—
      East Yorkshire, 2nd Bn., 194, 299, 357
      Gloucestershire, 2nd Bn., 175, 176, 178, 195, 202, 243, 247, 248, 249, 250
      ——, 9th Bn., 310, 321, 324, 325, 326, 327
      Hampshire, 10th Bn., 51, 65, 66, 69, 70, 73, 81, 82, 202, 243, 246, 247
      ——, 12th Bn., 188, 307, 309, 310
      Inniskilling Fusiliers, Royal, 5th Bn., 66, 72
      ——, 6th Bn., 66
      Irish Fusiliers, Royal, 2nd Bn., 166, 176, 178, 179, 181, 202
      ——, 5th Bn., 66, 69, 164, 195, 202
      ——, 6th Bn., 66, 70, 72, 195, 202
      ——, 2nd Garrison Bn., 298
      Irish Rifles, Royal, 6th Bn., 51, 72, 175, 178, 180, 181, 182, 183
      King's (Liverpool), 14th Bn., 73, 76, 167, 168
      King's Own (Royal Lancaster), 2nd Bn., 194, 320
      ——, 9th Bn., 73, 76, 77, 167, 252, 329
      King's Royal Rifle Corps, 3rd Bn., 159
      Lancashire Fusiliers, 12th Bn., 76, 77, 167, 168, 329
      Leinster (Prince of Wales's), 1st Bn., 174, 183, 202, 336
      ——, 6th Bn., 51, 72, 175, 336
      London, 2/13th Bn. (Kensington), 227
      ——, 2/14th Bn. (London Scottish), 229
      ——, 2/15th Bn. (C.S. Rifles), 227
      ——, 2/20th Bn. (Blackheath and Woolwich), 315
      ——, 2/21st Bn. (1/Surrey Rifles), 264
      ——, 2/22nd Bn. (Queen's), 299
      ——, 2/23rd Bn., 299
      ——, 2/24th Bn. (Queen's), 264, 299

Infantry (*continued*)—
  Regiments (*continued*)—
    Infantry of the Line and Territorial (*continued*)—
      Loyal North Lancashire, 12th Bn. (Pioneers), 263
      Manchester, 13th Bn., 312, 313
      Munster Fusiliers, Royal, 6th Bn., 65, 66, 181, 182, 202, 262, 301
      ——, 7th Bn., 66, 70, 72, 73, 181, 182, 183, 202
      Northumberland Fusiliers, 2nd Bn., 164, 165, 195, 242, 262
      Oxford and Bucks L.I., 7th Bn., 155, 311, 322, 323, 324, 327
      ——, 8th Bn. (Pioneers), 278, 310, 321, 322
      Rifle Brigade, 4th Bn., 357
      ——, 22nd (Garrison) Bn., 298
      Royal Fusiliers, 3rd Bn., 337, 338
      Royal Irish, 1st Bn., 174, 183, 195, 202, 245, 250
      ——, 5th Bn. (Pioneers), 51, 66, 72
      Royal Scots, 1st Bn., 175, 176, 177, 178, 179, 181
      Scots Fusiliers, Royal, 8th Bn., 322, 324, 325, 326, 327
      Scottish Rifles, 11th Bn., 321, 324, 325, 327
      Seaforth Highlanders, 1st Garrison Bn., 298
      Shropshire L.I., King's, 2nd Bn., 126, 246
      ——, 8th Bn., 250, 312, 313, 315
      South Lancashire, 9th Bn., 189, 312, 313, 315
      South Wales Borderers, 7th Bn., 189, 330
      ——, 8th Bn., 190, 328, 329
      Suffolk, 1st Bn., 180, 181, 195, 242, 262
      Welch, 11th Bn., 190
      ——, 23rd Bn. (Pioneers), 180
      Welch Fusiliers, Royal, 11th Bn., 167, 168, 265, 330
      Wiltshire, 7th Bn., 251, 307, 310, 311

Index to Arms, Formations, and Units

Infantry (*continued*)—
  Regiments (*continued*)—
    Infantry of the Line and Territorial (*continued*)—
      Worcestershire, 11th Bn., 189, 308, 310, 311, 313, 324, 325, 326, 327
      York and Lancaster, 1st Bn., 192, 194
      Yorkshire Light Infantry, King's Own, 1st Bn., 194, 299
Machine-Gun Battery—
  6th Armoured M.B.—181

Machine-Gun Companies—
  66th—312; 78th—155; 81st—175; 82nd—244; 179th—227
Medical—
  Field Ambulances—
    31st—54; 2/4th London—227
  Hospitals—
    29th General—297; Scottish Women's—291
Trench Mortars—
  Batteries—
    66th—312; 6th Light—246

OFFICIAL HISTORY OF THE GREAT WAR
FRANCE & BELGIUM

Official History of the Great War — France & Belgium was the grandest official history ever produced in Britain. Its purpose was to provide "within reasonable compass an authoritative account, suitable for general readers and for students at military schools."

Due to the number of full-colour maps bound in each volume many previous attempts to reprint this valuable reference ether floundered, or were produced with the maps in monochrome.

We have reissued our derivative editions NOW in both regular softback and hardback bindings, with smart new jacket artwork, and a refreshing of the internal pages with semi-silk paper for better reproduction of the important colour cartography.

Order directly from
www.naval-military-press.com

The Complete France & Belgium Series, text volumes with colour bound-in maps volumes included are:

1914 Volume I
Mons, the retreat to the Seine, the Marne and the Aisne

1914 Volume II
Antwerp, La Bassée, Arnetieres, Messines and Ypres

1915 Volume I
Winter 1914-15: Battle of Neuve Chapelle: Battles of Ypres

1915 Volume II
Battles of Aubers Ridge, Festubert, and Loos

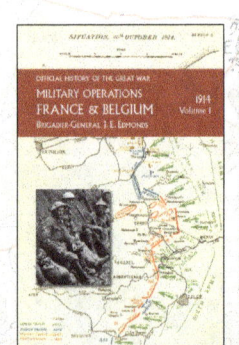 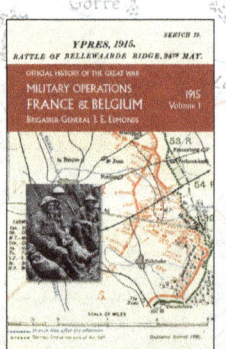 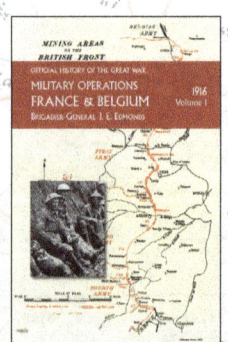 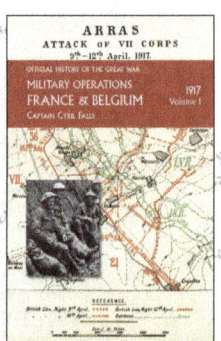

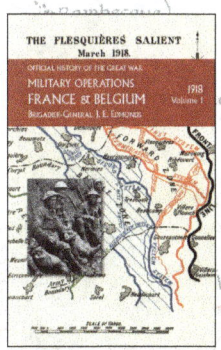 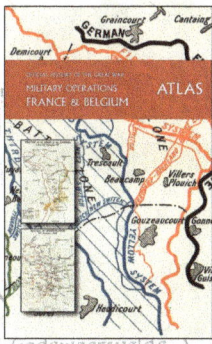 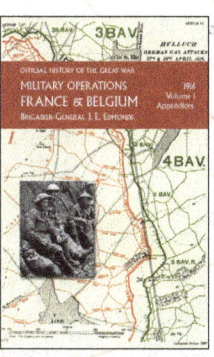 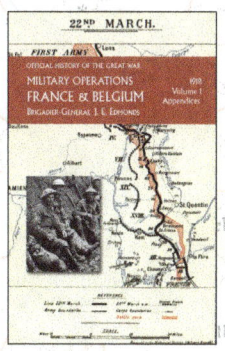

1916 Volume I
Sir Douglas Haig's Command to
the 1st July: Battle of the Somme

1916 Volume II
2nd July 1916 to the end of the
Battles of the Somme

1917 Volume I
German Retreat to the Hindenburg
Line and the Battle of Arras

1917 Volume II
Messines and Third Ypres
(Passchendaele)

1917 Volume III
The Battle of Cambrai

1918 Volume I
The German March Offensive and
its Preliminaries

1918 Volume II
March-April: Continuation of the
German Offensives

1918 Volume III
May-July: The German Diversion
Offensives and First Allied
Counter-Attack

1918 Volume IV
The Franco-British Offensive

1918 Volume V
26th September – 11th November.
The Advance to Victory

1916. Volume I. Appendices

1916. Volume II. Appendices

1917. Volume I. Appendices

1918. Volume I. Appendices

**Transportation on the Western
Front**

**The Occupation of the
Rhineland 1918-29**

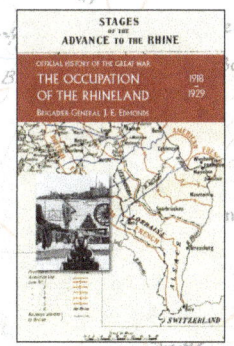 

www.ingramcontent.com/pod-product-compliance
Lightning Source LLC
Chambersburg PA
CBHW070803300426
44111CB00014B/2413